P9-DVJ-710

REPORTING

REPORTING

Fourth Edition

Mitchell V. Charnley
University of Minnesota

Blair Charnley
Minneapolis *Star*

Holt, Rinehart and Winston
New York Chicago San Francisco Atlanta Dallas
Montreal Toronto London Sydney

Library of Congress Cataloging in Publication Data

Charnley, Mitchell V
Reporting.

Bibliography: p.
Includes index.
1. Reporters and reporting. I. Charnley, Blair, joint author. II. Title.

PN4781.C43 1979 070.4 78-16594

ISBN 0-03-018871-7

Printed in the United States of America

9 0 1 2 3 039 9 8 7 6 5 4 3 2 1

This book owes more
than we know how to say
to
JEAN CHARNLEY
who—wisely or not—seems
to believe in both of us

CONTENTS

PART TWO NEWS WRITING AND STYLE 85

PART THREE NEWS NEWSGATHERING PROCESSES 177

PREFACE

Reporting is craft, and it is art. And it is much more.

It is a principal instrument for building and holding firm the kind of society a democratic people wants.

As craft, reporting is a practical blend of skills and stratagems that grow from thought and experience. It can be described and it can be learned. It can be passed along by those who have mastered it to others who reinforce their own capacities with dedicated desire.

As art, reporting feeds only on fertile soil. Artistic expression in journalism, as in music, marble or line and color, flowers when intuitive awareness and private gift are guided by craft. A journalist whose brain cells and nerve ends tingle at the creative possibilities of the materials at hand as well as their latent impact must, to be called artist, first command the craft; art follows the growth of control over skills. But the journalist must provide the artistic impulse. It cannot be drawn from books, a voice behind a lectern, even from painstaking sweat and toil.

Reporters use their craft in everything they do. Newsgathering—the fundamental act in reporting—knows a thousand proficiencies; its companion, newswriting, has as many. It is in the writing that reporters apply their talents for evocation of subtle meanings and emotions. Great reporting combines the character, understanding and insistence of the craft with the embellishment and vitality added by the art.

• • •

This fourth edition of *Reporting* differs in several ways from its predecessors:

- It enlarges emphasis on the social and contextual responsibilities of newsgatherer and newswriter. It suggests the increasing perplexities an ever more sophisticated and troubled society imposes, and many of the failures as well as the successes in modern news presentation.
- It brings current journalistic practices to date, from the booming interest in investigative reporting to the electronic takeover of the newsroom; from contemporary intricacies of libel, access and other news problems to changing views of ethical and professional obligations and modifications of news media purposes and functions.

- Its recommendations about craft and art are illustrated by scores of "new" examples to replace or amplify those of earlier editions. Some that we think timeless, or for which we have found no better substitute, remain. (A considerable number come from Twin Cities or other nearby media. Excellent "cases" are ready at hand here; furthermore, their appropriate use reflects the fact that differences in news practices are declining, as are differences between city and village, between audiences and between newsgathering facilities.)
- The end-of-chapter projects have been considerably expanded and divided into study suggestions and practice assignments.
- Each chapter is preceded by a Preview that summarizes the important points in the chapter.
- The book has been completely redesigned to make it both more inviting and more clear. It is now illustrated with a number of photographs; these photographs are not meant to be decorations, but are intended to convey additional information—either specific or general—about the work of newsmen and newswomen.
- The book now follows the styles of *The Associated Press Stylebook* throughout (except for names of publications).

• • •

In structure and purpose, this fourth edition of *Reporting* resembles its predecessors. Emphasis on the nature and environment of news journalism continues, in keeping with our conviction that learning reporters learn best when they see the land around them. The sequence of subsections of the book has been altered in response to suggestions from journalism students and instructors (the option to use the subsections in different order of course remains open).

Among those whose suggestions have helped, we are grateful especially to: Charles Eisendrath, University of Michigan; LaRue Pollard, Iowa State University; Sonya Zalubowski, University of Illinois. We also acknowledge valuable comments from: Maureen Beasley, University of Maryland; John V. Chard, Gloucester County College; Warren Francke, University of Nebraska; Charles V. Genthe, California State University/Chico; Richard W. Hainey, Northwestern University; William C. Harrison, Texas A & M University; David M.

Jones, Point Park College; Sharon Murphy, University of Wisconsin; Thomas Simonet, Rider College; Charles F. Slater, American River College; M. Neff Smart, University of Utah; Robert Taylor, University of Wisconsin.

No book is ever the product of its authors alone. This book has had help from students and instructors, from reporters and editors, from those who have granted permission to use their work, from critics who have sometimes been sharp in more ways than one and from the editorial staff at Holt, Rinehart and Winston—especially the patient and discerning Pamela Forcey. To all we pay tribute.

M.V.C.
B.C.

Minneapolis
September 1978

REPORTING

PART ONE

NEWS CHARACTERISTICS AND ENVIRONMENT

1 Reporting Today

PREVIEW

News reporting, a force in the world today as never before, faces critical external and internal challenges:

- Pressures from outside pose urgent questions about journalism's intent and performance, economic and social constraints, sophisticated manipulation of news sources and events for private purposes, and changing popular tastes and customs.
- Pressures from within include concentration of ownerships, reluctance to hear criticism or to inform the public of media problems and objectives, and a tendency to look on news as entertainment rather than substance.

There are counteragents, however: Improved writing and production, a vitalized interest in investigative reporting and news interpretation, the rise of self-criticism, a sharpening of professional standards, and refined technological facilities.

News, an indispensable agent in democracy, can be defined as knowledge of current life made available to wide publics. The number of channels that deliver news continues to grow. The broadening impact of mass communication adds weight to the responsibility of the men and women who gather and write the news.

News reporting in the late 20th century serves more people than ever before, and it serves them better. Yet never since America's first newspaper came off its clumsy handpress in 1690 has so much been asked of reporting, and never has it faced challenges so pressing or criticisms so trenchant. Some of its real or alleged failings are homegrown—seeded and nourished in the newsrooms themselves; some just as severe arise from society. Not all of the criticisms are angry or malicious. Some are both.

The world changes attitudes and values according to its needs; it makes new demands as it satisfies old ones. It challenges journalists in many ways, moral, social, economic, legal and legalistic, ethical—ways that were hardly thought of in a simpler and less sophisticated world.

This does not and should not discourage young men and women from "going into journalism." For every riddle there is a key, for every quandary a solution. To newsmen and newswomen the discovery of solutions is both a mandate and a fulfillment. That is one of a number of reasons that so many collegians try journalism of one kind or another; and it is a reason that in so many ways, in spite of stumbling and sometimes stupidity, the level of journalistic achievement continues to rise.

OUTSIDE PRESSURES

Among the significant external forces that bear on the news media are these:

Concealment and deceit Sources of news have developed sophisticated skills to make news events look like what they aren't. Half-truths—designed to serve the interests of the people who devise them—are routine. Misdirection, double-talk, innuendos and flat lies—from Pennsylvania and Madison avenues to rural Main streets—are everyday tools. "Management of news"—telling reporters what you want them to know but not what you think may hurt you—has become a high art, and its practitioners include senators and scientists, preachers and teachers, butchers and bartenders. It often is practiced by the very people who condemn it when it is revealed. Institutions trying to divert criticism, deserved or not, unwinkingly color or invent what they tell reporters (and often deny later that they said it).

Freedom Most citizens don't understand "freedom of the press." To many it means license, permission to report falsely. Though in fact it permits just that, false reporting is neither common nor commonly intentional or malicious. Freedom of the press is at base the freedom to say anything you like *without government interference.* It bears responsibility for the good or evil it may cause. Government may not, says the First Amendment, keep you from saying or publishing what you like, about government or anything else (and whether its object likes it or not); but your unlegislated obligation to report truly and to render opinion fairly remains paramount. You may publish whatever you will; but falsehood can cost you legal penalties or, worse, lack of credibility.

That the freedom-with-responsibility balance is not generally understood means that the news media that try to live up to it—most

A reporter questions President Carter during a televised news conference in Washington. Some reporters take notes; others use cameras. *(Wide World Photos)*

of them do most of the time—are often suspected of being self-serving, not because they are but because a superficial public expects them to be.

Votes of no confidence For this reason among others, popular confidence in the news media is frail. Lack of trust is sometimes justified; but it is unfairly fed by shockingly unsupported attacks by disappointed figures in the news.

Spiro Agnew called the Eastern press an "effete corps of impudent snobs" when he made it a Nixon administration scapegoat. Nixon himself, in 1962, had told the press, blaming it for his loss when he ran for governor of California, that "you won't have Nixon to kick around anymore." Eugene McCarthy complained in 1977 that the media didn't report "things that made sense" (which he identified as McCarthy campaign speeches), forgetting that the media nine years earlier had made him a formidable candidate for the presidency. Blaming loss of an election on the press is routine in American politics. And the public recklessly accepts statements of opinion as statements of fact.

A broad misunderstanding of what is referred to as "the power of the press" also leads to distrust of the news media. As press analysts have pointed out, the news media have little *power*—power to control or mold public attitudes or actions. What they do have is influence—the capacity to give the public materials on which attitudes are based. But the materials are news facts. Newspaper editorials were massively opposed to Franklin Roosevelt during all his presidential campaigns. But the papers reported the facts about what Roosevelt was doing, and the people liked what was reported. Facts, not editorial opinions, won votes.

The readiness to disbelieve is inevitably fed by a pervasive every-man-for-himself temper, the fear that nobody will serve anybody but himself. If a president tells you a lie, why should you believe the newspaper or TV? If Washington fabricates a story about the Bay of Pigs disaster in the 1960s or the Bay of Tonkin "incident" in the Vietnam War era, whom can you trust? If the grocer marks moldy vegetables "fresh," if Ford Motor hides for years the knowledge that 400,000 1972 cars are unsafe, if pharmaceutical houses knowingly peddle dangerous drugs, why should you expect the media to behave? Congress and legislatures pass laws to assure "ethical" conduct by their members, whose individual self-respect sometimes isn't enough; physicians, undertakers, and labor unions have to come up with tough sanctions to try to assure behavior in the public interest. The Institute for Social Research at the University of Michigan, reporting on 20 years of study of public opinion polls, reached the conclusion in 1977 that Americans have progressively intensified their suspicion of government in particular and authority in general. They continue to smoke, leave seat belts unfastened, fail to immunize children, and reject competent advice about the effects of Laetrile.

And yet news readers and viewers ask a higher standard of proof, a more relentless level of accuracy of the media than they do of themselves. News sources with no compunctions about embroidery or distortion of what they tell reporters—or each other—will not brook anything less than the impeccable in what reporters tell them. This is, ironically, a back-handed vote of confidence. "We don't have to tell the truth, but you can—and must." In Ohio in 1976 it was proposed that editors and publishers ought to register as lobbyists if their media discussed legislative matters.

"The First Amendment Belongs to the People . . ."

writes Lewis W. Wolfson in the *Progressive.* He goes on: "But the press must mind it when the people cannot be there. The people do not need direct access to the press as much as they need to trust newspapers' judgment. Readers may still resent the messenger that brings the bad news, especially when there is so much of it. But newspapers do not need to be loved; they just need to be believed. They can show that their First Amendment freedom is everybody's freedom by spurring debate on their pages by all voices, and by leveling about their own shortcomings . . ."

The suspicion that newspapers and newscasts are "just like all the rest"—that they will serve with integrity only if they are forced to—is easy to reach. When the mayor has to be drummed or shamed into moral behavior, why not the reporter?

This is the most alarming external problem journalists face today. Others—economic, legalistic, social, selfish—are examined in Chapters 19 and 20.

The look ahead Whether today's trends forecast tomorrow's is always uncertain. Some of the currents of change in journalism as this is written, however, suggest directions "the news business" may take.

- Newspapers, with declining circulations (most marked among 18- to 30-year-old readers), are seeking new formulas. Some are frankly cutting serious news in favor of entertainment. A Louisiana editor explains that "most editors won't eliminate stories that disturb or that deal with complex issues, but most will accommodate to readers' desires for lighter and more entertaining news." Many newspapers—the sober New York *Times* among them—are modifying makeup and using more "soft" material. Many have instituted or enlarged home care and personal improvement sections (under titles like *Trend, Tempo,* and *Ultra,* which the *Columbia Journalism Review* says "sound like laundry detergents," or folksy ones like *Home* and *YOU*). In some, crime news has begun to recall the tabloid orgy of the 1920s. Suburban coverage is getting more attention in metropolitan areas, and the number of suburban papers is increasing. Longer (and often better) human-interest features have become more common in all kinds of newspapers.
- Television news, though increasing technological skills help to expand its share of the younger audiences, is growing chiefly among the less educated and the lower economic levels. It has thrown out taboos on some types of news, and relies more and more on features and entertainment at the expense of local news and solid ma-

jor coverage. TV news shows often sound like three-minute hit-and-run radio news programs.

- The trend toward ownership concentration continues. Though Congress has moved closer to prohibition of single newspaper-and-broadcasting ownership in one community, chain ownerships are growing in number and strength. In 1978 about 170 chains controlled 60 percent of daily newspapers and had 72 percent of daily circulation. Rising mail costs threaten small newspapers and magazines that seek intellectual and news-interested audiences; specialized magazines and human-interest publications such as *People*, *Playboy*, and *Reader's Digest* seem safe.

PRESSURES FROM WITHIN

The news media are responsible for some of their own problems. Douglass Cater has put it positively: "The task of organizing intelligence and presenting a more adequate picture of reality is going to require initiative and discipline by those involved with communications." All kinds of journalists must spell out what "initiative and discipline" mean in their daily work.

The media are sometimes guilty of the very misbehavior charged against them: News selection that cannot be defended, lack of the aggressive reporting that digs behind facades, failure to follow a stream of news to its source or conclusion. Reporters too often leave a story before it is finished; they satisfy themselves with learning *what* happened but stop short of learning *why*; they report events but shirk the hard search for changing life patterns, for social or economic trends—the search that spots a fire when it is a mere glow.

The thoughtless acceptance of reporting stereotypes, of repetitious coverage in old patterns, marks every newsroom. "We always have reported the first birth on January 1—why stop?" Groundhogs on February 2, however banal the stories, always get space. Is this the fifth, or the 15th, Howard Hughes will?

And if the banal is also lurid, so much the better: "Can the congressman's secretary really type?"

Reluctance to respond thoughtfully to criticism is a news media characteristic. Newspapers scorned the searching analysis of the Commission on Freedom of the Press in 1947—a warning of the restrictive effect on the free flow of opinion and ideas that might result from the concentration of news media ownership. And they have consistently failed to inform the public of the social, ethical and procedural bases on which journalistic work rests. Communications law attorney Lee M. Mitchell told the 1972 Aspen Workshop on Government and the Media that "greater public exposure to the mysteries of how the press operates and the limitations under which it functions could lead to more intelligent and realistic public expectations."

Such currents, little and big, flow in a setting of complexity not imaginable a generation ago. No reporter can master more than a few fields of today's knowledge. Not college professors, not high school kids, not journalists can know enough to make quick and reliable analyses of the federal budget, the city sewage disaster, the inability to limit nuclear weaponry, juvenile vandalism—especially all on one day, all in time for the evening newspaper or the noon broadcast.

One consequence is that we all come to know less and less about more and more. Though the media deliver more substance and do it faster, only a shrinking percentage of all the information about what is happening can be passed along. News space and news time are finite.

So . . . can the media really be expected to keep people adequately informed?

If the answer to that question were a flat "no," books like this would be merely rhetorical exercises. But *Reporting* rests on the premise that such a goal is at least approachable. Whatever they do wrong, the news media's history of continuing progress and service seems likely to persist. Most men and women in journalism believe deeply in the gravity of their task and give it the dedication it demands; for most its challenge has not become an excuse for shoddy performance.

Some counteragents It is hard to recognize today's newspaper as the great-grandchild of that 1690 newspaper. The Hearsts, the Pulitzers, and the Henry Gradys of 100 years ago would rub their eyes. The world has never had so rich and productive a news service as it gets today. Some of the reasons—and some of the answers to the problems cited above—can be summarized:

- Journalists know the tricks used by news sources to silence them or blind them, and continuously develop countertactics.
- Popular concern about the news media and the quality of their service, though it is often naive or self-centered, is intense. It gains strength from the growing mass of thoughtful analysis in print and in college classrooms.
- The news media are growingly critical of themselves. The 1960s saw an outburst of reporter-produced "journalism reviews" that were merciless in their strictures. A number of newspapers, from the Port Huron (Mich.) *Times Herald* to the Washington *Post,* put

their own self-critics to work (see Chapter 4). Some news staffs have gained voice in policy-making.

- A National News Council and a number of local news or press councils, organized by professionals and laymen, examine complaints about news and editorial performance and make public judgments about it.
- Momentous feats of investigative reporting exemplify the levels of excellence reporters sometimes reach. As Norman Cousins has said, an example like the Watergate reporting of Bernstein and Woodward can "produce a moral consensus . . . more powerful than the highest elected official in the land," and such examples increase interest, both outside and inside the newsrooms, in investigative reporting.
- Improvement in craftsmanship—writing, editing, display, evaluation—makes news service more effective. The American Society of Newspaper Editors in 1978 established a series of annual awards "to honor quality of writing in journalism." TV managements followed the lead of their news departments toward meeting their responsibility as the primary purveyor of news to much of America. Among newsworkers the devotion to news achievement, and the joy in it, do not flag.

In short, today's reporters—though they too often fall short of perfection—cover more news of interest to more people, and do it more responsibly, than did the journalists they learned from. They are better educated and better equipped than their older sisters and brothers; and the trend toward specialized expertise expands their potential.

As important as any other factor: They live in a world which, however skeptical it may be about the motives and behavior of its neighbors, nevertheless seems not about to stop thinking about human freedoms, civil and social rights, personal privacy, and individual dignity. The effort to put news events into context, to explain and make them meaningful, gains ground year after year.

Factors and concepts like these define the purpose of this book. The chapters that follow deal with many of them.

• • •

The true role of the press, says the Washington *Post*'s in-house news critic, Charles B. Seib, is "to give the public what it needs to know in order to participate in and help shape society." Walter Lippmann said the same thing: to provide "a picture of reality on which men can act." Both say that the public needs the news of the day—tomorrow's history done up in today's package. A city editor of the New York *Herald-Tribune* in its great days used more florid language: news is "the best record we have of the incredible meanness and the magnificent courage of man." It is the fuel that powers the wheels of change and growth.

Put it pragmatically: News is not an event, but rather the concise, dependable report that tells people of an event. It isn't the threat to murder hostages or the fire at the corner grocery; it is the news media's report that the threat or the fire took place.

The concept that news is report rather than event poses this puzzler: That an event nobody hears about is not news. Suppose a car tumbles off a mountain road into a ravine: If no one misses or finds car or driver, is it news? The murders of a score of California laborers weren't news until, years later, somebody found the graves and reported them. *Knowledge plus report* creates news.

This definition implies three components of news: an *occurrence*, some kind of mental or physical action; a *report* that can transmit knowledge of it from one mind to another; and an *audience*—reader, listener or viewer—to whom the report is offered in print, on the air, by mouth, by smoke signal. The news may provoke a response in some of the people it reaches, or it may leave them untouched. Usually a happening is reported because a reporter or editor believes that it will have meaning for a group of consumers (and, to be practical about it, that it will sell papers or build audiences).

There are scores of channels for delivering news. The mushrooming of news media is a 20th-century phenomenon. Until the end of World War I there was no serious threat to the newspapers' domi-

---

What Is "Mass" Communication?

The term *mass,* widely but often loosely used in such phrases as *mass media* and *mass communication,* deserves delicate handling. Its loose application to all news media is sometimes taken to imply that all seek one audience: everybody. It's easy to spot the fallacy. In New York City the *Times* and the *Daily News,* each with huge circulation, are both mass media. But the *Daily News* "mass"—its audience—differs from that of the *Times* in interests, education, income, tastes, sophistication. Differences among radio programs and magazine contents illustrate even more sharply how drastically "masses" differ—from country-and-western buffs to lovers of Prokofiev, from body-builders to mind-builders. In many cities a single ownership offers AM and FM stations whose principal resemblance is in call letters.

Thousands of publications and broadcasters do not seek across-the-board audiences. Trade and technical journals, house and industrial organs, and scores of other specialized periodicals publish material that their carefully selected readers eat up but that would bore others to death. Does an IBM secretary want to be informed of a new machine used by a Chrysler assembly-line worker?

---

nance of mass news dissemination. But 1920 saw radio getting feebly into the act, and 1923 brought the modern weekly newsmagazine. Movie theaters, before World War II, offered skimpy newsreels; they disappeared when television broke its cocoon in the 1950s. Proliferation of news media in other parts of the world, though on a different timetable, followed a similar pattern.

The impact of news media on the lives they reach is easy to see and hard to erase. South Carolinians today know a lot more about peasants in China, as well as about their representatives in Congress, than they did a generation ago, thanks largely to what the news media have told them. And they know more about the man across the street. If you measure the responsibility of newsworkers in the number of lives their work affects, they have never before been so heavily burdened.

The advent of new media and the fearsome speed of technological change widen news responsibilities. But in the broadest sense the concepts of news and the techniques of reporting change little. Reporting, though it is using new tools to gather information and to package its reports, is stable in purpose. The manner of presentation, the shape and content of the package, differ from one medium to another, and all respond to the winds of thought and fashion. But the basic nature of reporting is a constant. Professional performance is based on a common set of ethical and social principles and on essentially the same techniques and skills. This fact is a keystone of this book.

STUDY SUGGESTIONS

1. How do concealment and deceit affect news coverage?
2. Whom is the freedom of the press clause in the First Amendment to the Constitution intended to protect?
3. Evaluate in your own terms the statement in this chapter that lack of public confidence is the "most alarming external problem journalists face today."
4. What do you consider the principal manifestations of the "power of the press"?
5. Why is the trend toward entertainment as a major news media function looked on as a cause for concern?
6. If you agree that concentrations of ownership of the news media reduce the "number of voices" to which the public has access, do you consider this a problem? How serious? Why?
7. What "counteragents" to support the press in the face of possibily debilitating pressures can you cite?
8. Explain your view of the meaning and validity of the statement that "news is not an event."
9. Define the term *mass communication.*

PRACTICE ASSIGNMENTS

1. Ask five or more men and women who in your opinion "keep up with the news" whether they have confidence in the news media they use. If any do not, find out why. Write a report with their comments and your own.
2. Ask several reporters about their experience with news source effort to conceal or distort news information. Write a commentary on what you learn.
3. Question 20 or more of your peers as to whether there are public institutions whose statements they sometimes mistrust—religious, educational, business, scientific, social service, philanthropic, journalistic, governmental. Summarize their views and add your own commentary.
4. Keep a precise one-week record of the time you spend in "news intake," medium by medium, from newspapers, magazines, radio, TV, and word of mouth. After thus defining your principal channels for getting news, write a statement to explain your choice and offer your judgment as to whether your pattern of intake makes you a well-informed citizen.

RELATED READING

Bordewich, Fergus M. "Supermarketing the News." *Columbia Journalism Review,* September–October 1977. New trends in editorial packaging.

Commission on Freedom of the Press. *A Free and Responsible Press,* University of Chicago Press, 1947. The Commission's report on its several years of study. Foreword by Robert M. Hutchins.

Knepler, Michael K., and Jonathan Peterson. "The Ombudsman's Uneasy Chair." *Columbia Journalism Review,* July–August 1978. A careful look at the development of newspaper "in-house critics," with the conclusion that there ought to be more of them.

Swan, Jon. "The New Ballyhoo." *Columbia Journalism Review,* September–October 1976. The comeback in sensationalizing news.

See also Related Reading, page 30.

2 What "Freedom" Means

The press must be totally free with respect to anything external to it. But internally it has to control its freedom—to be responsible, wise, just.
Aleksandr Solzhenitzyn, Russian Nobel Prize author

PREVIEW

Freedom of the press means the freedom of the public to learn what it needs to know to make its decisions. In America freedom of the press surmounted repressions of Colonial days, became public policy under the First Amendment to the Constitution, and stimulated the development in the 19th century of reporting news for its own sake.

As personal journalism declined, objectivity in reporting became a basic principle of news journalism. In the last century the press in America has been marked by:

- Insistence on access to news sources
- Examinations of press as well as government credibility
- The advent of new channels for news dissemination
- Definitions of the limits of government controls (including those on broadcasting)
- The movement of news toward the entertainment function

Your city is to hold a referendum on whether it wants the new freeway to cut through a park. As a good citizen, you want to vote "right." You have questions: Will it speed up traffic? Dissolve that 8 a.m. bottleneck on the way downtown? Save commuters money? Add to your tax bill? Grow obsolete as new kinds of mass transit come in?

How do you learn what you need to know?

You have all kinds of sources. Word of mouth is one: your buddies at the office, your bowling teammates, friends and neighbors and acquaintances (some of whom tell you "facts" that aren't so). You get a nonpartisan analysis in the mail from a civic association, with views on one side from paving contractors and from reluctant taxpayers on the other. You can bury yourself in "advice."

But if you're like most Americans, you rely primarily on the news media—newspapers and television. They give you facts you need, and often advice, to reach conclusions about things you consider important, whether highways, high finance, or hijackings. They help you decide whether you like the Republican candidate better than the Democrat. They give you tonight's TV schedule, let you know that the ball game or the symphony you want to attend is changed to Thursday, tell you that that pretty kid down the block has been voted Miss Baton Twirler of the Year. They inform you about matters momentous and trifling. They give meaning to the American principle that all citizens have the right to know about things that concern them.

Through its three centuries, as the American news system has come to put its informative function foremost, it has developed a pragmatic interpretation of the freedom the Constitution promises. "Freedom of the press," in the First Amendment sense, means "Government, keep your hands off!" But it connotes an unwritten corollary that is its real significance: ". . . so that the people can make informed decisions about the democratic system." Freedom of the press is the means, not the end; it protects the public, not the publisher.

Constitutional protection against governmental restriction is no bar against other kinds of attempted or actual interference—political, economic, social, religious . . . well-meant, malicious. This book will consider many such inhibitors.

The right to free expression was won by a fight in the nation's birth throes. Its evolution into the people's right to know articulates the recognition that without unhampered newsgathering and reporting there can be no actual democracy.

It is a sober fact that after 200 years both of these elementary rights are under attack.

THE GROWTH OF THE NEWS IDEA

News grows out of its era and society's demands. Patterns of news have existed as long as there has been what we call civilization. Caesar's Rome had its *Acta Diurna*, news sheets posted in public places; more primitive societies had runners from tribe to tribe, smoke signals, deep-voiced jungle drums. The Chinese had a court "gazette" a thousand years ago; what we now call newspapers appeared in western European countries, after modern printing was born, some 400 years ago. Some were government-inspired, issued

The Histories of Journalism

The first three editions of *Reporting* devoted more space to the development of the press than does this edition. Most schools and departments of journalism and communication now offer courses in the history and meanings of mass communication, and most users of this book have ready access to fuller treatment of such subjects. Students who want deeper penetration can find it in books like those listed at the end of this chapter.

to counteract political or religious dissidence; others, such as the German and English newsletters, were designed to provide business information.

Thus the newspaper was well-established by the time revolution had begun to stir in American Colonial hearts. The first attempt at newspaper publication in America came in 1690, when a Boston bookseller named Benjamin Harris issued a four-page leaflet (one page blank) called *Publick Occurrences.* It came out only once because, though today its content seems tame, Harris had not bothered to obtain a government license to publish.

At first slowly during the century that followed, other papers appeared. They were usually weeklies, of four blotchily printed pages. Their circulations were tiny, but their audiences were often considerable, for they were read aloud in taverns and passed from hand to hand among the lucky ones who could read. They dealt mostly with local events; their news from afar might be months late, for slow sailing ships had to bring word of what Parliament or Marie Antoinette had been up to.

But they could be vigorous and outspoken. John Peter Zenger's New York *Journal* was brought to court in 1734 by an outraged governor for "raising sedition," and Zenger's trial and acquittal get credit for establishing the principle that a jury makes decisions about libel. James Franklin in the *New England Courant* made history with what is called the first newspaper crusade (he fought *against* smallpox inoculation, and won). Sam Adams' fiery opposition to the Stamp Act and other despised British restrictions earned him the title "Father of the Revolution"; James Rivington won respect for the Tory cause by his measured and careful reporting of facts and issues. Benjamin Franklin made newspapering respectable, influential and often witty. Thomas Paine used newspapers for some of his *Crisis* papers.

The first American daily appeared in Philadelphia in 1783; by that time some hundreds of papers had started and stopped (two years was their average life). Little progress had been made in the technical production of newspapers—the handpress was a tyrant, and type was laboriously handset. The newspaper was established

A printing shop before modern machinery took over. The printer at the right sets type by hand, picking individual letters from a "California job case." The printer in the center "makes up" type for printing, fitting and then locking it into a "chase," a metal frame. A chase ready to be inserted in the steam-powered press in the background leans against the table. The printer at the left operates a small press by foot power. *(The Bettmann Archive, Inc.)*

in American life, but only in part as an information medium. Some papers had no purpose but the propagandistic; almost all were organs for the expression of their owners' views—views that might be freely injected into "news."

But new forces were appearing. The First Amendment introduced a new journalistic era. Added to the Constitution in 1791, it declared that

> Congress shall make no law respecting an establishment of religion, or prohibiting the free exercise thereof; or *abridging the freedom of speech*, or *of the press;* or the right of the people peaceably to assemble, and to petition the Government for a redress of grievances.

Each of the 50 states includes similar provisions in its constitution. In the 20th century they are taken for granted, but in 1791 they exemplified the respect for human dignity that was a keystone of the new nation.

There were other social and technological advances. Free education was helping thousands to read and write. Increase in newspaper advertising began to free publishers and editors from dependence on political subsidy. By 1830 steam-powered presses could print more than a thousand papers an hour—ten times as fast as Ben Franklin and Sam Adams had been able to produce them. The price of papers went down.

And in 1833 a canny young printer in New York, Benjamin H. Day, put the new technology to use to produce America's first successful penny paper. More important: he also developed for his New York *Sun* a new definition of news. He did not ignore the sober news of business and politics, but he cut down the space it received. His reporters covered New York's police courts daily, and each morning the *Sun* gave its readers vignettes of the drunks, brawlers, petty thieves who faced the magistrate. The pictures were often sordid or maudlin; but they were human, and they dealt with ordinary people. The new public to whom Day appealed, a public able to afford a penny paper and able to read it, grew greedy for the new kind of fare.

Day's new formula drew imitators, and soon one of them—James Gordon Bennett—brought it to maturity. Bennett was more imaginative, more talented and wittier than Day; his New York *Herald*, started in 1835, soon took the play away from the *Sun*. It introduced better writing, more thorough reporting—Bennett adhered stoutly to the belief that the public must be fully informed—and a broader view of news. Bennett is often credited with invention of the interview as a news form. And he confirmed the pattern of news for its own sake—earlier editors ignored news events they didn't like or views they disapproved, but Bennett held that all the news he could get was the least he should offer.

TOWARD NEW DEFINITIONS

Bennett and Day were called everything from heretics to pimps; but in the 30 years after the Civil War the American press followed them from its opinion-forming orientation toward the information function. Horace Greeley, whose editorials had guided the thinking of millions through his New York *Tribune*, died in 1872, his influence waning. Thurlow Weed, for 30 years a political power and king-maker with his Albany *Evening Journal*, failed in the 1860s to re-establish his journalistic authority in New York City. In 1885 the

---

What Is "The Press"?

Literally, the term "press" denotes communication in print. Today, however, it usually has an umbrella meaning that covers all journalistic, and especially news, activities: news on the air as well as in the newspapers, sex magazines as well as *Newsweek*, the country weekly or *The Times* of London. This book uses the term in this wide sense.

Liberty . . . License?

License in news treatment is taken to mean news practices that, however legal, are not consistent with the responsibility to provide balance and fairness and to keep within the bounds of accepted taste. License means indulging in practices that offend public mores and judgment. If it is accurate and properly weighted, a news story dealing with corruption, sodomy or teenage use of heroin is not "yellow journalism." But it is license to overemphasize the gaudy or salacious aspects of such news, to distort it by scare headlines or photos, or to let it crowd out news of significance. It is license to give the public a false impression of relative values or to overdramatize in order to let a news audience lick its lips over indencency, cruelty, suffering or human frailty.

editor of the respected Springfield (Mass.) *Republican* said that his prime purpose was to "furnish the raw material" so that the reader might "compare and weigh and strike a balance for himself." By that time a quarter of U.S. daily newspapers labeled themselves independent, and by the end of the century the frankly political newspaper, the journal that tailored its news to support its views, was becoming a curiosity.

Additional technological advances swelled the current. Bennett and others had formed a cooperative newsgathering group in 1848 to use the new telegraph and the fledgling railroad to move news faster. The Crimean War in a corner of Europe and the Civil War in America were reported to the world as no wars had ever been. The telephone came in the 1870s, the Linotype setting type at "fantastic" speed in the 1880s. Low postal rates to aid in getting more newspapers and magazines to more people were instituted.

"Yellow journalism" came to blatant visibility in this period. There had always been excesses—from the lurid broadsheets of Elizabeth's England, the libelous falsehoods and what Benjamin Franklin called the "scurrilous reflections" that led to the short-lived Alien and Sedition Acts, and Bennett's spectacular crime news reporting, to the New York newspaper wars of William Randolph Hearst and Joseph Pulitzer. The Hearst-Pulitzer fight for circulation produced feats of sensationalism that Bennett had not dreamed of. Hearst's *Journal* and Pulitzer's *World* made crime, violence and outrage their staples; their insistence on war with Spain, though it had less to do with starting the shooting than some historians have judged, yielded vast readership. And it left a mark on American news judgment—especially in the cities—for a good 50 years.

The fact is that yellow journalists have always been a minority, even when they were most visible. The New York *Times*, taken over by Adolph Ochs at the peak of the Hearst-Pulitzer struggle,

News? Or Editorials?

To a reporter or editor the distinction between the news columns and the editorial page is obvious. To a reader or listener the difference is not so clear. In theory, the editorialist is expected to comment on or explain the news; the reporter provides the facts. The layman's problem of discriminating has been made more difficult in the last half-century by the development of "news analysis," the treatment of news that couples acknowledged commentary and evaluation with factual reporting. A radio or TV newscaster is not a commentator, and a reporter is not an editorial writer.

promised soberly to present news impartially and fully, "regardless of party, sect or interest." The yellow in journalism, though it shows through more often than critics like, continues to pale.

NEWS RESPONSIBILITY

By the middle of the 20th century the American press had established a practical definition of news responsibilities. Such a code can never be fully spelled out. But its major tenets can be summarized:

1. A responsible press recognizes the peremptory obligation to give its audiences the news of significance to their lives as fairly and completely as competent professional practice and judgment permit.
2. The press must give people the opportunity to know, to understand and to evaluate all facets of significant news events, especially events involving social controversy and partisan politics. Declining media competition emphasizes the obligation to present all relevant news and views, including those that might have been offered by a nonexistent opposition. It also emphasizes an obligation to make sure that voices with no channels of their own are provided opportunity to be heard.
3. The press needs to be strong financially, so that it can use its strength to support the views, attitudes, groups or parties it believes in, and reject pressures that it considers selfish, antisocial or misguided.
4. The press recognizes the principles underlying laws that make malicious defamation subject to legal controls.
5. The press believes that its freedom to make final decisions about news is complete, and a necessary part of its ability to serve its function.

That these principles are generally accepted does not mean that they are universally observed. Some news that ought to be published is suppressed; political or emotionally charged news is not always presented fairly; financial muscle can be used against the public interest as well as for it; standards of decency and the dignity of privacy are not honored as they merit. But journalistic performance more than pious editorial protest testifies that most journalists seek to follow such tenets.

This chapter has talked principally about the newspaper. This is for convenience only: the principles of the First Amendment and its implications of media responsibility toward news consumers apply to all forms of journalism. Limitations on broadcasting through the Federal Communications Commission impose a number of restrictions on radio and TV. But freedom to portray the contemporary scene responsibly is tacitly assumed and loudly proclaimed.

Broadcasting and its controls No one denies that the First Amendment protects broadcasting, but few doubt that some kind of government "regulation" is a necessity. Before TV arrived in the late 1940s, technology permitted fewer than a thousand radio channels, and it seemed reasonable that government allot them so as to serve the greatest number of people. Today there are thousands of channels for broadcasting, and more thousands for wired community dissemination of programs; some say that anybody who can get a microphone should be permitted to broadcast at will. But the belief prevails that wide-open access, uncontrolled, would mean chaos (Secretary of Commerce Hoover's refusal to assign radio frequencies, in the 1920s before he could persuade Congress to act, led to what were called "nights of anguish" because everybody interfered with everybody else). So the FCC dictates a Fairness Doctrine that assures equal time for differing views on controversial public issues; it grants, withholds or cancels licenses; insists on a proportion of "public service" in station schedules; and considers "monopoly"—for example, ownership of both the single newspaper and the single broadcasting station in a community—a criterion in issuing licenses. The industry opposes such control. Richard Jencks, a CBS vice president, said in 1973 that the First Amendment might

---

"Public Interest"

The term "public interest" is easy to misunderstand and misuse. In the Federal Communication Act it denotes service to the citizenry. But what interests the public is not always in the public interest. The death wishes of a Utah murderer interested the public profoundly—a nation hung on the click of the executioner's trigger. But was the abundant news of the event "good for" anything but a morbid public curiosity? Not everything that is **of** public interest is **in** the public interest.

---

better read, "Congress shall make no law abridging the freedom of speech or of the press, except a law . . . that advances freedom of the speech and of the press."

In spite of the controls on broadcasting, its news services are governed by little except the special nature of the business and the competence of those who put news on the air. Broadcasting is primarily an entertainment business, secondarily a news medium (though its news services can do things no others can do), and owners and managers are usually more concerned with news as moneymaker than as information carrier. Daniel Schorr, who as a CBS correspondent won both cheers and jeers (and lost his job) because he refused to tell a Congressional committee where he obtained certain information, put it this way:

> The problem with television news is that it is trying to present reality but is forced to use the tools of fantasy . . . anything you do in it uses the tools of theater. [He added that] when the corporation, which stands above the news department, has to choose between independence for its news and risking its larger interest, almost always it will come down like a ton of bricks on the news department.

TV has improved its news services in recent years. It has developed more revealing documentaries, longer newscasts, better staffs. Its impressive possibilities emerged when millions watched the Watergate drama, the Sadat visit to Israel, the National Organization of Women's conference in Houston. The weekly examination of current topics in CBS's "60 Minutes"—some of the topics trivial, many of manifest meaning to all of us—not only enlightened America but in 1977 became one of its 10 most-watched "shows." All the networks, including public TV, extended their public affairs broadcasts; and some individual stations began to rival the nets with local documentaries and news coverage that departed from the 30-words-a-story pattern.

The arrival of new channels for news has not altered basic news concepts; but each medium has its own requirements. Each reports events in a manner that suits its peculiar facilities, audiences and methods of delivery. Within each medium, moreover, individual outlets are as night and day. *Time* could hardly be confused with the sober, conservative *U.S. News & World Report,* and the New York *Times* and the New York *Post* (especially under Australian Rupert Murdoch, who took it over in 1976) are as unlike as a robin and a roadrunner.

Improved communication processes in the latter part of the twentieth century have extended the reaches of news. Communication is more rapid in words and pictures (both bounce nicely off satellites);

their rapidity has shrunk the world and made its people more sophisticated, interdependent and eager for knowledge of each other. In an age when two world wars, a world depression, inflation, and unbelievable realignment of national identities, boundaries and loyalties have crowded into barely more than half a century; when Concordes cross the Atlantic between breakfast and lunch; when Alaskans can watch an American boxer in a prize fight in an African country that didn't exist a few years earlier—in such an age the interests and concerns of people everywhere are inevitably more expansive and at the same time more uniform than they were in a simpler era.

But the obligation of the newsworker is a constant: to provide dependable information.

THE CONTEXT OF NEWS

News events can be understood only against their backdrops. Most major news stories do not explain themselves—they need what journalists call analysis or interpretation. Reporting that ignores context and relevance is unfinished reporting. News possesses not only length, breadth and height, but also depth and perspective—not the personal or political perspective of the 19th-century editor, but a cause-and-effect perspective validated by true objectivity (see Chapter 3).

This kind of approach involves showing, for example, how a Supreme Court decision about public housing may affect a local urban-renewal project; or explaining how Australia's sale of two million tons of wheat to Russia may make re-examination of Congress's farm subsidy program imperative. Reporters and their editors today think and talk a lot about news analysis. Nearly all of a three-day conference of the International Press Institute in London was devoted to this theme.

That news analysis raises a quandary is apparent—the puzzle of explaining without pontificating, reporting without editorializing. This is one of the puzzles today's press faces.

Access and the need to inform An axiom of news journalism is that "you can't report it if you can't get it." If the facts about an arrest are hidden, you have either no news or only the news that something is hidden. Some of the practicalities of this question (examined in Chapter 12) make it clear that restriction of access to news sources is a principal constraint on full and revealing reporting. All levels of government, business and public and private organizations choose at times to keep information under the rug.

A trend toward opening doors and windows that ought to be open has marked the 1970s. Congress and state legislatures wrestle with "sunshine laws" to assure that the people's business is open to the people (usually by guaranteeing reporters' and others' access to public meetings and records). The federal Freedom of Information Act gives news media access to many government documents that had been habitually, for good reason or bad, held secret. Though a rash of court orders sought to limit reporters' use of trial information, the higher courts usually upheld the First Amendment principle that such processes must adjust to the public's need to know what's going on. (But the Supreme Court, in 1978, upheld or refused to review judges' "gag orders"—the press's term—as well as two cases in which reporters had been ordered to reveal sources of information.) The Pentagon Papers were opened to publication. The monumental revision of the U. S. Criminal Code, as it first reached Congress, included proposals that would have hamstrung certain news-gathering processes; but the outcry in and out of Congress compelled modifications. A Senate subcommittee held that closed proceedings and restrictive orders "constitute a serious threat to First Amendment interests." The Minnesota Supreme Court ordered release to press and public of documents in a murder trial sealed by a judge to protect the defendant's rights. The American Bar Association moved toward relaxation of its traditional exclusion of cameras from courtrooms, and the House of Representatives authorized TV coverage of its sessions 30 years after it was first proposed.

Credibility gaps This shopworn phrase is used to describe two kinds of phenomena: popular belief that government does not always tell the truth, and lack of confidence that the news media report fully and accurately.

Why Do You Believe What You Believe?

A curious contradiction appears in the nature of public confidence in two American institutions, press and government. In the Nixon years public-opinion polls revealed a public "pessimistic and alienated" in its attitude toward government; at the same time it expressed fear that the press was not informing it fully. Its confidence in both government and the press moved upward during the Ford and early Carter years. In both cases it based its opinions on reports in newspapers, newsmagazines and broadcasting; that is to say, it based its doubts about government on reporting it said it did not trust.

For some years TV has been the news medium in which Americans place greatest confidence; the apparent reason, since TV news is the same news that appears in print, is that when you see it, or see the newscaster, you find it more convincing.

The Hard Decisions

A reporter seeks out facts, often facts that a news source, public or private, wants to keep under cover. On the other hand, a news source may want a set of facts broadcast, but only when, as and with the perspective he dictates; and the reporter may refuse to go along. It is no wonder that the term "adversary" has been applied to the press, sometimes with approval but usually critically. Those who shrink from "adversary journalism" look on reporters as intruders, the enemy: "You're interested only in making us look bad," they say. Most journalists and some thoughtful analysts of journalism see it differently. Though reporters often reveal—or decide not to reveal—information, their proper role is to do what their judgment dictates and let others rule on whether their judgment is defensible. The press has for three centuries been termed "the watchdog of government"; and a watchdog barks when it finds something that others ought to know about. Reporters mostly think of themselves as disinterested observers who neither favor nor disapprove.

Of course it isn't that simple. For one thing, the love of the chase is a part of reporting—often to reporting's debasement. Journalists do indeed take satisfaction in giving the public information that—pleasant or unpleasant—they think the public has a right to (or will enjoy). But they also squirm at some of the facts they have to report. They don't like to think of themselves either as flaks or patsies. They see their position as one that requires them to make news judgments, and that denies the right of others—legally and philosophically—to make judgments for them.

The gap in public confidence in government agencies, from the White House down, traces to solid sources. From Cold War days a series of what can only be called lies issued from the White House (Eisenhower, U-2 spy planes; Kennedy, Bay of Pigs; Johnson, Marines in the Dominican Republic; Nixon, Watergate, and so on). Carter was accused by a columnist of "obfuscation" that "had a stalish Washington smell" in pleading ignorance about the perjury admitted by a former CIA director. "National security" became to the Washington press corps a tired cliché.

Reporters and the media, believing it their obligation to inform, earned credit for opening the nation's eyes in such instances. Yet accurate reporting of inaccuracies can damage the reporter. The public gets its information not directly from the source, but through the news channels. So "the media said it," and the hasty news consumer can easily attach the error or the lie to the news carrier rather than to its origin. Moreover, the correction never fully overtakes the error. Add to this the fact that the news media all too often justify mistrust by their own errors or mistakes in judgment. Newspaper readers do not often distinguish between the miracle of daily news service and the fact that some press performance is shoddy; being human, they look at all performance through biased glasses.

Who calls what black? News media, proud and jealous of their duty to reveal wrongdoing and spotlight misbehavior, often find the critical finger pointing at them. Indefensible is the word for the self-serving kind of attack employed by Spiro Agnew before the 1972 presidential election—attack characterized by misleading or clearly false statements and political inspiration. The loudest noises have often been made by the candidates who got beaten: "[The press] won't have Nixon to kick around anymore!" stormed Richard Nixon. "You can't believe anything you get in the news," says the doctor whose malpractice has been uncovered. "I didn't say it!" shouts the man whose foolish words are correctly reported—"the reporter made it up."

Journalists scoffed at the thoughtful evaluations of the Commission on Freedom of the Press because the Commission "had no journalists on it." When the American Newspaper Guild presented lectures on the press by such notables as theologian Reinhold Niebuhr, historian Henry Steele Commager and the curator of Harvard's Nieman Foundation, Louis Lyons—not to mention journalists like James Reston, Eric Sevareid and Elmer Davis—an important publisher exploded, "I'm not going to sit there again to hear somebody call me an idiot!"

Two salutary kinds of self-criticism, however, have come on the scene. One is the growing number of in-house critics who monitor and appraise their own media's "fairness, balance and perspective" as well as review complaints. The *Columbia Journalism Review* suggested that a large newspaper should employ two critics, "one to see that management's standards are applied to day-by-day operation, the other to serve as a public critic." The *Review* reported 15 such "ombudsmen" at work in 1977, on papers varying in size from the Port Huron (Mich.) *Times Herald* to the Washington *Post*, the Louisville *Courier-Journal* (which started the practice in 1967) and the Boston *Globe*. The next year "consumer advocate" Ralph Nader, in a manual designed to help readers criticize and evaluate newspapers, praised such papers and asked that voluntary citizens' groups go further by organizing local press councils.

The second type of self-criticism has come from the newsrooms, in publications that flourished in a dozen cities from 1965 to 1975. These "reviews" were unsparing in appraisals of the shortcomings of the papers and broadcast stations that paid their writers' salaries. They were often badly financed, and most of them disappeared by the late 1970s. But they brought fresh air into American newsrooms.

Pre- and postpublication controls The clearest meaning of the First Amendment is that government at any level may neither pre-

The Professional News Magazines

The *Columbia Journalism Review,* cited frequently in this book, is the kingpin among American magazines about newswork. Established by the Columbia School of Journalism in 1961, it is a forthright, dependable and often sharp-tongued commentator on the news media's sins and excellences. . . . The *Quill,* published for more than 50 years by the Society of Professional Journalists, Sigma Delta Chi, carries news and features about editorial journalism of all kinds, and advice to young journalists (colleges are the Society's prime recruiting grounds). . . . The *Guild Reporter,* the twice-a-month organ for the members of the Newspaper Guild, devotes most of its space to news of Guild organization and salary negotiations. . . . The *Masthead* is the house publication of the National Conference of Editorial Writers. . . . *More,* started as a New York City journalism review, went national after two changes of ownership; it died in 1978. In its last months it usually dug deep into two or three subjects (one issue examined media monopolies at length; one wondered "Can the [New York] *Post* Survive Rupert Murdoch?").

vent nor compel publication. Laws that make the press liable for damage caused by what it publishes—laws of libel are the best example—penalize those who do the damage when they have not met certain measures of permissibility; but they do not prohibit publication. The 1798 Sedition Act was a short-lived effort to abort the First Amendment; it fell of its own weight. The so-called Minnesota Gag Law was thrown out by the Supreme Court because it permitted prior censorship. On the other hand, the Court has made it clear that law cannot force publication—Florida law requiring newspapers to give "free space" to respond to editorial criticisms was invalidated in 1974. The Court agreed that fairness might be violated under its ruling, but it said that "press responsibility cannot be legislated" and that freedom to criticize, fairly or unfairly, is an imperative social value.

It appears that the literal meaning of the First Amendment is likely to remain its pragmatic interpretation, with regard to the press. And even when the FCC requires that part of a broadcaster's air time be devoted to "public service" programs and that some types of TV fare be broadcast after the children are in bed, it is neither forcing nor denying the use of particular material. The FCC's Fairness Doctrine requires reasonable opportunity for presentation of conflicting points of view on issues of public interest. Both the Fairness Doctrine and the FCC's "equal-time" requirement referring to political candidates, according to critics within and without the industry, violate the First Amendment to the Constitution. Both have received congressional approval, however, the basis being that the airwaves are public property and that limited guarantees of public access must be provided.

News as entertainment As editors run through the day's copy, deciding what to use and what goes into the wastebasket, they have more in mind than providing information. They also want to attract audiences. To interest or to entertain is to attract, and to do it regularly is to build audience and financial strength. Entertaining was one of Ben Day's goals when he established the *Sun*. He did it by giving his readers human-interest news—news of the pangs and pleasures of New York's back streets—and by a light touch in his reporting.

The formula is the same today. Entertainment is added to the news by selection of events that are amusing or exciting or tear-laden, with emphasis on their human-interest qualities; or by skillful writing. Much of the most admired journalistic writing is of this genre; *The New Yorker* has capitalized on it in the work of reporters like Lillian Ross and in E. B. White's essays on New York City and on the joys of raising geese. H. Allen Smith built a national reputation with this kind of writing for the United Press; Ernie Pyle did it for the New York *World-Telegram*, Ring Lardner for the Chicago *Tribune*, Ellen Goodman for the Boston *Globe*, Tom Wicker and Meyer Berger for the New York *Times*—the list is long.

Some critics of journalism look down their noses at efforts to build large audiences. Big audiences give a publisher or a broadcaster strength because they mean financial security. Advertisers, who contribute the bulk of the financial support of the news media, want the media whose audiences promise to buy the largest number of deodorant or Pintos; though catering to advertisers is one of the failings of TV and some newspapers today, the need for audience is a fact of life. Popular legend to the contrary, a particular advertiser can seldom dominate the newspaper or broadcasting station that has a stable audience; every reporter knows at first hand of attempts at pressure that failed.

When a Light Touch Hurts

That Ben Day's light touch was not always gentle may be seen in this example from the *Sun*'s police court news:

Catherine McBride was brought in for stealing a frock. Catherine said she had just served out six months on Blackwell Island, and she wouldn't be sent back again for the best glass of punch that ever was made. Her husband, when she last left the penitentiary, took her to a boarding house in Essex Street, but the rascal got mad at her, pulled her hair, pinched her arm, and kicked her out of bed. She was determined not to bear such treatment as this, and so got drunk and stole the frock out of pure spite. Committed.

The readiness to ridicule that Ben Day permitted himself is not common today.

No responsible journalists condone, in their own work or in others', distortion, over- or under-emphasis or sensationalizing news. All journalists who respect the profession, the public or themselves work at writing stories for the largest group to whom they are likely to appeal.

News as history Reporters don't see themselves, as they write, as historians. Yet they are just that, for their stories are often the only permanent records of contemporary lives and events. As Chapter 1 says, news is "tomorrow's history. . . ." At any future time, tomorrow or 2184, a news story may be exhumed; every newspaper is a potential source for the historian, the sociologist, the political scientist or the politician. Most newspapers, it is true, give little daily thought to their historical function; but "newspapers of record" such as the New York *Times* see their role as historians one of the valid controls on their decisions about which news, and how much, to print.

Although the uses of news as historical raw matter broaden the news concept, the requirements of history do not change its meaning or add to the responsible journalist's burden. The main purpose of news remains to provide current information, to inform a contemporary audience. The reporter who meets today's news demand is, nevertheless, inevitably enriching the files of history. A news story that is accurate, complete, objective and balanced (and sometimes when it is none of these) is a document that may be of value on a thousand tomorrows, to thousands of different readers, in thousands of different places.

Broadcast news is as much the stuff of history as news on paper, but it rarely is preserved as long. If permanent recording becomes general, newscasts will be as valuable to historians as newspapers.

STUDY SUGGESTIONS

1. Write brief definitions of the terms *press, media, mass communication, liberty* and *license, the public interest, access to news.*
2. What are the principal purposes of news reporting?
3. Describe the principal differences between news treatment today and that of 200 years ago.
4. Why is Benjamin H. Day sometimes called "the father of modern journalism"?
5. What does the term *yellow journalism* mean to you?
6. Define the "major tenets" that define the responsibilities of news reporters.
7. What is the major difference between the public controls applied to broadcasting and those applied to print journalism?
8. Cite as many of the obstacles impeding access to the news as you can.
9. What agencies are there that comment on or criticize news handling?

PRACTICE ASSIGNMENTS

1. From histories of journalism or other sources, review carefully the John Peter Zenger case of 1734. Write your opinion of the plea of lawyer Andrew Hamilton and the decision of the jury and relate them to later developments in American journalism.
2. Read carefully the news story from Ben Day's New York *Sun* (page 28). Compare it to police court news in the press today; write a statement of the differences you find and add your opinion as to which approach is to be preferred.
3. Draw from your experience or from interviews with peers, teachers, merchants, public officials, clergy, or blue- or white-collar workers several examples of "news" that was not published but which, in your opinion or that of others, should have been. Interview reporters or news executives of media that might have carried the news. Write your opinion about the propriety of the omissions.
4. Select a current news topic on which there are wide differences of public opinion (the abortion dilemma, the Equal Rights Amendment, Laetrile, or a local topic such as location of a highway or school busing). Interview six or more citizens (those with strong views will be most responsive) to learn what they think of news coverage of the topic: overdone? about right? underdone? biased? Summarize and comment on others' opinion and your own.

RELATED READING

Arlen, Michael J. "The Air: 'The News.'" *The New Yorker,* Oct. 31, 1977. Audiences are demanding, and broadcasters supplying, more and more trivia.

Barnouw, Erik. *History of Broadcasting in the United States.* Oxford University Press, 3 vols., 1966, 1968, 1970. (A shorter version is available in paperback.)

Branscomb, Anne W. "Citizen Access to the Media," in *Aspen Notebook on Government and the Media.* Praeger Publishers, 1973. Panel discussion on the Fairness Doctrine and other aspects of media availability to laymen.

Buck, Rinker. "Can the *Post* Survive Rupert Murdoch?" *More,* November 1977. The *Post* owner defends the direction in which he is taking the recently purchased New York newspaper.

Burgoon, Michael, and Michael Ruffner. *Human Communication.* Holt, Rinehart and Winston, 1978. Chapter 10 summarizes with clarity and wit the rise of mass communication, its processes and functions and its impact.

Dennis, Everette E. *The Media Society.* Wm. C. Brown, 1978. Facts and opinion about mass communication in America.

Emery, Edwin, Phillip H. Ault and Warren K. Agee, *Introduction to Mass Communication,* Harper & Row, 1976. A complete, sometimes overpowering, treatment of a vast subject.

Emery, Edwin, and Michael Emery. *The Press and America.* Prentice-Hall, 1978. A widely used and authoritative history of U.S. journalism.

"Inhouse Press Critics." *Columbia Journalism Review,* July–August 1977. Excerpts from comments by the ombudsmen of the Boston *Globe,* Louisville *Times,* Sacramento *Bee,* Washington *Post* and Washington *Star.*

Masters, W. H., Rinker Buck and Peter M.

Sandman. Articles on media monopolies and cross-ownership. *More*, October 1977.

McGehee, Fielding M., III. "Exemption 1: F.O.I.A.'s Catch-22." *Columbia Journalism Review*, March–April 1978. Classification of information as "top secret in the interest of national security" offers an access-to-information loophole that courts uphold.

Rivers, William L., Theodore Peterson and Jay W. Jensen. *The Mass Media and Modern Society*. Holt, Rinehart and Winston, 1965. The media and American culture.

Rivers, William L., and Wilbur Schramm. *Responsibility in Mass Communication*. Harper & Row, 1969. Second edition of a "classic," sponsored in part by the Federal Council of the Churches of Christ in America.

Schwarzlose, Richard A. "For Journalists Only?" *Columbia Journalism Review*, July–August 1977. The Supreme Court moves toward classifying the public's "right to know" as a legal rather than an implied right.

Shaw, David. *Journalism Today*. Harper & Row, 1977. The subtitle, *A Changing Press for a Changing America*, is appropriate.

Sterling, Christopher H., and Timothy R. Haight. *The Mass Media: Aspen Institute Guide to Communication Industry Trends*. Aspen Institute Publications, 1978. Carefully gathered and marshaled information about U.S. and foreign mass media: growth, ownership and control, economics, employment and training, content and extent.

Wicker, Tom. *On Press*. Viking Press, 1978. Carefully gathered and marshaled *Times* reporter, analyzing press responsibility and performance in light of 30 years' experience and observation, concludes that more "robust and uninhibited" news coverage is needed. He asks not only for less timidity but also for more reporting of important news in which "nothing happens," news of big money and big government, even when no terrorist threat or human drama is involved.

3 Characteristics of News

PREVIEW

News reporting has characteristics that are often difficult to describe and more difficult to put into practice:

- Accuracy—fidelity to actuality in fact and meaning
- Balance—emphasis where it belongs; weighting elements in news reports so that they represent their subjects justly and truly
- Objectivity—reporting that excludes personal opinion or slant. That impartial observation and account constitute "an ideal difficult to attain . . . does not excuse [the reporter] from a constant and vigilant effort to attain it." The New Journalism rejection of unbiased reporting as sterile and unworthy, a phenomenon of the Vietnam War period, failed to distinguish between informing and persuading.
- Currency—by custom and common consent a property of most news
- Concise writing—prose that goes directly to its point, without unneeded delay or adornment

---

Raw cotton can be used in making either diapers or high explosives. You can use the raw material of news—facts—for sociological exposition, propaganda, fiction . . . or reporting. The realities from which news stories grow respond to an extravagance of influences. Although the stuff of news can, like cotton, be woven into many patterns, its master pattern has a distinctive profile. A news story is more than the sum of its facts; it is the sum of the facts plus the form and perspective a reporter gives it. Its characteristics distinguish it from all other forms of writing.

Chapter 1 said that modern news is expected to be concise and dependable. Ideally it is fair and genuinely objective (not always the same thing), and it is clearly and accurately told. Without these qualities a report of an event is not true to the news model, though it may be high art, incisive scholarship or masterful persuasion. Truman Capote's *In Cold Blood* is a masterly report of a series of occurrences; but it is not news because it was not current when it was published, and it was not selectively concise.

The distinguishing traits of news are so firmly built in that they not only determine the forms of news practice but also serve as guides in the evaluation and presentation of news. They establish the working principles that condition a professional's approach to news and guide his daily functioning.

NEWS IS ACCURATE

Students on American campuses decided, on learning of the mining of Haiphong Harbor late in the Vietnam war, to protest what they considered the outrageous prolongation of the war. None of the protesters saw the mines being laid; none were there; few had first-hand word of what had taken place.

News reports were what provoked their anger.

Thus is the accuracy of news taken for granted. Much of the public superficially questions it. "You can't believe what you read in the papers," they say, or "That announcer always gets it wrong." A university dean once said he had never seen an entirely accurate news story about an event whose facts he knew. Yet that same dean, like most nonbelievers, not only accepts what the news media offer but bases his daily life on what they tell him. He knows by experience that when a news story says that the blackout was caused by a broken power line in a suburb, that the driver ignored a red light, or that President Carter went to a town meeting at a Massachusetts village, he can rely on the facts as stated. Even those reluctant to admit that news is a guide for their acts and opinions agree, if they are pressed, that the vast bulk of news is dependable.

Accuracy means literally that every element in a news story, every name and date and age and address, every definitive word or phrase or sentence, is an unequivocal statement of a verifiable reality. Not only that: it means fidelity in the general impression given by the way details are put together and by the emphases put on them.

If the meaning of accuracy and the imperative need for it are easy to understand, the quality itself is not easy to attain. A news story with fewer than a dozen specifics is rare; most stories contain as many facts as they have verbs, nouns and phrases. Even the seasoned reporter finds it hard to make certain of every detail. A reporter fights the pace of newswork; a story may be changed by a copy editor, by typos, by the nuances of a headline or an announcer's inflections. Any issue of a newspaper or any newscast offers literally thousands of opportunities for mistakes. Most errors, such as typos or mispronunciations, are little ones. But an error is an error; and the chances for error are so vast that the wonder is the level of accuracy of news, rather than of its blunders.

Nevertheless, there is that charge that the media never get things right. This is a model of the human gift for generalization from little evidence. Most newspaper readers see only the stories that interest them or the news columns dealing with subjects they know something about (few readers see more than 25 percent of their favorite dailies). So the errors they find get disproportionate attention. If the paper spells Smyth's name Smith, if it calls a yawl a ketch, if it reports as one paper did that a president's body was borne to the cemetery on a motorcycle ("motorcade," for the record), if it says that a hundred were at the PTA meeting when only 70 signed the roll, the confidence of the reader who spots the error is eroded. And people are likely to draw unjustifiably broad inferences rather than to complain only of what they are sure of. Only when errors are habitual or repeated are generalizations justified.

What are reporters' safeguards? How can they protect themselves, their medium, their readers against false statements?

Patient vigilance is the first protection. Make legible notes of every fact, particularly of such specifics as names, ages, dates, times, addresses. Take nothing for granted. Was it really Smith? Or could it have been Schmidt, or Smeeth, or even Psmythe? When the secretary said the meeting would occur Friday, August 17, was he sure August 17 would be a Friday? And if you find it's a Thursday, which did he intend? Are you safe in calling the professor "Dr." Brown? Maybe she's not a Dr., but a Ms. Or does she prefer some other title? If she does, she'll call you wrong even if you're right.

Patience needs as partners skepticism and a passion for double-checking. Skepticism means that the story clipped from another paper can't be accepted at face value—it isn't accurate just because it was printed. A number of American papers reported that enormous quantities of military supplies had been buried at an Air Force base in South Carolina; the Detroit *News* didn't believe it, and proved it false. A wire service opened a nostalgic feature story thus: "Orville Wright made history when he flew to a height of 120 feet in 1903." There's no record that any of the papers and broadcasters that used the story went to an encyclopedia to discover that Wright flew 120 feet from one point to another, but never more than 10 feet above ground.

These cases are, fortunately, atypical. Most of the time relentless use of everyday reference tools is enough—city and other directories, telephone books, dictionaries, the New York Times Index,

Facts on File, Who's Who, government manuals. Sometimes nothing but a dogged search for the person who really knows the answer will do.

Patient vigilance also means awareness that such a source may not, or for any of a number of reasons cannot, tell the answer. It is a plague of reportorial life that information sources are so often less reliable than reporters.

What errors? How many? A number of American newspapers and researchers have conducted surveys of their own accuracy. They commonly use a technique developed in university schools of journalism: submission of hundreds of news stories to individuals close enough to the events to know the facts. These sources are asked to report on accuracy of detail and of general meaning or connotation. Most responses in such studies show extremely high factual accuracy (correct names, times, dates, titles, statistics and other specifics). In half a dozen studies that covered more than 3,000 stories, the incidence of errors was about one per story.

The kind of error cited most frequently was "mistake in meaning," usually the opinion that the story—from the source's viewpoint—gave a faulty impression. Any reporter, however, would point out that the news source and the news reporter are likely to see a given set of facts in differing perspectives. The man who gives a talk on the use of marijuana, let's say, wants to express his belief that smoking pot is relatively harmless. The reporter's judgment, however, is that readers or listeners will find more significant the speaker's statement that legal penalties for marijuana use should be abolished. Who's right—the speaker, who knows what message he hoped to stress, or the reporter, who thinks that for the audience involved a different element was more important? It is the reporter's responsibility to make the decision. Might not a reporter, because of experience, purpose and perspective, make a more appropriate decision than the man who sees the event from the inside out?

NEWS IS BALANCED

Facts, however accurate, don't always insure accuracy of meaning. Accurate facts loosely or unfairly selected or arranged can be as misleading as outright error; from too much emphasis or too little, from irrelevant facts or omission of facts, a false impression can be drawn. A reporter for the journalists' union newspaper, the *Guild Reporter,* writing about a conference on liberal education and the mass media, included only the remarks made by a Guild representative. The report gave an erroneous view of the event.

True accuracy thus requires not only literal fact but careful balance of fact.

A reporter is the reader's or listener's representative, and so must work constantly to place facts in proper proportion, to relate them meaningfully to each other, and to make clear their relative importance. A sportswriter misses the boat if his story tells about the home team's homers but skips the opponents'. A report of a campus "riot" (the word itself may weight a story falsely) that pictures swinging police clubs but ignores protesters' rock-throwing is a bad report. It would be unfair and unprofessional, in reporting a Rotary meeting, to fail to mention the speech (even if it's dull) and concentrate only on the Good Citizen Awards.

A news story is complete when it presents a competent summary of all parts of the event relevant to its audience. The summary need not include every trifling detail; literal completeness, indeed, is seldom desirable. News stories are not minutes of meetings. Some get close to it—play-by-play sports stories, texts of speeches or court testimony, stories whose purpose is to reconstruct with photographic fidelity the Ruby shooting of Oswald, for example, or such dramatic events as the inauguration or the funeral of a president. Completeness usually means fair, well-chosen summary rather than second-by-second minutiae.

Reporters look on themselves as agents of the news consumer. They go to the baseball game, gather facts about the upcoming city budget or cover the flood so as to give information to the thousands of readers or hearers who can't be there themselves. From a reporter's statement of selected particulars these "clients" should be able to reconstruct the main lines of the events and to put them into understandable context.

One way *not* to achieve balance is to count words, minutes or lines of print. Radio stations and newspapers that seek "absolute impartiality," giving all the candidates for a particular office pre-

---

Out of Balance

A news story about a legislative hearing on the Equal Rights Amendment, calling the hearing "one-sided" because opposition was sparse, devoted most of its space to what proponents said. Off balance? The reporter said that the weight of the story accurately represented the weight of the hearing.

Balance can be lost wholesale or retail. A Texas paper whose editor was personally involved in a money-raising campaign gave so much space to the campaign that it slighted other local news. That was open imbalance. But when a press service said of the Senate Watergate hearings that "the witness will have his chance to counter-attack tomorrow" though in fact he had not been attacked, the imbalance was subtle and hard to spot.

---

cisely equal time or space, have discovered that news events don't balance. In 1972 McGovern ran a frenzied campaign, with lots of speeches and scads of newsy statements (some of which he regretted); Nixon "campaigned in his bedroom." The result: news about one, no news about the other. A bill introduced in Congress would have required that candidates who thought themselves criticized on the air must be given second-for-second rebuttal time; the bill deservedly died. In facts, thoughts and ideas, mathematics is no guide to equality.

WHAT IS OBJECTIVITY?

Objectivity in news treatment was called by Alan Barth of the Washington *Post* "one of the principal glories in American journalism." For half a century it had been revered, often uncritically and superficially, as a guide to responsible reporting. But in the next quarter-century critics, journalists as well as "outsiders," became doubtful. The development of the change is worth examination.

Beginning with seeds planted by Ben Day and Bennett, when the notion of reporting facts for their own sake was new, there grew the recognition that editorial opinion and news are not the same. The personal journalism epitomized by Horace Greeley's New York *Tribune,* often as much a propaganda organ as a newspaper, waned and by the turn of the century had almost disappeared. Even William Allen White's Emporia *Gazette* and Marse Henry Watterson's Louisville *Courier-Journal,* both better known for their editors and editorials than their news content, were devoted to the principle that editors' opinions must not monkey with the city desk. The American Society of Newspaper Editors in its 1923 code of ethics asserted that partisanship in the news columns must be looked on as "subversive of a fundamental principle of the profession." In 1943 the respected Paul White, then director of CBS News, expressed his conviction that "the fact that objectivity is an ideal difficult to attain ... does not impair the ideal itself nor excuse the broadcaster from a constant and vigilant effort to attain it."

So objectivity became a fetish. It said that news is the factual report of an event at the time it occurs—not the event as preconception pictured it, or as the reporter and editor would like it, or as those involved hoped it would be seen. It is the event as reported by a capable observer, without prejudice. It is report un-

---

Epigram . . .

. . . from an unknown source: "Objectivity is the search for evidence, which is truth. Subjectivity is the acceptance of guesses, which is magic."

---

tainted by bias or other influence that makes the event appear what it isn't. The reporter is expected to look at events through glasses neither rose-colored nor smoked. Only assurance that news is "pure" can give its consumers confidence in the reports on which they base their opinions.

There are two obvious flaws in this principle. One is that no reporter can escape being human and, therefore, possessing views, emotional as well as intellectual responses and subconscious predispositions. It is no problem to write simply that a speech will take place on a given subject at a given time and place. Facts so simple put no strain on the blood pressure. But suppose, reporting the speech, a reporter who happens to be an employed mother finds the speaker straying into a tirade about working mothers who "abandon" their infants. Keeping out of the story what she thinks of the so-and-so may be something else again. If she is alert and determined about her responsibilities, she has a good chance of coming up with a "straight" story. But if she gives the tirade more space than it deserves, or if wittingly or unwittingly she lets prejudice or annoyance color what she writes, both objectivity and the reader's chance of true understanding go out the window.

The second flaw in the principle is more serious. Sometimes the most undeniably objective reporting of the facts of a news situation does not tell the whole truth. A simple example is the photograph: it's more accurate than words in what it shows you, but it fails totally to show the image of the other side. Objective reporting may assume that news consumers, with whatever resources and outside help they can muster, can apply proper perspective to the facts a story supplies—can separate the genuine from the phony, the chaste from the poisoned, the complete from the fragmentary. Even in the 19th-century era of political and personal journalism, only a few citizens could do it for themselves; in today's complex world none, however much news they take in, can untangle the aggregate of facts. The very mass of news may so overwhelm them that they escape to the comics, a bridge game or a snooze before dinner—hav-

"We Cannot Be a Little Bit Impure"

So wrote an assistant managing editor of the New York *Times* just after the convulsions that shook the 1968 Democratic national convention in Chicago. He went on: "It is understandable that a reporter, viewing . . . the violence of Chicago, will be moved by normal human feeling; it is his job to report what happened without adopting a subjective approach . . . . It is neither necessary nor desirable to prefix the loaded word 'brutal' to the strong word 'clubbing' . . . a sharp line must be drawn between desirable interpretation and undesirable subjectivity, characterization or editorializing."

ing only a dim notion of the meaning of what they have just read or heard.

When one-dimensional objectivity collides with complexity, the reporter has to help the consumer out, often by providing background or tangential information. Listen to the perceptive observations of Elmer Davis:

> This striving for objectivity was in its beginning a good thing; but it went a little too far. From holding that newspapers ought to present both sides it went on to the position that it was all right to present only one side if nobody happened to be talking on the other; and it was not the business of the newspaper to tell the reader if that one argument happened to be phony.
>
> This . . . reached its peak, I think . . . in the administration of Calvin Coolidge, when it was the opinion of a great many American citizens that things are what they seem. In those days, if the Hon. John P. Hoozis was important enough to be interviewed, you might see half or two-thirds of a column embodying his views on some topic or other, with no indication that what he said was a lie from beginning to end—even if the editor who printed the story happened to know it—and no indication that the Hon. John P. Hoozis might have a powerful personal interest, financial or otherwise, in getting the view over to the public. He had said it; and if it was important enough to be news, it would not have been objective not to print it.[1]

Walter Lippmann, commenting on the problem, added a facet:

> [Senator Joe McCarthy's] charges of treason, subversion, espionage, corruption, perversion, are news that cannot be suppressed or ignored. . . . But with what are the news editors to balance the news of the McCarthy charges? Not, I take it, with news of inspirational talks to the Girl Scouts. . . . Had President Eisenhower . . . refused to cooperate with this gross perversion of the congressional power to investigate, that would have been news that news editors would have been only too pleased to publish. . . . They would treat it as very big news indeed if it were reliably reported that a President had raised a standard to which the wise and the honest can repair. . . .

Instead, as Lippmann explained, Eisenhower was silent. And silence rarely makes news.

These declarations say that objective reporting, admirable as it may be in itself, is in itself not enough. It is admirable to report a speech by a political leader accurately and completely, but not so

[1] Elmer Davis, in *The Press in Perspective* (Ralph D. Casey, editor), Louisiana State University Press, 1963, pp. 60–61. Davis was director of the U.S. Office of War Information in World War II, and a respected newspaperman and radio news analyst.

Guesswork

President Carter, after a two-hour conference with Premier Begin of Israel in their search for Mideastern peace, walked toward the White House, his back to the cameras. Passing a shrub, he plucked something from it and flung it sharply to the ground. A TV news announcer in a distant city described the gesture as "possibly indicating the frustration Carter feels." Reporting or opinion?

admirable to fail to report that another leader—or perhaps the same one—had earlier contradicted some of its "facts." (And naive news consumers don't want objectivity. A reader once complained that a newspaper report of a speech "could have been used as a vehicle to express the Chicano struggle"—a purpose that was neither the reporter's business nor his intent.)

Observations like these were forerunners of the New Journalism revolt of the 1960–1970 years against the concept of objectivity. The New Journalism was a partner, or at least a contemporary, of the youth rebellions; it ran parallel to outrage at the Vietnam war; it was part of the response to those in positions of power who, in the eyes of thousands of young Americans, were ignoring their obligation to exercise social controls. This was the period of the burgeoning underground press, much of which was irresponsible and bitterly biased but all of which was inspired by resentment at society's ills. It was the period that culminated in Watergate. And it was the time when much of America's ablest journalistic talent rejected, at least for a while, such restrictions on their freedom as the requirement to seek objectivity—that is, to hold back personal views of the facts as you report them. Bruce Brugman, the incisive and angry editor of the San Francisco Bay *Guardian*—known for its successful campaigns against public and private wrongdoing—asserted, "I tell every reporter I don't want to see objective reporting." In 1973 David Halberstam, who won a Pulitzer prize for Vietnam war coverage, substituted vigor for elegance when he told a dinner meeting of newsworkers that "objectivity is bullshit." Molly Ivins, who signed out of conventional journalism in 1970 to join up with the militant Texas *Observer,* said acidly that "objectivity is getting the facts straight and letting the truth go hang." Writers like Norman Mailer, Gay Talese, Jimmy Breslin and others of acknowledged talent pooh-poohed objectivity, as did publications like the *Village Voice*, the Texas *Observer* and the Bay *Guardian.*

The observation of Dennis and Rivers in *Other Voices: The New Journalism in America* that "the objectivity question is a debate between generations" seems valid. Reporting freed of the restrictions

"Existential Journalism"

This name for New Journalism is offered in a book whose burden is that a reporter released from the fetters of "corporate journalism"—who works ethically and with social orientation and is allowed to report "judgmentally"—is the one who attains "ultimate freedom and self-respect." With the New Journalists, the book's author holds that freedom and self-respect cannot be attained by journalists who report not what they would like things to be but what they are. This is a concept that the writers of this book reject.

of objectivity is more attractive to young writers and reporters than to older. For one thing, it is easier. You can cover the readily observable part of a story and comment entertainingly about it with less effort than you need to dig out all the facts and present them in meaningful context. And it's often a lot more fun to let yourself go, display your writing virtuosity and tell readers what to think instead of letting them decide for themselves.

But as the underground press and college-age enthusiasm for sit-ins ran their courses, anger at the principle of objectivity turned toward a definition that, though not really new, throws it into clearer light. It is significant that Halberstam followed his irate outburst by saying that competent reporting is "realistic, analytic, and fair-minded"; and that Ivins says that "there has to be an internal attempt to abide by the standards of professional journalism—accuracy and fairness." Both statements are part of the definition of objective reporting. The traditional principles have not evaporated. A news story should offer, in addition to the clear facts, whatever related information may be necessary to expand the consumer's perspective. Though objective reporting is the "report of an event as it occurred," a good reporter must frequently report pertinent background as well as literally observable facts. Unless balanced and complete information is presented in appropriate context, objectivity of the "old" kind may only add to confusion.

Objectivity is not attained, as one might infer from the last sentence of the Davis quotation above, by withholding publication of the dishonest claim or the deceitful speech. The reporter's obliga-

"My Job Is to Inform, Not Persuade"

The words are from Dan Rather, as White House correspondent for CBS. Rather, in *The Camera Never Blinks,* writes of the problems of a reporter who has strong feelings about a subject he is covering. "I do not subscribe to the idea of the reporter-as-robot," he explains. "But . . . every day that I went to the White House I left my emotions behind me. One test of the professional is how hard he tries and how well he succeeds in keeping his own feelings out of a story."

tion is to print it so that the reader may know that somebody did it, that an event took place, that a candidate lied; but the obligation is fully discharged only by printing the lie *with*, or closely followed by, whatever clarification is called for.

In short, objectivity is not only alive and kicking; it remains a "glory" of American journalism, properly understood and properly practiced. Objectivity is not a technique; it is an attitude.

ADVOCACY JOURNALISM—ADVERSARY JOURNALISM

An easy assumption might be that the terms "advocacy journalism" and "adversary journalism" signify opposite sides of the same coin—that one means journalism in favor of something and the other journalism against something. But journalistic usage gives them different denotations.

Advocacy journalism This term means what you expect it to mean. It means journalism—either reporting or editorializing—whose purpose is to show a writer's support for a cause or position. It's the kind of reporting you get from those who believe that objectivity is passé. "Nobody can be objective—everybody has attitudes. Reporting that doesn't reveal where the reporter stands is gutless and deceitful; it's desensitized, dehumanized, vacuous." Such comments defend the conviction that honest news exposition demands response to an event. Reporting, say some, isn't self-respecting if it doesn't reflect the reporter as well as the fact.

A well-thought-of liberal journalist and critic, Nat Hentoff, as a writer for the *Village Voice*, asked the question: "If to be neutral all the time is the only way for a reporter to assure 'credibility,' has such desensitized reporting of outrageous events contributed to the deep detachment—or cynicism, if you will—of much of the citizenry?" Hentoff implies a "yes" answer, writing in *Civil Liberties*, but he qualifies his meaning by distinguishing between reporting facts and commenting on them.

And a *New Republic* critic, John Seelye, says in reviewing a book by one of the high priests of New Journalism, Tom Wolfe: "On its plus side, the New Journalism is basically satire—tough, witty, unmerciful to all manner of pretense, immediate, jazzy, alive, and terribly readable. On the negative side it is cold, hard, often piously smug, blind to any but urban values (including pastoral sentimentality), phonily 'honest,' and willing to sacrifice a fact for the Larger Truth."

The writers of this book believe, as most newsmen and newswomen do, that advocacy reporting is not fair reporting. Perhaps it should not be called "reporting." Objectivity is a tool designed to gain impartial perspective—a reportorial attitude that is fair both to facts and to their recipients. It demands a great deal more than mere lack of bias, however, and more than mere superficial coverage of observable and provable facts; it means both of those qualities but also emphasis on what is salient, selection of news topics that serve the selected audience, vigilant search to find out what the needs are. None of these is likely of achievement without the objective orientation that starts the whole process going.

This view does not imply that there is anything wrong with advocacy. Tom Paine was an advocate; so were John Milton, Lincoln Steffens, Walter Lippmann. They held views, and they made abundant use of fact in arguing their positions. But when their purpose was to persuade—to advocate—they left reporting to become pleaders. They were not revealing actuality in order to let readers come to uninfluenced opinions, but rather were leading readers to view actualities from the advocate's perspective. Advocacy is a high calling and an honorable one. It shouldn't be called what it isn't.

Adversary journalism This term often expresses the concept that the press and government are inherently at war. The notion has been traced to a number of sources. One is the implicit suggestion in the First Amendment that government might seek actively to interfere with press performance, and must be forbidden to do so—an idea that has had support from the naked efforts of the Army, the White House and other federal agencies in recent years to bend the press to their will. Another is the fact that news of conflict is often more interesting than news of untroubled seas, and that reporting governmental conflicts is something the government doesn't often like. To some extent the growing emphasis on investigative reporting is a cause: Misbehaving politicians and misbehaving government often get a bigger share of the press spotlight than they merit. Moreover, the press has been called the ally of the intelligentsia,

---

Appearances May Deceive

Reporting sometimes looks "adversary" when it could be described better as aggressive, insistent, zealous or even intrusive, insensitive, combative. Reporters, believing in what they are doing and determined to meet what they see as their obligation (and sometimes driven by fear that somebody will beat them to a story), may push too hard for facts a source is trying to protect; they may use methods they'd find hard to defend. Irving Kristol, writing in *More,* speculates that reporters' assumption that they alone have the right to decide whether facts should be published or not is a source of the adversary theory of journalism. Most reporters would say that they don't look on news sources, in the Senate office building or a neighborhood bar, as enemies—not adversaries, though often obstacles.

---

whose alienation from government is common. Spiro Agnew railed against the "effete" press whose views of Nixon's government he derided. The press is called the watchdog of government, and a watchdog does not come up wagging its tail.

But to conclude that all this adds up inescapably to preordained warfare is bad logic. The press's function vis-a-vis government is not to fight it, not even essentially to criticize it. It is rather to report so that people can form sound judgments about it. A Department of Defense public affairs officer said that "the press is not a partner of the people with both arrayed against the government, but rather a bridge between the two." Ithiel de Sola Pool, a communications scientist at M.I.T., says that "society must have media that are the government's voice as well as media voices that oppose it."

The purpose of the press, and its justification, is to report. It is misbehaving grossly when it reports only bad behavior; but the fact that it does report such behavior—and comment unfavorably on it when it wishes—does not mean it is antigovernment. It is acting not against government but rather for its clientele.

NEWS IS NEW

The word *news* signalizes the emphasis on the instant—information that is new. Caesar's *Acta Diurna* on a wall in the Forum did not always recite today's or yestersay's facts, but the facts were the latest available. The advent of printing 500 years ago gave the word *news* new meaning. The first daily journal in England emphasized currency in both of its title words, *Daily Courant.*

Stress on the time context of a story is today taken for granted. The world moves fast, and its citizens know that they must run, not walk, to keep up with it. What seems true today may seem, or *be*, untrue tomorrow. Because news audiences want fresh information, most news stories report events of "today" or, at the most distant, "last night" or "yesterday." News media are carefully specific about time factors to show that their reports—more than merely "recent"—are the last word.

The media handle news fast to preserve this last-second flavor. A prime stimulus to speed is competition; every reporter works to spread the good or bad tidings before anybody else does. American news offices, and most of them throughout the world, are organized to gather, write, edit and circulate the news swiftly.

The print media accept the fact that they have lost the race for speed. There is no current way that newspapers can get news to customers as fast as broadcasting delivers it. As the newspapers' competitive positions have changed, their staffs ask themselves questions they might well have pondered before: How valid is

Television reporters and cameramen race to record an encounter between police and demonstrating construction workers. *(United Press International Photo)*

speed as a measure of news value, or as a factor in its presentation? Does a reader of the evening paper really care whether the legislature's vote on public housing reaches him two hours after it happens rather than two days? If reporters and editors had those two days instead of two hours, might they not turn out more carefully edited, better documented and more useful stories?

The torture of accuracy in the name of speed showed up dramatically when a jet plane slammed into a California apartment building. A TV report within an hour said that 200 people had died. The news the next morning changed it to "200 lived in the building—nobody knows how many got out." That evening: "Forty or 50 may have died." Next morning: "Eight bodies found, 14 missing." And

Spot News

The term *spot news* means hot news—news that is reported at the first possible time after its occurrence or surfacing. Most straight news is spot news, as is most hard news. (The time element in news gets further attention in the next chapter.)

so on until the third evening's report was that "eight bodies and a portion of a ninth" had been found.

Reporters and editors get cautious with news of this kind. First estimates of "death tolls" (large-scale catastrophes always produce "tolls") are inevitably exaggerated. It's fair to ask: What would be lost by reporting the major lines of such events but leaving details for the time—it won't be long—when you'll have the right?

And how much are the news media the victims of their own passion to get it first? Would their customers demand frenzied speed if the media had not trained them to expect it?

The newspaper extra has joined the dodo and the Model T (there were no extras reporting Ford's pardon of Nixon or the collision of jet planes in the Canary Islands). A thoughtful mid-century newspaper editor likened reporters to farmers "rushing through the fields grabbing handfuls of grain and leaving the real harvest to the gleaners . . . the weekly and monthly periodicals." Eric Sevareid, the respected CBS commentator, proposed shortly before his retirement, only half in jest, a policy of "news every other day—no newspapers, no news broadcasts Monday, Wednesday, and Friday" in order to give journalists time to think and evaluate. The quality of news coverage is more to be prized than its glitter.

NEWS IS CONCISE

News reporting exists to serve, and to serve best it has developed conventions of form and manner. At its optimum, it must serve fast. That means rhetoric that is concise, clear and simple. Effectiveness dwindles with diffusion, ambiguity, disorganization. Newswriting should be terse, direct and coherent. It should be well paced. And above all it should never require a double take.

Newswriting is tight for good reasons. One is that tight writing, without side trips or fancy decoration, is easy reading. Another is that a story that doesn't waste a reader's or listener's time has a good chance to hold attention; the story that bores doesn't bore for

---

When News Comes Flaming . . .

Complexity of a news event combined with the urge to get it out fast may make accuracy the victim. When Vietcong sappers attacked the U.S. Embassy in Saigon as the 1968 Tet offensive opened, some reporters had the enemy invading the embassy offices, others kept them outside (the "others" were right). When rebel forces attacked Kolwezi, Zaire, in 1978, 80 Western journalists put out almost as many estimates of whites killed, blacks killed, rebels killed, civilians killed. Some wrote only of the "massacre of whites," others reported "black bodies lying all over the streets." The reporters both times were a handpicked crew, experts in observing and fact-finding. Haste and emotion may play hob with facts.

---

long. And another is that no newspaper's columns, no news broadcast's precious seconds, can accommodate all the news that is available. If you report every play in a ball game, you have to leave unmentioned the new coach at Whatsis College. Tell the first story in its essentials and you have room for the second.

Good newswriting (and bad) are examined in later chapters.

STUDY SUGGESTIONS

1. What do you make of the fact that many people who deny the reliability of newspapers seem nevertheless to rely on them heavily?
2. Can you make a distinction between literal accuracy and effective accuracy?
3. Name as many reportorial methods of assuring accuracy as you can.
4. In studies of news accuracy, "mistakes in meaning" are more commonly alleged than other kinds. How do you account for this?
5. Write a definition of balance in presenting news and suggest some of the strategies for attaining it.
6. From your own experience, name examples of news reports that appear out of balance (the examples may be single stories or continuing news).
7. Give your own definition of objectivity.
8. Describe briefly what appear to be the two principal obstacles to fully objective reporting.
9. Describe characteristics of the New Journalism.
10. Do you believe that objective reporting is the kind that serves the public best? However you answer, defend your position.
11. Define *adversary journalism.* Do you accept the statement that it is not consistent with objective reporting?
12. Do you support or deny—and why—the position of this book that "advocacy journalism is not fair reporting"?
13. Give what seem to you the reasons that news media put such heavy emphasis on news currency.

PRACTICE ASSIGNMENTS

1. In most newsrooms stories that have just been published become news tips for folo or second-day stories. Responsible practice demands that they be thoroughly checked. Assume that you, as a reporter on an afternoon paper, are asked to rewrite a local story from a morning newscast. Select such a story, take complete notes from the broadcast, and check every specific in it: addresses, names, times, dates, places, dollars, quotations. Use all the sources you think appropriate, both people named in the story and printed or other sources. (When you ask questions, identify yourself as a student reporter.) Once everything is checked, compute a batting average for the story—percentages of hits and misses. If you have found errors, rewrite the story to correct them.
2. Select a newspaper report of a speech given locally by a speaker you can reach. Take the story to the speaker

and ask for comment, with particular attention given to whether or not he thinks it accurate in meaning and emphases. If he thinks it is in error, find out why. Then take it to the reporter who wrote it (a call to the city desk will identify the writer). Examine critically the statements by both sources.

3. Examine half a dozen stories in a newspaper or news broadcast to see whether you can find instances of reporter intrusion—the reporter's views instead of the accurately observed facts. You may need to consult both reporters and people involved in the story to test your observations. Write a commentary on what you find.
4. Examine all the news stories on the front page of a newspaper with two questions in mind: Is each clearly a report of the event's most recent developments? Does each make the time element entirely clear? Correct whatever faults you find.

RELATED READING

Bethell, Tom. "The Myth of an Adversary Press." *Harper's,* January 1977. Is the press an adversary of government, or has it become an arm and part of government? (The Washington *Post* in-house critic, Charles N. Seib, analyzes and disagrees with Bethell's thesis in the *Post* of Dec. 17, 1976.)

Dennis, Everette E., and William L. Rivers. *Other Voices: The New Journalism in America.* Canfield Press, 1974. A brief, readable, perceptive history and commentary about the new currents in news journalism inspired by the "turbulence of the 1960s."

Epstein, Edward Jay. "Peddling a Drug Scare." *Columbia Journalism Review,* November–December 1977. Subtitled "How Nixon and His Aides Sold a Heroin Horror Story to the National Media."

Fallows, James. "Ben Bradlee and His All-Star Revue." *Washington Monthly,* January 1975. Fallows scorns "shallow objectivity" and asks more thoughtful and carefully labeled "analysis."

Powers, Ron. *The Newscasters.* St. Martin's Press, 1977. Powers, one of TV's severest but best-informed critics, presents a somber picture of the accomplishments of TV as a news medium. He is concerned about the cult of personalities, the use of consultants to tell station management what the public wants, nomadic anchor-gods and -goddesses, and "marketing priorities and absentee ownership."

Rather, Dan. *The Camera Never Blinks.* William Morrow, 1977. Rather writes vigorously, humorously and entertainingly about his experiences as a reporter for radio and TV in the 1960s and 1970s. You learn what it is like to be a first-rater in the business, and you meet many big names, political and journalistic. (Available in paperback.)

4 Evaluation, Selection, Emphasis

PREVIEW

News—the timely report of facts of interest or importance—is evaluated under established criteria:

- Importance—the likely impact on the lives of those who receive it
- Interest—potential to stimulate recipients' emotions, to make them laugh, cry, shudder, go into action, come back for more
- The "best" news is news high on both importance and interest scales
- Identified factors help journalists to make news decisions. Among them are: proximity or distance, economic impact, familiarity, prominence, humor, pathos, currency, emotional stimulus

News decisions, often made initially by reporters, are subject to review by news executives. Among traps that beset news judgment are: copy-catting, sensationalizing, catering to public taste for crime, violence and sexuality.

Only a handful of a day's events become news. Most things people do or say go unchronicled and unremembered. Most men and women pass days, weeks, months and years without experiences considered newsworthy. Sometimes they edge into the periphery of news events: they go to baseball games, watch parades, vote. But they are rarely more than secondary participants.

Once in a while their personal ventures get into the papers. They upset their sailboats and need the Lake Patrol. They receive mail with 15-year-old post marks. Or they get fingers crushed, after 20 years of running an elevator, when the safety doors of the new elevator take them by surprise. Somebody decides that an event should not be tossed into limbo, that it merits a place in the daily record. It—and they—become news.

How is the decision made? On what rationale? What makes some events "better" than others? How are stories selected?

The news experts who make these decisions are not demigods with celestial intuition. They work and make their judgments in an environment studded with guideposts.

First of all, news stories do not develop in a vacuum. On the contrary, they are part of their era and their society. Social customs, history, geography, economics and a host of such conditioners affect the outreach of events and determine their value as the stuff of news. The factors are so familiar to newsworkers that in many cases any two, 20 or 200 would make substantially the same decision. On the day that Anwar Sadat breaks the solid Arab front by traveling to Israel, a fender bender isn't likely to get much play. But in news huddles everywhere professionals go at each other hammer and tongs in arguments about what deserves emphasis.

Should a local tax increase be played over the congressional inquiry into Korean bribery in Washington? Is the small fine paid by a nursing home for an unsanitary kitchen worth page one? One metropolitan "page-one editor" reluctantly—on orders from higher officers—gave the upper right corner of page one to a story about a chemical that retarded grass growth (less mowing!). By the final edition the story had moved to page 27 (where, said the page-one editor, it belonged; his judgment was borne out by the fact that six years later the chemical had not reached the market).

Judgments vary because of differing audience requirements and explicit medium limitations—some news that gets newspaper space is ignored on the air. But the processes are similar, and similar guideposts apply. The difference is often in their interpretation.

No rules are absolute. A reporter does not have over his desk a list labeled "Components of News"; the VDT of the modern news-

---

". . . A Proud Tradition"

Daniel Patrick Moynihan, later U.S. ambassador to the United Nations and senator from New York, wrote in 1971 that "the fact that news will be reported whether or not the reporter or his publisher likes it is a proud tradition. However, a decision must be made as to whether an event really is news or whether it is a nonevent staged for the purpose of getting into the papers or onto the screen."

News Defined

Among many definitions of news:

"News is anything timely that interests a number of persons, and the best news is that which has the greatest interest for the greatest number."—Willard Grosvenor Bleyer, distinguished journalism scholar and teacher

"News is what a well-trained editor decides to put in his paper."—Gerald W. Johnson, Baltimore *Sun*

". . . to many newspapermen no news is bad news, good news is dull news, and bad news makes marvelous copy."—Leo Rosten, writer, critic, humorist

". . . news is a picture of reality on which men can act."—Walter Lippmann, "dean" of newspaper commentators. Lippmann added that "news and truth are not the same." The function of news, he held, is "to signalize an event," and that of truth "to bring to light the hidden facts, to set them into relation with each other, and to make a picture of reality on which men can act."

This book's definition: *News is the timely report of facts or opinions that hold interest or importance, or both, for a considerable number of people.*

room doesn't think for its writer or editor. But even beginners in newswork, thanks to their newspaper reading and broadcast listening, have an idea about what makes news, and news veterans have subcutaneous rules of thumb ready for instant application.

Any professional can describe "good" news—usable news. It is news worth carrying to an audience. As reporters collect facts and write stories, as editors evaluate the stacks of copy that cross their desks, two questions continuously occupy their subconscious: "Will this story affect our particular audience? Will it 'grab' readers?" Reporters and deskmen rarely resort to so precise a significance-interest analysis, but they go through the process a thousand times a day. They do it at top speed, for news practice gives little time—more's the pity—to stop and think it over.

Newsworkers know that to be either significant or interesting a news story must relate to a particular audience—*their* particular audience—whether national or bounded by geographical, cultural, economic or emotional factors. Development of a new fertilizer means more in Iowa than it does in Pittsburgh; it is a better story today, in an age of irrigation problems and tired soil, than it would have been in 1880.

The significance and appeal of any event have to be evaluated in terms of a specific group audience, not of an individual. Since no audience is homogeneous—every group larger than a golf foursome has individuals with widely differing characteristics—a journalist always hopes to find news that will appeal to as many interests as possible.

WHO MAKES THE NEWS DECISIONS?

No news responsibility is heavier than that of the reporter or the editor who decides what ought to be reported. Their judgments govern whether a newspaper or a newscast serves well or badly. If decisions are made with scorn for the audience, with an eye only for the size of the audience or what the competition is doing—if they don't keep abreast of their time—they're likely to fail. They must grow not alone out of experience but also out of humane sympathy and recognition that a society depends on the quality of the information it gets.

Lines of responsibility The organization chart of a newspaper usually is headed by a publisher, that of a broadcasting station by a general manager, either of whom is likely to be the owner or the representative of ownership; and in the American economic system the buck stops there. But in large newspaper and broadcasting operations the news-decision buck rarely gets that far. In most newspapers the head of the news operation is the managing editor; his colonels, captains and corporals are news editors or desk editors of one kind or another. Major decisions in large newspapers are commonly made at daily news huddles in which principal editors examine the day's prospective news and decide how to use and emphasize it. The wire services, like many individual newsrooms, term their daily schedule of expected stories the "news budget." Lesser decisions are made by the city and wire editors and their assistants, often following the recommendations of the men and women who actually gather the news, the reporters.

News for Whom?

"Why didn't the radio tell about Aunt Emma's golden wedding party?"

You've heard the question—why do you know about events that the news media ignore?

One important reason is that a news pro, though he reports and writes for the individual eye or ear, nevertheless learns to see audiences not as individuals but as groups of people. He knows that though *you* may be offended that Aunt Emma didn't make the paper, most readers couldn't care less. There are more than enough subjects about which thousands of people care a lot. And so, since space and time aren't stretchable, the pro leaves out Aunt Emma so as to have room for the city council.

Smaller newspapers and broadcast newsrooms, though their staffs are smaller, follow similar lines of organization and procedure.

Reporters make a flood of initial news decisions—whether to spend time on this event or that one, what to put in a lead, what to leave out. Their judgments, as recommendations subject to review by their desk editors—city, sports and others—are usually honored.

What qualifies a newsworker to make decisions? A journalist should be equipped with perception, social purpose, a brain that doesn't limp, and personality traits such as skeptical curiosity, imagination, what is loosely called liking for people, and energy. Today the equipment usually includes specialized news training and education; a newsworker should begin building on-the-job news experience before graduation from algebra if he can, and keep adding to it unceasingly. There are other roads: William Randolph Hearst got to put his talents to work because his father was a millionaire; Bob Woodward studied law and served in the U.S. Navy, and Carl Bernstein got a newsroom job as a copyboy at 16; Edward R. Murrow came to radio from a background in education, the theater and public affairs. At least two excellent reporters had their first journalism lessons on state prison journals. For the most part the news decision makers are well grounded in professional experience. Their responsibility rests not only on copybook qualities but also on journalistic practice. That they perform so generally "in the public interest" is a continuing marvel of 20th-century journalism.

DECISIONS ABOUT SIGNIFICANCE

News is "significant" when it affects the lives or welfare of a considerable share of its audience. News of war in Vietnam touched everything from pork prices to styles of shoes and movies; news of fighting between two small nations on the west coast of Africa did not have such impact. News about a drought that threatens food supplies around the world can't be ignored; a potato blight in Idaho or Maine affects millions of dinner tables, but one in Rhode Island gets only local attention.

Geographical factors It's easy to see how location affects significance. The election of a senator in Arizona is big news in Phoenix, Tucson and Flagstaff, whose media cover it hungrily. In Pennsylvania it has no local significance, though it gets modest attention because the choice of a senator anywhere affects Pennsylvanians. Pittsburgh media find the election of a mayor in Youngstown, Ohio, just across the state line, worth little space and time. Youngstown media, however, play it big; those in Cleveland, Columbus and Cincinnati give it modest attention.

Geographical factors show themselves in other ways. Suppose the Department of the Interior opens previously closed areas of a Maine national forest to big-game hunting. Indiana, which boasts neither a national forest nor a wild animal bigger than a buck deer, ignores the event. Oregon media, whose forest lands and wildlife resemble those in Maine, report it because the same thing might happen there. Newspapers and broadcasters in Maine report not only the Washington decision but also develop "local angle" stories that show what it could mean to local hunters, the state resort industry, and the conservation of moose, bears and deer.

The geographical factor varies with media, areas and decades. Radio stations of different powers have different ranges and therefore quite different audience areas—a county for a 250-watt station, half of the Mississippi Valley for a 50-kilowatt clear-channel station. Airfreight and fast trucks make it possible to "lay down" a morning paper at 7 a.m. on doorsteps hundreds of miles from where they are printed. As audiences widen, relative importance changes, and the news selected reflects the change.

The numbers game News significance may be determined by the number of people it affects. Every citizen in Youngstown is somehow touched by a mayoral election, but the choice of a chairwoman of the crewel-and-macramé section of the Women's Library Club gets four lines in the paper, not even a bow on the air.

Community size affects news selection. Big-city media give little notice to the day-by-day affairs of private citizens or to organized and semipublic activities like the choice of a sewing group's chairwoman. It's common for city journalists to snicker at the small

---

Audience Interests—Editors' Interests

The Indianapolis *News* asked its editors responsible for news selection and a cross section of its readers to select the 10 most important news events of 1976. Only three selections coincided—all "human-interest" news: congressional sex scandals, kidnapping of a school bus, "legionnaire's disease." On the readers' list were the Patty Hearst trial, the Bicentennial, the swine flu scare, whether a New Jersey woman in a coma should be kept alive, the death of Howard Hughes, and the landing of a space vehicle on Mars. None of these were on the editors' list; in their place were illegal acts by the CIA and FBI, the deaths of Chou En-lai and Mao Tse-tung, racial upheaval in South Africa, civil war in Lebanon and the killing of U.S. soldiers in Korea. Readers attributed more significance to news that aroused their emotions than to news the editors thought of genuine importance. But observe that editors sometimes play up the emotional news above the other kind. If the customers want it, they get it.

It isn't hard to get an actor to pose or talk. Here, Liza Minnelli has just arrived at a Paris airport. *(United Press International Photo)*

newspaper that reports blessed events in the barnyard or write that "Grocer Sam Bilker has painted his front," but their barbs ignore the relative significance of the small event in the small world.

"Big names" Though the run-of-the-mill doings of the butcher, the baker and the candlestick maker do not make news, the slightest variation in the routine of a VIP is reported. Nobody notices when most of us have colds, but sniffles at the White House can be heard worldwide. A round-the-world vacation of an Atlanta manufacturer is worth only a note in the gossip column; but a modest weekend of a British princess is under a news microscope from Ketchikan to Khartoum. What for one person is a private affair becomes for another a matter of concern to millions.

Extent of audience Comparatively unimportant events may achieve a spurious significance if they arouse wide interest. The Super Bowl each January has lasting effect on only a few hundred Americans—the participants—but no yearly one-shot event gets more at-

How Much Detail?

The clinical detail with which illnesses of the famous are reported has deservedly drawn critical fire. Nobody denied, when President Eisenhower had heart and intestinal ailments, that the news was important. But the intimacy with which the President's symptoms were described was thought by many to be "bad taste." Bad taste was also a charge against the protracted, detailed and repetitious reports about Harry S Truman's final illness, the breast surgery performed on President Ford's wife, and Senator Hubert Humphrey's long struggle with ultimately fatal cancer.

tention. The World Series for a full October week holds 50 million Americans glued to TV sets and thus for a brief period alters the pace and texture of national life. Such events acquire impact that has nothing to do with their intrinsic significance.

Significance is relative Thus, because there are many measures, the significance of news is relative. Some news is important for everybody, everywhere. But much news is important only in restricted context. The conditioning facts are the radius of an event's influence, its power to attract attention and stimulate response, and its relation to a community's size and composition.

Hard news, soft news News that has significance for a considerable share of the target audience—usually the latest information on relatively sober matters—is called hard news. This is the news of government, politics, international relations, religion, legislatures, courts, civic activities. To most audiences hard news is dull news. Not always easy to understand, it makes for difficult reading or listening. Hard news, commonly of greater moment than soft news, draws smaller audiences. Human-interest tales, news of minor crime, stories of lust and comedy attract people readily. This anomaly is the challenge and the despair of newsworkers. No graphs are needed to prove that most people would rather hear about the latest nose bloodied by a movie player in a Las Vegas casino, remote as the event may be, than about the fall of another Italian government or last year's increase or decline in the gross national product.

"INTERESTING" NEWS

Reporters play an after-hours game: speculation about the event that would develop into the "biggest" news story. Their inventions range from the solemn to the absurd, the irreverent to the catastrophic. During World War I the death of the Kaiser was a favorite

News Can Be Both Hard and Soft

A hurricane hits the Florida coast. It levels towns, destroys shipping and fruit groves, kills and maims. Clearly this is a hard-news event—its effects reach far beyond the area it devastates. But it is also soft news because readers and listeners are moved by it: "How dreadful . . . that's the part of Florida where Josie and Bill were going . . . will it raise the price of grapefruit?" War news is often hard and soft at the same time; so is much political news, especially during campaigns.

"event," and in World War II this became the deaths of Hitler and Mussolini (fantasy that became spectacular fact and drew enormous headlines). Some suggest the Second Coming; discovery of a cancer cure; the first giant step on Mars. Each such event would be of high importance, but each would also carry powerful popular interest; each would not only shake the world but also make brisk conversation over breakfast tables, lunch pails and cocktails.

But news high in public interest is not necessarily high in public significance. Just as some important events leave the public bored, so some of great interest are genuinely important only to their participants. When the two qualities come in tandem, journalists beam. They have news that not only gives their customers something solid but also something that will be listened to, read, remembered.

Reporters and editors know that people give attention to news when they can expect to "get something out of it"—pleasure or profit, fun or security. It may be something that meets conscious needs or desires, or it may fall below the horizon of awareness. Sometimes it is the hard or important news; sometimes it is news that pricks the emotions (the New York *Post* sold 400,000 extra copies the day it reported the capture of the man accused of being the "Son of Sam" killer). A third such category: material that may not be news at all—self-improvement columns, bridge columns, how to grow tomatoes, how to lose 20 pounds in 20 days.

HUMAN-INTEREST NEWS

A human-interest story stirs the emotions. It makes you say "hurray," "what a shame," "wish I'd been there" or "glad I wasn't there." Hard news often has human interest—the shooting or resignation of a president, the adoption of a 55-mile-an-hour speed law. It establishes emotional contact quickly. When a story horrifies readers or makes them laugh, saddens or angers them, appeals to their self-interest, they become a vicarious participants. Such a story requires less concentration and effort than hard news demands.

Some of the components of news described in Chapter 3 may be

Surefire Ingredients

A sardonic view of "best news" inspired a reporter's musing, at an after-hours seminar, that four elements sure to grab readers are sex, royalty, the deity and mystery. Get them all together, said this reporter, and you have the biggest of all news. His model: "My God," said the duchess, "I'm pregnant. Who done it?"

of little importance in human-interest news. If a story makes readers laugh, they don't care that it's a week old. If a reporter is touched by what he writes about a battered baby, objectivity may seem unimportant.

It is rare that a newspaper goes to press without a seasoning of news that entertains—news of a child rescued from a well, of a student who breaks out of jail to take his final exams, of a starlet who marries a prince. Such stories are easy to digest even though they are not very nourishing.

Among characteristics of human-interest news are these:

Adventure and conflict The ready human response to adventure and contest leads to priority for news of war, sports and controversy. The extent of sports sections and the domination of weekend afternoons by play-by-play broadcasts measure the media's awareness that America worships men and women who can run faster, throw straighter or punch harder than anybody else. A writer in the Harvard alumni magazine points out that when scientists and astrologers disagree about the validity of astrological predictions, "the media, properly sensitive to our delight in a good catfight, play up" the news. Attempts to climb Mt. Everest—conflict between men and nature and, perhaps, abominable snowmen—are covered so routinely that they all seem alike. Hard political news wouldn't get nearly as much space were it not that somebody wins, somebody loses. Ellen Goodman of the Boston *Globe* comments that overzealous reporting of petty infighting in the National Women's

Human Interest on the Air

Radio newscasts carry a smaller proportion of human-interest news than either TV or the printed press. Radio, with its capsule newscasts, often has less elbow room. Television is charged with devoting too much time to news that can be pictured—fires, accidents at the beach, pretty faces—but TV news has made long strides toward finding human interest in stories of conflict and personality rather than of petty disaster and cheesecake. Because TV's great advantage is its video, however, its temptation to use news of sunbathers rather than devaluation of the dollar will continue.

How Much Crime News?

Dependable studies show that from 2 to 10 percent of news space goes to crime news. The decline of newspaper competition has decreased newspaper dependence on crime as audience bait. In the 1920s, when New York City had three screaming tabloids, the good gray *Times* gave more actual space (though less prominence) to a juicy love-nest murder than any of its blood-and-guts rivals. But the two sensational papers outdistanced the *Times* in the 1977 "Son of Sam" tempest.

Conference can "turn a conference into a fight-and-folly show for the evening news."

Crime and violence This kind of news has the magnetism of news of adventure and conflict. It may be either hard or soft. Social critics consider media emphasis on violence far overweight; the extent to which it is the stimulus of violent behavior is a major concern of today's sociologists, psychologists, journalists. A Florida jury rendered an opinion that TV violence was not the prime cause of a 14-year-old's murderous behavior, but that doesn't settle the question. Journalists and criminology students alike point out that failure to report criminal activity would surely have disastrous social effects, and would be dishonest reporting as well. (The movie "Star Wars" triggered a wave of inquiries to the National Space Administration about space exploration, and scientists forecast that a movie about unidentified flying objects would bring a new flood.)

A question asked at a journalists' convention in 1974—"Is the press being held for ransom?"—underlined a modern problem in crime reporting and news evaluation: the "publicity crime" or "media event." The Patricia Hearst kidnapping was a case in point—a case in which it seemed, as *The New Yorker* said, that a powerless group committed an outrage "in order to gain visibility and a small amount of leverage." The puzzle of how kidnappings should be covered is a journalist's headache: Do you report all the news you can get as fast as you can get it? Do you listen to law officers who want cover-up for the safety of the victim or the recovery of the ransom? The question has been answered both ways: In a California case the media were silent about a kidnapping until the victim was found unharmed. In another, scare headlines (and, said police, pinpoint shadowing by reporters) helped to stretch police work from days to years. Most media are inclined to hold back on police request, as long as the cover doesn't leak; but covers are notoriously holey.

"Publicity crimes" put hard questions to the media. An Indianapolis man with a shotgun muzzle wired to a hostage's neck de-

The Right Not to Know?

The Russian savant Aleksandr Solzhenitzyn, in a Harvard commencement address, argued for the right of people "not to know . . . not to have their divine souls stuffed with gossip, nonsense, vain talk." He said that "we may see terrorists treated as heroes, secrets pertaining to national defense revealed, shameless intrusion on privacy." Thus the man imprisoned in and exiled from his own land for outspoken views seemed to express an elitist view of who ought to know what. The First Amendment principle is that people should be told when lies are lies, when fact is fact. The dangers in freedom to speak, says this principle, are overweighed by the dangers in darkness.

manded, and got, three-network prime time (during which he proclaimed himself a "goddamn national hero"). Journalists, political leaders and peace officers agree that much of the 1970s' terrorism in Europe and the Middle East was actuated more by desire for attention than for money or strategic advantage. An Israeli TV reporter told an international TV audience that his news broadcasts had been boons to the Mogadiscio hijackers. Nevertheless terrorist crimes are real events, and the public has to know of them. When, and with how much glare, are painful quandaries.

No computer has puzzled out the answers to these dilemmas. Public knowledge of any kind of behavior, "good" or "bad," is a stimulant to imitation—airplane hijacking and hostage-holding were theatrical examples in the 1970s. But social psychologists speculate that notoriety is more likely to affect the form of criminal behavior than to act as its germ. And journalists know that deviant activities cannot be corrected or controlled if they are not known. Suppression of news of violence because it is a repugnant model may be self-defeating.

Proximity An auto smashup on your front lawn interests you more than one on the other side of town. If you see a picket line, you're more likely to want to know something about it than if it's in another state. Readership studies say that you will more probably read about a football game you've seen than about one you have missed. And if the winning touchdown was made by the kid next door, your interest is heightened.

Humor The leaven that humor provides in the daily diet of sober news is in high demand. It is also in short supply. Genuinely comical news is hard to find; a humorous or ironic story can rarely be planned in advance. Usually unforeseen, it has to be caught on the wing—the fire delivered to the fire station (page 305) or the safecrackers who got away safely with $500,000 in stage money. Some papers are blessed with writers who turn out humorous features several times a week, but even "funny" writers produce their share of duds. The "brights," brief oddity stories that some newscasters choose to conclude their programs, are often pretty dull. Humor is hard to write.

Pathos-bathos One of the products of the yellow journalism era were the "sob sisters" (often cigar-chewing males) who supplied daily tear-jerkers; their excesses and their cynical insincerity brought news of individual human distress under suspicion. Though the sob sister is no longer a staff fixture, news media are alive to the human-interest appeal of news of a baby orphaned by a tornado or an invalid who died just before help reached him. A reporter is expected to be able to write effectively about suffering and sorrow. The mode today is one of restraint and moderation; the fine art of understatement has kept many writers on the safe side of bathos.

The sex angle Since Queen Victoria died, it has become respectable to acknowledge that people are interested in sex. Even during Victoria's reign, "love crimes" and unconventional man-woman relationships were overplayed. Love triangles, scarlet divorces and adultery reached their news peak in the 1920s, during the circulation wars among New York tabloids. Since then, most media have held such news within bounds.

Serious news about sexuality, however, receives more attention today than ever before. Increasing understanding of homosexual life and activity has led to straightforward treatment in the press. Pornography and obscenity—the first well understood, the second not yet satisfactorily defined—are no longer backroom mysteries, thanks to news treatment. Feature sections thrive on articles examining aspects of sex. Where people once smirked as they used the euphemism "four-letter word," they now use the word itself. Newspapers were about equally divided, when a U.S. secretary of agriculture "talked dirty" in a racial reference, on the propriety of reporting it verbatim. Today TV has followed movies into the bedroom. Writers and editors are using the words that mean what they want to say—even four-letter colloquialisms when they clearly fit the needs of accurate reporting.

The odd and unusual Critics sometimes deplore news emphasis on the freak accident, the two-headed calf, the man who mislaid an elephant. The atypical provides one of the bases for news selection:

A wedding in church is society page stuff, but if its bridegroom shows up on a stretcher it makes page 1 and if it links a pair of nudists there's a three-column photo (taken from the rear). The news media are eager to present the odd and the unusual because readers pay quick attention to deviation from routine. News high on the oddity scale doesn't have to be important. Few lives are affected when a family in the Ozarks names all of its five sons Joe. But the news story about it is the one that a reader will repeat at the office.

Emphasis on the unusual, say some critics, leads to glorification of the unique or the atypical. The comment has merit. Yet if the media excluded all news of "abnormal" events (and who is to decide what is normal?), they would be implying that every current in their communities runs flat and placid—no misbehavior, no accidents, no change from yesterday. To reject news because it is not representative would create a worse kind of misrepresentation: That there is no abnormal or antisocial behavior. Just as society must in self-protection pay attention to asocial members of minorities who rob, slug, defraud or undress on Main Street, the news media must report their activities. You can't bandage a sore thumb if you don't know it's sore.

"Good" news A letter to the editor that comes in a thousand versions but always says the same thing goes like this: "Why don't you give us good news along with the bad? Let us hear about husbands who help with the dishes as well as those who beat up wives." The *Saturday Review* once published a column of "good news" for a few months, but let it die a quiet death. A weekly column devoted to such material, used for a time by 200 newspapers, was given up (said its author) because it had become repetitious: "The differences in good news were only in datelines and names, not in 'news plots.' "

A selection of stories composed entirely of rays of sunshine, whatever their glow, fails to picture the world as it is. The *Saturday Review* is quick to report that some plays, books and movies aren't worth your time. Charles Seib of the Washington *Post* says that "the true role of the press is not to paint the world in rosier hues than the facts warrant . . . not to tailor the national news diet in order to spread sweetness and light . . . . It is rather to give the public what it needs to know in order to participate in and help shape society." James Reston of the New York *Times* says, "Though we should give space to the quiet news," the news media must report the news about violence or anything else.

News about murders in Uganda, that is, as well as about progress toward a cure for cancer. About a killing frost in Florida as well as about a bumper wheat crop in Kansas. You report the bumper crop so that people can rejoice and expect to pay less for bread; you report the killing frost so that they won't be surprised when the cost of oranges goes up.

"What's good for me . . ." A psychological truth that journalists translate into copy is that humans are interested in events that affect their well-being. Self-interest leads them to read about a social security plan rather than a foreign-aid program; one may benefit them directly, the other at long range or not at all. In the fall of 1976 a Gallup poll showed that 93 percent of Americans knew something about the swine flu vaccination program. Advances in one's own profession or business, medical developments that may mean better health, the promise of better housing, better foods, better shampoos—subjects like these get wide and instant attention.

Names One way to give a reader or viewer a sense of association with news is to salt it with names. Thus the shopworn but valid axiom that "names make news." Small-community papers build clientele on the fact that almost everybody knows almost everybody, and that almost everybody's name gets published now and then.

"Big" names or names in the news have similar pull. It's hard to think that a story with the name "Carter" in it would not have had instant meaning to any American in 1976 . . . and the name Evel Knievel to most. A name you recognize means a ready-made contact between reader and event.

The small event attached to the big name—that sniffle in the White House—may have importance as well as interest.

THE TIME ELEMENT

The time of a news event—when it occurred, when it will occur—is an essential component of any news story. Time is a vital consideration in the selection and evaluation of news. (*Time* and *speed* are not, in news, equivalent terms. One is a statement of the time of an event; the other the relation of time of publication to the time the news became available.) A story reports, for instance, that the mayor announced *yesterday* that he will appoint a new tax commissioner *next Tuesday*. Here are two time elements—*yesterday* and *Tuesday*. Should the story go on to say that the commissioner will take office *July 1*, there would be a third. But there's a difference. *Yesterday*, the time the information became available, is the prime time element in the story, the element that gets it published today. It may not be the most important, for either of the others could give the event special meaning. "Readers often like to identify themselves with news stories," says a New York newspaper editor. "It's satisfying to think, 'Five minutes more and I'd have been walking right past the accident.' "

Timeliness, seasonableness A story is *timely* if it is appropriate to the audience at the time it is printed or broadcast. The difference between spot news—news with a strong time element—and timely news appears in what news media do when the city has its hundredth birthday. The local paper puts out a special edition with both types of news: spot or current news about the parade, the governor's proclamation and the collapsing grandstand; timely material with historical pieces, speculation about the future, a biography of the city's founder. These are timely because they relate to the particular date, though they have no element of currency.

Timeliness tied to a period of the year that keeps coming back—football season, Christmas, high school graduation—is called *seasonableness.* The familiar stories about Halloween, Groundhog Day, the cherry tree that either was or wasn't chopped down—these are seasonable.

Much timely or seasonable material may be without spot news value. But some stories gain interest because of fortuitous seasonableness. A story on February 12 about the discovery of a batch of Abraham Lincoln letters is always important, but it has extra punch because of its date.

FOLLOW-THE-LEADER NEWS

A little Nebraska girl was sent to an Eastern hospital for surgery to correct a congenital disarrangement of her abdominal plumbing, and a reporter coined the phrase "upside-down stomach." The wire services loved it, and upside-down stomachs became a journalistic obsession. Upside-down stomachs were discovered in hospitals everywhere, and reported everywhere. The mania didn't die until a reporter with more enterprise than his fellows discovered that neither the condition nor its correction was uncommon.

Time Copy

Not everything a news medium presents has relation to current affairs. Bridge columns, comic strips, sewing hints, medical advice and historical or personality features have little "today" relevance—they could be used as well next July as this January. Such material is called time copy ("timeless copy" might be a better term). It is something the editor keeps under his desk blotter, or stored in the computer, against the day the news slows up. You can use a story on how many people have tried to go over Niagara in a barrel any day of the year when there is a hole to be filled.

The newswriters and editors had given so much rope to a sometimes defensible news principle, "give the audience what interests it," that they hanged themselves. Nobody wanted to know that much about intestines, even though the subject at first had oddity, as well as a touch of pathos and suspense. Though the story had originality, warmth and human interest when it was new, it quickly became banal. Journalists did the same thing when Amy Carter was enrolled in a public school, with the same result. The cases are examples of follow-the-leader reporting: "If it was good yesterday, it's good today." News consumers were for a time surfeited by stories about flying saucers (none of which ever landed).

Why news fads? Because it's easier to follow a well-marked news trail than to blaze a new one; audiences are long-suffering; and merely reporting an event, particularly an offbeat one, may lead to its replication. Reporting the annual sophomore high jinks at Fort Lauderdale used to be an annual must. But it got less interesting the 10th time than when it was new. Thoughtful reporters and editors know that when they follow fads they may find themselves coming back on their own trails—and boring customers as well.

There are other kinds of journalistic stereotypes. Another section of this book examines clichés of diction. Some editors can't resist stories about lovable pets. A wandering bare-bottomed 2-year-old is pretty sure to make the front page.

It's not always easy to avoid the stereotypes of routine reporting. Woodward and Bernstein, by refusing to ask only the usual questions and accept only the usual answers, helped overthrow a president—but it wasn't easy. It's not hard to report the surface of today's school board story if you look to see how last week's was handled. Political events, baseball games and commencement speeches have familiar patterns, but no two are identical, and re-

---

Critics and Critics

Popular criticism of American news performance is often superficial and uninformed. But notable critics of the press have surfaced in recent years. One is Ben Bagdikian, once the Washington *Post's* in-house critic, widely known for his articles on the press. Others worth listening to are Harry S. Ashmore, of the Center for the Study of Democratic Institutions, and Douglass S. Cater, director of the Aspen Program on Communication and Society. Among significant and often erudite examinations of the media have been such conferences as the Liebling conventions held in Washington and New York, the Aspen conferences, and those arranged by the Center for the Study of Democratic Institutions. The study by the Commission on Freedom of the Press in the 1940s yielded books on press freedom, broadcasting, movies and international mass communications.

---

ports of them shouldn't make them seem hatched from identical eggs. A revealing reporter finds what makes today's event different rather than what makes it conventional.

SENSATIONAL OR SENSATIONALIZED?

Much news is "sensational"—it heats the blood, it gives off sparks. The capture of hostages in three buildings in Washington early in 1977 by a group of Muslim "terrorists" was a sensation, a spectacular event that frightened, excited and angered thousands of people. But it quickly became a media event of which, as Charles Seib said, "the media were as much a part as the terrorists, the victims, and the authorities." Print and TV reporters doubled its dimension with live interviews, rehash of what happened yesterday, and a plethora of forgettable details. An event that was sensational enough in itself was sensationalized. As one commentator put it, the assertion that the event "terrorized the nation's capital" was true only because the media made it true. A reporter who worked on the story said in a memo to his editors:

> How much does the public need to know in these situations and when? What function are we serving—to satisfy some primeval urge for gore and sensation, or a real need for information? How much more did we add to the real horror of the situation with our flourish of reporting at the end (when reporters engulfed the exhausted hostages)?

Among other cases of overreaction:

- The blowup of a throwaway remark by President Ford (that he would give amnesty for Vietnam deserters "another hard look") into a promise of sweeping change in government policy (see page 274);
- The news orgy after a report that a congressman maintained a non-typing stenographer on his federal payroll (when an overdose of sleeping pills sent him to the hospital, 30 reporters and three TV network camera crews went to Ohio to make sure nobody missed a breath);
- The repetitious and overdetailed reports of hijackings and hostage-kidnappings;
- And one of the most blatant in the last decade, the explosion of news and non-news over the "Son of Sam" murders in New York City—an event that took two New York papers back 50 years into the journalistic debauchery of the 1920s.

Sensational news draws audiences; most of it ought to be reported. But it is what one observer calls "journalistic overkill" to

How Careful Is Too Careful?

In the 1960s, when "racial incidents"—bar brawls or street fights between whites and blacks—were frightening America, a number of broadcasters and newspapers agreed to delay reporting such events, or to downplay them, to forestall public terror or attempts to get into the act. Thus they avoided sensationalizing what were undeniably sensational events. They achieved their goal in some cases, failed in others.

But this question was always asked: What if withholding news of a slashing street fight at city center permits citizens to stray into the war zone? And what if, later, they say of a news medium, "It should have warned me. It can't be trusted"? The National News Council, debating this topic in 1977, suggested case-by-case decision. A reporter who covered the Council meeting, Austin Wehrwein, concluded that though "the media bristle at suggestions of 'self-censorship,' restraint in the form of playing it smart in specific cases may contribute to a solution."

magnify it beyond its real size. The sin is not in reporting the sensational event, the sin is in building it larger than life. You don't call a neighborhood rumble between teenage gangs a riot; you don't call an automobile sideswipe a crash; you don't say the Blues destroyed, routed, overwhelmed or crushed the Whites when a tight game ended in a 2–1 score.

No newspaper or news broadcast can hope to be forever free of sensational news. And it is a perverse fact that sensational events are not only more interesting but often more important than those that come every day.

STUDY SUGGESTIONS

1. Using materials in this chapter or from other sources, or both, compose your own one- or two-sentence definition of news.
2. What are the principal values on which journalists base the decision to publish or not to publish an account of a current event?
3. Diagram the "decision flow" by which news decisions are made—where they start, what influences them, where final decisions occur.
4. What values, in the eyes of most news editors, make an event *significant* news?
5. How do you explain the differences between editors' interests and those of their audience (see page 54)?
6. Define *hard news* and *soft news*.
7. What are the prime elements that mark news as *interesting* in contrast to *significant?* Cite a dozen actual examples of news that has both qualities.
8. Write your own definition of human-interest news (see also Chapter 15).
9. Distinguish carefully among: *timeliness, currency, seasonableness.*
10. Distinguish between the terms *sensational* and *sensationalized,* as applied to news. Give several examples of each kind of news, then several of news items to which both terms apply.

PRACTICE ASSIGNMENTS

1. Observe carefully, taking notes if necessary, all the local news in a week's issues of the paper you see most often or on a week's dinner-hour or late-evening TV news program. From your observations, try to arrive at a description of the news values that seem most desired by the medium. Write a descriptive statement of what you discover and follow it with an evaluative or opinion statement.
2. Repeat the process, using both a print and a broadcast medium. Again, write two kinds of statements.
3. Conduct a similar observation to discover the relative weight given by a medium or several media to local as opposed to nonlocal news. Basing your conclusions on your evidence, state your opinion of the merits of the editors' news judgments.
4. Study printed or broadcast news for a considerable period, a month or more, to observe the use of news fads, news apparently selected because it resembles other current news. If you find examples, answer these questions: (a) What news event got a fad started? Would you have used the story in the first place? (b) What are the arguments to support attention to news fads—the news, for instance, of upside-down stomachs?
5. Find 10 or more stories selected because of the quality of oddity—departure from the familiar. Discuss their use with a number of friends, instructors, family members, and others. Then write a report evaluating the news judgements that led to their use.

RELATED READING

Braestrup, Peter. *Big Story: How the American Press and Television Reported and Interpreted the Crisis of Tet 1968 in Vietnam and Washington.* Westview Press, 1977. Report on a six-year study (two volumes, 1446 pages, $50) of what major American media did—and failed to do—in covering the Hanoi offensive. Overpowering in documentation, controversial in some of its evaluations. A vastly impressive scholarly and informative achievement.

Tate, Cassandra. "Conflict of Interest: A Newspaper's Report on Itself." Columbia Review, July–August 1978. A remarkable self-examination by an Idaho daily of conflicts of interest that may have affected its news coverage.

See also Related Reading for Chapters 2, 3, 5, 19, 20.

5 Audiences and Channels

PREVIEW

Every viable news medium identifies and studies its particular audience, an audience with many common or similar interests. Many media conduct extensive audience surveys to determine precisely whom they are reaching and what the audiences like or don't like. Among guides to audience identification are:

- Geographical location
- Economic, social and cultural interests
- Attitudes on political, religious and "moral" issues
- Age, sex and ethnic characteristics

A news medium operates a carefully organized newsgathering system to minimize the chance that it will not be aware of news information that may concern its audience. News is delivered to audiences by established carriers or channels; the principal ones are newspapers, radio and television, and magazines. News from outside a medium's immediate area is usually provided by a wire service, a wide-reaching reporting service that goes to thousands of individual media.

Second in importance only to *what* the media report—and to their newsworkers often just as important—is knowledge of *whom* they are talking to, and *how* to reach their particular whoms. This chapter describes some of the implied questions and describes some of the steps the media take to arrive at answers.

NEWS MEDIA AUDIENCES

Through the middle years of the 20th century the New York *Daily News* and the Chicago *Tribune* were the most widely circulated daily newspapers in American history. The *News* was first, the *Tribune* second. They were under a common ownership. But not even the hastiest reader could have mistaken one for the other. The

News, a tabloid (one means of making subway reading easy), was a picture paper. It hit you in the eye (its most famous front page was covered by a stolen photo of a woman dying in an electric chair); it exploited sex and crime; it was unconcerned about either human or journalistic dignity. Its circulation was almost entirely within New York's five boroughs, and largely among lower-income groups. Its politics were comparatively liberal. Its cousin the *Tribune* was conservative in appearance and social attitudes; its circulation and news covered "Chicagoland" – major portions of five states; it carried a big and admired sports section, many columns of food features, first-rate comics and first-rate news and arts criticism. Its contents were chosen to appeal to conservatives throughout the Midwest agricultural area, to women and to readers in their homes.

These contrasts say, first, that no single formula will produce success everywhere; second, that the differences – governed by the nature of the audience, of the setting and of publishing philosophies – are not matters of chance. They are carefully designed.

To put it more simply, every successful news medium is plotted to meet one set of circumstances and is unlikely to be successful in others. A welter of technological, geographical, economic, cultural and social factors determine what a medium's audience is or can become.

Narrow-interest content – for small groups, specialists, minority concerns – is therefore necessary. But journalists try to make contact with as large a share of the potential audience as possible, as much of the time as possible.

AUDIENCE IDENTIFICATION

Most of the factors that define media audiences are obvious. The most apparent is geographic – the extent of territory a newspaper or station hopes to cover.

Paradoxes

1. Sometimes a newspaper or broadcasting audience is of a consistent texture – largely of one religion, say, or of one occupation, one political persuasion, one community, one ethnic character. But most so-called "mass" audiences comprise many small audiences. The larger the paper or the broader the broadcast range, the greater the variety of news and other kinds of content chosen to meet the variety of interests – farm news, financial news, bridge and gossip columns, scientific news, gardening hints. Major sections like those for sports or the stock market are dedicated frankly to fractions of the audience.

2. Any mass audience, big or small, must be reached through the eyes and ears of individual men and women. No two humans are duplicates, and no single news story is expected to interest everybody. A story seen and remembered by 25 percent of those who see the paper carrying it is considered widely read.

Geographical limits For every kind of medium a territory has known physical limits. A clear-channel radio station may have a radius of a thousand miles; a low-power station may cover only a county. TV and FM radio waves reach only to the horizons. Newspapers today, with airplanes and fast truck service, may reach out to entire states or regions; the Des Moines *Register* covers Iowa from corner to corner. But most papers seek to reach only the communities within the limits of easy circulation—a town or county, a well-defined area. Newspaper and broadcasting advertising departments produce careful maps to show where their audiences are concentrated, so that advertisers may know what area they're buying; such maps, often prepared with utmost care, are useful to news staffs as well. An advertiser does not want to spend money trying to sell skis where there isn't any snow; the news department wastes little time covering a Syttende Mai celebration when only one remote community in its area has enough Norse to observe such an event.

Other factors Every city editor has to know intimately the principal interests of the entire area and its enclaves. Economic and social conditions are primary influences. A broadcaster in a part of Georgia must keep his listeners abreast of the market for goobers; one on the New England seacoast makes the fishing industries a principal interest.

National origins, religious traditions, political attitudes and all such social and cultural elements help identify the audience. A paper in El Paso may have thousands of Chicano readers, one in Milwaukee few; but Milwaukee residents of German ancestry get lots of attention. The Miami *Herald*, at the northern edge of the Caribbean, has used a page headed "Around the Americas" for news of nations to the south; the *Herald* also has a Spanish section for Miami's Cuban community. Detroit newspapers and broadcasters have regular reporters in Windsor across the river in Canada.

Such obvious factors guide editors in planning and making assignments. Many use not only the usual reference sources in the libraries but also intensive studies of audiences. Door-to-door interviews, telephone surveys, "aided-recall" studies in which you tell a researcher what you remember out of last night's paper—all these tell the media the things they need to know. Data provided by national surveys of broadcasting's audiences—Nielsen, Arbitron and others—influence what radio and TV offer and what advertisers buy.

Audience research means that the media now know more than ever before about the impact and effects of news, and that they can tailor their work with surer hands. This may be bad as well as good—the medium that is "edited by arithmetic," as one editor has put it, may miss its mark. Properly used, however, such aids help the media to surer and better service.

AUDIENCE RESPONSES

Responses to news differ as widely as the respondents themselves. Constant patterns develop: most people are repelled by a photo of a mangled body; most approve of news about the "war" on cancer. But no two react with precisely the same thoughts or reflexes.

Some responses are anything but subtle. Let an announcer report that there's an out-of-control fire at Main and Fourth streets, and in minutes police lines are straining to hold back curious spectators. Let the newspaper report that the local NOW chapter wants a porno movie closed because it is debasing to women and the box office is swamped. But the media with enough money to use audience research, and hence to know exactly what this group likes and that one dislikes, can gauge audience response in advance. The wealthier newspapers, the networks, many magazines spend millions to find the answers.

Nose-counting and numbers, however, must not blind an editor or a reporter to individual responsibility. Facts the employer finds out through surveys usually are open to reporters, but the right questions in the right places, individual observations on and off the job, are as important to a reporter's arsenal as a portfolio of surveys. News must always be collected, winnowed and written to serve an identified and well-understood body of readers or listeners; the reporter who does best is the one who knows more about the audience for each story than anybody else.

THE FLOW OF NEWS

News reaches its audiences by a number of complicated processes, most of them carefully organized and planned. The familiar phrase "nose for news" suggests to laymen that newsworkers have extrasensory perception, a kind of built-in antenna that shivers when a dam is about to burst or a cabinet officer to quit. Not so. It is rarely by luck or intuition that a reporter is on hand at the critical moment; more often it's because of scrupulous advance ground-breaking. Much reporting occurs after the event—after the burglary, the election or the Supreme Court decision. Reporters get their stories because they have taken pains to identify events that make news and to be there when they take place.

Different purposes, different channels Channels for the delivery of news differ according to who the desired audiences are, where they

The Luck of the Draw

The radio reporter whose horrified tones described the explosion of the dirigible Hindenburg at a New Jersey airport wasn't there to cover a catastrophe, merely to report the conclusion of a transatlantic flight. If a Tacoma newsman had left work a few minutes early on a certain November afternoon, he would not have been in his car on a Puget Sound bridge that was heaving in high winds. Before the structure and his car plunged into the Sound, he crawled along the writhing bridge to safety and called his office. This was a rare case of reporter's luck; but the firsthand story of the Hindenburg disaster was possible because of advance planning.

Of 76 general news stories (excluding specialized news) in one edition of a metropolitan morning paper, only five involved no advance reportorial planning. Of 44 in another issue, only two.

are and what their interests are. Geography is a major influence. People in Yuma are interested in news that those in Youngstown or Yakima don't give a rap about. But some news carries across state and regional lines. Newsmagazines, wire services, the networks select most news according to its breadth of interest or importance, ignoring individual localities. The New York *Times* covers its own area; so do its two competitors. But the *Times*, with circulation throughout the country, sends reporters nation- and worldwide. Like the *Times*, most media offer something of a mix. The typical smalltown weekly and some small radio stations ignore nonlocal news and hammer hard at events they can reach and touch.

Some newspapers and broadcasting outlets, moreover, select audiences almost solely by particular audience characteristics: the Chicago *Defender* serves black citizens, *Women's Wear Daily* the garment industry, and *Civil Liberties* those who support the American Civil Liberties Union.

NEWSGATHERING SYSTEMS

The captain of the news team in the typical newspaper organization is the managing editor. It is up to this editor to make sure that the paper presents a fair and complete picture of the news of importance or interest to readers. The details are delegated to subeditors and staffs.

At the top of the typical newspaper organization (see the chart on page 74) is the publisher—the owner or ownership's representative. On the next level are the executive editor or editor-in-chief and the principal business executive. The editor is responsible for all "editorial" content (everything that isn't advertising): the managing editor is usually second in command. The business manager is charged with management and financing. Immediate subordinates direct the circulation, advertising sales, promotion, production and

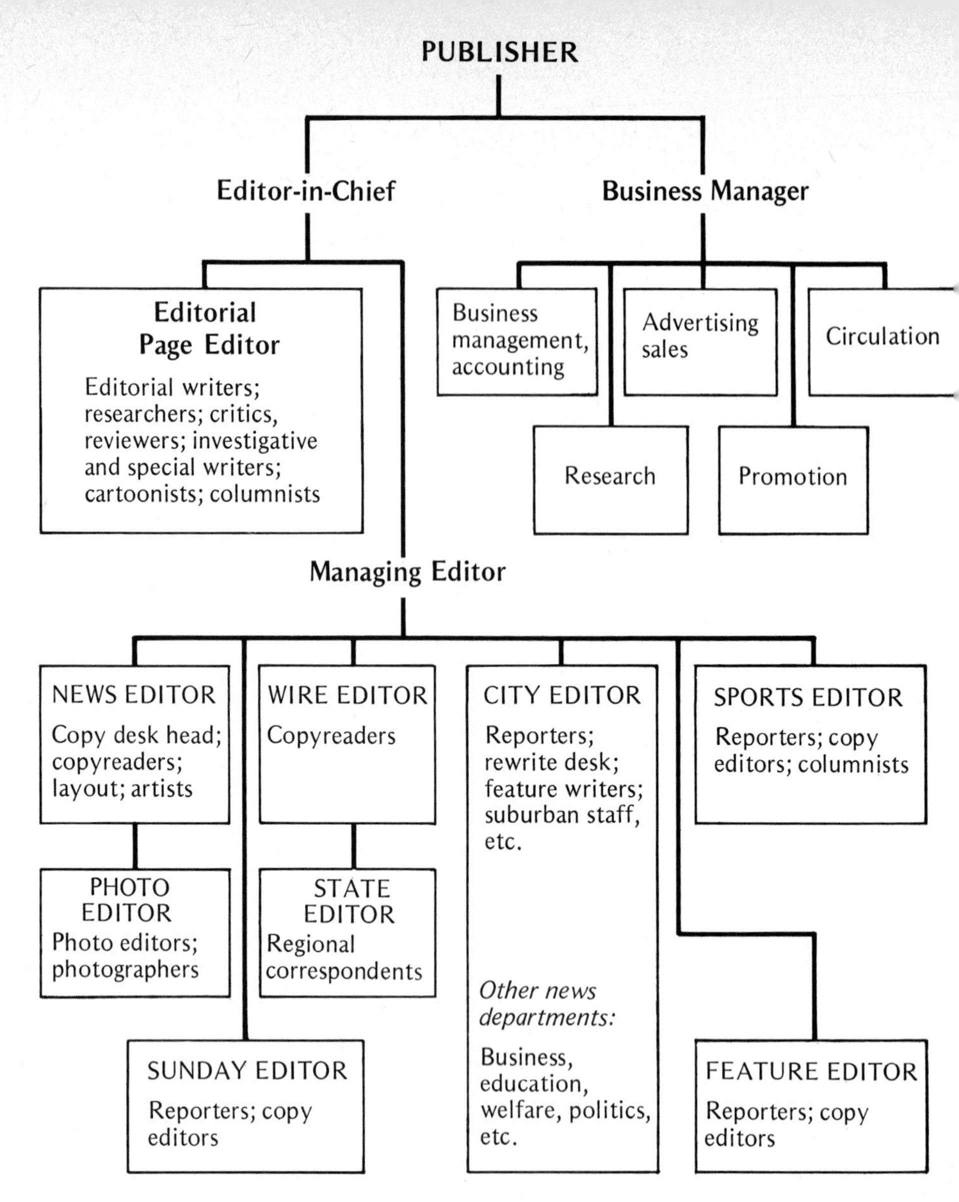

No single chart can show the organization of all newspapers. In many, photo assignments come from city and other department editors; sports, for example, often has its own corps of photographers. This chart shows typical, rather than specific, patterns.

other departments concerned with noneditorial operations. This pattern of newspaper organization, though not the only one, is typical of most and similar to all.

The newsroom On most papers the most important staff group is under the direction of the city editor. He may be responsible for covering an entire city and its suburbs, a small town and some surrounding communities, or—for a "neighborhood newspaper"—a section of a city. It is his mission to see that his staff brings in the area's news each day. And what the staff provides gives the paper a personality different from that of any other news medium.

Fiction and popular misconception—from "The Front Page" to Hollywood's fantasies—make the newsroom (city room) a madhouse, and its city editor profane, harried and always in a lather. Sometimes he (or now and again she) is all of these. But more often a city editor is a contained, orderly news professional who gets results by careful planning rather than by shriek and shout.

A city editor bases planning on the fact that news information centers on identifiable hubs. News of city government is found at the city hall and other municipal offices. County news comes from the county offices; crime news from police headquarters, sheriffs, the FBI, the courts; business and financial news from banks, the chamber of commerce, trade associations, labor unions, individual businesses; news of social welfare from service agencies. Sports news, transportation news, school and education news, church news, health and science news, suburban news, all flow through appropriate centers.

To each such news center the city editor assigns a "beat" or "run" reporter. Sometimes several reporters cover a large beat with many news sources; sometimes one reporter covers several. No two beats are alike. Covering the waterfront is an important beat assignment in New York, Houston, Seattle and Honolulu, but it's nonexistent in Butte and Indianapolis. The varying methods of reporters as they learn and mine their beats are given attention in Chapters 11 and 12.

In addition to beat reporters, whose work schedules remain about the same from week to week, the city editor has at his disposal "general assignment" reporters to whom he assigns specific stories. Tips for such assignments come from all directions: beat reporters who don't have time for them, citizens's tips, other media. City editors take many of them from their "futures books," from the calendar, from publicity releases. They also use a corps of photographers, one or more rewrite experts who write stories from information telephoned in by "legmen" outside the office; secretaries, copy aides or messengers; and others.

Usually specialized departments are supervised by the city desk, often by assistant city editors. "Society departments" are passé, but reporters on feature sections that replace them may cover women's activities. There are business departments, and reporters assigned for education, religion, environmental concerns, politics, government, social welfare and science. The sports department is often jealously independent. The larger departments follow procedures similar to those of the city desk.

News from "outside" On larger papers a second news subdivision receives and edits news from nonlocal areas. A wire or telegraph editor receives copy from one or more of the news or wire services, Associated Press and United Press International (supplemented sometimes by the British Reuters and others). A major metropolitan daily or a broadcasting network may also get service from the Canadian Press, the Los Angeles Times-Washington Post and New York Times services, and other such agencies.

Many papers have correspondents in their circulation areas. Everybody knows of the correspondents of the county weekly whose chore is to mail or phone in "personals" and other news of neighborhood events big and little. Some papers maintain reporters at the state capital and a few in Washington, in adjoining states, abroad.

Electronic magic and the computer, technological developments of mid-century, have modified wire-editing operations. Typesetting may be done by computers rather than fingers; "cold type" and offset printing, a photographic process, have replaced hot metal. But all such changes affect editing and production procedures more than basic newsgathering.

The chart on page 74 shows a typical staff organization of a metropolitan newspaper; with obvious modifications, it represents broadcasting news structure. Radio and TV news systems, like those of newspapers, range from the far-reaching and complex to the single jack-of-all-trades. Producers, announcers, directors, cameras and microphones replace composition and printing presses; but newsgathering, evaluation and editing are basically similar.

Other editorial functions If news media provided only news, the facilities just described would do most of the job. But newspapers not only inform but also offer views, opinions and entertainment. This means more departments.

The views-and-opinion section of the paper comprises the editorial page, sometimes a facing ("op-ed") page and allied sections. An editorial page editor, under this or some other title, is responsible for these sections. This department usually includes editorial writers, researchers, columnists and feature reporters; many papers assign critics and reviewers to it. It may occasionally borrow investigative reporters or feature writers from the city side, just as city may call on it.

There are many kinds of entertainment and service material. Much is in the form of news features, prepared by the city staff or

Informality and, often, cramped quarters characterize the newsroom of a small radio station. Here, newscasters work close to the typewriter. *(Mimi Forsyth photo from Monkmeyer Press Photo Service)*

furnished by outside services. Much is syndicated material that can be used with minimum editing. Comic strips are in this category; so are many health and home-service columns, Broadway gossip columns and humor features like those from Art Buchwald and Erma Bombeck.

Papers with Sunday editions have separate Sunday departments. Much of the content of the Sunday paper, however (half of which is printed in midweek before the date of issue), is turned out by the city and editorial page staffs or comes from outside suppliers.

In contrast to a small radio station, a large station has elaborate facilities. And VDTs have now invaded broadcast, as well as newspaper, newsrooms, as shown here: a newswriter at KCBS in San Francisco edits a story. Using the microphone next to him, he can talk to the announcer in the "on-air" booth (see next photo) during commercials, telling him that a late-breaking story will soon be on the VDT in the booth—or he can read a story over the air himself. KCBS, an all-news radio station, converted in 1977 to an electronic news-processing system that is hooked by satellite into the UPI master news-transmitting computer in New York. KCBS was the first U.S. radio station to adopt such a system. *(KCBS, San Francisco)*

BROADCASTING NEWSROOMS

Radio and TV newsrooms operate much as do print newsrooms: they identify audiences, decide what news to cover, write it in broadcastable form and disseminate it. But there are marked differences between print and broadcast, between radio and TV, and among individual stations.

This is the main "on-air" booth at KCBS, San Francisco. A newscaster is reading the latest weather report, which he has "called up" on the VDT next to him.
(KCBS, San Francisco)

The prime product of newspapers is news; for most broadcasters news is second to entertainment. News gets a small part of the day's schedule even on stations that take news responsibility seriously (one reliable study discovered commercial stations giving about 20 percent of prime evening time to public affairs programs, a genre that includes news; noncommercial stations gave about 30

Counterfeit

Most newsworkers, print or air, decry the bombast of the "big 24-hour newsrooms" that claim to present news from "Mr. News himself," all without news professionals, newsgathering and newswriting, or effort at balanced, complete coverage. Rip-and-read broadcasts—rip from the teleprinter and rush to the microphone—present only a shadow of the news; they contribute to public suspicion of all news media. This kind of newscasting, which used to be common, is properly going out of style.

The artfully stylized television news showcase gives little notion of the complex system of reporting, photography, studio production, preparation of "visuals" and careful timing lying behind it. These men are about to go on the air at WTOP–TV in Washington. *(James H. Karales photo from Peter Arnold Photo Archives)*

percent.) Pride in news and editorial quality is a newspaper publisher tradition (though not all share it); broadcasting owners for whom "news comes first" are in a minority.

Broadcasting, with only a fraction of its day's schedule assigned to news, offers fewer stories, in fewer words, than do newspapers. It has less "space" for news and uses fewer reporters to cover the same sources.

Broadcast news, nevertheless, is "better" year by year. Longer news shows have been introduced, particularly by television stations. Network and local operations have increased the number of news documentaries. Staffs are bigger and more experienced (and more often female) and photography continues to improve. Maturation has made broadcast of news lifted from newspapers rare (the practice was common in radio's early days). Cross-channel credits have become almost routine. When ABC broadcast the David Frost-Nixon interviews, all media recognized them as news and gave ABC credit.

Most broadcast newsrooms look and sound like print newsrooms,

Where Do People Get Their News?

This question is as hard to answer as the one about the chicken and the egg. For years after the rise of television the number of TV watchers and the percentage who reported TV as their major news source rose. According to one study, 65 percent preferred television to newspapers in 1974 (a slight decline followed). A study in 1974 reported that fewer than 20 percent of adults watched evening network TV news on an average weekday, but 80 percent "read" newspapers. The figures, though something like apples and oranges as contrasts, show conflicting "facts."

According to most studies, most people think the reliability of TV news higher than that of print. But it is also shown that those who prefer TV also believe TV most readily, and those who prefer newspapers believe newspapers. You might speculate that seeing is believing. One unmentioned factor in any comparison is that, for all their efforts to compete with TV as entertainers, newspapers offer more hard news and present it more completely.

though on a smaller scale. A news director has a staff of reporters, writers, TV photographers and announcers, along with teleprinter services ranging from one regional wire to a clattering battery of machines. Network affiliates enjoy one facility newspapers lack—teams of reporters in Washington and around the world to supplement the wire services.

OTHER NEWS CHANNELS

The newsmagazines *Time*, *Newsweek* and *U.S. News & World Report* have wider range than most other news media, and maintain newsgathering and editing corps that run into the hundreds. *Time* uses what it calls "group journalism"—many reporters and editors working together to produce one anonymous story—but its editorial procedures are blood relations of those of the wire services and the networks and large newspapers. After almost half a century of unsigned stories (it was frequently accused of biased reporting), *Time* moved in the 1960s to occasional use of bylines.

The wire services Though gathering news for the two American wire services—Associated Press, United Press International—is much the same as any reporting (except that it is gathered for distant rather than local audiences), its distribution is complex. One story may be written for hundreds of audiences, worldwide. A story about an oil slick in the North Sea or a political upheaval in Honduras must be relayed from local reporters through regional centers to New York, thence to members or subscribers throughout the world. Computerized control systems now facilitate the flow of news, sometimes by use of codes that direct stories instantly to members or clients of the services for whom they have interest. The Associated Press, a cooperative association, operates largely on a membership basis; the UPI is a profit-making business that contracts with members on a fee basis.

The stories that reach broadcast newsrooms are usually written for vocal rather than printed delivery. The wire services once presented news for print only; but they now provide "radio wires" as well.

Word of mouth One of the principal channels of news transmission is totally unorganized—person-to-person communication. The reason is obvious: Such communication, haphazard and lacking planned "reporting," is a sociopsychological rather than journalistic channel. Those who stop to figure how much "news" they get from others' lips will be astonished. Researchers who got busy instantly after the murder of President Kennedy in 1963 learned from 200 telephone calls that everybody reached had heard of the shooting within about three hours; that half had heard it first from another person; and—not surprisingly—that the accuracy of what the respondents thought they had heard varied from pole to pole.

Dynamic news like this travels fast by word of mouth; the statement that every kid at Blank High School smokes pot moves about as fast. That it often changes shape as it travels is an indication of the need for organized, dependable mass communication systems.

Feedback In face-to-face communication the process called "feedback" is what keeps it going. Feedback is the return message given by receiver to sender: "Is that so!" or "That's not the way I saw it" or "I better call Joe." In most mass communication there is little feedback. The newspaper reader may write a letter, cancel his subscription, order extra copies. Broadcast listeners may call the station, scold or praise sponsors, write postcards. But the mass communication systems make little provision for instant response, and they get little.

This is one of the reasons that some broadcasters and newspapers go to costly length to stimulate feedback, to find out what their audiences think of what they're getting, and why.

STUDY SUGGESTIONS

1. Faithful readers of the New York *Times* outside the New York area sometimes ask, "Why can't we have that kind of paper in our own city?" How would you answer their question?
2. State the two "paradoxes" that mark "mass" audiences.
3. List and describe briefly the factors common in audience identification.
4. How do news media know what their audiences like and want?

5. Describe the principal differences between news for a small-town radio station and news for a small-town newspaper.
6. Define *beat, wire service, editorial* (as a journalistic writing form), *syndicate.*
7. Why is there little feedback in news journalism?

PRACTICE ASSIGNMENTS

1. From a library or newsstand get several copies of two newspapers published in different geographical areas. Analyze their content; then describe your conclusions about the similarities and differences of the audiences they are seeking.
2. Immediately following two striking but dissimilar news events—a major prize fight and a natural disaster, for instance—question at least 20 people in each of two clearly defined groups (perhaps high school students and hospital nurses or members of a football squad and factory workers) to learn how much they know about the events, the depth of their interest, and the chief sources of their knowledge. Write your findings and conclusions.
3. Examine two issues each of five magazines in the "intellectual" group—*Harper's, Saturday Review, Atlantic, Yale Review, Nation, New Republic, Progressive, Chronicle of Higher Education,* and the like. Study their advertising as well as their editorial content. Then summarize and comment on what you believe are the differences in their audiences.
4. Off the top of your head, list what seem to you the 15 or 20 principal audience interests of the citizens of your community—political, industrial, occupational, religious, educational, cultural, ethnic, and so on. Check your list with reliable source books such as encyclopedias, census reports, fact books, and library materials. Confirm, supplement, or modify your own off-the-cuff list.
5. Compare the findings of Assignment 4 against the content of your local newspaper or news broadcasts and decide whether any interests are being ignored or unduly favored.
6. Interview 10 or more members of one of the subgroups you have identified, asking their opinions on local news coverage of their special interests. Summarize and comment on what they tell you.

RELATED READING

Barrett, Marvin. "Broadcast Journalism Since Watergate." *Columbia Journalism Review,* March–April 1976. An "interim report" on the state of the industry, based on comments from 1,600 news directors and corespondents.

Meyer, Philip. "In Defense of the Marketing Approach." *Columbia Journalism Review,* January–February 1978. Contention that careful use of audience surveys will both improve and profit American newspapers.

Powers, Ron. "Eyewitless News." *Columbia Journalism Review,* May–June 1977. Severely critical report on tendencies in television news.

UPI

PART TWO

NEWS WRITING AND STYLE

6 News Story Form and Organization

PREVIEW

A standardized news story form developed by American newspapers a century ago is now being relaxed to serve new purposes, but the form remains the base of American news writing. Its characteristics:

- A "lead" or opening section that summarizes the principal facts of an event
- An "order of decreasing importance"—elaboration of the lead facts, arranged with important facts first and least important last
- A structural pattern that makes it easy for reader or hearer to leave a story when he's had enough

Unity of structure, a prime attribute in news story organization, is attained by including only materials logically related to the story's central concept.

Important news or news offered primarily to inform (called "hard" or "straight" news) normally employs the standard form. Human-interest and feature news often uses other forms, such as the narrative or suspended-interest form. Broadcast news uses a modified form, designed for the ear.

Condensed summary of earlier news ("tieback") is often desirable in news that continues from day to day.

Newswriting in America has moved into its third style period. Through its first 200 years it was diffuse, editorialized, often chronological—wandering, wordy, careless of space and time. As 19th-century personal journalism was modified by the telegraph, tight deadlines and the new "objectivity," it adopted the AP lead and the inverted pyramid form (also called order of decreasing importance form—major facts first, narrowing progressively to least). Along came radio with a new view of what makes prose easy to

Facts Come First

By definition, you can't write a news story until you have something to write about. Reporting—fact-gathering—comes first. Why, then, start with newswriting? One reason is that some teachers of reporting—aware that knowing something about how you are likely to treat a set of facts helps to collect and select among them—ask students to grasp news story form first. A pragmatic reason is that writing news stories can be learned more easily in the classroom than can fact-gathering. But the learning order can be reversed.

take. "Scientific" readership formulas pointed out practices a reporter who wants an audience should avoid.

Today a basic rule for newswriting is "say it quickly, understandably, interestingly." This does not proscribe either the basic lead pattern or the inverted pyramid, but it uses them with a liberated hand. Though it asks scrupulous elimination of unnecessary detail, it demands well-ordered contextual and structural facts. It holds that the form and flavor of a news story ought to fit its character.

You see the rationale of the formula if you take one step backward: The newspaper headline (or its broadcast cousin) prepares the ground for what is to follow—it is the story's marquee, its condensed table of contents. Reader or listener uses it to decide whether to bother with what comes after. (The delicate and often-abused techniques of headline writing, with their occasional absurdities, are not within the range of this book.)

If the head catches the reader's interest, the lead helps to a decision whether to stay with the story or go do the dishes. The selection process continues. When the invitation to stay with it is accepted, the readers go on. Perhaps after a few paragraphs they have had enough; the episodic form provides easy "breaks" where they can leave the story. If interest persists, so do the readers—to another break or to the end. The design shows clearly in this wire-service story, written in the Minneapolis Associated Press bureau:

Briefcases bump lunch pails and three-piece suits sit beside blue jeans. The Joneses of a moneyed Minneapolis suburb are going to work.

Three colorful paragraphs introduce the subject.

And thousands are keeping up with them, leaving their two-car garages in their moneyed suburbs behind for an air-conditioned ride costing 30 to 60 cents.

Half the people who enter downtown

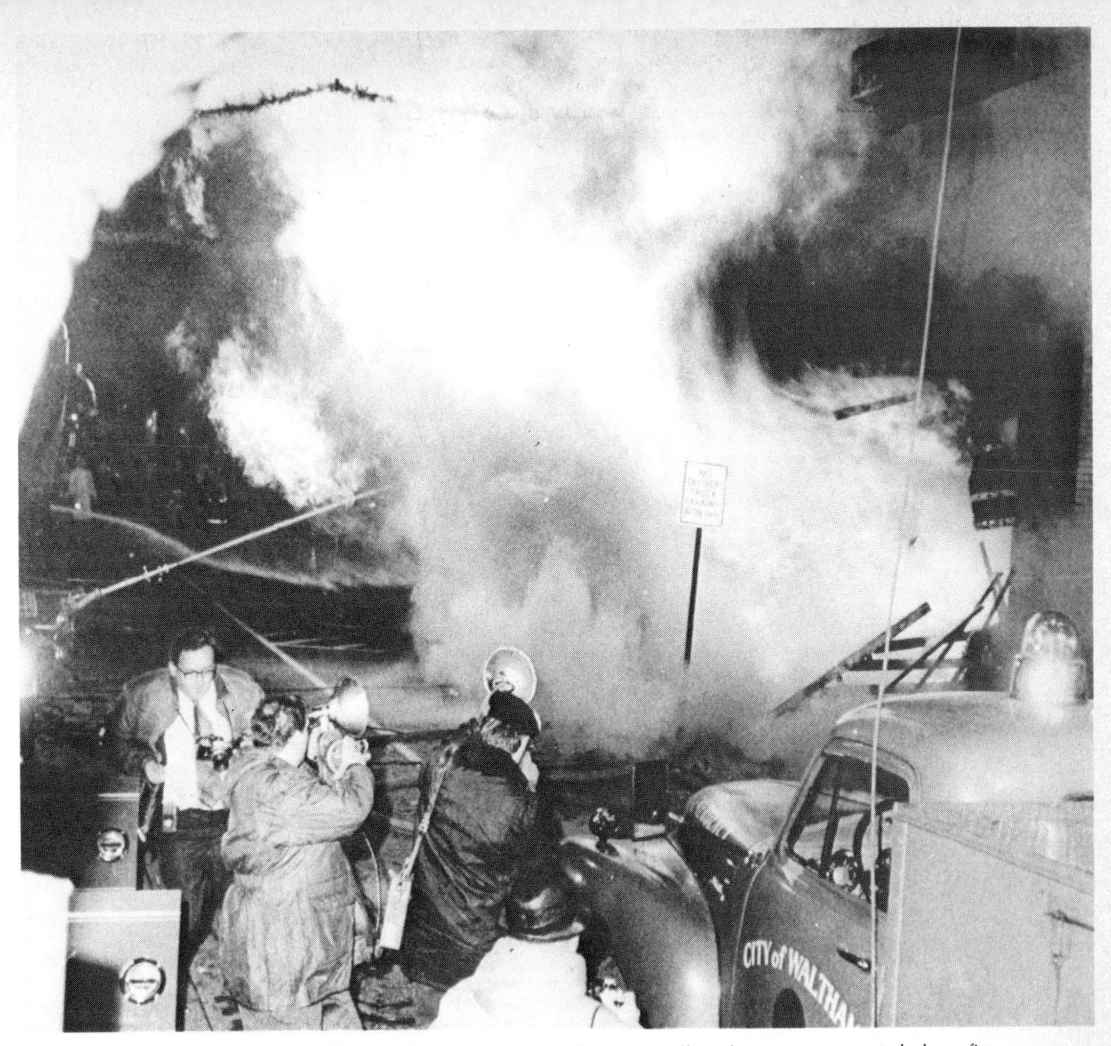

News photographers run from a collapsing wall as they cover a general-alarm fire. *(United Press International Photo)*

Minneapolis during peak commuter hours are on buses. The clean red vehicles carry 63 million people a year, an increase of 40 percent since the Metropolitan Transit Commission took over a run-down private busline seven years ago.

First break

Now a firmer statement of the topic the story is to develop.

Using a savvy advertising and marketing program, the commission has made bus riding in Minneapolis and St. Paul the thing to do—almost fun—and has certainly changed the image of the bus rider.

"In 1969 the person on the street would say the buses were for the poor and the infirm," Lee Lynch, president of the firm that handles the bus advertising, said recently. "In 1973 they looked at buses as kind of a smart alternative for a few people. And now a lot of people say, 'I wish I could ride a bus.' "

A quotation to add color to the summary.

Second break
Now come details of the purpose and methods of the campaign.

The commission went after the affluent adult male, telling him it cost $1,900 to drive a car to work each year compared to $900 to ride the bus.

"We tried to persuade him that the bus was similar to a car, dependable and cost efficient," said Greg Fern, the commission's marketing director. The secret, he said, was getting someone to try a bus once.

[*Four paragraphs describe similar programs in Atlanta, Seattle and Salt Lake City—comparable cities. The story then reverts to the Twin Cities:*]

Seven closing paragraphs complete treatment of the topic.

Sixty percent of the Minneapolis-St. Paul bus operating budget of $52 million is tax supported. Building ridership—not breaking even—is the transit commission's mandate.

Mass transit in the Twin Cities used to mean streetcars; at one time 220 million riders used the trolleys every year. But the automotive age after World War II led to buses that could maneuver among cars, and eventually to a vicious cycle of ridership decline and service cuts by the private bus line.

The commission had to start practically from scratch. But with the zest of Madison Avenue selling a bar of soap, the commission and the ad agency began selling the joys of bus riding.

The commission bought 900 new buses with comfortable seats and air conditioning and built 343 shelters, half of them heated.

Telephone operators were hired to answer route questions from 6 a.m. to 1 a.m., the buses were washed every day, fares were reduced, and the media campaign was begun.

Three final paragraphs add expendable, though interesting, details.

The current advertising calls the bus the "Oughtamobile." An "owner's manual" tells riders where to catch it, how to read a schedule, and how to get off the bus: "You should pull the cord about three-fourths of a block from your stop. One pull is enough. No, people won't point and stare."

"Set your jaw with firm determination," the manual says. "Walk right past that car of yours and down to the corner bus stop."[1]

The bus story, though it concerns one city, was written—says its writer, James Carrier—for the national AP wire, and it was used by papers throughout the nation. The material from other cities was supplied, on Carrier's request, by local AP bureaus. (One paper cut off the last two paragraphs, for lack of space—thus achieving an abrupt and unsatisfactory ending.)

The four short stories that follow exemplify the inverted pyramid. The first story falls neatly into four sections: lead, amplification of the summary, identification of the major figure, and the entire event in detail.

An intoxicated surgeon started shooting at police Friday while holding his infant granddaughter in his arms. A policeman braved the fire until the doctor put the baby down, then shot him dead.

The lead paragraph summarizes the major facts. Its two sentences rather than the one more common in leads give it clarity and force.

First break
Summary of two important elaborating facts.

The slain surgeon was Dr. Arthur A. Arthur, 59. Coroner Joseph Hilginson called his death "justifiable homicide."

Second break
Summary of additional background facts.

Police said Arthur, for many years a prominent surgeon but lately less active, was paroled recently from a hospital for narcotics addicts.

[1] Copyright © 1977 by the Associated Press. Reprinted by permission.

Third break
The last four paragraphs reconstruct the event chronologically for a reader who continues beyond break three. But those who stop sooner already have the essential facts.

Yesterday police were called to the family home. There Patrolmen B. L. Buchanan and C. D. Guy found Arthur on the second floor holding his granddaughter, 11-month-old Helen Jane Smithson. Arthur started cursing them, the patrolmen said, and Guy went for help.

Before he returned, the doctor whipped out a pistol and fired three shots at Buchanan. The officer backed away rather than fire while Arthur held the baby.

Arthur then put the baby down and followed Buchanan downstairs, cornered him and announced, "We'll shoot it out here."

Buchanan drew his service revolver and fired five shots. Two struck Arthur, who was dead on arrival at a hospital.

A two-paragraph lead gives principal facts.

MIAMI BEACH, Fla. (AP)—A court order says workers at the Fontainebleau, largest of Miami Beach's plush hotels, must end a strike and return to bed-making, food-serving, and other duties.

But there is nothing to prevent picket lines from remaining up in front of six other resort hotels hit by a five-day-old strike that has forced high-paying guests to carry their own luggage and clean their own rooms.

First break
Summary of results of the facts above.

The strike has added to the financial woes of the luxury hotels which, recently hit by a decline in tourism, had hoped to be full over the year-end holidays.

Some guests have left in anger, checking out in favor of smaller inns here or in other Florida cities.

Second break
A new subtopic. Note that the final paragraph might better be logically placed here.

Federal mediators, meanwhile, are meeting behind closed doors with negotiators for the union and the Southern Florida Hotel and Motel Association.

Third break
A subtopic, giving background.

The walkout was started against selected hotels Christmas Day by the Hotel, Motel, and Restaurant Employees Union, Local 355. Its 11,000 members had been working without a contract since September.

Fourth break
Another subtopic.

James Scearce, director of the Federal Mediation and Conciliation Service in Washington, flew in yesterday to help local mediators.[2]

Don't look for relief from the heat today. The weatherman says it will be 95 again.

Quick lead summary of major facts, and a quick answer to "How hot?"

First break
Related facts summarized in short paragraphs.

The northwest portion of the state may get a break—a low-pressure area is moving in.

But there will be nothing but continued heat, and very little wind, in the metro area.

Second break
Secondary facts.

The U.S. Weather Bureau says tomorrow may be better. A few showers and a top of 78 are expected.

Third break
"Old" facts.

Yesterday's high in the city was 96 between 4 and 5 p.m. Relative humidity was 41 percent.

Fourth break
"Expendable" facts.

In states to the east the temperatures were even higher . . .

A local couple were killed in a home fire yesterday.

Laconic summary lead.

First break
Expansion of lead.

Found dead by firemen in a burned-out house at 417 16th Ave. S. shortly after 1 a.m. were John Doe, 67, and his wife, Mary, 62.

Second break
Background, elaborating on major facts.

David L. Jamieson of the arson squad said neighbors told him Mrs. Doe often threw extra fuel into the oil heater. Sudden ignition of the extra oil, he said, would blow open the heater door and flame and smoke would puff out.

Third break
Further elaboration.

Doe's charred body was found under a pile of debris. Mrs. Doe was declared by the medical examiner's office to have died of smoke inhalation.

Fourth break
Expendable facts. Should they have been omitted? or expanded? Was the heater old?

Neighbors said Doe was retired.

City Hall records show that the house and the one next door were built in 1902.

These examples show, among other things, the flexibility of the formula. Even sticking to the formula, two competent reporters may assess them differently. Chapter 15 describes an alternative form, the suspended-interest story.

UNITY IN NEWS STORIES

The key to effective news story structure is unity.

Unity in a news story is achieved when the story is built tightly around one central idea and the facts that relate to it. A unified story has only one tale to tell. All its details are relevant to the central core, the major meaning or theme; materials that don't develop the theme are firmly thrown out.

It isn't always easy to bind a story tightly around its core. News events are seldom simple. People do a lot of things at a speech, in an interview or at a parade that have no significant relevance to the event, the parts that *must* be reported. To include everything around the periphery, however accurately, might cloud the reader's view of the center of the ring. Selection on the basis of relevance to a story's essence is the key.

The conventional news story pattern is a guide to unification. A

Pyramids Sometimes Get Truncated

The order-of-decreasing-importance form helps both the copyreader who decides to shorten a story and the makeup editor who puts it into a page. The last two paragraphs in the fire story above could have been left out, with minimum effort. But a careless editor or makeup man can cause trouble. One morning paper used a Washington story whose lead said that New England states would get an extra day of grace in a certain April for income tax payments. That's where the story stopped, its last paragraph dropped off. The afternoon paper used the full story. (Note the bus story ending on page 91.) This error is disastrous when it occurs in a suspended-interest story, the kind with its kick in its closing lines.

"Straight" News

Newsworkers classify most news under the labels *straight* and *feature*. Straight news is news in the conventional form; its purpose is primarily to inform; it is usually news of some significance, news that people "ought to get," or bulletin board news that needs no ornament, such as "Kiwanis members will meet Wednesday to hear . . . ." The term *feature* (see Chapter 15) describes news whose prime purpose is to entertain or supplement rather than inform. Either kind of news may be hard or soft.

good lead in a straight news story says to the reader or listener, "*This* is what this story is about—this and nothing else." If the writer remains true to the lead's promise, the story isn't likely to wander.

Look again at the story of the intoxicated surgeon (page 91): Every paragraph provides pertinent background. The four closing paragraphs tell the story in time sequence. The chronological pattern, either as part of a story or as the whole story, is one primary method of assuring unity—if you stick with the sequence and keep out extraneous matter, unity is certain. Part of the story about Howard Wigfield's vodka (page 103) is narrative; the story about the stumbling derelict (page 313) is entirely narrative.

The following story's lead paragraphs promise three major elements, and the story delivers them, in order:

Half the city's elm trees will be destroyed by Dutch elm disease in the next five years, according to a state Department of Agriculture expert.

And whether the destruction can be halted there, he says, is questionable.

"Our best hope," John F. Herring, state agronomist, told the Argus this morning, "is an organized war with everybody in it—state, city, property owners."

The first paragraph states the story's theme. Two succeeding lead paragraphs add to the theme and tell what is coming in the story.

The number of elms along city streets will drop from 8,200 to no more than 4,000 in five years at the current rate of loss, Herring said.

"We are losing close to 1,000 trees a year," he added. "And nobody is sure what can be done about it."

First break
Support for first lead point, the rate of loss.

Tree scientists have not found a surefire preventive against spread of the disease,

Second break
Development of second lead point, deficiency of scientific knowledge.

Herring said. Some types of chemicals, injected annually into infested trees, have achieved some success, but they are stopgap rather than curative, he said. And they have not been used long enough to establish certainty about their results.

Third break
Development of third lead point, what can be done.

Herring advocates "organized war" by every element that is concerned about the problem.

"No one body can do it alone," he said. "The state and the city can provide a certain amount of scientific help—tree inspection and funding for preventive work and tree disposal. And private owners can aid both in spotting diseased trees and in getting them treated. Community efforts have been helpful in a number of cities.

"But we've all got to work together—and even then we may lose."

The confusion when a story does not stick to its lead theme, or the lead starts with one topic but turns to another, is shown in this Washington dispatch:

Lead promises information about training military volunteers.

A former chief of covert operations for the CIA says that the United States gave paramilitary training to Eastern European volunteers for intervention in potential national uprisings in Hungary, Poland and Romania in 1956.

Second paragraph continues lead theme but suddenly moves to another topic.

James Angleton, head of special operations and counterintelligence in 1956, said that the agency began training hundreds of Eastern Europeans after . . .

. . . one of his operatives obtained a text of one secret speech in which Nikita Khrushchev denounced Stalin's crimes before the 20th Congress of the Soviet Communist Party in February 1956.

Angleton, who retired from the CIA last year, maintained that his motive was to "balance out" an account of the CIA's handling of the speech published by Ray S. Cline, then a top-ranking intelligence analyst at the agency. Cline, who was in charge of Chinese-Soviet affairs in the Office of Current Intelligence and later became deputy CIA director before going to the State Department, included the account in his newly issued autobiography, "Secrets, Spies and Scholars."

A sentence whose details seem to confuse more than illuminate.

[*Four long paragraphs go on to report the speech and its use. The last two paragraphs return to the initial topic.*]

This story disappoints readers' expectations by not following its own lead; it also confuses them thoroughly by inserting names and long titles of a handful of government agencies. Much of this detail should be omitted. Introduction to the Khrushchev speech element in the second paragraph might be construed as a device to glue the lead to what follows. But the speech report goes on so long that the readers have forgotten the first element before they are yanked back to it.

A university newspaper story, reporting the result of a month-long dispute over a campus election, left readers gasping by retelling the entire story in detail—a story the paper had already told half a dozen times. Here is the story's lead:

> The University Elections Commission voted unanimously Monday to seat six students elected to the Board of Publications a month ago, and dismissed an appeal from the Campus Committee Against Racism (CAR) to rule the election invalid.

Seventeen paragraphs of rehash followed. Instead, the story might have been completed thus:

> The six candidates seated are . . . [names inserted].
>
> Their election was protested because of a CAR complaint that the University Daily had improperly endorsed them. The commission denied jurisdiction after the University Press Council declined to hear the complaint.
>
> A joint Commission-Board of Publications committee has been appointed to draw up regulations for Daily endorsements.

The following story falls into pieces that seem only distantly related:

An Australian sailor was found innocent Wednesday of a charge of rape in a court-martial at the Washington Navy Yard.

Able Seaman Kevin J. Clarke, 19, was found innocent of the alleged rape of a 20-year-old Baltimore woman on a barge in Baltimore Harbor following a party on July 10 honoring the Tall Ships.

Two-paragraph lead that repeats itself.

First break

Two paragraphs describing the unusual characteristic of the event—not introduced in the lead.

Clarke's trial was authorized by a 20-year-old law that permits a foreign serviceman charged with a crime to be tried by a court of his peers. The Baltimore woman assented, so the American prosecutor turned the case over to a tribunal from Australia.

The Australian government paid an estimated $100,000 for travel and legal expenses for the tribunal participants. The court-martial was marked by Australian accents and British customs, including curled and powdered wigs, black robes, and the accepted form of address: "my learned friend."

Second break

Dangling paragraph. (The hyphen in "missile-firing" makes the phrase nonsensical.)

The Australian naval attache's office said Clarke would return to duty aboard the Hobart, a guided missile-firing destroyer now in Australia.

Third break

The law that permitted the trial is called the Friendly Foreign Forces Act. It was passed in 1944.

A leisurely story written by James (Scotty) Reston of the New York *Times* when he was a Washington reporter is held together by opening and closing paragraphs with a tongue-in-cheek theme that sandwiches solid matter between them:

WASHINGTON (AP)—The usually solemn Secretary of State Dulles was in a mood of relaxed good humor at his news conference Tuesday.

He expounded to the reporters the glories of being fingerprinted, disclosed that he is the first pistol-packin' Secretary

The opening paragraph establishes the story's unifying theme, the "relaxed good humor" of the news conference. The theme is supported in the second paragraph by introduction of topics not usual subjects of a State Department news conference.

of State since Cordell Hull, and announced he is going off on his first two-week vacation since taking over the State Department almost three years ago.

First break
A carefully designed transitional paragraph moves from the story's structural theme to a sober subject.

This last point may have explained his sense of well-being, but the real reason probably is that his foreign policy ideas are back in ascendancy in Washington.

[*Nine paragraphs now develop the subtheme just introduced. Then back to the original theme:*]

Return to the opening theme holds the story together and satisfies the reader's curiosity.

As for the lighter portions of the conference, it went like this:

Dulles said he himself gets fingerprinted a couple of times a year. Why? asked a correspondent.

Because, said the secretary, he has to be fingerprinted in order to get his pass to the State Department building. And also, he added with a rather sheepish grin, in order to get a permit to keep his pistol. This drew considerable interest.

Reston has tied the news elements in a not-very-productive news conference into a unified package by a contrived but skillful and convincing use of a major theme.

Fortunately, said the secretary, he hasn't had to use his gun at all. Apparently aware that he had dashed the hopes of the whodunit fans in the news corps, Dulles explained that his revolver is one he was given in 1917 when he made his first trip to Central America. He has kept it ever since.[3]

Examination of these examples leads to some generalizations about unity in news stories:

1. *Sticking to the theme* A story is unified when its central topic states the major facts and the supporting facts develop it. Essential in the process in a straight news story is selection of materials that support the theme. Thus there are two decisions: first the choice of theme, then the choice of supporting facts. Whatever doesn't contribute toward understanding or distracts attention from meaning must go. In this sense the Reston story is not uni-

[3] Copyright © 1955 by The New York Times Company. Reprinted by permission.

fied—it's two stories. But a reader goes away from it remembering the pistol-packin' cabinet member rather than "foreign policy ideas."

2. *Unity of mood and structure* In the story above and the Wigfield story (page 103), the mood of relaxed good humor is a unifying adhesive. In the Dakota blizzard story (page 147), a counterbalanced narrative pattern makes one story out of several.

Structural or rhetorical devices like these are rarely for beginners. Chiseled by the instruments of experience, they show up more often in feature writing than in straight news. But even in routine news a reporter can frame a unifying theme by tying separate-but-similar facts together: "Seven drownings occurred in four state boating accidents over the weekend." Broadcast news, which has to say everything in a hurry, uses this device constantly: "The world's three shooting wars are quiet today for the first time in a month."

Dilution of unity Even when details hang logically from a lead's thematic frame, unity may be diluted by their careless use. A story about a police chase of a car thief confused its readers by the lead's unfulfilled promise that it would tell about minor injuries to policemen, wrecking a squad car and "ingredients of a movie thriller." A street-by-street description of the route of the chase and of policemen's radio intercom chatter interrupted the flow of the story without adding to its meaning. Often such details, if they're worth reporting, can be given in sidebars.

A story loses unity when a subordinate fact, especially a sensational one, is given lead emphasis. Overemphasized minor facts are likely to frustrate any attempt to organize a balanced or orderly structure. You'll see this happen when, in a speech story lead, the speaker's throwaway is made the lead. Asides may be loaded with reader interest, but only occasionally with primary news value. A reporter who plays up a speaker's accidental tumble from the dais may conceal the gist of the speech.

Leads with too many facts, as well as leads with too few, make unity hard to achieve. When a lead promises story development that doesn't come, or fails to forecast what is to come, it has undermined structural strength. One gifted writer got both faults into one lead:

Axioms

Better that the news consumer see the forest than each separate tree.

Better to grasp the meaning of a news story than to be confounded by its virtuosity.

Sidebars

A sidebar is a secondary story that develops minor facts or related angles of a news event covered by a principal story. Its value in maintenance of the main story's unity is easy to see. It fleshes out and adds color to the principal event.

Sidebars often report human-interest adornments of straight-faced news. When the carnival comes to town, the routine story tells how many attended, what time the shows open, where to park. Sidebars report seven heat prostrations the first day; more visitors in town than at any time since three astronauts were on hand; the absence of the fat lady because she's honeymooning with the mayor of the last town the shows played. With a principal front-page story on the anniversary of the Hiroshima atomic bombing, sidebars reported a propaganda broadcast from Peking, comments by the chaplain who counseled the bombing plane's crew, refusal of the plane's pilot to talk about it, and the wreath laid at the Unknown Soldier's tomb by a Hiroshima survivor.

(The two paragraphs above are a kind of sidebar.)

> A special alarm fire that sent a pall of smoke over the Whitney district Friday night caused damage estimated at $80,000 . . . .

From this lead you expect to hear more about the special alarm and the smoke cloud. Neither gets a nod in the story that follows.

On the other hand, the following three-paragraph lead tells readers precisely what they're going to get:

> Rejection of a civil rights ordinance ended a six-hour City Council meeting last night.
>
> The council voted 9 to 4 to table the proposal whose purpose was to make racial and religious discrimination illegal in employment in any business in the city.
>
> The council also turned down a proposal that all schoolchildren must carry identification cards.

First the story's chief topic, then warning that a second topic is coming. Fourteen following paragraphs develop the civil rights ordinance topic; the remainder deals with identification cards. If paragraph three were omitted or placed after the civil rights topic, a reader might well ask, "How did this get in here?"

Unity in long stories The longer the story, the more room for it to wander. Specific cases or attention-getting illustrations of the subject matter to follow are strong openings because their focus is narrow and pointed. But they need to be tied to the major topic by summary or transitional paragraphs to prepare readers for what is coming. In a series that depended heavily on specific case studies of the plight of the elderly poor, one story went along for a dozen paragraphs about the predicament of "Mr. and Mrs. N"; it then switched abruptly to summaries of the city's housing problems and policies, and the Ns were forgotten. Either a transitional paragraph or a return to the Ns at the end would have pulled the story together.

Transitions Transitional passages, properly prized in essay writing, are not common in newswriting. A newswriter depends on the *sense of transition* rather than on literal mechanics. This sense derives from the unity of a story—from the selection of a dominant theme and the flags in or near the lead that say that secondary topics will be coming along.

Straightforward rhetorical transitions, nevertheless, are devices a newswriter ought to master. Long stories, particularly those built in unusual news form, often have to acknowledge explicitly what direction is changing.

VARIATIONS IN STORY FORM

American newspapers have broken from confinement to upside-down pyramids and "stories that all sound alike" or stories that ignore the time-sequence logic. Traditions die hard, but a prediction of a United Press International editor in the mid-1960s was prophetic: "The inverted pyramid style . . . will remain a useful tool, but the narrative news story is more fun for the journalist"—and often for readers as well. Classification of the unorthodox forms is impossible (and when they fall into patterns, they lose their freshness). But one ancient pattern gaining wider use is the chronological or narrative (see page 307); so is the anecdotal opening, a device once thought the property of the popular magazines. What is new in application of such forms is their appearance in stories about news once considered suited only to "straight" treatment.

Newswriters who successfully break the shackles of news story

---

Excellence Was Not Born Yesterday

A book in most journalism libraries shows that high skill in news writing has a long history: *A Treasury of Great Reporting*. Its more than 125 stories cover more than 350 years. Its authors run from Daniel Defoe, Charles Dickens and Rudyard Kipling to Edward R. Murrow, William L. Shirer, Ernie Pyle, John Hersey, A. J. Liebling and Lowell Thomas. It is a history not only of events but also of journalistic style, form and attitude.

DEE = Description, Explanation, Evaluation

The *Wall Street Journal,* one of America's best-written papers, talks of its DEE story form. The acronym stands for description-explanation-evaluation, the three parts of long "trend" stories that report tendencies among human beings and institutions—a developing idea in farming, a change in legislative support of education, fans' desertion of baseball for soccer. Such stories follow their leads with DEE, the three types of exposition. Description is likely to come from observation or other "simple" fact-gathering. The two E's may derive from outside expertise gained by interview or research, or subjective treatment by a qualified reporter.

---

conventions do it by viewing both materials and audience needs with an imaginative eye. They don't select form first and then apply it to a set of facts; rather, they perceive that a given set of facts can be brought to life through custom-made contrivance of pattern.

The example below shows adaptation of manner and reportorial attitude to subject and audience. The paper is a weekly in a small community where most people know most other people (hence no identification of Howard Wigfield). The subject is high on the interest scale, low in importance; thus the whimsical treatment. The story form, after a lead that does more to intrigue than inform, is narrative, conversational and at times personal. If it were presented straight, with a flat summary lead ("Howard Wigfield discovered recently that he was being overcharged for vodka,") followed by a summary of details, it would be short, flat and dull. Instead, an amusing yarn (it was reprinted in dozens of papers) was developed. The story:

If it looks like a half gallon of vodka, costs like a half gallon of vodka, and pours like a half gallon of vodka, is it a half gallon of vodka? Ask Howard Wigfield.

Every once in a while Howard takes a ride to his favorite liquor store to pick up a half gallon of vodka. He brings the half gallon home and pours the contents into a couple of decorative bottles. One of the decorative bottles is a quart and one is a fifth. The two bottles filled, there's still enough left for a few one-ounce drinks. This overage he's traditionally shared with his good wife, as they chat together that evening.

Recently our friend, no doubt in preparation for the holidays, made his trek to the liquor store, went to the familiar shelf, and secured his bottle of Nicholas Vodka. Many vodka drinkers agree that vodka, unlike Scotch, should be bought by price, not by taste, since the latter isn't detectable anyway. Wigfield's bottle cost $7.77, and soon he was home with it and ready to fill his decorative bottles.

The quart was carefully filled and capped. Then the fifth. He topped that off, but as soon as he finished he knew something was drastically wrong. For five years he'd been filling those bottles, and every time there was enough left over to share a drink with his wife.

Howard's wife wasn't even home yet, but her ration was gone. What's more, so was Howard's. You see, after the two small bottles had been filled, there wasn't a drop left in the big bottle.

A case of evaporation? Magic? A hole in the bottle? No chance. Wigfield was just another victim of metric manipulation. It looked like a half gallon, cost like a half gallon, and poured like a half gallon, but it wasn't a half gallon. It was 1.75 liters.

And it took a bit of detective work on Wigfield's part to determine that. The label itself said nothing about the volume of the bottle. The spot that says "One Quart" on little brother's label said "Supreme Quality" on big brother's label. But if you look close on the bottom edge of the bottle, slanting down toward the earth is the embossed message "1.75 liters, 59.2 fluid ounces."

A half gallon has 64 fluid ounces in it. That's why Wigfield and his wife had to break into their holiday reserve to share a drink. That five-ounce overage just isn't any more.

Wigfield, showing the perspicuity of a man who knows that the huge economy size box of soap isn't necessarily a better buy than the regular size, took his investigation further. You can do a lot of things with one of those little pocket calculators. Here's what our man Howard did.

A quart of the same vodka sold for $3.98. That's 32 ounces of booze. And it works out to 12.4 cents per ounce. How much did the big 1.75 liter bottle work out to? The 59.2-ounce bottle at $7.77 costs, by Howard's calculations, 13.1 cents per ounce. Howard would have been better off buying two quarts of vodka to fill his decorative bottles.

And he would have had enough left over to share a few drinks with his wife.[4]

Ask some questions about this story:

- Should "Howard" be identified and given an address?
- Is the repetition of phrases ("a half gallon of vodka," "decorative bottles," "share a drink with his wife"), obviously a planned rhetorical device, effective?
- Is "perspicuity" the right word?
- Would the Wigfields or anybody else be offended at the story's bantering tone?
- Can "breaks" like those in the examples earlier in this chapter be identified?

RADIO AND TV NEWS FORMS

Broadcast news, though its form is close to that of news written for print, also has important differences. The one you see first is that news on the air gives fewer details. Newspaper editors are less threatened by the chance that readers might get tired in the middle of a story, for they can move easily to something that pleases them better. Not so the radio or TV news editor. If the listeners-viewers turn away from a story, they may never come back. Moreover, lis-

[4] Reprinted by permission, Carver County (Minn.) *Herald*, 1977.

teners' attention span is brief. So radio and TV news stories often run only a few seconds, rarely more than a minute (about half a page of double-spaced copy).

The summary lead and inverted-pyramid structure, however, are both found in broadcasting, though radio-TV leads contain fewer facts and are more informally written than print leads (see Chapter 7). Broadcast news makes wider use of the leisurely narrative pattern, a form which, more conversational and "natural" than the inverted pyramid, is easier for the ear to take. Its sentences are shorter, the facts less specific ("about a million dollars" instead of "$992,475"; "the county social welfare director says . . ." instead of full name (and identification). It uses sentence fragments.

And TV's style is often conditioned by the necessity to write to the picture—to make the audio follow the video, no matter what violence it may inflict on the logic of story structure. TV writing can take advantage of the facts given on the screen.

One story written for radio will illustrate some of the differences. Compare the following treatment with the treatment of the same hotel strike on page 92.

> Well, the guests in one of Miami Beach's big luxury hotels won't have to make their own beds any more.
>
> A court order has told workers at the Hotel Fontainebleau to go back to work, after five days of picketing.
>
> But the employees of six other big resort hotels are still on strike.
>
> All of this is hitting the big hotels hard—coming on top of a surprising slowdown in the Florida tourist trade.
>
> There's some hope of ending the strike. A federal mediator has just gone to Miami Beach, and closed-door meetings with the hotel association are going on.

REVIEWING THE BACKGROUND

Not everybody gets to the news every day. This fact of life has led to the journalistic device of briefing readers or listeners on what happened earlier—yesterday's, last week's or last year's events out of which today's story grows. The running story, with new developments daily, must summarize previously published facts.

There is no "best" way to manage such review (many newsrooms call it *tieback*). It may be placed early in a story; it may come at the end. Feature and long straight news stories may put it into a "precede," a separate short passage placed ahead of the lead. It must be tightly condensed. A good example is the following paragraph, the fifth of 17 in a wire service story several days after the arrest of the man accused as the New York "Son of Sam" killer.

> David Berkowitz, 24, is charged in the murder and wounding of Son of Sam's last two victims. The gunman, who used the same 44-caliber pistol in all his attacks, killed six young people and wounded seven in little more than a year.

Occasionally the flavor of a story betrays a writer into doing it too well. Americans were retold *ad nauseam* the story of Clifford Irving's attempt to counterfeit a biography of Howard Hughes. For years the media wasted space by repeating what everybody knew about the kidnapping of Patricia Hearst (often taking pains to refer to her as "newspaper heiress," which she wasn't).

The tieback, however, provides a service. There are always news consumers who scratch their heads and ask "who dat?"

GETTING STARTED

Only newswriting novices permit themselves the luxury, when they come with a batch of notes for a straight news story to the VDT or typewriter, of sitting and thinking it over. The mark of the pros is the dispatch with which their fingers begin to fly. They get at it fast because, between fact-gathering and desk, they have planned ahead. They have decided on the lead and the opening paragraphs; often they have plotted out the entire story.

Experienced reporters are able to follow this businesslike procedure because they know the patterns for lead writing—often more patterns than they know they know. Some of the guides for lead writing are described in Chapter 7. Among the questions a newswriter should ask and answer are:

- What is the dominant theme in this set of facts?
- What facts denote and illuminate the theme?
- What principal impression do I want reader or listener to carry away?
- What are the focuses for emphasis?
- What is most significant? What most interesting? Are they the same?
- What should I leave out?

The significance-vs.-interest conflict may be a puzzle (see Chapter 4). Sometimes this conflict takes care of itself—when what's important is also interesting. But often the trivial will grab an audience when the important is dull as dust. The fact that a senator dedicating a building discovers, as he rises to speak, that he has forgotten his suspenders, and pays a public penalty, is not usually as significant as what he has to say; but it's more entertaining. The reporters have a richness of choices. They could emphasize the senator's moment of truth; they could ignore the episode; they could, probably with some difficulty, build a unified package. Any choice is hard to defend as *the* right one. The news media are lambasted for emphasizing popular interest rather than public significance; but they usually try to cover the news in self-respecting perspective.

In the following example of the conflict, there's modest significance in the crime itself; there's amusement in its setting. Which should a reporter stress? Both? See what one reporter decided:

Brazen thieves got by with burglary and arson within eye-view of the county sheriff's office and a stone's throw from fire department headquarters at 1 a.m. today.

The lead combines both elements, significance and human interest.

First break

The thieves broke into the Weston Engraving Co. on the third floor at 415 S. Fourth Street. From its window you can look down into the sheriff's office on the ground floor of the courthouse across the street.

However, the sheriff's office was unoccupied. During night hours, the sheriff's radio tower is the nerve center of patrol activities.

Second break

Now the story leaves its theme—the thieves' brazenness—and goes on to detail.

Firemen were first on the scene, summoned by an alarm that was set off by a sprinkler, which in turn was set off by a fire set by the burglars.

Investigators found evidence they had started three fires—one in a trash container, one under a desk with papers pulled out of drawers, and a third among papers in an open area between the safe and a desk.

Detectives who were called in said the burglars probably became disgruntled when they were unable to open the safe. The dial had been knocked off but no entry made.

Fire damage was almost negligible, with sprinklers checking the blazes and firemen finishing the job. However, water damage was heavy in the engraving firm and in the second floor office.

Third break

Why include this detail?

The firemen's cleanup job lasted an hour and 45 minutes.

The story shows what happens when the long reach overplays common sense. The "got by" in the lead is not justified. A more routine lead would have served: "Brazen burglars failed in attempted theft and arson . . ."

The Reston story (page 98) fares better. Reston seems to have decided that although the news conference didn't yield much, its human-interest angle was intriguing.

No sweeping rule helps newswriters make such decisions. They approach each story with all the judgment and experience they can produce, and each time come to a new conclusion about order and emphasis. The design is often suggested by the lead, sometimes mandated by it.

To repeat: A reporter should, before starting to write, make two decisions:

1. The story's theme—its central substance, its unifying core.
2. How the facts can be arranged so that first things come first, and secondary facts can be deployed to conform to theme and to order of declining importance. In newswriting, as in war or politics, unity and strength are partners.

STUDY SUGGESTIONS

1. Describe the conventional straight-news-story form.
2. How does this form differ from news forms in early American journalism?
3. What is the rationale of the order-of-decreasing-importance form?
4. Why is the bus-riding story (page 88) suitable for distribution to papers throughout the United States, though it deals largely with a situation in one city?
5. How does the unity principle help in news story construction?
6. How is unity maintained in the Dulles story, page 98?
7. What causes of disruption of news story unity can you cite?
8. Why are transitional devices used less in straight-news stories than in essay or other forms of writing?
9. In what ways does the Wigfield-vodka story (page 103) depart from straight news story form?
10. Cite and explain the principal differences between news stories written for print and those for radio.

PRACTICE ASSIGNMENTS

1. Rewrite and condense the Australian sailor story (page 98) to reduce its length by one third.
2. Rewrite the Wigfield-vodka story as a brief straight news story, using the lead suggested on page 103 or designing a new one. Is the new form an improvement?

3. Rewrite the bus-riding story for use by a local radio station.
4. Study the tiebacks (see page 105) in five or more newspaper stories dealing with continuing news. Write an analysis of their content (too much? too little?) and their placement in the stories.
5. Select a major local news story from your newspaper and rewrite it in form suitable for wire service use.

RELATED READING

Burken, Judith L. *Introduction to Reporting.* Wm. C. Brown, 1976. A textbook that treats fundamentals of reporting carefully and clearly.*

Hohenberg, John. *The Professional Journalist*, 4th ed. Holt, Rinehart and Winston, 1978. Newswriting and newsgathering.*

MacDougall, Curtis D. *Interpretative Reporting.* Macmillan, 1977. A textbook treating all aspects of reporting (originally titled *Reporting for Beginners*).*

Mencher, Melvin. *News Reporting and Writing.* Wm. C. Brown, 1977. A new and well-received textbook, thorough and "professional."*

Mott, Frank L. *The News in America.* Harvard University Press, 1952. A readable book, informative on news values and practices.

Ryan, Michael, and James W. Tankard, Jr. *Basic News Reporting.* Mayfield, 1977. Another useful new reporting textbook.*

Snyder, Louis L., and Richard B. Morris, eds. *A Treasury of Great Reporting.* Simon & Schuster, 1949. More than 125 examples of outstanding reporting and newswriting, from the 16th century through World War II.

*These books contain materials that relate also to several of this book's later chapters dealing with newsgathering and newswriting.

7 News Story Leads

lead *(pronounced leed) The opening segment of a news story, usually a one-sentence paragraph, that summarizes the story's content or keys its mood*

PREVIEW

For most news stories the "lead" or opening section is a compact statement of the report's principal facts. Usually a straight news story lead presents:

- One sentence, rarely more than 35 words
- Emphasis on the event's principal element, often achieved by stating the element in the opening words

Feature and human-interest stories are likely to use more leisurely patterns (though by definition their openings remain their leads). Scores of lead patterns are in use, and more will be invented; variety is prized if it does not confuse or retard a story's pace. Leads for news on the air are also leisurely and often informal. Their example has helped newspaper reporters to make their writing sharper and clearer. Laborious five-Ws-and-an-H leads are now passé.

On June 9, 1864, readers of the New York *Times* had to labor through four columns of agate type (14 lines to the inch) to learn that Abraham Lincoln had been renominated for the presidency.

On July 15, 1976, *Times* readers found the Democratic national convention story opening thus:

> Jimmy Carter of Georgia won the Democratic Presidential nomination last night.

The lead had kept pace with the times.

A "good" lead, one that not only helps its writer organize and unify a story's facts but also takes readers quickly into them, has two primary characteristics:

1. A short, sharp statement of the gist of the story, the topic or theme upon which the story is to center. (Suspended-interest leads, which depart from this pattern, are described in Chapter 15.)
2. Compression of major facts into a one-idea sentence that prepares the reader for what is to come, without confusion of detail.

Newswriting today—today more than ever—demands terse expression. The straight-news lead, as Chapter 6 demonstrates, sometimes runs to two or three paragraphs; but its facts are the essential facts, and its sentences are short and pointed.

COMPONENTS OF STRAIGHT LEADS

When news story form jelled at the end of the 19th century, straight-news leads were painstakingly complete, long and confusing. The stereotype, graven in stone in the "AP lead," required a lead to answer six questions: who? when? what? where? why? how? The five-Ws-and-an-H requirement gave birth to the term "clothesline lead" because everything hung on it. This AP lead shows its virtues and its faults:

> Two men, Guglielmo Fenestrada, 24, 4627 Amsterdam Ave., Centerdale, and Brooks Smith, age unknown, of nearby Connerstown, were instantly killed at 7:15 a.m. today at Liberty Blvd. and Skystone Ave. when a tire on Fenestrada's small car blew out, causing the car to overturn and pin its occupants beneath it, both with broken backs.

In this lead you find:

What?	Two men killed accidentally
Who?	Fenestrada and Smith, with identifying information
When?	7:15 a.m. today
Where?	Liberty Blvd. and Skystone Ave.
Why?	Tire blew
How?	Car overturned, broke both men's backs

It's all there—54 words (13 lines of newspaper type) and nearly 20 specific facts—presented with magnificent impartiality and ponderous confusion. When you get to the broken backs, how many of the early facts can you remember?

The AP lead was the model for American newspapers for more

The mayor of Atlanta talks into a battery of microphones at a city hall news conference. *(Michael Kagan photo from Monkmeyer Press Photo Service)*

than half a century. But radio intruded, and the pace of life increased. Radio news announcers learned (often as they read into microphones the news stories they lifted from newspapers) that a listener's ear was a poorer recorder than a reader's eye. The eye can retrace a printed lead if it has to. But the ear may miss it all if it misses a word. Radio news must "sound like people talking"—it must have simplicity of structure, content, language and fact sequence. Its writers adopted a form which, if not new, met their purposes—often a narrative conversational pattern:

> Another pair of auto deaths today—two men killed in an auto accident in downtown Centerdale.

The radio lead has seven facts and 15 words; it makes no pretense of giving all the answers; it consists of two sentence fragments. But it gives the essential facts in a way the ear can take easily. It prepares the listener to accept added details as they come along.

Radio's undeniable claims started newspaper writers wondering whether a simpler lead might have something for them. Readers were (and are) devoting fewer minutes a day to newspapers as demands on their time grew stiffer—not only radio-TV demands but also those of more money and more opportunities for play. The conclusion: The newspaper could make stories in print more quickly meaningful, easier to take, faster to read.

The wire services and a number of magazines and papers hired readability experts to analyze their styles and suggest improvements. Twenty-five years ago the managing editor of the New York *Times* posted a memo in his city room: "We feel it is no longer necessary—perhaps it never was—to wrap up in one sentence all the traditional five Ws."

The effects of this interest in simpler writing, though it didn't revolutionize writing for print overnight, are unmistakable. The Associated Press, a dozen years after its expert made his recommendations, declared that the ease-of-reading level of its copy had reached the desired plane. The clothesline lead became passé. An up-to-date print version of the accident story might go like this:

> Two men were killed early today in downtown Centerdale when their car overturned.

If you contrast the three leads, you find the third lead closer to radio than to the first. It is two words shorter than the radio leads which, in good broadcast style, repeats a major fact, the *what*.

The move to a simpler pattern does not make a newswriter's task easier. The ready-made formula is no longer a routine guide. From the five Ws and the H writers must choose what most truly catches the flavor and meaning of an event, then express it in half as many words as their grandfathers used. One newsroom has this rule: "If you write a lead longer than 35 words, write it again." Some put the limit at three typewritten lines.

Today's news lead, then, is both more and less demanding than yesterday's. The old formula isn't discarded, but in most stories it's modified. From among six concepts containing perhaps a score of facts, a reporter must select those that stand out. Which concepts best represent the meaning of a story? Which can come later? Which can be left out entirely?

Leads Now and Then

The leads of front-page straight news stories of two 1924 metropolitan papers (picked at random) averaged 53.2 words. Those of a 1955 paper averaged 26.4, of a 1965 paper 25.9, of a 1977 paper 23.8. With one exception, the 1924 leads were longer than the longest of the leads of 30, 40, and 50 years later. The 1924 exception—shortest of any—was a 14-word sentence under a famous byline: Elmer Davis.

The clothesline lead on page 111 includes all six elements. Its modern versions offer the *what* and the *when*, suggest the *who*, *where* and *how*, and ignore the *why*. Time and place (*when* and *where*) can usually be given in phrases, and *who* in a few words; but *what*, *how* and *why*—especially *why*—can rarely be neatly compressed. If the last three get into a lead, they usually are promises of later elaboration.

THE LEAD ELEMENTS

For quite different reasons the *what* and the *when* are almost always included in leads. They earn first attention.

When The time element is firmly established as a major factor in news, and straight-news leads are rarely acceptable without it. In this high-speed era of SSTs and pictures bouncing off satellites, the meaning of an event is often delicately related to the time it occurred. The news media's recognition of this fact—as well as their sometimes frenzied sprint to get news first—have conditioned audiences to think that only "hot" news is worth their time.

The basic *when* is the time information becomes available. This means, in one sense, that every news story is in the past tense: A reporter must have learned, at a given past instant, what he was going to write about before he began to write. An event had occurred, or a specific set of facts had become available.

Here are simple examples of the time element:

> Twenty groups demanding support for equal rights *met* in the Mayflower Hotel *last night.*
>
> Centerdale does not have enough policemen, Mayor John Wilcox *said today.*

The time element does not alter the principal substance of either story. News of the meeting and the statement could stand alone without "met last night" or "said today." But readers find the meeting story more satsifying and meaningful if they know that the event is current; they can relate it to what they were doing, or wonder whether that's where Nancy was going when they saw her near the hotel. And they can respond to the immediacy of the lack of policemen; "today" may tell them that the mayor is reacting to the rash of grocery store holdups.

Placement of the time word or phrase needn't, and usually shouldn't, be anything but where you'd put it if you speak it. Look at what happens when rhetoric gets fancy:

Parking on most of Newark's streets *for more than two years* has been dictated by the rush-hour tide.

Swimming today was prohibited for all of next month by . . .

What The primary purpose of news is to communicate something that has happened or is about to happen. So this something—the *what*—appears in straight-news leads more often than any other element. Today's straight-news lead tells what the story is about—what its main facts are—to let its readers decide whether to spend time on it and to give its writer a center around which to group its facts. (Suspended-interest stories use a different approach to emphasize the *what*.)

Once a reporter decides on the theme of a story, writing the *what* into the lead imposes little problem. The news columns of any newspaper or the contents of any newscast offer many examples of *what* leads, most of them illusively simple. A tightly written summary of an event or a definition of its principal meaning usually suffices.

Many writers of *what* leads are snared by their zeal for brevity. A reporter who has been covering a beat or a month-long continuing story sometimes assumes knowledge of a topic that readers don't have. In these examples readers might be unable to identify the *whats*.

The Council decided yesterday not to make the projected improvements on three areas of the city.

What Council? What improvements? Projected by whom? What areas?

Extension of some types of education in Centerdale, expected since last year, has been stalled by four subcommittee votes.

Would all readers know what types of education? What subcommittee (and of what body)?

Leads that don't say it all can be used when there's no question that everybody knows the circumstances. You could have written in 1974, for example:

The President resigned last night.

The Centerdale Yacht Club's Electra is leading in the Chicago-to-Mackinaw race.

Present tense makes the time clear; the time is NOW.

The implicit time element is common in broadcast news, whose emphasis on news currency is continuously suggested by present-tense verbs.

The lead that follows, from a wire service story, shows how lack of time element may mislead a reader:

Four German students who spent six months at the local university studying American educational techniques reported that controls imposed on American students are "shocking."

The lead makes the complaint appear current. As the story lengthens you learn that it occurred two years ago and had been reported at that time.

An "old" event, however, may acquire legitimate current interest. Twenty years after Franklin D. Roosevelt's death the news media used a story about an occurrence not reported during his lifetime. The Associated Press story said:

> President Roosevelt opposed the return of Indochina to France at the end of World War II, according to historical papers published Monday.

A 1944 act became news in 1965 because it became public in 1965; *Monday*, not 1944, is the story's time element. In 1977 handwriting experts produced evidence that some of Joseph Smith's 1830 "golden tablet" *Book of Mormon* had been written a generation earlier by a scholar they identified.

Thus a story might have two or more *whens*. A local theater manager announces that Lena Horne will be in town for a recital next December. The time of the recital is far in the future. But the *when* of the story itself is the "today" or "yesterday" of the announcement. The lead will spotlight the story's main fact, the *what*.

Should the time statement open a lead?

The news columns of any well-edited newspaper answer "rarely." Seldom is the *when* a story's most meaningful or interesting element. And since a lead should concentrate on its strongest element—more about this principle soon—the time element is seldom the opener. It is more common in broadcast than in print leads, because of radio and TV emphasis on currency.

On occasion, however, the *when* is the focus of a story:

> April 15 has replaced March 15 as the date on which income tax returns are due.
>
> Jan. 28, for the third year in a row, was winter's coldest day.

A final comment: News stories are, whenever possible, the latest word, and sometimes reporters (or copydesks) are reluctant to admit

Giveaway

One of the signs that a story is the work of a novice is absence of the time element. Don't let the customer wonder whether the time is today, yesterday or last Thanksgiving.

that they are not. Failure to write "yesterday," "recently," "last week," "early in March" when appropriate may be confusing. It is less than honest, and there are always some news customers who will know it. It erodes audience confidence.

Who Though the *when* ought to be in almost every lead and the *what* is rarely absent, the *who* is often the opener—sometimes even if it carries less weight than other elements. The commonest reason is also the poorest: that the *who* opener is easy.

A better reason is that the *who* is the human element, and that often it is the element most familiar to the customers. If the President of the United States appears in a story, chances are nine in ten that his name will open it. The name attracts readers; it suggests something about the nature of the story; to most people it is a point of ready contact.

The name opener may, however, depart from the logic of structure or emphasis. Sometimes *what* the President says or does is a better index to the event than his name. Note how changes in the openers alter story emphases:

> President Carter said today he will nominate Cyrus Vance secretary of state.
>
> Cyrus Vance is to be nominated for secretary of state by President Carter.
>
> The next secretary of state will likely be Cyrus Vance.
>
> Nomination of a new secretary of state was announced today in Washington.
>
> Successor to Henry Kissinger as secretary of state is expected to be Cyrus Vance. . . .
>
> One more name for the Carter Cabinet was presented today.
>
> A former secretary of the army, Cyrus Vance, is to be nominated as President Carter's secretary of state.
>
> Cyrus Vance is to be asked to return to the Cabinet.

When the *who* lends neither prominence nor distinctive meaning to a story, it should rarely open the lead. But unusual characteristics may justify a *who* opening, even when specific identification is not needed:

> An 11-year-old boy, scolded for practicing the wrong music lesson, smashed his violin and tried to hang himself today.
>
> A blind man was today made chairman of Nyack's new commission to rid the city of pornographic movies.

Some leads contain no *who* element:

> Nineteen trucks, buses and passenger cars piled up in smog on the New Jersey Turnpike this morning.
>
> The new heliport will be only two blocks from City Hall.
>
> Rain this spring has already exceeded the local annual average.

A contrived variation of the *who* uses a pronoun instead of a name—an engaging device but one that is wearing thin. The example below is effective because its reference is to a typical representative of a group rather than to a named individual:

> Every season, it seems, somebody picks on him. Newspapers expose him. Reformers denounce him. Prosecutors indict him and send him to prison.
>
> But this much has to be said for the crooked politician—he endures. He is a permanent fixture, it seems, of American politics.
>
> Looking at the recent past, one might even say that old-fashioned public corruption flourishes today. An impressive number of public officials have been called to account in the last few years, from a vice president to city meat inspectors and a mayor's press secretary. The common denominator in their indictments was money.

Note that the "he" is specified at the start of the second paragraph.

Where Proximity or its absence can influence audience response, and a statement about it is often essential to understanding or interest. The location of an event, when it is not explictly stated, should always be suggested. In wire stories the dateline often serves.

The place element, like the time element, rarely opens a lead. In some cases, however, it merits first position:

> Houston gets the nod over Seattle as the site of this year's Super Bowl.

A billiard table in a saloon became an emergency operating table this morning.

How and **Why** The *how*—the explanation of an event—usually does not gain priority in lead structure. Few leads explain *how*; the manner of an event cannot always be summarized briefly. Its development is often presented later in a story; sometimes, especially in brief stories, it is omitted altogether. *How* may be implicit rather than spelled out. When a lead says "Congress declared war," it isn't necessary to add "by taking a vote on a resolution." A story about panic in a burning nightclub describes the course of events and thus suggests the fear and hysteria. But not in the lead.

Much the same can be said about *why*. Only a few leads show causes of the events or actions they describe. One that does is the lead about the boy violinist; the highway pile-up is partly explained in the lead. But most leads omit *why*. It would be difficult to explain in tight phrases why the fire started or why people panicked.

Why often is left out for an obvious reason: the reporter can't find out. We still don't know why John F. Kennedy and Martin Luther King were shot. You can't find out on the instant why a dam broke, why the lights went out, why a five-star general defied a president. Some *whys* you never learn.

The urgent need to inject more *why* and more *how* into reporting is recognized as one of journalism's imperatives, nevertheless—sometimes more emphatically by critics of the press than by journalists. More delving into what made it happen, more time spent trying to find answers—either before or after events—is one way, and perhaps the best way, to improve news reporting.

WRITING LEADS

Three rules of thumb for writing summary leads:

1. Open the lead with a capsule expression of the story's strongest element.
2. Adhere to the one-idea-to-a-sentence principle as far as your materials and good rhetoric will let you.
3. Either suggest in the lead the story's substance or write it so that what comes later will relate clearly and logically to the lead theme.

The strongest element You can put rule one in other words: Get the most substantial fact of the story into its first word or phrase.

What facts are "strongest"? The facts that most sharply define the heart of the story—those to which everything in the story relates, those whose quick summary establishes the story's dominant import. Here are examples:

> A jack-o'-lantern crisis is expected in Arizona. Not enough pumpkins.
>
> Two hundred Tampico residents died yesterday when hurricane Ione hit.
>
> Homes for 175 families are to be built here next year.
>
> Repavement of Centerdale's main streets will be debated at . . .

Opening words in those leads summarize the key facts—three, five, four, and five words. One group includes the verb, a bonus. Most rearrangements would not summarize so succinctly:

> Drought and curly top virus have all but wiped out the pumpkin festival in central Arizona.
>
> A hurricane that hit Tampico caused . . .
>
> Home construction here next year will . . .
>
> A debate on whether Centerdale's main streets . . .

The rephrasings also have merit. But each takes longer to bring central facts into focus. The key is to choose a statement (there may be several ways to do it) that stresses central meaning in a hurry, one that starts telling the story instantly.

In some cases the interest-versus-importance conflict may be resolved in favor of reader attraction. The jack-o'-lantern lead is an example. Here are others:

> A quarrel over a recipe for chili sauce upset a Latin American government today.
>
> Dollar bills showered out of a sunny sky on a Centerdale home this morning.

And sometimes, as has been said, the prominence of a participant takes over:

Even the English

The Manchester *Guardian,* one of England's most distinguished newspapers, says in its style sheet: "In news stories, would writers and subeditors please put the point at the beginning? . . . Opening sentences are always important, both to capture the reader and to inform him."

> Queen Elizabeth will go to the races at Epsom Downs tomorrow.

The strong opener principle is an excellent guide to unification of a news story. If the right facts have been chosen for the opening, building the body of the story around it becomes easy.

SKEWED LEADS

The *Progressive* magazine once complained about an Associated Press lead that said:

> Government outlays for support of farm commodities are expected to run close to a record $7 billion this fiscal year.

The story later reported that sales and repaid loans would reduce the actual outlay to a tenth as much.

> Fire broke out at the Prince River Lumber Co., Winston, Wednesday, causing almost total loss.

The significant fact is not that fire broke out, but that the loss was heavy.

> In a hearing before the state Council on the Economic Status of Women Friday at the Capitol, representatives of various metropolitan women's groups testified that the middle-aged former housewife—the displaced homemaker—faces job discrimination because of age, sex and work background. [42 words]

Try turning the sentence around (opening with a variant of the last nine words) and cutting out half the verbosity, and you get something like this:

> Job discrimination because of age, sex and work background faces middle-aged former housewives, women's groups testified at the Capitol yesterday. [21 words]

A story about a tornado's destruction of a trailer camp opened with four paragraphs on the disconsolate little boy who lost his toys.

Maybe Better Next Year?

"Motorists are killing pedestrians in the state at a near-record rate" says a lead on a traffic story. Is the reporter hoping the record will be smashed? (One of the common—and legitimate—criticisms of American journalism is its love affair with the ultimate—biggest, smallest, first, last, longest, hottest, tallest . . . uniquest? deadest? saturatedest?)

The story then reported the death and devastation at the camp. The opening gets attention, but it doesn't key the story.

Other leads that misfired:

The library at Hayfield Elementary School in Fairfax County contains more birth control information than an article school officials would not allow to be printed in the high school's newspaper, according to a suit filed . . .

This lead opens with the wrong facts, and compounds the sin with clumsy rhetoric.

A federal grand jury in Baltimore yesterday indicted two men arrested separately in connection with attempts to tamper with the jury in the political corruption trial . . .

Not the grand jury, the locale, the time or the separate arrests is the key. Jury tampering should open the lead.

One idea to a sentence This principle—that most "good" sentences express only one concept—is parallel to what has been said about the modern as compared to the clothesline lead. A reader, and even more a listener, can rarely swallow a jumble of facts one on top of another; an effective sentence offers only one idea before it arrives at a period. Multi-idea confusion is compounded when the overloaded sentence is a lead, for the consumers aren't prepared—they can't see the concept in advance, they haven't been given guides to meaning or direction. Two heavy leads and rewrites that compress them make the point:

Originals	*Rewrites*
The first three concerts of the 1978–79 Imperial Orchestra season were canceled Friday as negotiations between the Imperial Orchestra Association, governing board of the orchestra, and the orchestra musicians, members of Local 129, American Federation of Musicians, bogged down again after almost eight months of bargaining. [46 words]	The first three concerts of the 1978–79 Imperial Orchestra season were canceled Friday after negotiations between the musicians' union and the orchestra's governing board broke down again. [26 words]
Sixty-eight hijacked passengers were released from an Amman, Jordan, hotel and flown to Nicosia, Cyprus, Friday, and 23 passengers held aboard a British Overseas Airways Corp. (BOAC) jetliner—one of the three planes with 300 people captured and taken to the Jordanian desert—were transferred to Amman. [48 words]	Sixty-eight passengers from hijacked planes headed home from Amman, Jordan, Friday, and 23 more of the 300 aboard the three planes held in the desert were transferred to Amman. [31 words]

Some questions about the rewrites: Are they *too* brief? Do they leave out essential facts? Which of the facts omitted ought to be worked into the stories later? Can any be omitted entirely? Note that neither rewrite observes the one-idea-to-a-sentence formula—each has at least two; can either be brought down to one central idea?

Three more leads that mislead:

Wyn Sargent, a sociologist who married a New Guinea tribal chief, said she was ill Saturday and refused to discuss her life among the stone-age natives.

Nothing in the story that follows relates to the phrase "said she was ill Saturday."

University President William McCabe has appointed a seven-member committee to evaluate the performance of Dr. Avery Force, University vice president for humanities. The review is the first step toward what may be periodic review of all administrative offices.

A nearly inescapable implication in the first sentence is that the evaluation has to do with supposition of malfeasance. The second sentence softens the implication; a later paragraph reports that Force volunteered as a guinea pig in a study of evaluation procedures.

Three men, one of them a local organizer for the National Socialist White People's (Nazi) Party, were arrested Wednesday and charged with trying to steal plumbing fixtures from an unoccupied South Side residence.

A paragraph near the end of the story says that one of the men had recently been identified as a spokesman for the Nazi Party. But it shows no reason for mention of the fact in the story.

GETTING LEADS STARTED

The first rule of thumb on page 119, many newswriters believe, says it all: Open a lead with the story's dominant fact.

Specifics support the principle. One is that strong leads usually start with the subjects of simple declarative sentences—nouns or noun phrases. Another is that the verb or verb phrase should not be long delayed. You'll find examples in the leads on page 120. Any reporter could write these leads in other words, and most could find other emphases. You can always argue that Geri's lead is "better" than Burt's, or weaker; even when there is no argument, the rhetoric chosen is a matter of judgment. Once an emphasis is chosen, however, the number of vigorous alternatives may be limited.

Names You don't have to look or listen long to find support for the faded bromide that "names make news." A count of major general leads in three different newspapers produced 43 opening with personal names, 41 with titles or names of groups or associations, and 32 with "other."

Not every name opener is well selected. Prominence of a name makes it an attention-getter, but it often fails to get the story going. When a tornado ravages a prairie town, for example, and a senator driving through is among the 100 dead, should his name open the story? Circumstances alter decisions; here are some possibilities:

> Senator John Doe lost his life in a tornado here yesterday.
>
> A senator and 100 others were killed by a tornado . . .
>
> A hundred deaths were counted here after yesterday's tornado.
>
> A tornado that killed 100 persons, including a U.S. Senator . . .

Other patterns could be developed. Some questions about these four:

- Using the name to open slows up arrival at what most would say is the major fact: 100 deaths.
- Is the opening "Sen. John Doe" preferable to "A senator"?
- One lead does not mention the senator. Right or wrong?
- Can the phrase "were counted" be strengthened?

Quotations Quotation marks—around words, phrases, clauses—attract attention (most fiction readers prefer pages with lots of dialogue to those with little). Often they add meaning:

"Fog" from a broken steam line caused two auto collisions . . .	*The quotation marks say quickly, "It wasn't really fog."*
"Crime always pays," an ex-convict told an audience . . .	*The quoted clause is attractive, and presumably it sums up the talk.*
"The Merchant of Venice" will be given by home talent . . .	*A play title, say most style sheets, must be in quotation marks.*
"The three musketeers" of Grantham Park were arrested last night.	*Quotation marks call attention to a familiar nickname.*

The writer of the "musketeers" lead might be reaching for effect. If facts published earlier or in the story that follows don't justify the metaphor, the reader feels cheated.

A caution: A long quotation as opener is usually to be avoided. It takes too long for either reader or listener to find out who is talking, or why. Moreover, it's rare that a reporter comes upon a long quotation, however witty or pungent, that provides a sharp summary of the story's facts. Speakers are not often that obliging.

But a short quotation that also summarizes—such as "crime always pays"—is to be prized. Other examples: "Win for Wilson!" for a pep rally story; "What Washington needs is a good five-cent lie detector"; and "No man ever dominated me—I think."

Question leads

Can the police close down a movie they call obscene?

Will the rains ever stop?

Is polio really licked?

"Who won the turkey? is the question everybody is asking . . .

Question leads like these meet the criteria suggested at the beginning of this chapter. Each gives the topic of its story quickly and directly, and suggests that an answer is coming. But the suggestion raises a problem: If readers are not to be left dangling, the newswriter must take them off the hook soon. Police can (or can't) close "dirty" movies, says a court; the weather bureau promises a week more of rain; local doctors say polio is reappearing because complacent parents aren't getting their children immunized; five citizens held winning raffle tickets.

A trap set by the question lead, for unwary reporters, is that it may not produce the expected answer. "Would you like a free look at Tahiti?" asks a lead. Some readers would glow and read on; some might answer, "Hell, no!"; and some might ask, "What's a Tahiti?"

Short leads What is sometimes called the cartridge lead (it packs power in a small packet) is often just right for major news or familiar news. If you can safely assume that your audience has the background to know what you are writing about, you can use leads like these:

Lyndon B. Johnson died today.

The new mayor—Richard Roe.

Rain today ended the drought.

Rain!

Cartridge leads don't appear often, largely because the right circumstances don't often arise. They should be used sparingly. They are defused by overuse.

"You" leads The informal "you" lead is suitable when most readers or listeners are likely to relate easily to the story. If the "you" clearly helps a reader to identify with the news, it may be a plus. It usually suggests that the news it introduces could be written, "Did you think the rain would never stop?" or "you may have given up on the sun" or "you'll be safe in planning that weekend picnic." But its informality makes it suitable only for informal or familiar topics. It ought to appear chiefly in stories in which consumers can picture their own participation.

Longer leads Some news events are complicated enough that terse leads will not do. Increasingly this problem is being met by leads of two or more sentences or paragraphs (the old "rule" that a lead is one paragraph is passé). The following examples, as well as those for a number of stories in other sections of this book, introduce news situations too complex for short leads.

> One of the year's steamiest battles between legal and social work viewpoints is rumbling through the County Government Center.
>
> The issue is child abuse: Under what circumstances should the county Welfare Department's child protection unit turn complaints of physical or sexual abuse over to the police?
>
> All complaints about child abuse should go to the police, insists Ann H. Alton, assistant county attorney and one of the chief protagonists for the legal or criminal justice view.
>
> Police should be called in only under restricted conditions, says Phillip Colinger, child protection program supervisor and advocate of the social work view.

Those four paragraphs, completely outlining the story, are followed by factual development and the contrasting views of the two schools of thought.

> As crime rises and becomes more sophisticated, Washington businessmen fight back by pouring millions of dollars into modern security measures and agencies. The constant search for new crime-fighting weapons is making the security-conscious take a new look at a group of men who know the criminal mind inside out—the ex-convicts.
>
> Yesterday, Bishop Smallwood E. Williams of the Bi-

> bleway Church explained why he became the first businessman here to fight the war on crime with the help of ex-cons.

This two-paragraph lead first states the story's general subject, then shows specific application—the news peg.

> A funny thing happened yesterday to the shade-tree disease bill on its way through the House Tax Committee. It became the Dutch elm and eastern timber wolf bill.
>
> The bill, passed by the Senate (without the wolf provision), was amended today in the tax committee, 15–13, to provide that the state compensate farmers who lose livestock to wolves.

Easy, informal introduction to the subject in first paragraph; specifics in the second.

Radio and TV leads Leads for stories on the air—like the stories themselves—are more leisurely and less detailed than those in print. People getting news by ear must be eased into stories gently. They are accustomed to the looseness and generalities of casual conversation rather than the plunge into concentrated facts common to printed leads. Friends don't say to them, "Hampton will have two new fire stations next year," nor do they organize patterns of facts carefully as in the long lead on the crime-fighting story above. They might begin, "Here's a surprise. A bishop is using ex-convicts to help fight crime."

Many of this chapter's observations about leads hold for air as for print. If the lead paragraph merely suggests the substance of the story, the second paragraph ought to clarify it at once.

Name leads, cartridge leads and *you* leads are common in radio-TV newswriting. One taboo for leads on the air: Don't open with a quotation. Listeners can't hear quotation marks—they think they're listening to the announcer until they're told otherwise.

LEADS AND STORY ORGANIZATION

The third lead guideline on page 119 says that a summary lead provides a skeleton for story organization. It says that development of the facts a lead states or suggests can be expected as the story moves along. Often it helps a writer decide on the order of materials in the body of the story.

Carelessness in relating lead to story may produce either of two errors: inclusion of material that doesn't show up later, or failure to include important topics that do appear later. The story about the

Australian sailor (page 98) is devoted to unusual circumstances not mentioned in the lead. On the contrary, a wire story whose lead talks of lifetime security for steelworkers gets to the topic only as an afterthought in a final paragraph.

Another example:

> A controversial plan to construct lanes exclusively for buses on two downtown streets was presented to the Transit Commission Wednesday.

The story devotes half a column to details of the plan and the controversy surrounding it. So far so good. But it goes on, without warning, into five paragraphs about a city car-pool plan. Reader A complains that the car-pool proposal doesn't belong in the story. Reader B, who couldn't care less about bus lanes but yearns for a car pool, failed to get that far in the story. One easy device that would serve both readers and at the same time preconstruct the story: insertion after the first paragraph of a second to show that the commission also talked about car pools. Another would be a lead saying that "the Transit Commission discussed two city traffic problems . . ." Multiple-paragraph leads often have advantages (see those on pages 126–127).

"DIFFERENT" LEAD PATTERNS

Beginners often strain for "different" leads. When their inventions add life, variety or clarity to writing, they may be gems; when they stretch too far, watch out. Most stories can be written with a dozen or more leads; but some too-familiar patterns should be sidestepped. One is the routine lead that "writes itself"—the lead that is like a thousand others because it fails to capitalize on the unique fact or spirit of the story material. Here are some of the routine leads to watch out for:

Preposition leads Observing the first-things-first guideline with an opening prepositional phrase may be difficult, and it's rarely an attention catcher. Examples:

> At a meeting of the Kenworth Keglers last night, a six-team bowling tournament was . . .
>
> For the first time in 10 years, members of the Kenworth Keglers will . . .
>
> With cheers of enthusiasm, Kenworth Keglers decided last night to . . .

> In an unprecedented decision, the Kenworth Keglers voted last night to . . .

Not one of those opening phrases tells you anything about what the Keglers did that made news. It wouldn't be far wrong to call "at a meeting of" the worst of all leads (it turns up often in novice copy): (1) it says nothing of what happened; (2) it could open a dozen or more stories in any issue of any newspaper; and (3) it's hackneyed. The others, though not quite so stale, waste words, space and time without advancing knowledge of what went on. If an "unprecedented decision" made the event newsworthy, why not name it at once?

Participle leads You can say about the same things of most participial phrase openers:

> Meeting at Pinky's Bar and Eatery, the local Rotary Club . . .
>
> Faced with certain defeat, rebels in the Trinidad jungles . . .
>
> Cheering as it took the final vote, the Senate yesterday . . .
>
> Bringing its membership near the 500 mark, the Harris PTA . . .

Sometimes one can argue for a participial opener. A participle is a verb form, and verbs are action words (note that "cheering" has more life to it than "with cheers." Either might say something significant about the event). But it's often likely that a gerund (which looks like a participle) will do the job better:

> Cheering that interrupted his sermon took the Rev. Adam Bates by surprise . . .

Dependent clause leads Opening with a clause used like a noun, especially if rhetoric demands that it begin with *that*, is pretty sure to be stilted:

> That all schools should long ago have been integrated was the conclusion of a Student Forum meeting . . .
>
> That America is drifting far from fundamental spiritual values was the declaration of . . .

Recasting either sentence to open with strong words or phrases (*school integration, America's spiritual values*) is usually to be preferred. Purists moan at a common journalistic sidestep:

> Schools should have been integrated long ago, a Student Forum . . .

Though this usage draws frowns, it is direct and forceful.

Weak folo leads A businesslike lead for a short *prelim* (an announcement of a future event) is one that is posterlike, one that gives principal facts fast and then stops:

> Mayor Henry Oakes will speak on air pollution before the Kiwanis Club at Pioneer Hotel this evening.
>
> Air pollution will be Mayor Henry Oakes's topic before the Kiwanis Club's annual meeting tonight.

But repeating it with only time change in the folo story the next day (Mayor Henry Oakes spoke . . . Air pollution was . . .) is a journalistic sin. Folo leads usually ought to throw emphasis on facts not available for the prelim. What the mayor said, or the fact that half his audience walked out on him, is the news.

Upside-down leads Some leads end where they should have started. This long-winded example is from a Florida paper:

> Even without formally receiving the Broward County court order demanding it provide more rehabilitation services for dependent children, the Florida Health Department in Tallahassee today began a study of needs and available financing.

You read 24 words before you reach the *when*, the action verb, and the *what*. As in many such leads, a long title and details that ought to come later slow up getting to the core of the story. In the following examples you read 17 to 34 words before finding out the *what*:

> A 25-year-old law-school student confirmed Thursday night that he and some others who survived a plane crash and 70 days in the Andes mountains had . . . *what*?
>
> Dr. Norman Borlaug, an American agricultural scientist who by developing new high-yield types of wheat and corn may have done more than any other individual to fight starvation among the world's growing populations . . . *what*?

An appeal board of the Atomic Energy Commission (AEC) recommended Wednesday that more information be given opponents of . . . *what*?

The U.S. Food and Drug Administration (FDA) announced Wednesday night that it will advise doctors to curb drastically . . . *what*?

The heart of these stories is not the *who* but the *what*—what somebody said or did. It shouldn't be relegated to the back yard. Stand such leads on their heads. (The *what* in the first example was "eaten the flesh of dead companions to stay alive." Try inverting the sentence.)

Credit-line openers Many leads need credit lines; but many don't. If the credit line ("so-and-so said yesterday") starts the lead, it may blunt the story's point. If it comes at the end, it weighs the lead down. The following credit-line openers throw emphasis where it doesn't belong:

Weak	*Better*
Police Chief Ralph Johnson said today that local crime has decreased 13 percent under last year's.	Local crime has decreased 13 percent under last year's, according to Police Chief Ralph Johnson.
Secretary of Agriculture Robert Berglund said today that he has begun investigation of charges of fraud in grain shipments to Russia.	Charges of fraud in grain shipments to Russia are being investigated. Agriculture Secretary Robert Berglund described the charges today to . . .
The Rev. Henry Peterson said today that Gethsemane Lutheran Church will be torn down at once.	Gethsemane Lutheran Church is to be torn down immediately. The Rev. Henry Peterson said . . .

These leads close with unnecessary credits:

The city has taken delivery of six new police squad cars, Police Sgt. Elmer O'Ryan said today.

Halfback Otto Fink, who won a game for Franklin High Saturday, broke his leg in the game's last play, team physician Howard Wilson said today.

All but one of the hundreds of forest and range fires that had ravaged Western states for 11 days were under control Saturday, Gov. Cecil Andrus of Idaho reported this morning.

In these leads the story can be told without attribution. Tagging it on at the end slows the reader, and might suggest the reporter's doubt. Usually it should appear later in the story.

"The" leads To some copydesk chiefs a lead that opens *a*, *an* or *the* is anathema. These editorial despots distort leads to avoid *a* or *the* openers. Simple articles, however, are often less intrusive than artificial contrivance. A reader usually doesn't see them, and a listener certainly doesn't hear them. Some newswriters self-consciously avoid *a* or *the* simply by omitting it. Broadcast writers, seeking conversational ease and flow, wouldn't think of foregoing it when it "sounds natural."

Strong leads This chapter has emphasized what not to do in lead writing. Here is a small library of leads that succeed. Note how many use more than one paragraph.

Mr. and Mrs. James Baer had their first five children here today—three girls and two boys.

• • •

BUENOS AIRES—In March, housing rents increased an average of 95 percent here. In April, the price of gasoline doubled to around $1.30 a gallon. A loaf of bread costs 23 percent more than it did last week.

Despite these dismal figures, financial sages here and abroad are calling the Argentine fiscal recovery "an economic miracle."

• • •

Vice President Spiro Agnew was balked yesterday in his attempt to get Congress rather than the courts to investigate allegations of corruption against him.

• • •

The good news is that water levels in Minneapolis lakes are rising, after sinking to near-record lows last winter.

The bad news is that drought may be better than a lot of rain for the water quality of those lakes.

• • •

"It's all over. The President has directed everybody to tell the truth."

That is how Jeb Magruder, deputy director of President Nixon's re-election campaign, told a friend April 17 that their Watergate cover had blown.

• • •

The nudist from Illinois isn't on the Minnesota ballot. The guy who favors tax loopholes isn't there. The guy who would legalize prostitution but shoots drug peddlers on sight isn't there.

And Lester Maddox isn't there.

Nonetheless, Minnesotans who don't want to support President Ford or Jimmy Carter will find a wide range of alternate candidates on their presidential ballots Nov. 2, candidates ranging from left to right to indescribable.

• • •

The state Senate's 18 Republicans met yesterday to lick their wounds, admire their three newcomers, and cast fearful glances in the direction of the Democratic caucus.

The swollen Democratic caucus—now 49 strong—was meeting downstairs in the same hotel, and Sen. Carl Pitkin, Warfield, expressed a lot of the Republican' thoughts: "God, there's a lot of people down there."

The GOP caucus, with 11 fewer members than it had before Tuesday's election, had something of the air of a combat unit that had just suffered heavy losses. The members made light of their plight, with jokes about how the press at the meeting outnumbered the caucus (not quite true.)

• • •

The county tax assessor's office will stay open Saturday and Sunday for last-minute homestead exemption filings.

• • •

Robert Spanier, 42, closed his auto shop, put away his police badge, and headed north Thursday with his wife and six children to visit relatives for the day.

By early Friday, all but one were dead, killed in a head-on auto collision in central Minnesota. The driver of the other car was also killed.

• • •

Two conservatives from the second congressional district were selected Saturday to lead the state Independent-Republican Party through its 1978 comeback campaign.

Vern Neppl of Mankato, an aide to U.S. Rep. Tom Hagedorn, won a five-way race for the party chairmanship. Loanne Thrane of Chanhassen, a former University regent, was elected chairwoman in a two-way contest.

• • •

White businessmen have reaped millions of dollars in noncompetitive federal contracts that were intended to help struggling minority businesses become self-sufficient, the Washington *Post* said this morning.

Some of these leads depart from the patterns recommended in this chapter. When are newswriters justified in freewheeling?

1. When they are so fully the master of basic newswriting, so entirely aware of the logic of the patterns, that in departing from them they still honor the need for unity, clarity and appropriate emphasis. This usually means that it is the old hands, the reporters who have written thousands of leads, who are qualified or allowed to do it.
2. When haste in making the story's point isn't important, when making it too fast would puzzle more than enlighten, or when the story molds readily into suspended-interest or narrative form.

SUSPENDED-INTEREST LEADS

A teaser opening, one that reverses the purpose of the straight news lead, is the suspended-interest lead. This lead does what its name suggests: holds you away from the heart of the story. Its purpose is to make you keep reading to find out what the story is about. Though it's a trick, it's legitimate when properly used: when attention must be seized to lead to substance; when the impact of the story lies in its human interest; when a quick statement of content is less significant than mood; when the story is treated in narrative form. One such lead comes from the Miami *Herald:*

> Most of them never knew Meredith (Skip) Runck, but he was a cop killed in the line of duty, and that was enough.

The story goes on to tell of the throng of Florida policemen at Runck's funeral.

You will find suspended-interest leads opening a number of stories in this book. See pages 88, 98, 103, 145, 147, 150, 151, 252, 255, 275, 293, 294, 305 (two), 306, 307 (two), 309 (three), 311 (two), 313, 318.

Suspended-interest leads and story treatment get further attention in Chapter 15.

STUDY SUGGESTIONS

1. What are the purposes of a news story's lead?
2. In what respect does a radio or TV news story lead often differ from one written for print?
3. Comment on the relative importance, in a lead, of the traditional lead components (five Ws and an H). Can you say which are most likely to be included?
4. A lead example in this chapter says, "The new heliport will be only two blocks from City Hall." Do you consider its treatment of the *when* element adequate? Can you suggest alteration or improvement?
5. Name some of the justifications for opening a lead with a name; with a location or place reference; with a time element.
6. This chapter advises you to "get the most important fact of a story into its first word or phrase." Are there circumstances when this might not be the best advice?
7. Define, and give examples of, the *upside-down lead.*
8. Define *suspended-interest lead,* explain its use, and give several examples.
9. How does construction of a lead relate to the story that follows it, and how does lead construction aid in story construction?

PRACTICE ASSIGNMENTS

1. After examining the original and rewritten leads on page 122, write at least two more versions. Be sure not to change the original emphasis.
2. From a daily paper pick six news stories, each of which emphasizes a different lead element (W or H). After studying each story's content, rewrite its lead to emphasize a different element. Criticize the new leads.
3. Cover a news event of which you have read or heard a prelim. Write as many leads for your folo story as you think its facts might justify. If any of the

leads repeats the emphasis of the prelim's lead, show justification for it.

4. The one-sentence lead below contains 53 words. Rewrite it in two or three sentences, trying to follow the one-idea-to-a-sentence principle:

   The Eastern financial leader, long an active supporter of more cooperation among corporations, who risked losing his job when he agreed to consult on sales policies with a competing company, said in an interview that he is "bitter and disillusioned" over the refusal of his own company and its rivals to get together.

5. You are told on page 117 that the *who* element is a common lead opener "because it is easy." Pick a dozen or more *who* leads from newspapers or broadcasts that are, in your opinion, "easy" but not necessarily the most effective or appropriate. Rewrite them.
6. Rewrite a number of suspended-interest leads (a good example is that on the young doctor story, page 150) in straight-news form (which presupposes rewriting the entire stories). Evaluate gains or losses resulting from the changes.

RELATED READING

See Related Reading for Chapter 6.

8 News Story Style 1: Elements and Guides

There is no such thing as good style or bad style. The question is, does it accomplish its intention?
Christopher Morley, critic, essayist, novelist, editor

PREVIEW

News story style is to be judged by its effectiveness rather than its literary grace. Journalistic writing is often of highest effectiveness (as examples in this book demonstrate). Learning to write news well is one avenue to skill in any kind of writing. Among qualities that make news style effective are concision, directness, simplicity, lack of pretense and respect for the audience.

Five guides to effective news writing:

- Thorough reporting—you can't write what you don't know
- Logic of fact selection and story structure
- Observance of the tenets of grammar and diction.
- Avoidance of overwriting, either by ornateness or wordiness
- Injection of color and imagination into writing when such qualities are appropriate to subject and purpose

There is no royal road to "personalized" style. Though the conventions of newswriting may seem constrictive, a writer of imagination and inventiveness finds constant opportunity for using his highest skills.

Morley, talking about "literary" writing, asks that its form suit its purpose. Not is it graceful? moving? colorful? exciting? learned? Rather, does its language carry facts, ideas and emotional impulses to the particular audience its writer wants to reach and with the meaning he intends?

To put it differently: Morley means that there is no absolute criterion by which to judge style. Nobody would hold that *Who's Who* or a telephone directory has literary style. But each has simplicity, directness, concision and lack of ornament; the style of each accomplishes its intention.

Morley's aphorism applies in spades to journalistic writing. The style of a news story may be effective or ineffective. And a style that hits its mark in one area of journalism may wander in another. What works well on the sports page is silly or offensive in church news. What is "good" for the *Christian Science Monitor* may not do at all for the New York *Daily News*.

Nonetheless, the guides to effective journalistic style have more similarities than differences, and the similarities are basic. In most examples of "good" news style, as in styles with other labels—literary, expository, narrative, technical, pedagogic—there is a common core. The familiar qualities are constant: simplicity, directness, economy, color, pace, precision. You evolve guides to word choice and complexity of thought and structure according to audience characteristics, then write as simply as your time, purpose and patience allow.

Self-respecting journalists are profoundly weary of a pair of fallacies: the assumption that simple writing is simplistic (the prose of the Twenty-third Psalm, Charles Lamb, Ellen Goodman and Harry Reasoner is one but not the other) and the generalization that because some journalistic writing is shoddy, all journalistic writing is shoddy. These conclusions reflect ignorance and mental laziness. Only those who think that polysyllables spell elegance or a high IQ deny that simplicity in writing is desirable.

The second fallacy, though you'd be hard put to construct a syllogism from its premises, has more flesh on its bones. Much of the writing in newspapers, on the air and in advertising accomplishes its intention as well as any writing anywhere. But a lot of it is flawed by curbstone diction, imprecision, sloppy grammar and lazy acceptance of today's fads or yesterday's clichés. Some of this arises

---

How Many Ways Can You Skin a Cat?

Traditional handbooks on grammar and usage employ a carefully systematized style, straight-faced and strait-laced, businesslike, clearly suited to their function. But an admired and respected book, Fowler's *Dictionary of Modern English Usage,* offers wit and now and then caustic barbs along with its precepts about rhetoric, grammar and diction. And the widely used *Elements of Style,* by Strunk and White, is anything but starchy or pedantic. Theodore Bernstein's several books on language and writing make you chuckle as they guide you. They would grace any writer's desk.

Scores of reporters for every kind of news medium are provided elaborate work facilities at "big" news events. This is the newsroom at the Democratic national convention in Miami in 1972. *(Jan Lukas photo from Photo Researchers, Inc., New York)*

from the haste of journalism, some from incompetence, some from failure to respect the dignity of writing.

Nobody realizes the problems more painfully than newsworkers who take their craft seriously. They are often their own severest critics. Agencies of the press have taken on "readability experts" to help improve staff writing. Scores of local and national awards—under sponsorship of individual newspapers, the Society of Professional Journalists-Sigma Delta Chi, wire services and others—attest to the professionals' desire to do their work better. A comparison of the press in recent years with that of 50 years ago shows that contemporary newswriting is surer, sharper and clearer than its ancestors.

English or composition teachers sometimes tell journalism students that "journalism will ruin your writing." Certainly some of the influences in newsrooms must be countered. But others help: the demands for tight writing, for accuracy, for telling clarity and vividness—not to mention the competition with the man or woman at the next desk. One can gain facility in a newsroom more surely than almost anywhere else; whether facility comes at the expense of quality depends on a writer's artistic and professional integrity.

Style and Stylebooks

The Associated Press and United Press International compete in quality and speed of news serivce and in number of media served. But in one kind of "style" they work for uniformity. This style is not rhetoric, good writing, "perfection of good sense," "the choice and command of language," the way words are put together. It is "a customary manner of presenting printed material, including usage, punctuation, spelling . . ." It is the decision on how to govern the mechanics of writing. Every publication has its rules of style, chosen to make writing and reading easy, and to assure consistency—that you won't write *Company* one time and *Co.* the next, or find *cigaret* and *cigarette* in one story.

To make work easier for everybody—reporters, editors, typographers, students—AP and UPI have agreed on substantially similar style rules. Each has its own stylebook, with most rules mutually accepted (the AP book includes dozens of factual aids and a useful "libel manual"). Most printed news media and most journalism students use one or the other, though individual papers adopt variations to meet particular needs. *Reporting* uses the styles of the AP stylebook (except for publication titles).

Newsroom workers aware of the Buckleys, Herseys, Lardners and hundreds of others who have moved from reporting experience to profit and critical acclaim rather than disaster are piqued at the counsel that "it will kill you as a writer." They know that it will kill no writer but the one who, for laziness or lack of purpose, is not going anyplace anyway.

STYLE FOR "THE MASS"

Journalistic writing is conditioned by its character as "mass" communication. A news story or magazine article is not written in the hope that it will reach literally all 225 million of us. Rather, it is designed to reach a significant share of a defined audience. Some journalism frankly seeks audiences of millions: network news broadcasts, national advertising and the kind of magazine fare that *Reader's Digest* and *People* publish. None is designed for one set of eyes or ears and only a small percentage for limited groups. This puts double emphasis on the basic virtues—simplicity, clarity, directness. The broader the audience, the more necessary that vocabulary and rhetorical patterns rate "easy" on the readability scales.

Yet incompetent or slovenly craftsmen, even when they try to follow these precepts, may produce the inelegance and oversimplification that critics of journalism deride. Their products contribute to the cult of the lowest common denominator, the descent to banality.

The search for simplicity, however, need not lead to the shallow or the crass, to lack of precision. Newswriting that has meaning for the largest audience has sure diction, artful and often artistic design, subtle and discriminating selection of word and fact.

The Direct Road

Reed Whittemore, poet and English professor, says that "journalists are conservative writers . . . . A reporter, new or old, continues to like to put a subject down, a verb and an object—and to proceed that way until he has reached the bottom of the page and can go home. His job demands that he be methodical, straightforward, and obedient" to "a strict norm of accent, syntax, and style." The comments are from Whittemore's article "The Newspeak Generation" in *Harper's* of February, 1977.

The writer of this sort of journalistic prose respects the audience and has an informed desire to serve it. One of the emptiest of clichés is that the "mental age" of the average American is 14 (or 12 or 10) years. Whatever validity such loose talk may have is complex and involved; it is not the simple, flat aphorism its proponents would have you believe. Just as exceptionable is H. L. Mencken's caustic observation that nobody ever went broke by underestimating popular intelligence. Even if these were dependable guides, they would not justify "writing down" or condescension.

Moreover, they would not make writing easy. Young hopefuls dreaming of literary careers say glibly that they'll "start with stories for children because they're easiest." This is hallucination; writing simply and with crystal clarity is hard work.

GUIDES TO JOURNALISTIC STYLE

Just as there are pitfalls to bypass in newswriting (some of them pinpointed in Chapter 9) so there are signposts that are to be observed. Among them:

1. Thorough fact-gathering
2. Orderly structure
3. Precise diction and grammar
4. Economy
5. Vitality, color, imagination

Thorough fact-gathering No one has discovered a substitute for scrupulous reporting. Writers must have all the findable facts relevant to the story they want to tell. Without the facts they cannot lo-

How Many Facts Are Enough?

Magazine writers say that they throw away twice as many facts as they put into their finished articles. "This is not waste," they say. "This is making sure that only relevant materials get into the story. You have to know *all* the facts before you can judge what you don't need."

cate the center of the material—they cannot decide on the story's pith. And they cannot determine how to move toward the flavor the finished story should present. It is basic to the concept *objectivity* that the writer decide what the facts ought to denote and connote ("ought" not moralistically but realistically).

For these reasons, among others, *know your facts* is the newswriter's first commandment.

Orderly structure The structure makes and follows a story plan. Without logical organization, no piece of writing can be successful.

Your story plan gives form, logic and unity to what you write. It starts the story at a point that defines its substance or its nature (the lead), then lets your readers follow it in comfort. It brings the readers and the facts to conclusion at the same time. And it guides your decision about what to include and what to leave out.

Few newswriters beyond the novice stage put their blueprints down on paper (though sometimes you wish they had). Usually reporters depend on clear mental images of what they want to achieve.

Precise diction and grammar *Words* are agreed-on symbols that represent specific meanings. In the rich but sometimes confusing American-English language one symbol may have a number of meanings. But it has only one meaning at any one time.

Sentences are combinations of words brought together to form a more complex meaning.

Grammar is a system of rules for putting words and sentences together in an orderly and familiar pattern. The rules of grammar are the traffic laws of Communication Avenue. They grow from centuries of experience, from agreement by a people that they help build words into phrases and phrases into digestible sentences. Ignoring or fracturing them is a good deal like making your own rules for driving in traffic. Suppose you violate a "no left turn" sign. You may get by with it. But more likely you will snarl the purposes and tempers of a swarm of other drivers, and maybe get a bashed fender to boot. You have failed to achieve your objective, or worse.

Rhetoric, says Jacques Barzun, is "the craft of setting down words and marks right"—the art of prose composition that puts words, sentences and grammar to work to accomplish a desired effect. You can use words correctly in grammatical sentences but achieve clumsy or confusing rhetoric, as well as nonmeaning:

The girl was hurt only yesterday.
Only the girl was hurt yesterday.
The girl was only hurt yesterday.
The only girl was hurt yesterday.

Same words and grammatical sentences—but four different meanings.

We may expect by the year 2000 three-quarters of the people of the nation will have significant hearing impairments.

Does the date apply to the expectation or the impairments? Insert a "that" at either of two places, and the correct meaning—whichever it is—emerges.

The rules of grammar are not inviolable. Like traffic laws, they change as the needs of people change; they bend and give way before stresses of social and intellectual climate. Sometimes the effect a writer wants can be gained only by breaking them.

In general, however, English that observes the rules is the clearest and most forceful English. It gives the eye or ear what it is accustomed to. It doesn't stop the reader with uneasy suspicion that something is wrong. Ordinarily it lays down the easiest, the most economical, the surest path to understanding.

The same comments apply to the use of words. People skilled in a craft wield their tools with pride and tender regard. Good writers want their style strong and exact, and they know that each time they misuse a word—each time they let slip *flaunt* for *flout*, *literally* for *figuratively*, *nominal* for *small*—that word is degraded. The sloppy writer asks, "If everybody knows that I mean *small* when I say *nominal*, why not say it?" The answer: What do you use when *nominal* is precisely what you mean? Five cents is a small sum, but it's a nominal price only when it's the price named. A million dollars would be the nominal price for a rowboat if that's what you are asked to pay for it, but it's hardly a small price.

Economy—tight writing A quip attributed to a business executive is that "I didn't have time to write a short letter." Its wit has been dimmed by overuse, but its truth is as good as new. The leanness, the word economy, the concision characteristic of good journalistic writing are not easily come by. It takes time, thought and will to pare cherished rhetoric to its marrow.

Tight writing means: Say it briefly; say it simply; crop excess fat; cut decoration that hides. It means: Speak your piece and stop.

Copy editors believe that there never has been a piece of writing that could not be polished to advantage. Experienced writers don't enjoy surgery on their work, but few deny, when time has eased their pain, that competent surgeons help.

The key to successful paring is rarely in sweeping discard of paragraphs or sections. If selection and organization of a story's material have been properly managed, there should be no major segment that can be cut. Trimming means deleting a phrase here and a sentence there. And it is often expedited by increasing the number of periods (there are four in the original example below, eight in the edited version).

Original version

WASHINGTON–Republican members of a Senate interior subcommittee concluded that President Ford's former campaign manager, Howard H. Callaway, used "very poor judgment" in his alleged efforts to expand a Colorado ski resort during earlier service as secretary of the Army, Sen. Mark Hatfield, R-Ore., said yesterday. [45 words]

However, Hatfield added that the Republicans have determined that there was "no evidence of abuse of power" by Callaway, who headed Ford's drive through the initial GOP primaries before resigning when questions were raised about the resort matter. [38 words]

Last week the four Republican members of the subcommittee on environment and land resources objected to a 250-page report approved by the five Democratic members which Hatfield said suggested that Callaway, as a government official, had used undue pressure. [40 words]

Callaway resigned as Ford's campaign manager after allegations that while he was Army secretary he had intervened with Forest Service officials in 1975 in an effort to obtain approval of a proposal to allow expansion of the Crested Butte ski area, which is on federal land. [46 words]

Edited version

WASHINGTON–President Ford's 1976 campaign manager, Howard H. Callaway, used "very poor judgment" in alleged efforts to expand a Colorado ski resort while he was a member of the Ford cabinet. [30 words]

This is the conclusion of the Republican minority on a Senate subcommittee, Sen. Mark Hatfield, R-Ore., said yesterday. [18 words]

Hatfield added, however, that the Republicans found "no evidence of abuse of power" by Callaway. Callaway, formerly secretary of the Army, was Ford's campaign manager through the initial primaries until the resort question was raised. [35 words]

The four Republicans on the environment and land resources subcommittee objected to a report approved by the five Democratic members. Hatfield said the report suggested that Callaway, as a government official, had used undue pressure. [35 words]

Callaway resigned as Ford's campaign manager after allegations that in 1975 he had asked Forest Service officials to approve expansion of the Crested Butte ski area. The area is on federal land. [32 words]

One aid to the paring process is rare in newswork: the advantage of "letting it cool." When the writing is a day or a week old it is easier to recognize words and phrases you don't need than when they are still smoking. A newswriter's product rarely gets time to cool. Fast, sure editing judgment, which is usually the product of experience, is the nearest thing to a substitute.

Vitality, color, imagination These qualities give life and movement to writing. To gain them, you guard against the perils of haste, of bromides and sloppy diction, of verbosity . . . and then use all of your skill to gain vigor, pace and richness. The more these qualities style a reporter's work, the more satisfying and successful it is.

You follow a wealth of specific guides. You remember the counsel of your composition teacher to use active verbs instead of passive:

"The jury indicted Smith" rather than "Smith was indicted . . ." You keep at forefront the precept that verbs and verbal derivatives are strong because they connote action; that concrete nouns (*touchdown* instead of *score, bananas and oranges* instead of *fruit*) represent specific and easily identifiable concepts; that you can smother a noun by overdressing it with adjectives (especially when you use *good* when you could say *pious, sterling, safe, skillful, gracious*). You remember John Ciardi's advice: "Never send an adjective on a noun's errand."

You learn other means of injecting color and life into copy. You become aware, in spite of Ciardi, that adjectives and adverbs that "move" are life-giving. You underscore such suggestions as these:

- Don't choose a term simply because it's different or interesting. Your question must be: Is it *right*?
- Search for the simple word, the word your audience will know, rather than the erudite, the showy.
- Replace phrases with words, clauses with phrases. Keep sentences short, simple, mostly declarative.
- Look for illuminating figures of speech but don't reach too far. Don't write that "the baseball soared like a sparrow"—baseballs aren't good soarers, and neither are sparrows.

"Reading ease" and writing ease Writing by formula was explored in the 1950s by American "communication scientists." Rudolf Flesch developed what he called ease-of-reading scales, mathematical descriptions of samples of writing by the number of words per sentence, the number of polysyllables, the complexity of sentences and other such characteristics. Other researchers developed similar formulas, and the two major American news services as well as individual media experimented in applying them. Newswriting profited from the critical attention centered on it—more from the focus than from the formulas. Formulas don't teach writing, although they describe variations in it. In effect they say in a new way what writing teachers have always said: Write simply, use familiar language, don't overload or muddle sentences.

The work of the professionals, those to whom the practices urged in this chapter are almost reflex, is worth critical examination. Examples both good and bad appear in this book. But the daily world of news is full of them. You can pick your own examples for diagnosis.

The smoothly told story about a man and his vodka (page 103) is worth a second look for its simple directness, its use of specifics, its easy informality and good humor. Here are two more that show daily journalism as its best.

The first—one reprinted time and again as an example of telling selection of detail and of narrative that needs no adornment—won a Pulitzer Prize for its writer, George Weller of the Chicago *Daily News*. Even time and some abridgments do not dilute its artistry.

"They are giving him ether now" was what they said back in the aft torpedo rooms.

"He's gone under and they're ready to cut him open," the crew whispered, sitting on their pipe bunks cramped between torpedoes.

One man went forward and put his arm quietly around the shoulders of another man who was handling the bow diving planes. "Keep her steady, Jake," he said. "They've just made the first cut. They're feeling around for it now."

"They" were a little group of anxious-faced men with their arms thrust into reversed white pajama coats. Gauze bandages hid all their expressions except the tensity in their eyes.

"It" was an acute appendix inside Dean Rector, of Chautauqua, Kan. The stabbing pains had become unendurable the day before, which was Rector's first birthday at sea. He was 19.

The big depth gauge that looks like a factory clock and stands beside the "Christmas tree" of red and green gauges regulating the flooding chambers showed where they were. They were below the surface. And above them—and below them, too—were enemy waters crossed and recrossed by whirring propellers of Japanese destroyers, transports and submarines.

The nearest naval surgeon competent to operate on the young seaman was thousands of miles and many days away. There was just one way to prevent the appendix from bursting and that was for the crew to operate upon their shipmate themselves.

And that's what they did: they operated upon him. It was probably one of the largest operations in number of participants that ever occurred.

"He says he's ready to take the chance," the gobs whispered from bulkhead to bulkhead.

"That guy's regular"—the word traveled from bow planes to propeller and back again.

They kept her steady.

The chief surgeon was a 23-year-old pharmacist's mate wearing a blue blouse with white-taped collar and a squashy white duck cap. His name was Wheeler B. Lipes.

[*The story tells of Lipes' inadequate training; the grim courage with which he and his patient approached the operation; the tension aboard the sub as substitutes for anesthetic, antiseptics and surgical instruments were improvised. At length, the climactic point:*]

It took Lipes in his flap-finger rubber gloves nearly 20 minutes to find the appendix.

"I have tried one side of the caecum," he whispered after the first minutes. "Now I'm trying the other."

Whispered bulletins seeped back into the engine room and crew's quarters.

"The doc has tried one side of something and now is trying the other."

After more search, Lipes finally whispered, "I think I've got it. It's curled way up behind the blind gut."

Lipes was using the classic McBurney's incision. Now was the time when his shipmate's life was completely in his hands.

"Two more spoons." [*Bent metal spoons*

had become surgical retractors] They passed the word to Lt. Ward.

"Two spoons at 14:45 hours," wrote Skipper Ferrall on his note pad.

"More flashlights and another battle lantern," demanded Lipes.

The patient's face, lathered with white petrolatum, began to grimace.

"Give him more ether," ordered the doc.

Hoskins looked doubtfully at the original five pounds of ether, now sunken to three quarters of one can. But once again the tea-strainer was soaked in ether. The fumes mounted, thickening the wardroom air and making the operating staff giddy.

"Want those blowers speeded up?" the captain asked the doc.

The blowers began to whir louder.

Suddenly came the moment when the doc reached out his hand, pointing toward the needle threaded with 20-day chromic catgut.

One by one the sponges came out. One by one the tablespoons bent into right angles were withdrawn and returned to the galley. At the end it was the skipper who nudged Lipes and pointed to the tally of bent tablespoons. One was missing. Lipes reached into the incision for the last time, withdrew the wishbone spoon, and closed the incision.

They even had the tool ready to cut off the thread. It was a pair of fingernail scissors, well scalded in water and torpedo juice.

At that moment the last can of ether went dry. . . .

[*The story then reports the operation's success and Rector's return to duty; it tells the reader finally that on a submarine shelf in a bottle "swayed the first appendix ever known to have been removed below enemy waters."*]

It takes no Pulitzer Prize jury to see why this kind of newswriting remains compelling. The excerpts—less than half of the story—are a primer of the high competence that turns what could have been a two-paragraph filler into memorable prose. The reader sees the "flap-finger rubber gloves," smells the ether, hears the gobs' whispers and feels the propellers' throbs. The dialogue is gob language; you can count the medical terms on one hand. "Two spoons at 14:45 hours," noted the skipper. "The doc has tried one side of something," whispered a seaman. The story demonstrates the Theodore Bernstein precept: "To give a sense of immediacy in reporting, inject quotations—if possible, dialogue—into a story."

The next story is marked not only by low-key writing but also by artful structure. A good deal of its substance was "old" when the story appeared, but old news given new life by broadened perspective. The writer was George Moses, an Associated Press correspondent who had been a reporter in Bismarck, North Dakota, and knew the storm-swept plains he was writing about. The event covered four days; Moses decided it could be made fully vivid for readers by a "mop-up" that gathered scattered events into a single focus.

Spring is an elusive visitor to the northern Great Plains. It drops in briefly after the cold of January and February to set the snow melting and to remind the hardy plainsman winter won't last forever.

Then it usually gives way to another blast or two of icy air before it returns to stay.

March this year opened with such a promise. The sun squeezed water out of a sparse snow cover on the Dakota prairies. Cattle dozed in its warmth. Children brought out jump ropes and bikes.

But the harbinger was brief. By Wednesday, the second day of the month, gray clouds began to cover the sun. The Weather Bureau predicted snow ending by Thursday. Shortly before noon Wednesday the weathermen took another look, predicted heavy snow and strong wind farther east in the Dakotas. They still said it would end Thursday.

One who heard that snow warning was a hardy rancher named Otto Mettler, who lives 16 miles northeast of McLaughlin, S.D., near the North Dakota border.

Mettler, his wife, and their son, Lyle, 7, had been visiting a daughter in nearby Lemmon, on her birthday. As a light snow began, the Mettlers started home.

In McLaughlin they stopped for gas, and Mettler bought 50 cents worth of candy bars.

Across the North Dakota line, in Mandan, three basketball coaches from the Indian reservation town of Fort Yates were watching a basketball tournament. Their team was to play the next day.

Harlan Wash, Allen Mitzenberger, and James Barret eyed the thickening snow and the rising wind, decided to drive the 60 miles home to Fort Yates anyway.

In their car were three sweet rolls.

Southeast of Mandan, across the Missouri River, lies the little town of Strasburg, N.D. Fading road signs label it the home town of Lawrence Welk. A cousin, Eugene Welk, farms east of town. His 6-year-old daughter, Carleen, splashed around the muddy farmyard in her new overshoes. As usual, she was following her two bigger brothers as they did chores.

Many miles across the prairie to the northeast, at the Raymond Diede farm near another tiny town called Woodworth, the hint of spring had been in the air. The Diedes' daughter, 13-year-old Betty, was a seventh-grader in the Woodworth School.

Suddenly there was the snow, and the wind.

The weathermen had been watching an odd combination of low pressure cells. One developed in Nevada and a second in northern Colorado. Deepening, they moved slowly northeast on a collision course. They met that day over the northern plains, linking up with a third low already on the scene.

The snow thickened. The wind rose. Quickly it was hard to see more than a few feet in the white, or to breathe in it. Drifts formed on highways and stopped travel dead over all but northwestern North Dakota and southeastern South Dakota.

The Weather Bureau on Wednesday afternoon added to its prediction a word it doesn't use lightly:

Blizzard.

You can usually get an argument at any corner cafe in the north country on when a snowstorm becomes a blizzard. To the weathermen, this yardstick is simple: winds of more than 45 miles an hour, great density of snow, and temperatures of 10 or lower.

Though temperatures first were in the teens—probably sparing lives—there was no argument about the storm that swept over the Dakotas from the southwest that day. It packed winds clocked unofficially in some places at more than 100 miles an hour. It laid down a blanket of snow ranging up to three feet.

Despite its howling, blinding fury, it

lumbered northeastward across the Dakotas and northern Minnesota with punishing leisure.

Before it blew itself out four days later, the great blizzard of 1966 took 18 lives, stopped outdoor life almost dead in hundreds of towns, and killed unsheltered livestock in numbers that are still being totaled.

Homeward bound, the Mettlers and their boy fought mounting drifts and blinding snow until a tire chain broke. Their car went into a ditch. The Mettlers didn't know it, but they were two miles from their ranch.

Wise to prairie winters, the three put on heavy clothes from the trunk and began a lonely vigil that was to last three dark nights and two snowwhite days.

"I kept saying, 'We can't leave the car,' " Mettler said later.

To keep his family from suffocating as the drifts closed over them Mettler would roll down a back window and shovel until he could crawl through enough to widen the hole to the top of the drift. Then he'd crawl back into the car.

Often, in the frightening hours, Mrs. Mettler and Lyle sang the Sunday school hymn, "Jesus Loves Me."

Lyle ate the last of the candy bars Friday evening.

Saturday morning the Mettlers stirred under the feather comforter they shared. The snow and wind had stopped after 60 hours.

They fought their way free of the car and walked the two miles home across crusted drifts.

Some 40 miles to the northeast, the three young coaches from Fort Yates were stalled south of Mandan.

Without heavy clothing, they ripped out the back cushion of the car. There, in the back seat, they burned everything burnable—including some wooden fence posts near the road.

"We kept thinking with every sunrise or sunset it would break," said Barret. "Everybody was saying his own prayers. It got pretty quiet in that car."

The men shared the three sweet rolls, grabbed fistfuls of snow for water.

At 2:30 a.m. Saturday a rescue party from Mandan, led by a rotary snowplow, found them. All three were hospitalized for treatment of smoke-irritated eyes from the fire that kept them alive.

Thursday afternoon the blizzard eased momentarily at Strasburg. At the Welk farm, Carleen's two brothers, Allen, 13, and Duane, 11, went to the chicken coop 60 feet from the house, then to the barn another 20 feet away.

Carleen started out with them. When the boys got to the barn, they stopped, frightened. The little girl was no longer with them.

Welk and the two boys looked for her in the wind and snow until dark. Welk tried it again Friday. Search parties couldn't reach the farm.

The storm dying, Welk went out again Saturday, battling 12-foot drifts. A quarter of a mile from home he found Carleen's body. It was in a sitting position, upright in the snow. Her new overshoes were still on her feet, a stocking cap over her brown hair.

At the Diede farm Friday morning, the winds were screaming, the snow still falling. There'd been no school since the storm broke. Betty slipped out of the farmhouse to close a banging door on a chicken coop 100 feet away. Then Betty went to a barn close by, where a nephew had taken refuge. The girl started back for the house. She was not seen alive again.

Mrs. Diede, realizing Betty was missing, headed in a frenzy for the chicken coop, then the barn. The boy in the barn pointed in the direction Betty had disappeared—away from the house.

Mrs. Diede followed. She soon realized she too was lost in the blinding whiteness.

The woman remembered the lashing

wind was from the north, and that home was in that direction. She kept the wind in her face, and dropped on hands and knees so she could breathe and move. She crawled perhaps 300 feet that way, until her home loomed up in the snow.

Rescue crews from Woodworth could not break through to the farm until the next morning, when the storm slackened. With visibility still bad, they roped themselves together in teams of six.

One group found Betty's body at 11:15 a.m., half a mile from home. It was lying near a railroad track.

"She was a very pretty girl," said her family's minister of the brown-haired seventh grader, "quiet and well-mannered."

In the larger Dakota cities in the blizzard's path, traffic signals blinked foolishly for days, directing vehicles that were stuck in drifts. In some, office workers were marooned for days, even though home might be just a few blocks away. Emergency workers caught at home risked their lives to report for duty.

And in at least one Bismarck residential area, the first shortage that started neighbors bucking drifts to lend or borrow was in cigarettes.

The blizzard of 1888 is a legendary one on the northern plains. It raced out of Canada on Jan. 12, left at least 112 persons dead, and wiped out cattle herds wholesale.

On Nov. 11, 1940, a sudden blizzard struck Minnesota. The Armistice Day blizzard left 49 dead.

And almost 25 years ago to the day, on March 15, 1941, a blizzard pounced on the Red River Valley of North Dakota and Minnesota, trapping unwarned travelers wholesale in their cars. The loss of life in that one is put at from 76 to 90.

Better forecasting and speed and spread of modern radio may have helped keep the 1966 death toll relatively low. But in terms of ferocity of the storm itself, the blizzard of 1966 may well rank as the worst in recorded Bureau history. The weathermen are still checking their records.

Winds have been higher, and snows have been deeper. But it is doubtful that any other winter storm in history has circled on itself twice, as this one did, or hit so big an area with so much for so long.[1]

"How did the reporter get all the detail?" you ask. Moses explains: "I had a stack of stories from newspapers and from AP files. Stories of this kind are often loaded with specifics, and every detail I used—three sweet rolls in the coaches' car, the 'stocking cap over her brown hair'—came from those sources. One detail I added—the traffic signals blinking at nothing. That seemed legitimate." Three paragraphs about earlier blizzards were drawn from reference materials such as any news office maintains.

The story illustrates again the force of understatement. It lets the facts tell their story. It uses adjectives sparingly, and only when their validity is evident. And it depends heavily on short declarative sentences.

These two stories are drawn from dramatic stuff. A compelling story emerges easily from a stirring event if the writer resists temptation to overwrite, to adorn, to "improve" material that needs no improving. One of the marks of the able writer is that he knows when to say "no" to purple prose. Graham Hovey—World War II and Washington correspondent, journalism teacher, New York *Times* editorial writer—says that one of the best bits of advice he received as a journalism student told him to "eschew fine writing!"

For a story from more ordinary clay look again at the Reston dispatch on page 98. The Washington correspondent often works with what seems drab material—a Congressional debate on the balance of payments, though it is important to all of us, rarely makes the blood run hot (or cold). But Reston, by selection of detail, humor on both sides of the story's major substance, and unpretentious language, has given a routine piece movement and sheen.

It is hard to find fault with the story that follows. The event was charged with pathos, and its writer might have let it become maudlin. But his emotional control matched that of the participants, and both are transmitted to the reader. His simple narrative moves surely to the climax—the more graphic because it is starkly unadorned.

The young doctor leaned back in the chair and smiled. "I'd give the patient another few weeks," he said. "A month or so at the most."

The doctor himself is the patient.

So Dr. Napoleão Leaureano, 36-year-old Brazilian physician, is going home to die. His plane was to leave this morning.

"A man ought to die at home," he said. "We have a fine new home. We've been making payments three years . . ."

He looked at his pretty 25-year-old wife, Marcina, and she said, "Oh, yes, it's lovely. Very lovely."

It has seas of flowers spilling over the wide yards that border on a shady street, and a patio and small pond in back. It's summer in Brazil, and the flowers will be blooming now. Their daughter, little 4-year-old Maria, will be there too.

"We're in a hurry to get back," the doctor said. "So much to do, and so . . . well, so much to do."

About a year ago Dr. Leaureano, a surgeon, completed a specialty course in cancer in preparation for setting up a diagnosis and treatment center in his home town, João Pessoa, Brazil. Shortly thereafter, he discovered he had the virtually unstoppable lymph cancer (lymph sarcoma) that spreads relentlessly through the body tissue.

Hundreds of his patients and friends, many of whom he had cared for without charge, scraped together a fund to send him to Memorial Hospital here, a major cancer research center.

But the hospital specialists here found it was too late to help.

"Yes, it's a little hard at first to reconcile yourself to it," he said. "But then your perspective begins to change, and you're ready for it. You see things more clearly, more sharply."

And what, a reporter asked through an interpreter, do you see?

"Well, you see how very important work is, especially work that you want to finish. You cherish friendships more than ever. You recognize that affection, good will and love are the main things . . ."

He glanced over at his wife, who now sat silently in a corner of the room. He added: "And family, the ones who are close."

He got up and walked stiffly across the

room, and put his hand on his wife's shoulder. She stared down at the floor.

The reporter said to the interpreter: "Would you ask her how she feels to have such a courageous husband?"

"She's very proud," the interpreter said. "But I'm not going to ask her, because she's going to cry."[2]

Sports stories, though many grow out of color, conflict and excitement, don't always live up to their possibilities. This one by a syndicate reporter, however, turns an offbeat scene into a reader's delight. Satchel Paige, who went from black leagues to big leagues after he was 40, is its "hero." Its charm lies in what appears to be the absolute fidelity of the reporting, without additives.

TUCSON, Ariz. (NANA)—"I hear you got control," said Oscar Melillo skeptically.

"Man, you didn't hear no lie," Satchel Paige replied.

"How many strikes do you think you can throw outa, say, 10 pitches?" Melillo asked.

Satch considered this carefully.

"Maybe not over eight or nine," he said. "I ain't throwed since October. Gimme another week an' I'll throw 10 out of 10, all of 'em curves."

"A Coke says you can't throw eight," said Melillo.

Satch grinned. "Man, you got yourself a wager."

Jim Hegan placed a shinguard on the outfield grass to serve as a plate, and Paige recoiled at the implied insult.

"I c'n throw a thousand outa a thousand over that big old thing," he said. "Put a baseball cap down there. That's all the plate old Satch needs."

An audience had gathered, including Dick Roznek, the Indians' wild young left-hander. Roznek's eyes popped.

"Is he kidding?" he asked.

Paige withered him with a look.

"Sonny boy, you c'n get yourself a Coke, free for nothin', if you think I'm kiddin'."

He went into an elaborate windup and threw his first pitch, a sidearm fast ball that crossed the button of the cap-plate, waist high.

"Strike!" said Hegan.

"I gotta give you that one," Melillo conceded.

"Man," scoffed Satch, "you gettin' generous in your old age."

"Look who's talking about old age," Bob Lemon snorted, and Satch turned on this newest heckler.

"You talk like you pitch," he said. "Loud but not smart. What you know about anybody's age?"

"All I know," said Lemon, "is there was a colored man on that barnstorming team of yours out on the coast last winter. He told me he was 47 years old, and I heard you call him 'son.' "

Satch wound up and buzzed another fast ball across the cap. A plumb bob hung from the straight line of its course would have touched the cap's red button.

"Two!" said Hegan.

"Two," Melillo agreed.

Five strikes Satch pitched before he missed the cap's edge by a hair. He cut the narrow strike zone with two more, then missed again.

It was seven strikes, two balls, with one pitch to go.

"You're in trouble," said Melillo. "You're in bad trouble. Because you want to know why? Because the other ball club

[2] Copyright © 1963 by the Associated Press. Reprinted by permission.

just sent in a pinch hitter. A midget. He's only this big." And Melillo dropped to his knees. "To make it worse, he hits from a crouch. You only got about six inches between his shoulders and his knees."

"Shucks," said Satch.

He tied his long body into a tortured knot and as he unwound his whiplike arm came down. It halted suddenly in the familiar pattern of Paige's famous hesitation pitch. Then it resumed its motion and the ball left Satch's hand and whizzed across the cap.

"Strike!" said Hegan.

"I guess I used too big a midget," said Melillo.

"Gee," said Roznek, "I wish I had a million dollars so I could buy some of that."

And finally the shortest story on record, helped out by everybody's knowledge that Elizabeth II had been pregnant for what seemed a very long time:

LONDON, England—Not yet.

HOW DO YOU "PERSONALIZE" STYLE?

The conventions of newswriting—story forms, lead patterns, diction, editing—may seem to inhibit the development of individual styles. But the famous Cleopatra's Needles—one in London, one in New York—have proportions and hieroglyphs that at a distance look alike; yet they're not the same. Similar, yes; identical, no. Two or 10 or 100 newswriters covering the same event will produce a lot of look-alike stories. But they are not identical. The more the event departs from routine and the more it challenges reportorial inventiveness, the more will the stories bear the stamp of author individuality.

Style in writing has often been defined as personality. An intriguing area of psychological research deals with the disclosure of psyche through writing: How much can you learn from an essayist, a poet, a newswriter by psychoanalytic examination of their writing? Researchers and philosophers dispute the answer. But none deny that what is written depends on who writes it.

Expression of personality in newswriting, should it become an end in itself, might constitute a declaration of war on the purpose of news. A newswriter may not, as a responsible professional, make self-expression a primary goal; rather than ask how much personality can be allowed to show through, reporters have to make sure that whatever shows through does not distort substance. This is the point at which the New Journalism and the "old" clash. Self-proclaimed "new journalists" too commonly look on what they write primarily as opportunity to show who they are.

How to achieve "personal style"? There is no rule of thumb.

Start with the fundamentals. Do a professional job of fact-gathering. Know your audience. Select from the facts you *could* use the ones you *must* use. Choose a story form consistent with the theme.

What you do next will measure how much individuality, how much of you, will show through. You write your story in the way you think will make it most effective. You choose rhetorical forms and specific words you think the sharpest you can find to give the impression you want reader or listener to receive. Inject color where it adds to substance, leave it out where it doesn't. Stop when your story is told.

Inevitably your story will have "style." It may accomplish its purpose or it may not. It may move or it may lie flat. It may sing or it may stutter (either might be appropriate). The extent to which you as a unique individual contribute imagination and understanding, an eye for distinctive detail, a nicety of rhetoric and word will govern whether it is routine or a product undeniably your own.

Style and manner These terms are often taken to mean the same thing. But a distinction between them clarifies the approach to writing. Style applies both to the broad characteristics or effect of a piece of writing and to the writer's personal contributions. Manner means the approach adopted by a news medium, a group of media or a newsworker toward an audience.

For example: The characteristic manner of the writing in a weekly or community newspaper is intimate, personal, often folksy. The weekly is typically the servant of a closely knit community, and its manner shows it. Community newspapers today do not carry this trait to the familiar extremes of older generations, for their audiences more nearly resemble city folk; their interests, education and social patterns no longer make them a breed apart. As the isolation of the small town has declined, intimate community ties have faded. The manner of the weekly becomes less leisurely and casual, more like that of the daily.

Broadcasting's distinctive news manner is marked by conversational patterns and studied simplicity. It avoids the formalities of written language in favor of breeziness, colloquialisms and the ease of face-to-face communication.

PURPLE PROSE

"Purple prose" is *The New Yorker's* favorite label for overwriting—the substitution of verbal acrobatics and sentimentality for direct simplicity. The sob sisters of the late 19th century reveled in it; so, it seems, did many of their readers. One such writer opened a story about a small girl run down by an automobile with these paragraphs:

> None lives who can quite understand it. It isn't just death. Death can be kind as well as terrible. It's the taking of little children, cruelly, suddenly, almost as if some unknown power were striking in utter callousness. The crushing of the bud seems so needless, the heartbreak that follows so bitter.

The writer then slogs through the story with such rhetoric as "fragile loveliness of babyhood," "the world had been a bright and shining adventure since the very dawn of her existence," and "the car, a ton and more of metal and glass, rushing through the day . . . rushing on and on, its driver hurrying, hurrying." Thus you are prepared for the closing:

> And then it was a gray day, a dour and dull and tragic day, with a little figure in the dust, a voice that was still, and her frightened little dog standing there with puzzled eyes . . .

This writer had a killing disease: a love affair with his own words. He drowned pathos in gush, he lost truth in maudlin banality. You can hardly avoid asking: How many of his details did he invent?

Another sample with some of the same faults:

> When Margaret Wade talks you can hear a gentle Southern breeze stirring through the mossy cypress trees—soft, cool, unflappable, yet resolute. Her Delta State women's basketball team plays the same way—patient, under control, yet with a purposeful zest.

When you get an unflappable breeze in the mossy cypresses, you've got quite a basketball team.

A different kind of overwriting, the unbearably cute, appears in a story that begins with these paragraphs:

> Alors, mon enfant, shed a tear this mercredi for the French liner Flandre, très chic, très proud. What a day to weep for la patrie.
>
> She ended ze maiden voyage here—mon Dieu—at ze end of ze towline, 14 hours late . . .

Contrast these stories with the effect gained by the writer of the story on page 150, who "eschewed fine writing."

Fresh approaches in newswriting are jewels of great worth. But cuteness palls and defeats its purpose; revulsion is an appropriate response to the sobs of the auto accident story.

STUDY SUGGESTIONS

1. Explain Christopher Morley's dictum that "there is no such thing as a good style or a bad style."
2. What safeguards can a newswriter set up to avoid carelessness in writing?
3. Define *style* from each of the two approaches described on page 139.
4. Why is thorough reporting a prerequisite to effective newswriting? (Or, if you disagree, why not?)
5. Do you agree with the principle that orderly structure in a news story increases its impact? Explain your answer.
6. Make lists of the "color terms"—terms that provide life and movement, picture terms—in the appendectomy story (page 145) and the blizzard story (page 147). They may be nouns or verbs, adjectives or adverbs, single words or phrases.
7. A criticism of the young doctor story (page 150) is that it "ends abruptly." What do you think of this judgment?
8. From your acquaintance with the prose of five well-known writers (Capote, Bellow, Michener, Mailer, Buchwald, E. B. White, Didion, Reston, Ellen Goodman, others) and from reexamination of their work if necessary, write a comparative statement about their style characteristics.
9. *Reader's Digest* strives for a style that makes it easy reading for almost everybody. Study an issue, then write an evaluation of its style characteristics. Do you consider it "written down"? Does it offer one style or more than one?

PRACTICE ASSIGNMENTS

1. The 240-word news story below confuses readers with facts or phrases that are accurate and relevant but could be omitted. Rewrite it to take out what you think is not needed; end up with a story of no more than 175 words. Criticize the result.

Wilford College, Mountain View, Ark., was ordered yesterday not to withhold from a local school the federal money meant for tuition and loans to the school's students.

District Judge William Brownstone granted the temporary injunction to Extraordinary Learning and Educational Complex University, Inc.

The Communiversity, at 1708 Oak Park Ave. N., is an education program designed primarily for students who have been "bypassed" by traditional educational institutions, according to papers filed by the local group.

Wilford College has acted as liaison between the Communiversity and the U.S. Office of Education, and has disbursed to the school and the students grants from the U.S. agency amounting in the last year to more than $200,000.

The Communiversity charged that Wilford College said Oct. 4 that it would cease all distribution of money until a new contract is signed between the two institutions.

The school charged that the Arkansas college is trying to get complete control of the project because it has been transformed, since its founding six years ago, from a "marginal" institution to a financially viable one.

Brownstone's order provided that the school must file a $25,000 bond to reimburse Wilford College for the costs of the suit if the college prevails at trial of the case.

Papers filed by the school said it has 230 full-time students, 175 of whom are eligible for federal aid. It said it depends on the aid for 70 percent of its operating revenue.

2. Review the last five news stories you have written to discover whether any offend against the "signposts" named on page 140. Edit or rewrite those that do, to eliminate or mitigate the faults.
3. Procure one of the books that offer formulas to clarify writing (such as Rudolf Flesch's *Art of Plain Talk* and *A New Way to Better English*, Robert Gunning's *The Technique of Clear Writing*, or *Know Your Reader* by George R. Klare and Byron Buck). Using one of the formulas, analyze a half-column news story and an editorial from a newspaper or magazine; then analyze a story you have written. Compare or contrast your findings. Then rewrite your story to "improve" its ease-of-reading score.
4. Apply the same formula to several paragraphs of either the appendectomy story or the blizzard story. Compare and contrast all the scores you have found.
5. Find an example of "purple prose" or "fine writing" in a newspaper or magazine. Rewrite it to remove unnecessary adornment.

RELATED READING

See Related Reading for Chapter 6.

Angione, Howard, ed. *The Associated Press Stylebook and Libel Manual.* Associated Press, 1977. A careful, though slightly captious, review of both this book and the UPI style manual, pointing out occasional faux pas in both, appears in the *Columbia Journalism Review,* January–February 1978.

Lanham, Richard A. *Style: An Anti-Textbook.* Yale University Press, 1974. Witty, literate and engaging observations about effective prose; designed for college composition students, but, says Lanham, "not a textbook, but a counterstatement to the textbooks now in use."

Miller, Bobby Ray, ed. *United Press International Stylebook.* United Press International, 1977.

Strunk, William, Jr., and E. B. White. *The Elements of Style.* Wadsworth, 1972. Thousands of writers and teachers call this 78-page handbook "the best manual on writing ever produced"—a judgment hard to counter.

Zinsser, William. *On Writing Well.* Harper & Row, 1976. This brief "informal guide to writing nonfiction" comes from an experienced newspaperman and teacher of writing, and shows it. Extremely helpful.

9 News Story Style 2: Journalese and Other Sins

[My students'] papers suffered from obscurity, incoherence, ambiguity, jargon, pedantry, mannerism, or downright illiteracy—to say nothing of haphazard organization and fitfully recognizable spelling and punctuation.
Professor Jacques Barzun, Columbia University

Will America be the death of English? . . . My well-thought-out mature judgment is that it will. The outlook is dire; it is later than you think.
Edwin Newman, NBC newsman and house grammarian

PREVIEW

Journalese is the derisive term applied, by journalists and their critics alike, to the sins in English that occur in printed and broadcast news presentation. Journalese may be the product of laziness, ignorance, haste, an attempt to achieve informality, or, as one critic says, "the desire to achieve a tone of suppressed excitement." Among major causes:

- Writing under pressure—racing to meet a deadline
- Failure to follow accepted guides to verbal communication—usage, grammatical precepts, diction, spelling, rhetoric
- Leaning on others—accepting tired language, clichés, worn-out constructions and ideas
- Relying on others ("let the copydesk catch it") to clarify copy or check facts or syntax
- Using too much paint on the brush—overwriting, pomposity, substituting sentimentality for substance

---

The messages are familiar. For generations lovers of language that says what it means have writhed at the abuse it gets. It is common to place much of the onus for dulling the edges of words on mass communicators—newspapers, broadcasting, advertising, the lecture platform. Though all these have played their part, the blame isn't theirs alone. Ph.D.s in front of college classes say "he don't" and "I'll give an A to whomever gets it right." They mix singular nouns with plural pronouns and use the gutter *that* ("the show wasn't all that bad") without even a smirk. White House grammar has been mangled when speech writers have been on vacation—and sometimes when they should have been. Quarterbacks with good arms and starlets with good legs talk what would be gibberish if it were on paper.

So the professional communicators are not alone. But the responsibility weighs heavy on them—especially on those of the print media, whose sins are on record. What is on record is there for all to copy.

One of the weaknesses in the critics' case (see page 137) is the implication that everything the journalists produce is bad. Most journalistic writing is clear if not elegant. Typically it is simple, terse and accurate. But it is too often perfunctory, banal or scarred by avoidable blunders.

What are the barriers to "good" journalistic writing? What pressures, what laxities turn newswriting into journalese? What traps lure reporters who know better into writing prose that is pedestrian, muddled or worse?

Here are six principal traps:

1. Writing under pressure
2. Carelessness
3. Ignoring the guidelines
4. Following the leader
5. Writing what you don't mean
6. Overwriting

Journalese

When the word first entered the dictionaries, it was defined in terms like those of the American Heritage Dictionary: "Slick, superficial writing characteristic of newspapers." The Random House Dictionary did it more discerningly: ". . . writing or speaking characterized by neologism, faulty or unusual syntax, etc., conceived of as typifying the journalistic style." In newsrooms the word is used more harshly. It covers slang where slang doesn't belong, limping grammar, improper word choices, lazy repetition, fine writing, tired writing, loose writing. Wilson Follett's *Modern American Usage* says that it presents "the tone of compressed excitement. When the facts by themselves do not make the reader's pulse beat faster, the journalist thinks it his duty to apply the whip and spur of breathless words and phrases. . . . they get repeated, and repetition begets their weakening, their descent into journalese."

Reporting on Deadline

Deadline reporting—the movie cliché: "Sweetheart, gimme rewrite"—is a reality. This example is from a Minneapolis *Star* reporter's experience.

On an April day the state senate was laboring over a bill to provide funds to fight a disease destroying thousands of elms in the state. The disease had hit Minneapolis hard. At 1:15 the bill passed—and the *Star* deadline for city final and mail editions was 1:30. The reporter, in the capitol pressroom, called his city editor. "Keep it short," the editor said. The seven-paragraph story moved from pressroom to newspaper city room by VDT; it topped the front page.

The reporter now planned for the next day, remembering that broadcasting and the morning paper would have more complete stories. He wrote and dispatched a short rehash for the first edition.

At 8:00 the next morning he was in a house committee room, waiting for what would come next. It was an angry proposal from a rural legislator to take on "something for rural citizens"—a rider to pay farmers who lost livestock to protected timber wolves. This became the theme of the new story (see its lead, page 127). At 10:00 the committee acted—90 minutes before home edition deadline. This gave the reporter time not only to report the day's news but also to recap yesterday's and to provide background on the differences between house and senate bills. (The final compromise left out the wolves.)

WRITING UNDER PRESSURE

You may be weary of reading that time pressure—the news tradition of getting there "fustest with the mostest," whether it's "bestest" or not—is an enemy of good reporting. Of good writing, too. Writers with a deadline driving their typing fingers have little time for the polishing and pruning that may turn good writing into excellent. News is called "history in a hurry." Experience reduces the casualties of speed—the more a writer has sweated under deadlines, the more nerves and fingers relax. Some old-timers boast that pressure starts their juices flowing. "Best piece I ever did," said a Detroit *News* rewrite man, "was with the city editor breathing 'deadline' down my neck!"

But nobody can say how much stronger the story might have been had there been time for cutting a line here and revising one there. Any piece of copy—journalistic, literary, imaginative, any kind—can be improved by expert second judgment.

Haste in newspaper production has declined a little thanks to the pace of broadcasting. But not more than a little. The pressures on wire service reporters are unceasing. Deadlines are here to stay—in the weekly newspaper shop with one edition every seven days almost as relentlessly as in the big-city newsroom with five every day. In broadcasting the stress is greater. There is no avoiding the newsroom clock. Newsriters must live and prosper with it, develop skill in planning, learn to make pressure a lubricant and not a frustration.

When Pressures Lit the Fires

Jack Lait wrote his brilliant story about the shooting of hoodlum John Dillinger with INS editors begging for copy. George Hicks delivered one of the greatest of war broadcasts—the story of D-Day on Normandy beaches—with shells and planes screeching overhead. Will Irwin's "The City That Was" was written while the fires were red in earthquake-ridden San Francisco. Russell Jones wrote Pulitzer Prize stories from Budapest with revolution outside his door and hourly deadlines pressing in.

CARELESSNESS

A companion of haste is the I-don't-care syndrome. It's the disease of the writer whose patience isn't up to the job, who is geared to the energy-saving shortcut. It is the tool of the reporter who finds it easier to borrow another's imagination than to brush the dust off his own. Its product is called by many names—cliché, bromide, stereotype . . . writing that is trite, banal, hackneyed.

It is easy to see how a cliché grows. Once in the dim past a sportswriter said that a running back who made a touchdown "hit pay dirt." Strong picture language, that first time; other sportswriters liked it and repeated it (without credit). One liked it so much that in his newsroom the weekly football pool was based not on game scores but on the number of times *pay dirt* showed up in his copy. Repetition made it flat and pale—a cliché.

City and copy editors denounce such banalities, reporters satirize them, and humorist Frank Sullivan turned them to advantage in a wryly amusing form of literary criticism. Here is a brief sample of one of his series of dialogues with his fictitious cliché expert:

Q. Mr. Smith, how is the first quarter of a football game usually referred to?
A. As the initial period.
Q. What does a young football player show?
A. You mean an *embryo* football player? He shows great promise in high school.
Q. Why?
A. Because he is husky, powerful, stout-hearted, sturdy, fast on his feet, and a tough man in a scrimmage. He tips the scales at 200 pounds.

A powerful stimulant to use of clichés in newswriting is the American newspaper headline. Imprisoned in a column of less than two inches, a one-column headline must be written in short words. The result is headlinese, a language in which verbs become nouns, nouns become verbs, sentences become fragments, and the parlor type of four-letter word is king. From headlinese come such usages as *probe* (a verb meaning "explore") for investigation, *panel* for committee or any other small group, *gut* ("remove the insides of") for destroy by fire. These words and their brethren, imprecise as well as trite, move quickly from headlines to the prose below them, thence into the vernacular. Few of them enrich communication.

This does not mean you should avoid *gut* if "gut" is what you want to say. If fire burned out the insides of the building, the building was in fact gutted. But if the fire merely damaged the basement, say that precisely.

New York *Times* writer James (Scotty) Reston scolded both Republicans and Democrats for their bromidic patter after one election. The Democratic candidates had talked about "freedom and progress," "powerful selfish interests," and "the belief of the Democratic party in the people." The Republicans declared the need for a "rudder to our ship of state" and "a firm hand on the tiller," and found the Democratic party "coming apart at the seams" and the United States facing not only "a rendezvous with destiny" but also "the crossroads of its history."

The irony of such language is that it makes no difference what candidate uses it. It is all-purpose and interchangeable. The *Masthead* of the National Conference of Editorial Writers once published an acid "utility editorial," offered free to all editors, with options to suit the writer's persuasions:

> We must all (*get behind, oppose*) this (*promising, threatening*) development in the (*ever, never*) changing rhythm of time, in order that the (*Republicans, Democrats*) may (*wax more powerful, be sent about their business*).

And the New York *Times' Winners & Sinners* approached the problem more caustically:

> Fill in the following blanks with exactly two words: "Telephone switchboards throughout Manhattan lit up like a ________ ______."

The right word Using words that say exactly what you mean to say is fundamental to any writing. The English language is one of the world's most versatile and punctilious communication tools. Treated with devotion and respect, it can inform, illuminate and, once in a while, electrify. Its toughness withstands constant manhandling; but slipshod writers content to choose words that are roughly in the vicinity of what they mean weaken it more than do the illiterate or the lovers of the cliché.

Among the worst offenders are those who believe "the copydesk will catch it." It's a creeping habit. It can start with impatience with details or unwillingness to learn the stylebook. Paradoxically, a good copydesk can help bad habits to grow; a skillful editor fixes mistakes and clears up shadows in meaning. But editors asked too many times to save lazy reporters may stop mumbling under their breaths and start talking right out where the boss can hear. Writers who feel such details beneath them aren't always novices; sometimes old warhorses get tired and lazy.

Those who shirk the hard work of writing have little chance of becoming writers. Men and women who deserve the name have too much respect for the sensitivity and cutting edge of word tools to ask somebody else to hone them.

IGNORING THE GUIDELINES

Usage The terms *use* and *usage*, applied to language, need not say the same thing. *Use*, the broader, means application of the tools without regard to quality. *Usage* means customary use. It is proper to say that a particular use of a word is good or bad usage. You could be pardoned for calling the concept elite, for it is judged by whether its endorsers are the right people—writers, editors, the careful and fastidious, teachers who watch their language (not all do). One handbook of English defines *usage* as "customary environments, social limitations, and special effects of various expressions."

Two examples: It is common *use* to say that somebody's girl friend is "quite pretty" when you mean "fairly pretty," but it's vulgar *usage* because the preferred meaning of "quite" is "entirely." Usage may in time make the sense "fairly" acceptable, though careful writers avoid it. Careful writers also avoid using the term "girlfriend" when they mean "sweetheart." It's an apt term for a friend who is a girl; it's often a puzzler in its other meaning. But it, too, is well on the way to acceptance; "sweetheart" brings to mind rumble seats and the Andrews Sisters.

You face another problem in the use of four-letter words that are timidly described as "four-letter words." One guide is social acceptability. Such words as *crap* and *shit* were once confined to the alleys and the books you had to smuggle into your bedroom; today they are constant on lip and in print. This is not a question of accepted meaning, but rather of taste. Would anybody be offended? Is there a strong reason to risk giving offense?

Conundrum

A puzzle for reporters is when—or whether—to depart from verbatim quotation. Literally, quotation marks mean that what they enclose is exactly what somebody said or wrote. But literal quotation is not always possible, and in some circumstances it may serve neither speaker nor reader best. This problem receives attention in Chapter 14.

A guide more persuasive to writers who respect the language came from Norman Cousins, as editor of the *Saturday Review:*

> The trouble with four-letter words and foul language is not so much that they are offensive as that they are weak precisely at the points where they are supposed to be strong. Through incessant, indiscriminate use, they lose their starch and produce flabbiness . . . .

Another way to put it: What do you mean when you say a speech was "nothing but crap"? Was it vulgar? nonsensical? filthy? obscene? erroneous? uncouth? discourteous? illogical? You might intend any of these qualities, or others. Who can be sure?

Reporters should know customary usages—through wide reading, careful listening in the right places and intimacy with a dictionary and an up-to-date book on usage—and also observe how they change. Unless reporters suit usage to their day and their audience, they run the risk of writing foolishly, opaquely or offensively.

The term *usage* has been stretched to include correct diction. Thus you may get, under "usage," counsel like these examples:

Wrong: Coach Munson was *literally* burned up . . .
Right: Coach Munson was *figuratively* . . . (unless he was destroyed by fire)

Wrong: Drinking violations are *very minimal* . . .
Right: Drinking violations are *minimal* . . . (*minimal,* like *unique,* is an absolute that does not permit modification); and *very* may be the least precise word in all of English)

Wrong: The speech *refuted* the biblical story . . . .
Right: The speech *contested, denied, challenged,* etc. . . . (*refute* means "disprove")

Wrong: The mayor *inferred* he would vote "yes" . . .
Right: The mayor *implied* . . . (infer means "deduce"; imply means "suggest" or "indicate")

Wrong: Heavy rains *mitigated against* the project . . .
Right: Heavy rains *militated against* . . . (mitigate means "modify" or "alleviate"; *militate* means "oppose with force")

Grammar Grammar, the traffic cop for language, is ever changing. Yesterday's error becomes today's vulgate and tomorrow's accepted usage. But some of the fundamentals are set in concrete, and observation of them is one way to help assure understanding. Because this book is not a grammar manual, it comments on only a few of the common journalistic gaffes:

- *The dangling modifier: Now 200 years old,* she was dressed in a costume inherited from her grandmother . . . . *Riding a bicycle*, the crowd cheered the high-wire performer.

- *Verb-noun and verb-pronoun disagreement:* The *effect* of all these laws and prohibitions *are* more violence . . . The *Foundation* granted wage increases to *their* employees.
- *Who* and *whom:* He sent 20 policemen, *whom* he thought could handle the crowd. He sent 20 policemen, *who* he commanded.
- *Tense sequences:* The figure *is* an increase over last year and *was* the 11th consecutive annual growth . . . . He *said* that this year's figure *was* an increase over last year's.
- *Nonparallel parallels:* They marched *silently* (adverb) and *orderly* (adjective) . . . The *firm could expand* its plant more economically than a new *installation could be built* (clauses with different structures) . . . They want only *their fair share* and *for their people* to be recognized (verb complements of different structures) . . . He *not only* likes wine but also beer ("not only" misplaced).
- *Sentences:* One way to make sentences unintelligible is to cram them too full. The best way to repair such sentences is, usually, to make more use of the second key from the right on the bottom row on the typewriter. Most overlong sentences break easily into separate though related parts: breaking them cuts the fog. The samples below illustrate:

Originals	*Rewrites*
Several thousand persons are reported to have been massacred during a week of indiscriminate and seemingly aimless killings by antigovernment forces in the tiny east African country Burundi where an attempt at a coup d'état was launched against the régime of President Michel Micombero at the end of last month. [49 words]	Several thousand persons are reported massacred in a week of indiscriminate killings by antigovernment forces in the tiny east African country Burundi. An attempt to overthrow the régime of President Michael Micombero had been made late last month. [22, 16 words]
The special House committee set up in September to investigate again the assassinations of President Kennedy and the Rev. Dr. Martin Luther King Jr. may be abolished this month, according to many senior House members, and its plight only six months after it was established by a vote of 280 to 65 provides an insight into the workings of Congress and the relationship between its members and their staffs. [69 words]	The special House committee set up in September to investigate again the assassinations of President Kennedy and the Rev. Martin Luther King Jr. may be abolished this month, many senior representatives say. Its plight provides an insight into the workings of Congress and the relationship between its members and their staffs. It was established only six months ago by a vote of 280 to 65. [32, 19, 14 words]

"Likes Short Sentences"

A classic in American newsrooms is one about Basil L. Walters, known affectionately for many years as "Stuffy" because he wasn't. His liking for capsule sentences and paragraphs was legend. After he dropped into the office of a North Carolina newspaper one day, the paper ran this story:

Stuffy Walters dropped by Charlotte the other week.
Visiting.
Nice fellow.
One of the boys.
One of the really great boys.
Big.
Almost a legend.
Maybe strictly a legend.
Who's to say?
Stuffy grew to size as a managing editor.
It's a title.
Means "boss."
Nowadays he's called "executive editor."
New age.
Same meaning.
Stuffy does most of his bossing around the Chicago *Daily News*.
Nice, nonetheless.
A little peculiar, maybe.
Likes short sentences.
Terse.
Gets 'em.
We're glad he came by.
Glad.
Honestly.

The in-house critic of the New York *Times,* in which the 69-word sentence appeared, said this about it:

> It contains at least two major ideas . . . . many readers would have . . . to go over it a second time to grasp its meaning, and . . . they haven't . . . the time.

That's the one-idea-to-a-sentence principle discussed in Chapter 7.

- *Modifiers* Place them clearly with the words, terms or phrases they modify:

> Judge Conroy recessed the hearing but *upon returning to the courtroom* Calzczyk again refused to be quiet. (Who returned?)
>
> Those were the first runs scored off Seaton *in his third inning this spring.* (First runs this spring, or first in his third inning?)
>
> The league title, after surviving the "longest 13 seconds in history," belonged to the Tigers Tuesday night.

- *That* Some writers, to tighten a sentence, omit a needed *that.* It often is dropped in spoken English—"he said ___ he'll be there." The omission may be confusing or clumsy on paper:

> Fire officials warned ___ the buildings contained flammable chemicals. ("Warned *that* the buildings . . ." would eliminate momentary confusion.)

Jenkins said ___ the red light at the crossing was not working, but that it would be repaired at once. (The "but that" demands a parallel *that* after "said.")

OTHER WRITING PROBLEMS

Two examples show reporters saying what they didn't intend to say:

> The President's popularity *fell 13 percent*, from 55 to 42. (The drop is in *percentage points*, not *percent*. It's a decrease of *24 percent*—13 is 24 percent of 55.)
>
> The Concorde flew the 3,000 miles in 2½ hours—*1,500 miles an hour*. (Simple division makes it 1,200 miles an hour.)

Maybe the reporters' calculators were broken. But in most cases of failure to say what you mean, the trouble is in use of words. This is the subject of the rest of this chapter.

Neologisms Words newly invented or used in new ways enrich and expand a language. Many of them make communication easier. *Radar* comes from *ra*(dio) *d*(etecting) *a*(nd) *r*(anging). Nylon was supplied by the textile and chemical industries so that we wouldn't have to labor with "synthetic fabric produced from high-strength,

---

Dictionaries, Style Manuals

Dictionaries: Webster's Unabridged (third edition) is complete and generally available; it defines more words than does the second edition, but doesn't help in usage judgments. Many newsrooms and publishing houses rely on the *Random House Dictionary* (college edition) or *Webster's Collegiate Dictionary*. The writers of this book find the *American Heritage Dictionary* most helpful, particularly in its usage comments by a panel of about a hundred writers, editors, teachers and public officials. The AP stylebook relies on *Webster's New World Dictionary of the American Language*.

Wordbooks, diction: The revised *Roget's Thesaurus* is best known, and easier to use than earlier editions. Rodale's *Synonym Finder* is exceedingly helpful. The more scholarly Webster dictionary of "discriminated" synonyms offers both usage evaluations and antonyms. The newer *Harper Dictionary of Contemporary Usage* has 648 pages of notes on usage, diction, spelling, grammar and other writer's concerns, with thousands of comments from its panel of writers and editors.

A list of more than 60 reference resources—"important written sources with which journalists should be familiar," says Michael Ryan, who compiled the list—is published in the March 1977 *Quill*, the organ of the Society of Professional Journalists. Ryan provides a number of hints on use of source materials.

resilient materials, the long-chain molecule of which contains the recurring amide group CONH." *Hippie,* though it means many things to many people, came along to identify a new social phenomenon. *Automate,* a back-formation from *automatic,* is a needed and accepted term. Thousands of new words and terms have entered the American and English languages as new technological and social forces have entered people's lives—*high-rise, bop* and *bebop, rip off, boob tube, cop out.* And English has adopted a horde of foreign words such as *chauffeur, spaghetti, boulevard, bikini.* It has given words appropriate new meanings (*jog,* "to jar or move by shoving," nowadays also means a form of exercise that many Americans hope will keep them alive longer). Some of the new uses are slang, some are approved usage. Most belong in the language, as long as they aptly connote concepts for which English has no term as good.

Twisting standard words into new meanings or forms, however, can cheapen the language. Bastard usages (*finalize, muchly, hosted* and *authored, forelady, chairperson, clichéd*) have been contrived to express meanings for which other choices exist. They clutter language and dilute it (one *American Heritage* definition of *neologism* is "a meaningless word or phrase coined or used by a psychotic"). Perfectly good words and terms have been given secondary meaning, sometimes to avoid words about which people are squeamish (the nice-nelly *have sex* for "have intercourse" and *bathroom* for "toilet") and sometimes in the hope of achieving elegance (*lady* for "woman," *presently* for "now"). Some terms invented to denote concepts once sidestepped in most spoken communication (*biffy* or *john*) have come into casual, and printed, use. Such words go through probationary periods, during which dictionaries list them as slang or colloquial. Careful writers, using them, remain just that: careful.

Honest words American journalism has become more honest, hence more accurate, in use of once-taboo words (a reflection of changes in 20th-century mores.) The word *whore* is used when appropriate, as are other words with sexual connotations: *sodomy, penis, uteral.* Rape is now called *rape* rather than *criminal assault* or *statutory crime. Nude,* however, somehow remains less naked than *naked,* and *disrobe* more genteel than *undress.* (At gab sessions reporters take acid pleasure in an unwritten story: "The lady ran disrobed down the street shouting, 'I am the victim of a statutory crime.' ")

Accurate reporting of some types of news that not long ago were ignored or disguised is now a fact of life.

Misused words 1. The adverb *that,* with a specific referent, means "to such-and-such a degree." But you hear it commonly thus: "Was the movie good?" "Oh, it wasn't that good." Thus it loses its force as a specific.

2. Many Americans, thinking they are using drawing-room English, hook *more importantly* onto sentences when what they mean is "more important." "More importantly, the Senate voted to abolish fishing in the White House pool." *Importantly,* an adverb, modifies the verb (*voted*); but the intended importance attaches to the fishing ban rather than the vote. This solecism may be a stepchild of the vulgar misuse of *thankfully* and *hopefully:* "Hopefully, I'll go to the ball game." The speaker *means* that he hopes he'll get there; what he *says* is that when he goes he will be hopeful about something unnamed.

Use may confer legitimacy on such bastard usages, but when it does the language will be poorer and communication more difficult. When you can't use *woman* to denote a female but must say *lady,* what will you use when you need a feminine equivalent of "gentleman"?

FOLLOWING THE LEADER

Fads Language fads should be approached with decent caution. The Ten Best-Dressed Women, whose annual selection is a familiar promotion put on by the clothing industry, are selected partly because they are prominent and partly because they make good use of contemporary resources and design. Whatever you may say of the concept "best," you rarely find these women guilty of overdressing or of following fads. By the time the fur-edged hanky and the porous umbrella are seen on Main Street, they have long disappeared from Saks Fifth Avenue.

Language and the Law

In court or crime reporting you sometimes have to write foolishly. A formal criminal charge must often be phrased, if you're to avoid libel, in stilted legalese. In one state you once had to say, instead of "burglary," that a charge was "breaking and entering a private dwelling in the night-time with intent to commit theft."

A word that might cause trouble, though for a different reason, is *pornographic* or *pornography.* You are on target if you shudder at the term "adult bookstore," but to write that a store sold a pornographic book is to risk a libel suit. Substitutions like *sexually explicit* are clumsy; but fastidious writers and editors vow to resist the substitution of *adult* for the rest of their—well, adult lives.

A careful writer sidesteps artifice—for instance, *Time*style. Though *Time* for 40 years found tricky diction a useful trademark, its inversions ("said Jones, 'I resign' ") and tortured inventions ("cinemactress") were little accepted in spoken language, and not much in written (*Time* has abandoned most of them.) They drew attention for the wrong reasons; their attraction was their glitter, and glitter can obscure substance or cover emptiness.

Contrived language patterns, therefore, are well avoided. Leave William F. Buckley's style, and Erma Bombeck's, to Buckley and Bombeck, who use them better than anybody else. Extravagant prose reveals its own pretense. Some vogue terms earn their keep, but most lose their market value when everybody puts them to work.

Journalese and headlinese These diseases are cousins. Headlinese is journalese at its lazy worst. Among words and habits that ought to be retired or used only when the writer means the same thing the words do are these:

at this point in time (now)
input (contribution, information, data)
quite simply (simply)
bottom line (total, sum, conclusion, result)
sum total (sum or total)
ongoing (continuous)
image (reputation, appearance, standing)
dialogue (conversation, discussion, argument, debate)
implement (put into effect, start)
structure (organize, plan)
cope (cope with)
counterproductive (ineffective, opposite, contradictory, hampering)
represents (is)
physical (rough, vigorous, muscular)
task force (committee)
directive (plan, order)
burgeon (beginning to grow, blossoming)
lectern (speaker's reading stand—NOT podium, dais, platform)
firm up (confirm, complete)
sift (examine, probe, explore, analyze)
ethnic (pertaining to one social group—NOT foreign, alien)
minority (less than half of a total—NOT a member of a minority)
ecology (science of natural interrelationships—NOT environment, biological or natural welfare or condition)
aggravate (make worse, exacerbate—NOT annoy or irritate)
defense (protection against—NOT oppose, NOT a verb)

By the time this book is published, there will be new verbal horrors to avoid. You support respect for writing by reading good current prose and using the dictionary when in doubt.

NEOJOURNALESE

The following errors are not yet true journalese. They can be helped not to get there:

from whence (whence or from where)
avow (flaunt, declare openly—NOT acknowledge, assert, confess)
culminate (climax—NOT conclude)
masterly (domineering, powerful—NOT masterful, skillful, deft)

Finally, some of the commonest and easiest-to-avoid:

Details were *not immediately available* (the subterfuge meaning "we couldn't, or didn't have time to, get them")
Doctors say the stabbed man *is critical* (of the doctors? the stabber?)
He was *convinced to* vote (*convinced* is followed by "that." "Persuaded to" is correct; so is "persuaded that")
He said bullfights make him *nauseous* (what he means is "nauseated")
He died of *an apparent heart attack* (write he "apparently died of" . . .)
Today marks the anniversary of . . . (wrong. The anniversary *marks today.* Write simply "Today is" . . .)
Namath *admitted* that he passes better . . . (*admit* suggests guilt or unwillingness. You *admit* guilt, but *assert* competence)
The body lay *prone* on its back (*prone* means "face down")
The critic gave it *fulsome* praise (*fulsome* means "excessive," "insincere")
The beer has *less* calories (*fewer* calories)
Police *revealed* that there were fewer burglaries . . . (*revealed* means "uncovered." It's more likely that they "reported.")

Gobbledygook and jargon Jargon, the specialized language of a distinct activity—sports, business, science, religion—is not a disparaging term; it often is a necessary tool. A sportswriter covering golf assumes that his audience knows the meaning of *eagle, bogey, lie, one up,* and *explode from the trap.* But the White House reporter covering a golfing President uses such terms sparingly if they're likely to end up on the front page. Newsworkers covering medical stories, the new discount rate ordered by the Federal Reserve, or insecticide research at an agricultural college must be equally cautious. Casual readers may be floored by language that is kindergarten talk to specialists.

Jargon, however, works its way into the vernacular. Government offices have a gift for prose that, as a *Fortune* editorial once complained, "made a perpetually ratcheting sound composed largely of

Nonexplanatory Explanations

Newswriting should never force a double take. It must be clear the first time through. Your reader may ask, "How far is that?" if you write "as far as from Montgomery to Birmingham." The reverse may be as bad: "That's about 100 miles." Better use both, especially in broadcast news.

Overexplanation is an opposite sin. Take this phrase: *"Close to 40 percent (39.6) of the black children in America and about 10 percent (10.5) of the whites . . ."* If painful accuracy is not required, leave out the precise figures; if it is, leave out the round numbers.

such terms as *setup* and *offbase* and *cutback*." *Fortune* pointed to terms like *processing, task force, operative, directive,* and *know-how* and wondered whether "any victory is to be achieved . . . over verbal ugliness." Many such terms that work their way into colloquial use are weak deputies.

Simplifying technical material for mass audiences can be a headache. Experts rarely like to have their language adulterated for the multitude. The heart surgeon wants the grocery clerk to hear about new cardiovascular surgical procedures, but he wants them described in heart surgeons' terms, a language that for most people is Sanskrit. A reporter may have to persuade the surgeon to accept lay language, then to get his help in telling the story accurately. Reporters who find experts unwilling to cooperate have to decide whether to flout the experts' wishes, to write stories that only experts can understand, or to forget the whole thing.

Gobbledygook is jargon turned pretentious—the foggy, diffuse prose common to bureaucracy and pedants. We have had it for centuries; writers of legal documents, for instance, have made gobbledygook a tribal rite (some lawyers are now working to put legal materials into layman's English). From the first *whereas* in a resolution through the mazes of military orders and on to government "directives," pompous or unperceptive writers have substituted verbosity for succinctness. For example:

> To all employees of this commission: Any employee who might be engaged in occasional outside activities and whose services are actuated by the experience or knowledge gained during the course of his or her employment by the commission or because of information available to him or her, the contents of which is [*sic*] directly or indirectly connected with said employment and by reasons of such experience, knowledge or availability of information receives benefit which such employee would not enjoy if he were not gainfully employed by the commission.
>
> It is therefore ordered that no employee of this commission shall engage in any business activity as a private citizen which may or might in any way directly or indirectly involve any matter coming under the juris-

> diction of this commission, or the outcome of which might be affected or influenced by the result of any action or duty performed by this commission.
>
> This order shall not be construed as taking away from any employee the right to work on his own time when such work is not contrary to the foregoing directive.

Those 178 words appear to mean this:

> Employees must not use knowledge or experience obtained through their commission work for personal profit. They are free to hold outside jobs that avoid such conflict. [26 words]

A wire service provides another example:

> HOUSTON—The parent of a Houston high school pupil received a message from the principal about a proposed educational program:
>
> "Our school's cross-graded, multi-ethnic, individualized learning program is designed to enhance the concept of an open-ended learning program with emphasis on a continuum of multi-ethnic, academically enriched learning using the identified intellectually gifted child as the agent or director of his own learning.
>
> "Major emphasis is on cross-graded, multi-ethnic learning with the main objective being to learn respect for the uniqueness of a person."
>
> The parent wrote the principal:
>
> "I have a college degree, speak two foreign languages and four Indian dialects, have been to a number of county fairs and three goat ropings. But I haven't the faintest idea what the hell you are talking about."

A reporter has first to decipher gobbledygook, then paraphrase it.

Slang is the informal and specialized spoken language of a particular group or culture. In the United States it has been considered the special property of the young; but as informality has increased the language of youth has spread to almost everybody. It remains a characteristic of conversation more than of written English; but the

---

Wherin Whereas Waxes Forthwith Null and Void

New York state law now requires that leases be "written in nontechnical language and in a clear and coherent manner using words with common and everyday meanings." William Safire of the New York *Times* made it the springboard for a witty column complaining about most legalese (some, he said, is "beautiful, like the sonorous, majestic King James translation of the Bible"). Even this law, however, has some "hereby designateds" and a "void and voidable." "Some legal draftsmen," comments Safire, "just never get the void."

---

written and spoken languages grow constantly closer together.

Slang, more than formal English, changes rapidly. Today's slang differs from yesterday's (somebody who "lost his cool" a few years ago was recently more likely to "freak out"—and "freak out" itself has more than one meaning; over the years the terms "twenty-three skidoo," "scram," "take it on the lam" and "get lost" have successively meant much the same thing). The inventiveness of slang has enriched and expanded the American language, even though it lacks respect for the conventions of grammar, traditional meanings and usage, and syntax. (The slang sentence "I could care less" means, in good English, "I could not care less.")

Most written English uses slang with care. But it is more widely accepted and understood than ever before. Newswriting, even when it is meticulous in propriety and meaning, has become more hospitable to slang.

OVERWRITING

Overwriting is laying it on thick, substituting the fancy or theatrical for the tellingly familiar. Its parent may be inexperience, incompetence or lack of discrimination and humor. It is pretentious, usually long-winded, sometimes dishonest; it is usually very, very earnest.

Every newswriter comes on news events with valid emotional content. Reporters learn to stimulate imagination by sensitive choice of detail and insinuation of mood (reread the story about the dying young doctor, page 150). Imagination responds more actively to the gentle nudge than to the bludgeon; the hint may hit harder than the haymaker. The hint sneaks into the reader's subconscious; the haymaker triggers the defense of skepticism.

Overwriting of the kind cited in the old-fashioned sob story (see page 154) belittles the reader and reveals a writer's incompetence; it is sometimes misleading in intent and deceitful in effect. It is often overnice, the kind Bernstein of the New York *Times* calls "writing with the little finger well out." One Bernstein example is "the Texan took things easily" (the idiom, which is good English, is *took things easy*). In the same basket are *"felt badly," "charlady"* and such pomposities as *mortician, beautologist, realtor, custodial engineer* (janitor) and, from Honolulu, *water waste engineer* (sewer worker).

The long reach Another form of stretching for effect appears in these news story excerpts:

> It was a pretty bad cuttin' . . . It was on account of Ben's gal friend's double wooin' and there's some that says they can't blame Ben much—cause of it happenin' twice, and all.

> McGintry had this comment: "Begorra an' it's sure Oi am that no girrul av moine wud dhrink loike thot."

The first tries too hard to establish mood and manner; the second exaggerates what its writer thinks is Irish vernacular. Mood or dialect can be suggested by a few strokes; attempts at literal reproduction stop readers in their tracks.

STUDY SUGGESTIONS

1. Define each of the terms given by Professor Barzun in the quotation at the head of this chapter.
2. Rate on a 1-to-6 scale the "principal traps" listed on page 158—1 least perilous, 6 most—and defend your rating.
3. In samples of your own writing—news stories, test papers, other written work—try to find 10 examples of tired or over-used words and phrases (clichés). Sometimes a cliché does the job better than any substitute could; but if you find any you can replace to advantage, do so. Support both the changes and the nonchanges.
4. Do you think the present use in news stories of terms once taboo—profanities, obscenities, and the like—improves the effectiveness of reporting, or debases it? Give your reasoning.
5. When you write that an article was bought at a "nominal" price, most readers will recognize that you mean "small" (though *nominal* means something else). Do you support the puristic admonition to "write it right"?
6. A news story says, "Marken *indicated* he would attend." Rodale's *Synonym Finder* offers these substitutes for *indicate:* "Be a sign of, debate, show, manifest, evince, designate, register, signify, make known, reveal, exhibit, present, bespeak, evidence, tell, display, disclose, point out, mark, connote, express, point to, mean, demonstrate, notify, betoken." Would any of these suit you more than *indicate*—or can you do better?
7. Make a list of 10 (or 100) current or recent "fad words" or "fad phrases."
8. On pages 169–170 you are told that "new verbal horrors" will appear before this book is published. List as many as you can find in print, on the air, or in the colloquial language of your peers.
9. What characteristics might lead you to describe a piece of prose as overwritten?
10. Why is sports writing so burdened with clichés?

PRACTICE ASSIGNMENTS

1. Procure an insurance policy, a formal lease, a legal document, a statement of rules for conduct, or some other example of formal prose that you think pompous, verbose, confusing, or roundabout. Rewrite it in layman's language—prose that says it all simply and directly.
2. From sports broadcasts and sports pages, list 25 or more clichés. Separate the old-timers from the current fads. File them away mentally for nonuse.

3. Find a news story or other prose that you think overwritten. Rewrite it to get rid of excesses: sentimentality, ornate or showy diction, phony elegance, needless embroidery. Cut it down to size.
4. Compare a newspaper story about a business or economic development with a story on the same subject in *Business Week*, *Forbes*, or some other specialized business publication. Are the differences in style or language appropriate?
5. Carry out the same process with a medical or scientific news story and its opposite number in a specialized journal.
6. The news story on page 165 is clearly tongue-in-cheek. Try writing its facts into a straight news story. Better or worse?
7. Rewrite the high school principal's message (page 172) in "ordinary" language, to make it more understandable.

RELATED READING

See Related Reading, pages 109 and 156.

Bernestein, Theodore E. *The Careful Writer.* Atheneum, 1968; *Miss Thistlebottom's Hobgoblins.* Farrar, Straus and Giroux, 1971. Two books by the witty producer of the New York *Times* "bulletin of second guessing" pinpoint newswriting sins and virtues of *Times* editors and reporters. *The Careful Writer* would be useful on any writer's desk. The second book attests to Bernstein's willingness to change with the times.

Fowler, H. W. *Modern English Usage* (rev. by Sir Ernest Gowers). Oxford, 1965. The classic book on its subject since first publication in 1906. Notable for completeness, good sense and engaging wit. (A modified version for American use is Margaret Nicholson, *Dictionary of American-English Usage*, Oxford, 1957.)

Grey, David L. *The Writing Process.* Wadsworth, 1972. This small book, subtitled *A Behavioral Approach to Communicating Information and Ideas,* sees writing as a systematic process to be understood and honed by analytic examination. It is well organized, highly specific and illustrated by carefully annotated examples.

Jordan, Lewis, ed. *The New York Times Manual of Style and Usage.* Quadrangle, 1976. A sometimes heavy-handed but remarkably complete and dependable guide to style that's fit to print.

Newman, Edwin. *Strictly Speaking.* Bobbs-Merrill, 1974. For a book that says so many helpful things about journalistic and other writing, this one is at times curiously self-conscious and overdecorated. But its good sense is enhanced by Newman's wit and caustic comments.

Rivers, William L. *Free-Lancer and Staff Writer.* Wadsworth, 1972. A compact manual that packs tight many of the things a journalist ought to know. It contains a lot of good advice on topics covered in *Reporting.*

Williams, Donald M. "Don't Call Her Ms.—It Was All a Mistake." *Quill,* July–August 1977. A witty and useful article (with which you may or may not agree) on the he-or-she problem.

UPI

PART THREE

NEWS NEWSGATHERING PROCESSES

10 The Newsroom

PREVIEW

Covering the day's news depends on careful planning—on knowing where news information centers and on getting reporters there to collect it. No two media do it in just the same way, but the lines of organization resemble each other everywhere. A central news office—the newspaper city room, the radio or TV newsroom—bears the responsibility for covering local news, which means assigning reporters both to beats and to individual events.

Most news media except those serving limited communities—community weeklies, for example—depend on wire services for news from other points (state capital, other cities and countries).

The larger the medium, the more elaborate the breakdown of responsibilities. Departmentalization may be by occupational activity (education, business, agriculture), by special interest (foods and cooking, travel, the arts) or by method of reporting (photography, rural or state correspondence, use of other specialists).

News reporting relies on imagination, fact gathering and competent writing. But it starts with organization. Some reporters work in an unorganized vacuum; featured columnists, for example, may write their own assignments. So do free-lance writers if they have ready markets—or wealthy grandmothers.

But reporters live with editors who direct their work, in greater or less detail. Newspapers, radio, television, newsmagazines—in each field an organizer tells reporters what to cover.

In newspaper organization, local newsgathering starts with the city desk, specifically with the city editor. (In electronic media the title is usually news manager or director, but the responsibilities are the same.) Here is a view of the city room operation of a daily in a middle-size city—an actual case that is typical of many.

This afternoon paper, the *Sun*, has a circulation of about 40,000; its presses start at 1:45 p.m. It serves a county seat of 44,000 population, the center of a farming region. A principal activity of the city

For a hundred years American newsrooms were "organized chaos"—typewriter clatter, overflowing wastebaskets, hurrying copy messengers and a general air of ferment. Compare this newsroom with the one on the opposite page. *(United Press International Photo)*

is an expansive medical facility. The city's power plant serves its area and sends power to the metropolis 100 miles away; the area has a small college, two high schools, some agricultural service agencies, and some light manufacturing. The *Sun* has no local newspaper competition, but there are two TV and two radio stations.

Make the city editor a man of 40, a college journalism graduate who has worked for the *Sun* ever since college. He reported for 12 years and has been city editor for five. Moonlighting for a TV station got him through college. Give him a name: Miller.

Miller gets to work at 7:15 each morning. He has listened to a radio newscast on the way to work and combed rapidly through the metropolitan morning paper. At 7:30, with his first cup of coffee, he tunes into a local newscast (one local station has a news staff; the "rip-and-read" station Miller ignores). Already he has an overview of the day's news.

The metropolitan paper has just opened a bureau in his city, and a good young bureau reporter has burned the *Sun* a couple of times. Today, thanks to advance planning, the *Sun* is what Miller would call well set on news from its area. He picks up two "local angle" ideas from the national news, however. One is so routine for an editor in a farm area that he doesn't really need the reminder: the national crop forecasts from Washington. The other may not be so obvious, and Miller hopes his competitors will miss the "short" in the

Video display terminals (VDTs) in the modern newsroom are silent and lightning-fast, and they are their own messengers, carrying news stories from one desk to another by electric impulses. *(United Press International Photo)*

metro daily about the unknown actor picked as a surprise lead in a forthcoming movie. He pegs those for the day's work.

THE CITY DESK

Miller's first task is to glance through the "slop" or overset—proofs or computer-stored copies of stories that didn't make yesterday's paper. Some get a bold black **X** through the middle; in others Miller changes "today" and "tomorrow" to "yesterday" and "tonight." One short story is marked "AAA": it *must* run today. The slop proofs go along to the news desk so the wire editor can go through the same process with wire news, then send the proofs to the composing room.

Next comes the day's news budget. The copy and news desks have to know just what Miller is offering for today's paper, how much space it will take, where he wants to "play" it (city desk doesn't always win, but its average is pretty good), and when it will be ready. Miller works with a "city staff" of 11 reporters. In addition, the "lifestyle" section has three and sports five, including the editor. Miller's sharpest competition for space comes from the wire editor, with whom he carries on a more-or-less friendly war. Miller's budget looks like this:

Power. Third in series on new plant. P-1, 35 inches. In type. Ostman

Governor. Finally got the interview with him on the new ag commissioner. P-1, 17″. Moved last night. King

Heaters. Three local stores sold those water heaters the FTC says will blow up if a gizmo isn't replaced. P-1, 2 pages. Moving soon. Mueller
Rape. Mailman in Sunrise arraigned for having sexual relations with 12-year-old. 4''. In type. Inside. Howell
School. School board meeting. Small stuff. 8''. Inside. Handberg
Actor. Robertson working on feature on Lance Elkins, who got that movie role. Turns out he's Bobby Ingebretsen (local boy who makes good). Moving late. P-1

The budget goes on through a score of items. One of the area reporters has a good piece on a jewel robbery two counties away; the city hall reporter has information on the cost of the new sewer line. Miller probably is being too hopeful in offering four stories for page one, but it never hurts to try; and he knows the ones that don't make it will get good play inside. He also lists three local pictures.

By 8 a.m. he's done with the budget. As he works, he deals with reporters and answers phone calls. One of the first tasks is to phone the entertainment reporter—who grumbles sleepily that he was up late the night before on a story—and ask him to come in to work on the movie star story. The reporter is new to the area, so Miller spends a couple of minutes explaining who the Ingebretsen family is and where to go for information on the next Robert Redford.

The budget completed, Miller turns to the copy on hand. He works swiftly at his VDT, deleting a sentence here, polishing a phrase there; and occasionally mumbling an indictment of reporters' command of English or the politicians at the school board. The eight-inch school story gets a complete rewrite because, though the veteran education reporter knows everything that's happening in the school district, she never has learned to pick the right lead in a board meeting story. At least, Miller tells himself, I've got her cured of writing 10-page narratives of everything routine everybody said.

With finished copy on its way to the copy desk, Miller turns to planning the day's activities—many of them directed toward tomorrow's paper. He starts with the "tickle file"—a daily file of upcoming activities. Everybody on the staff files notes on things that might be of future interest, and the city desk secretary sees to it that everything for today winds up in Miller's "in" bucket. Miller also has a large desk calendar covered with scrawled notes.

The "tickles" range from a note that it's time to start working on previews of state legislature elections to stories clipped out of yesterday's paper with a noted "folo?" The oldest tickle in today's file is 10 years old—somebody's suggestion that local cemeteries might be running out of space. "Maybe in 10 years," the memo says. Today Miller refiles it in the wastebasket.

"The System," VDT, and the Reporter

The scene: an up-to-date newsroom. The news editor and the copy desk chief, a deadline near, are talking urgently about a story—not what it says, but where they can find it in "the system." The acronyms and computer jargon they use, to outsiders, sound like gibberish.

"Some idiot put the wrong format on the Carter story," an angry copy editor snarls.

"The computer just ate my story," a reporter wails.

Typewriters out, tube in Reporters of a few years back would be struck dumb. The newspaper business, a backwater of obsolete mechanical procedures for the first two-thirds of the 20th century, has plunged into new technology. A breakthrough this morning may be passé this afternoon.

Newsrooms don't sound the same. The clack of typewriters has been replaced by the muted click of electric keyboards as reporters and editors work not on paper, but at what look like small TV screens—video display terminals, VDTs.

Copy pencils are hard to find in modern newsrooms. Reporters "type" their stories on the VDT, edit and alter them with correction keys, send them electronically to the city desk. A computer "stores" them until they're ready for editing (also by VDT). Most newsworkers adjust readily to "the system," though some copy editors find it a mixed blessing.

Newspapers today—many small ones as well as the giants—make the investment in "the system" because it's faster and a money-saver. It even sets type with a punch of the button.

But the new methodology does not change what a reporter does as reporter—gather the news and put it into words. Reporting is reporting.

Readers are a bonus news source. Tips on local events that escape the news net come into most newsrooms—if not in a flood, at least in useful quantity. Most of them are trivial: "there's an albino squirrel nesting in our oak" or "we have a sunflower that's 14 feet high." The albino squirrel might warrant a photo in an area that didn't have lots of them, but Miller gets the same call about once a month, and once he had a reporter follow it up unprofitably. Others are more useful: "There's a buffalo running down Maple Street!" two years ago yielded a feature about the chase and killing of an escaped "beefalo," a hybrid from a nearby farm.

Some media make pitches for audience help. The Kokomo (Ind.) *Tribune* wasn't unique when it established a "red alert" phone number for readers to report crimes in progress; in Indianapolis a similar program contributed to the capture of nearly a hundred lawbreakers. Such efforts draw favorable attention, and this may be more important than their value in news tips.

The 11 reporters Miller directs cover beats like those on most papers: environment-outdoors, medical-police, county government, city government, agriculture, politics, entertainment, schools, busi-

A reporter works at a VDT, making corrections and delivering finished stories to his editor by punching buttons. *(United Press International Photo)*

ness, "area" beats. Area reporters cover just about everything in the six counties of the *Sun* circulation area outside the "home" county. The *Sun*'s one beat unusual for a paper of its size is that of the part-time medical reporter.

Outside Miller's direct control are three reporters in the "lifestyle" section and five sports reporters. The *Sun* also has three photographers and a lab technician, and a full complement of copy editors.

By 9 a.m. Miller has things rolling. All the reporters are at work, covering beats or working on features. The stories called for by the budget have been written, and most of the day's copy has been given its quick city desk editing (the copy-desk does close editing and, sometimes, rewrites). It's time to go to the "huddle" to decide on news play for the day. The huddle is the daily conference of the paper's principal news executives. Often its decisions are obvious; there are usually both local and wire stories that merit page-one space. But today Miller and the wire editor each have four stories for page one; somebody's got to give. Today it's Miller. The decision is made that if the movie-star story arrives in time, the water heaters will go inside; otherwise, the movie star will hold for tomorrow.

Miller and the wire editor get in their usual good-natured debate: "how many of our readers care about a revolt in Afghanistan?" and "when is Ostman going to quit blathering about that silly power plant?" The "Old Man," the *Sun*'s 68-year-old owner-publisher, plays peacemaker; this time, along with the managing editor and news editor, he sides with the wire editor. Today's decisions made, the huddle turns to less immediate matters. The sports editor tells of a proposed series on high school football injuries. Miller reports that the county reporter is spending a lot of time looking at deeds because she smells a rat in a county land sale. (The Old Man harumphs; he has a hard time understanding why a mother of two would want to work. And he can't get used to women covering anything but "society" news. But mostly he keeps his views to himself, and women hold three of the top seven beats on the *Sun*.) The huddle breaks up.

The rest of the day, Miller says, is devoted to "playing city editor." He answers phones, arbitrates between reporters and the copy desk, edits copy and works on advance schedules. And he puts final touches on today's paper—the *Sun* goes to press at 1:45—and starts work on tomorrow's. The key job is the assignment sheet. Each reporter gets a daily memo about stories to cover, when they are due, probable length, special future assignments. A typical assignment sheet:

> OSTMAN—Fourth in power plant series runs tomorrow, fifth Friday. You're late with the fifth. I need it today.
>
> The governor told King that the environmental group over on the river is happy with him now. (He refused to meet with them last summer.) You might check and see if they really like him now.
>
> Remind me to talk with you about the wild-river canoeing feature. You've been doing so much environment there hasn't been much outdoors stuff.

What's in a Name?

On small staffs, titles may not mean much. On a paper not much smaller than the one described in this chapter, for example, the "city editor" might also cover city hall. The managing editor might be the wire editor and part-time sports reporter as well. Among larger newspapers, the duties of city editors, news editors and managing editors vary widely; each news system, with the people in it, molds its own pattern. The sum of all functions, however, is about the same on comparable papers, no matter how the jobs are described or the work divided.

MUELLER—The old man gave the go-ahead on the land deal. We've got to be really careful with this one; among other things, the county board chairman is the old man's hunting buddy. He won't spill it, but he's going to be looking over your stuff like a hawk.

Tickle file shows they should make a decision on fixing up the Hwy. 14 bridge soon. Anything on that?

Is Goldsmith going to resign from the county board to run for the state senate? I keep hearing rumors.

ROBERTSON—We're probably going to hold the Ingebretsen piece for Thursday. Sorry I had to roust you out of bed. Anyway, this'll let you do a more thorough job. Keep an eye out for art, pictures of him from the family scrapbook, or something we can shoot of the family. What do his folks think of his changing his name?

Lemme know what else you're working on. I don't like surprises.

HOWELL—Sunrise city council tonight. Anything from over there? When's the trial for that mailman? How are people taking it? It's not often you get sex crimes against kids in a town that small.

(The copy desk points out that you just about convicted that guy in your story today. Forget the word "allegedly." It doesn't protect you a bit when they come with the libel suit. We've got to play cases like this straighter than we used to. Take another look at the "free press-fair trial" guidelines I sent out last month.)

Have you got time to work up any features from your school districts?

JOHNSON—Localizer on the federal crop forecasts.

The process goes on. Beginners get detailed instructions. Veterans like the agriculture reporter need little direction.

Though the city editor on a paper the size of the *Sun* doesn't write straight news, Miller cranks out a couple of columns a week on local politics, social events or other topics that interest him. Today he uses his half-hour of lunch to interview a local high school teacher who is the center of a controversy on sex education. The education reporter has covered the issue in detail; Miller wants to try to capture the man's personality.

Back at the office, Miller edits the late copy. There's nothing major: the police reporter has a couple of shorts; the education reporter has a small story about hot school lunches served cold in one school because of an equipment breakdown; the two area reporters have routine government stories from the six counties they cover. The budget Miller wrote in the morning is his major working paper. Additions are penciled in at the end; stories that fell through are crossed out. As the city desk deadline nears, he photocopies the revised budget for the news and copy desks. He edits the final stories on his VDT and lets the news desk know, "You've got it."

Miller has had a fairly routine day. Some are more strenuous—the

No News?

"No news today," a reporter sometimes growls. He doesn't mean it literally; the paper will carry as much copy as usual. He means the news is dull, that there's nothing of commanding interest or importance.

No inhabited community is literally without news. The local news may not be exciting, but it's there. Reporters who complain about lack of news ought to examine their own imagination and enterprise; editors who make the complaint might ask whether they're loading their staffs with so much routine that they can't seek out revealing stories. The store of publishable news is limited by a lack of news imagination, not by lack of newsworthy material.

days of blizzards, elections, a major fire, a teachers strike. On those days the relaxed atmosphere of the newsroom vanishes. Reporters are yanked off their beats to help out, the city desk hums. But the daily schedule usually resembles this one, with its rhythm of covering focal news points, identifying salient events that must be covered, and seeing to it that staffers are where they ought to be.

Deadline and after Most of the day's work is finished by 1 p.m. Today's local copy has been written; the beats have been covered; the wire and local news for the day has been selected, edited and prepared for the press. The newsroom turns its attention to tomorrow. Robertson is at the Ingebretsen farm interviewing the actor's mother. Mueller is sitting through an interminable county board meeting, wishing she could be in the records room three doors down, finding out which commissioner owned what land. Johnson is sipping coffee in the county agent's office, learning how the crops are doing.

Back at the office, Miller updates the tickle file and gives reporters additional assignments. He gets started on his column about the sex-education problem and talks by phone with King, the political reporter in the state capital. He jots some story ideas for the paper's annual "Harvest Edition," which is coming up again (all too soon, reporters mumble darkly). He answers the ever-present telephone, and toward the end of the day he drops over to the mayor's office to defend the city hall reporter against His Honor's ire. He's likely to be at it after most of the reporters have gone home.

OTHER DEPARTMENTS

The city desk is the heart of most newspapers; but it's surrounded by other departments (see the chart of newspaper organization on page 74). Among them are the picture desk, the feature section, the state, regional and wire desks, the news specialists.

The picture desk Most picture assignments originate with reporters. What happens to them afterward varies from paper to paper. For many, however, the picture desk assigns the photographers, sizes the photos and writes the captions. On the *Sun* there's no photo editor. Miller directs the photographers; the news desk sizes the pictures, and the photographers, reporters and a copy editor share the caption-writing chores.

The feature section "Women's pages" are going out of style (and, most journalists say, good riddance). In their place has grown a varied crop of feature sections with such names as Style, Lifestyle, City Life, Variety. Some are hardly distinguishable from their predecessors; others range wide in topic and quality. The *Sun*'s lifestyle section runs family-related pictures and articles on such topics as interracial dating, teenage abortions, laws that allow adopted adults to find their natural parents, and so on. "And the old-fashioned women's stuff, too." By that Miller means wedding and anniversary announcements, social notes and the usual "women's section" features.

"Outside" news Stories from a newspaper's correspondents, if they come by wire, usually are routed through the wire desk (big papers have national and international desks). Area stories may go to a state or regional desk. A smaller newspaper that maintains regional coverage may have a correspondence desk in charge of stringers—correspondents paid by the published column inch.

Specialized coverage Large or small, any news operation is pretty sure to have news specialists. Giants like the New York *Times* and the Los Angeles *Times* list as many as 25 specialists, each assigned to one news field only. The Walla Walla (Wash.) *Union-Bulletin*, with a staff of about 10 reporters, lists almost as many specialists. Most of its reporters are "specialists" in two or three areas. Sports departments are almost universal; other areas that get special attention are business, agriculture, entertainment, health, welfare and science. (More attention to specialized coverage in Chapter 11.)

STUDY SUGGESTIONS

1. What meaning do you take from the assertion that news reporting "starts with organization"?
2. List at least 20 of the day-by-day sources of information routinely covered by a newspaper or radio station in a medium-sized city.
3. Define the terms *news budget*. How is the news budget used?
4. Define the terms *local angle, city edi-*

tor, copy desk, wire service, VDT, overset, tickle file, news huddle, stringer.

5. What are the principal responsibilities and duties of a city editor?
6. List the separate news departments of a metropolitan paper (study of several issues of the paper will help) and describe what you think are the news responsibilities of each.
7. Through what channels beyond its own local staff does a daily paper or a broadcasting station get its news?

PRACTICE ASSIGNMENTS

1. Identify all the news sources that seem to have fed into the front-page stories on a large daily newspaper. (Remember that wire services, like reporters, are news *carriers,* not news *sources.*) Can you offer generalizations from your findings?
2. From all local stories on a day's front page or in a 15-minute newscast, develop an assignment sheet for the next day. On the next day, compare your assignments with what the paper or station has reported. What were the story ideas and the information sources you missed? What did the media miss?
3. Using all the news tips and sources you can assemble, write an assignment sheet for the next issue of your school paper.
4. Interview a city editor, a radio or TV news director or an experienced beat reporter to learn in what ways, and for what reasons, news coverage has changed in the last few years.
5. Interview a sure-fire source of news—a police chief, a school superintendent, a county official, an airport manager, anybody in authority in an area where "things happen"—to get opinion as to the success of local media in covering the news your interviewee is close to.
6. Make up a "news flow" diagram, using information from this or other books and from interviews with news professionals, to show the path that a local news story follows from origin to publication: sources, hands through which it passes, processes applied to it.

RELATED READING

See Related Reading, page 109.

Etzioni, Amitai. "News That Is Both National and Local." *Columbia Journalism Review,* January–February 1978. A sociologist writes about local angles on nonlocal news.

11 Reporting 1: Reporters and Beats

PREVIEW

News beats are organized by geography—because news centers group within convenient reach of each other—or (more commonly) by subject matter. Beat reporters develop daily routines and regular contacts to assure efficient and thorough coverage. Guides for beat-covering:

- Detailed knowledge of a beat's functions, responsibilities, personnel and relation to other activities
- Close rapport with news sources, from doorman to board chairman
- Scrupulous observation, so that deviations won't go unnoticed
- Persistent digging behind the face of events, to find the *how* and the *why*
- Insistence on the reportorial rights of access to information the public ought to have
- Faithful regard for commitments, but wary avoidance of unnecessary promises
- Regular reports to the editor on what news to expect

Reporters today often move toward specialization, either because of personal interests or on assignment. The trend seems likely to continue.

News beats are organized in two ways: by subject and by geography.

The first, which zeroes a reporter in on one field or a group of related fields, is common to big newspapers, network news operations and newsmagazines. Most familiar beats follow the subject-matter pattern: police, city hall, education, sports, business, religion, courts, politics. Reporter-specialists concentrate on science and health, environmental concerns and other fields, some of them defined by local circumstances (Seattle has waterfront reporters, but

Butte doesn't). A sportswriter is as much a specialist (or ought to be) as is an agribusiness reporter. A newspaper that can afford a corps of specialists can do its job most effectively.

A geographical beat—the second kind—groups news centers that can be conveniently covered by a single pair of legs or a single automobile. It's the common beat on smaller newspapers and in most radio stations with genuine news operations. For example, a reporter may be assigned to cover a city's largest industry. This could be a full-time assignment by itself, with union problems, demands for better housing for workers, pollution questions, plant expansions or labor layoffs, management's response to a city plan to broaden the tax base. But, says the city editor, "The plant is way out there between Wilshire and Brighton. You might as well cover those suburbs too. And the veterans' hospital is on the way back to town."

COVERING A BEAT

Follow the medical-police reporter who works for the paper you met in Chapter 10 as she goes on her daily rounds. Diane Slovut is 40, married, mother of two and a thorough pro. She earned her B.A. after six years of raising children and started on the *Sun* covering three outlying counties—police, city and county government, social events, disasters, whatever the areas had to offer. She had a longstanding interest in medicine, and when the police beat opened up, she talked Miller into juggling other reporters' responsibilities so she could take on medicine as a sideline. The importance of the town's big medical center economically and in many other ways, she pointed out, made it sensible to devote more attention to medicine than most comparable papers would.

Though her heart is in the medical beat, Slovut knows police news is bread and butter. Accordingly, when she gets to the office at 7:30 a.m., her first attention goes to police news. She raps out a short story on a burglary she picked up the day before, then begins the day's rounds. The first "rounds" are by telephone: the county coroner's office, the hospital emergency ward, the fire department, the state highway patrol office. She chats easily with the people in all four spots, because she spends enough time there that they all know and trust her. She reminds herself to get over to the emergency room sometime this week—she hasn't been there recently, and there's a new nurse she ought to know.

This morning's calls yield little, but the coroner's assistant has heard a rumor that a coroner in a neighboring county is working on an "odd" case. "It may be nothing," the assistant tells her, "but they've been taking a long time on it, with a couple of calls to the pathology department at State University." She passes a note along to the reporter who covers that county, asking for a check on it; if it's a criminal matter, the reporter will cover it. If it's a medical oddity, she'll do it.

It's 8:15, and after conferring briefly with Miller, she takes off. Her first stop is at the city police station, where she chats with the desk sergeant, an old acquaintance. It's routine for both of them. The sergeant has already shuffled through the night's thin stack of reports and picked out the four he knows will interest her. One is on a minor traffic accident that produced no injuries but did heavy damage to a car and a streetlight. She takes quick notes, for a short: readers will be curious about the bent lamppost downtown.

The second is also minor—a fight in a bar that's been the scene of a number of brawls. She takes careful notes because she's building a file on the place. The repeated "incidents" may make it, eventually, a story of some importance. She's aware that similar incidents in other bars don't get more than one-paragraph attention; but the police would like nothing better than public notice that would move the city council to revoke the bar's license. She makes a comment about that, and the sergeant grins.

She ignores the report on another traffic accident.

The fourth catches her eye. Her city isn't large enough that rapes are common, but this is the fourth in six months, and there have been no arrests. Once again she wishes the police didn't forbid her to photocopy the offense reports; they're public records and she can hand-copy everything, but the police won't let her duplicate them. She suspects she could win if she made an issue of it, but victory might not be worth the ill will it would arouse.

As she goes over the reports, she chats with the desk sergeant. He makes his routine jibe that "dainty young women" aren't suited to police reporting, and she makes her customary offer to take him on in karate any time, any place. It's a tired routine, but it saves Slovut from more of his endless fishing stories.

Her next stop is the police chief's office. In the two years she's had the beat, morning coffee with the chief has become a habit (she has her own coffee mug by the coffee machine). Today she wants to find out more about the rape—whether the police see a pattern, what they're doing to identify the rapist, whether they think one man is responsible for more than one incident, what precautions women should be taking. She also knows the chief will try to jolly her out of doing more than a brief report of the latest incident.

That's exactly what he does; but when he realizes she isn't buying, he switches tactics. "Look, Diane—if you give this a lot of ink, you're going to panic everyone in town. We're making some progress on it, and when we catch the guy, you'll be the first to

A reporter interviews a police chief in his office. She takes notes as they talk. *(Hugh Rogers photo from Monkmeyer Press Photo Service)*

know." "Then you think it's one man, chief?" "Dammit, that's not what I . . ." Finally he gives up and decides to level with her. There is a clear pattern, and there are some clues. There are no sex offenders with criminal records living in the area, as far as the police know, but there are suspects. Gradually Slovut convinces the chief that careful reporting won't create a panic, and they work out a story pattern that satisfies both. The chief obviously is relieved when she turns to questions about precautions women should take, and talks at length. As she leaves, she realizes that the chief is exasperated with her, and it's going to be a while before their relationship is entirely mended.

Her next stop is the county sheriff's office, where the process is similar to that in the police station. Today's finding is petty: a burglary of a grocery store. The sheriff's on vacation, and his replacement is reluctant to talk. Slovut next checks the booking sheet in the city-county jail. Normally she picks all the major stories from the offense reports, but sometimes there's a surprise. Once she found that a prominent local doctor had been booked on drunk-and-disorderly charges, but the arresting officer hadn't completed his offense report. She might not have known about it without the extra check.

Her final check on the police round is at the two courts in town, county and district. Here, as at the other spots, her technique is to combine chatting with people she knows on the beat with close looks at official records. At the county court the clerk of court is helpful and interesting; the records and court docket get a cursory check in case the clerk forgot something or didn't recognize a news story. At the district court she has a different problem. The clerk is a fussy man who regards anyone meddling with his records as an intruder. Slovut once had to get the judge to remind the clerk that the records, by law, are open to the public, and she studies them closely. She gets no help from the clerk, though. She's not without sources, however; the office secretary has formed an alliance with the reporter.

There's nothing in the court records today—the day's trials will be dull. Knowing she has two medical stories coming up in the afternoon, Slovut heads back to the *Sun* office to write the morning's stories. All but the rape story get routine handling, but that one is written with great care, after a conference with Miller; they agree that the story should be played down. It goes on page one, at the bottom, under a small head. Sensational play, they know, might panic the community. Under the news policy common to most news media, the name of the woman will not appear, but other facts will be spelled out straightforwardly. Similarities to previous rapes are reported, along with the police chief's belief that only one man is involved, and that the police have some leads. No detail on the evidence—using it might help a suspect to cover up. Slovut decides to give space to the chief's suggestions on ways women can protect themselves.

It's 10:30, and time for Slovut to put on her medical reporter hat. The principal story is the regional medical association's annual meeting. Slovut had asked Miller for a substitute on the police beat today, but he couldn't accommodate her: "Two reporters on vacation this week," he explained. So she has missed some seminars that would have provided grist for her weekly medical column. She will, however, cover the important talk about a new approach to treating certain kinds of cancer.

At the hotel where the meeting is being held, Slovut passes a protest group passing out pamphlets and locates the Chamber of Commerce secretary who is acting as receptionist. From her the reporter gets a copy of the cancer speech, information about where to find the speaker, and a tip: "Dr. Osborn is furious about the people who are handing out a Laetrile pamphlet, and I think he'll bring it into his talk."

Slovut finds Dr. Osborn and reduces his initial reticence with questions that indicate she knows something about him and his topic. He assures her that he won't deviate from his text, "except that I'll probably have something to say about the Laetrile bunch." It's going to be a tight squeeze to cover the story by 1:30 deadline, so she heads back to the office. She stops to get a Laetrile pamphlet, and finds that the pamphleteers like Osborn as little as he likes them. They believe their drug is a cure for cancer, suppressed by the medical profession because it would hurt business; Osborn says Laetrile is a quack drug that keeps people away from appropriate treatment.

Back at the office, Slovut scans the speech and prepares "A matter" on it. A matter, ("advance matter") is used by reporters who have part of a story, but won't get the rest until just before deadline. Slovut's 10 paragraphs of A matter summarize the Osborn talk. She gives a copy to Miller (or stores it in the computer), warning him that Osborn might change it, and takes a copy (or a printout) back to the hotel.

Osborn is true to his word; he doesn't change his text. But he adds a stinging attack on "Laetrile quacks." Before the applause has died down, Slovut goes to a telephone and starts dictating her story. The lead paragraph is conventional: Osborn describes a new approach to cancer treatment at the medical convention. The second brings in the Laetrile matter. The third and fourth return to the cancer approach, with major details; two paragraphs then report the attack on Laetrile and quote the pamphlet. "Now," she tells the rewrite man on the phone, "pick up the A matter." Rewrite asks for a few clarifications; then Miller comes on the line: What about the hospital addition story for tomorrow? "After lunch, slavedriver. I'm starved."

She goes to a working lunch—an interview with a visiting physician about a flu epidemic warning and what people should do to protect themselves. Then she sits in on a medical seminar, which will produce a four-paragraph item for her Friday column. Her day is rounded out with another check of the police and fire departments, the emergency room, the sheriff's office and the courts—and writing the hospital addition story.

DEVELOPING A BEAT

When reporters have covered a beat for six months, they think they're "beginning to know it." As they tagged along with their predecessors for two or three days before taking over, they probably thought it was going to be a killer. How could they ever get to know everybody in the county building? After six months they may say cautiously that they have it pretty well under control. In another six months or so—if they're good, and if they work hard—they will have mastered not only the idiosyncracies of their own beats, but also many of the techniques of successful reporting.

Few reporters verbalize all the things they have learned. They know about their craft by experience and by repetition, but they rarely reduce their knowledge to formula or analysis. It's unfortunate, because there are few ways to improve one's own knowledge as effective as explaining it, precisely and in detail, to someone else. The organization process reveals gaps and faulty emphasis, flaws and strengths. It's as true for halfbacks, bricklayers and pastry cooks as it is for artists (reporting is a craft, and it is an art), all of whom are likely to do their work by impulse, instinct and reflex.

The memo from a beat reporter to a beginner that follows is a compendium of precepts and suggestions from a hundred sources, but principally from men and women on the job. This memo concentrates on a government beat, but it applies to most beats.

KNOW YOUR BEAT—The cardinal rule, underlying all others, is: *know your beat.*

That's easy to say and tough to accomplish because there are hundreds of things to learn about any beat. You've barely started when you've mastered the obvious indicators—the names on doors, the principal activities of the offices, the telephone numbers. You can absorb these in a few days. But the kinds of knowledge that make you a subsurface reporter instead of a skimmer take time and thought and a lot of pure hard work.

Your beat covers a certain amount of routine activities and responsibilities, and you might say that any kid in a high-school social-studies class could name them. But that's all he could do. *You* have to go much deeper. You should get the official government manuals, statutes and ordinances and learn the county organization in your state, especially if you crossed a state line to get into this job. No two states (and not many pairs of counties) have identical practices or laws. Official records and proceedings have different names from one state to another, and different areas allow public access to different records, either as a matter of law or of local practice.

You should also read up on public administration to see whether the offices you cover depart from standard practice, and find out why. You'll need time in the library, in your paper's morgue and in other sources of information.

In addition, you'll have to be thoroughly familiar with the issues on your beat. You can't cover the county recorder this year without knowing what news his office yielded last year. *Spend some time going through back issues.* If your predecessor was doing the job properly, last year's stories should give you material without which stories this year might be incomplete.

Research in back issues of newspapers is often an important part of reporting. *(James H. Karales photo from Peter Arnold Photo Archives)*

KNOW YOUR SOURCES—In major offices in the county building you'll find a principal officer—a county clerk, an auditor, an assessor, a sheriff—and a lot of second- and third-level employees. Beat reporters have to *know "their" people.* Sometimes they have to know the county recorder's staff better than they know the recorder. Most offices have an employee who keeps an eye on everything and who loves to gab. The office motormouth can be an invaluable source of tips, though most such tips have to be corroborated by the top man, by official records or by other sources.

Not everything a source—even a reliable one—tells you is fact. It may be opinion, or it may be just plain wrong. Your gabby receptionist may tell you that "a woman died in the courtroom today—I saw them carrying her body out." A check shows that she fainted and is at home cooking dinner.

Along with knowing your beat, *be sure that your beat knows you.* Reporters on their first visit to a news source introduce themselves so that they'll be remembered. Frequently they write down name and phone numbers (office and home) for each contact—a good way of making a firm initial impression. They get on informal terms with the staff; this is frequently easier than becoming friendly with the boss.

Nevertheless, you have to rely heavily on the men and women at the top. They have the last word, can hold back or release information. They usually know more than you do about the topic, and you have to depend a lot on their judgment. Beat reporters don't necessarily have to see the boss every time they step into the office, but they should touch base on a regular schedule, perhaps every other day. If you can get minor information without bothering the bosses, they'll probably appreciate it.

Word from the chief, however, is only one way of finding out what's going on in an office—and not always the best way—in a world where concealing news, for good reason or bad, is common. You chat with people who are knowledgeable—or who think they are. Bulletin boards can be a source of tips; so can the janitor or the girl at the candy stand. They may notice things "insiders" think too routine to mention. You can't be too curious. Get the head man to tell you what the most important work of his office is; then find out what the staff thinks. They may not agree. And, further, you may have your own ideas; when yours are different, remember that the employees know more than you do about the office. But also remember that your main interest is news; theirs is something else.

A beat reporter must be constantly aware of the politics of his beat. County Commissioner Smith, a Democrat, may loathe Commissioner Jones, a Republican. Auditor Johnson may be furious at Recorder Peterson. You can use that, but use it gingerly; if Smith tells you something Jones says ain't so, remember that Smith has an axe to grind. Use the information as a starting point for checks and double checks.

READ THE SIGNPOSTS—You quickly learn to watch for signposts that help you *establish rapport with your sources.* If you see a mounted northern pike on an office wall or a rod and reel in a corner, chances are that fishing talk will please the man behind the desk. If a secretary has a stack of travel folders about the Virgin Islands on her table, you've got an opening. You may be surprised to find how many questions you can ask about the Caribbean and how much they'll yield in goodwill, in news tips and in access to information.

This leads to a warning: *Don't be phony.* If you think fishing is for the birds, don't try to pretend. You'll be caught for sure, and you'll lose credibility. Confession of ignorance in such a case may be a door-opener. People respond to interest in their interests. Sometimes a reporter finds the role reversed—interviewer becomes interviewee.

GET UNDER THE SURFACE—Much significant news is under cover, either because someone's hiding it or because of its nature. Getting it requires imaginative questions and the drive to dig out answers. Digging pays dividends in readership; many surveys indicate people are more likely to read backgrounders than they are surface or "event" stories.

It's routine to report the motions passed at city council meetings. But suppose you note that every vote for six weeks showed the same eight councilmen on one side and the same five on the other. If it's not a party-line split, is it mere coincidence? Probably not. If instead of the usual two bailiffs stationed in a courtroom there are six, you need to find out why. If a local industry starts buying up all the property in an area south of town, there has to be a reason, and it's probably newsworthy. Suppose the county clerk tells you that twice as many marriage licenses—or dog licenses—were issued last month as in any previous month. If you can find a reason, it's probably a story. If you can't find out why, it still may be worth a couple of paragraphs.

DON'T BLOW SMOKE—Above all don't blow it in an office or living room where you can't spot ashtrays. Good manners—and that doesn't necessarily mean formality—are an important tool in any reportorial kit. The play called "The Front Page"—like most plays, movies and television shows about newspapers that have followed it—gives the impression that reporters are drunks and/or boors. "The Front Page" may give a reasonably accurate portrayal of one kind of Chicago newspaper life in another era and generation; it doesn't have much to do with today's journalists.

A New York *Times* staff memo insisted on a reasonably short haircut and "clean, business-style shirts with neckties where appropriate." Even the good, gray *Times* admitted that situations differ. Heavy boots, jeans and a sweat shirt may be appropriate for a story on farm life, but they could be resented at a governor's press conference. And that could interfere with getting the news.

BUT BUILD SMALL FIRES—Being courteous doesn't preclude being aggressive. Sources often don't want to talk for reasons good or bad. It could be that some sources simply don't know the answers; but they may be covering up private gain at public cost or hiding misbehavior. Sometimes it can take weeks of asking the same question, in different places and in different ways, to break the facts you need into the open. If you *keep digging* long enough and hard enough, chances are you'll find answers.

Sometimes publishing evasive, doubletalk answers dries up news sources. Reporters face a dilemma when they uncover information that damages or offends a productive source. A beat reporter who's only peaches and cream with his sources may be no reporter at all. But there is usually a middle ground. Every reporter has to define no-man's-land for himself.

If you're stuck, there's no virtue in not looking for help. Maybe the seasoned business reporter who has known the reluctant banker for years can get him to talk when you can't.

It's important to remember that *you, rather than a source, are the expert on news.* Everyone thinks he can run a newspaper better than its editor, and everybody tells reporters how to do their jobs. A news source may say that you "can't" run such-and-such a story—"that's not news, and it would wreck our negotiations"—or that you'd better run it or else. You don't have to get rough, but you may have to be tough. If it's important to the public, and if you've come by the story legitimately, you'll have to stick to your guns. In such cases it's a good idea to go over the conflict with your city editor.

Reporters increase their efficiency if they have cooperation from news sources. You'll probably be asked to hold off publishing some stories, and sometimes you can't honor the request. In other cases, however, the request is legitimate and you serve your readers just as well—or better—by going along with it.

One final word: if you are going to "burn" any sources, prepare them for it. You'll have a better chance of salvaging your relationship if they get the bad word before they pick up the paper.

REPORTERS KEEP PROMISES—A prime responsibility of reporters is to keep their word to sources. They don't loosely break release dates; they don't print information given to them in confidence; they don't reveal the identity of sources they have agreed to protect.

This, however, can be used against them. A news source can gag you by putting you "off the record." If you find you've been had by this kind of ruse, you may decide you have to break the promise (with due warning to the source). You can avoid this trap. A Boston editor once said, "I make it a practice to refuse to let people tell me news facts 'off the record.' In almost every case I can get the facts through other channels. Some news sources have said to me, 'Well, I'm going to tell you anyway. Use your own judgment as to whether to print it.' " Once in a long, long while it works to accept material off the record; but do it cautiously.

RELIABILITY—Responsibility means other things, too. It means that you *keep appointments and keep them punctually.* It means you return the stenographer's carbon copies as promised—in good shape and on time.

You don't have to see every source on your beat every day; some produce news only once or twice a month. And some executives and government officials are much too busy to *waste* time with a reporter. They'll resent wasted time, but rarely will they resent legitimate, well-thought-out questions. You usually can check things with their secretaries or others in their offices. And once they trust you to be respectful of their time—and to get the facts straight when you do talk to them—they frequently will call *you.*

Be specific. One of the most practical pieces of advice experienced reporters give is "don't ask general questions." "Why is the county spending $28,000 for new staff cars?" is likely to elicit a detailed, specific answer. "What's going on?" is likely to elicit a response appropriate to the question: "Not much." People think more clearly and respond more fluently to concrete questions than to vague or abstract.

Keep your own calendar or futures book. If you rely on memory, chances are you'll forget, especially if you have a large, complicated beat. In addition to noting upcoming meetings, report releases and other facts, the futures book is a good place to *jot down feature ideas* or hunches for pieces you can develop. Though beat reporters have the primary assignment of covering the regular news, they are doing no more than 51 percent of the job if they cover only events and neglect features, stories that may take extra time and digging. If you keep your eyes open, you'll soon have far more work than you can handle. Feel free to let the city desk know about story ideas you don't have time for; perhaps another reporter will have some spare time.

Always keep the desk informed of what you're doing. City editors rage about surprise stories that don't need to be surprises. Among other things, such a surprise can make the difference between good display for your copy and display on page 11Z, back with the truss ads. In addition, the city editor will know whether someone else is working on the same yarn you are.

GENERAL ASSIGNMENT

Ask students what kind of reporting they hope to do and you're likely to get one of three answers: features, their own columns or general assignment. Features get attention in later chapters. A column may be straight reporting, straight self-expression or anything in between; many of this book's suggestions can be applied to column writing. And anything you say about reporting applies to general assignment, because general-assignment reporters are jacks-of-all-trades. They are available for any assignment that doesn't fall under a beat, and frequently some that do. Young reporters consider "general" a plum, for it usually is earned by proven competence, and the variety of work frequently is more interesting than the "same old grind" of a beat. General-assignment reporters also are likely to get the more important and tougher stories and to have greater freedom of style and approach.

General assignment—because the reporters are assumed to have

How to Tell a Fictional Reporter

He races up to the district attorney (tie askew, hat back on his head, press card in the hatband) and pokes pencil and pad in the official's face. He growls questions—usually banal questions. He rarely gets an answer, and the last you hear of him is his "gimme a break!" as the D.A. slams the office door.

You don't often see real reporters acting that way. They'd feel silly and, like the Hollywood reporter, they probably wouldn't get the story. A recent TV series is closer to reality. The Lou Grant show has some tired stereotypes (news photographers grind their teeth at the cameraman called "Animal"), but one experienced reporter said, "That newsroom *feels* like a newsroom!"

---

skill and experience—frequently is freer of supervision than beat reporting. But the advantages aren't all one-sided. General-assignment reporters are dependent on the desk for tips and assignments; it means they may spend a lot of time sitting around the office or doing routine drudgery. Beat reporters use all the tools general-assignment reporters do and develop most of their own story ideas. Frequently beat reporters are more independent than are the "stars."

SPECIALIZED REPORTING

> *When I hire a sportswriter, I hire a reporter.* He doesn't have to be a sports expert. First of all he must have mastered the craft of getting news—preferably in a city room, on the police beat, covering schools and Rotary Clubs and the suburbs. Second, he has to *like* sports.

This sentiment came from H. G. Salsinger, the respected sports editor of the Detroit *News* back when Babe Ruth was hitting home runs. It has been repeated time after time in newsrooms across the country. It remains a fundamental of "the business."

This is an age of specialists. Newspapers, newsmagazines and to some extent broadcasters are peopling their newsrooms with men and women who can report with authority in circumscribed fields. There's a fine line between beat reporters and specialists. Beat reporters often cover an area without specialized training, no matter how much reporting experience they have. A specialist is a reporter who has advanced schooling considerably beyond what most college graduates have. Though reporting skills remain the constant, more and more of today's specialists have combined subject-matter training with journalism study and experience in college. The reporter assigned to cover politics is likely to be one who studied lots of political science.

That shouldn't surprise anybody. Before medical students get their M.D.s they learn a lot about anatomy, chemistry and physiology. Whether they go on to become neurologists, surgeons or psy-

---

Are Specialists Needed?

The few reporters who specialize in covering the oil industry agreed with industry PR men that coverage of the 1973–1974 energy crisis was "shallow, conventional and cliché-ridden." They say a prime reason was the reporters' lack of knowledge of financial, production and delivery problems of the petroleum industry.

The media, said PR men, overdramatized and oversimplified the problems of getting gasoline into automobile tanks. The qualified oil reporters concurred in terms such as "hurried" and "superficial." The lack of expertise, the reporters said, often meant that the right questions were not asked. (They also said the industry frequently tried not to answer any questions.)

---

chiatrists, their specialties are built on a bedrock of fundamentals.

The axiom that newsworkers need to know a little bit about everything confirms this principle. Reporters explore a thousand byways, and the need for specialists does not mean the end of generalists. Most well-trained news specialists cover fields broader than the ones they "own." Medical reporters don't know as much about heart surgery as the specialist they're interviewing, but they may know somewhat more about psychology and pharmacology. A newsroom staffed only by experts would be in real trouble when the unclassifiable comes along. Medical reporters got into politics when they were covering the news of Hubert Humphrey's cancer. The church editor may be asked to cover a plane wreck, the environmental writer a school board budget.

Toward specialization There's no specific path from general reporting to particular. Reporters get to their specialties in many ways.

Many food editors come to newspapers with double majors in journalism and home economics; others find themselves enrolled in courses in nutrition and in specialized cooking schools soon after they take the job. The interest in environment in the last few years means many reporters arrive for work with extensive education in that area.

Other reporters become so involved in their beats they take time off for further education. A long-time education reporter went back to college and got her master's degree in education; a business writer boosted to business editor promptly went to Columbia University for a year of graduate business education. Science writers frequently take a half year or year off to explore the fields they're covering. Most newspaper bulletin boards carry notices of fellowships for advanced study, either in specific areas or in areas at student option.

It doesn't always work that way. Some experts have been brought into journalism in the belief that they can acquire reporting skills on the job. Sometimes they can. But it's not surprising that most scientists write *like* scientists, and *for* scientists, rather than for a mass audience. (*Better Homes & Gardens,* a magazine with much specialized content, for years met the problem by having in each area not one but two top editors, a specialist and a journalist.)

Though the need for specialists is growing, the need for generalists is not dead. One school of thought urges journalism graduates to work at news jobs for a while before they go on for graduate work in a specialized field. It's hard to argue with the contention that some firing-line experience will help guide advanced work into the most fruitful paths.

To repeat: Reporters *may* be specialists; they *must* be generalists.

THE TOOLS OF REPORTING

There was a time when a soft black copy pencil and a wad of copy paper were enough equipment for most reporters. They were convenient and cheap. But copy paper is soft and perishable, and copy pencil notes can quickly smear into smudge. Hard pencil or ballpoint on notebook paper is neater and more durable. And, in these days of two-month investigations, lawsuits and press-council evaluations, reporters often want their notes to last for months.

The typewriter This workhorse of the newsroom may be heading for extinction (in newspapers, anyway) as the age of computers advances. Typing skills aren't extinct, however, and if you can't type 35 words a minute without your eyes glued to your fingers, if your copy is splotched with strikeovers, and if you haven't learned to compose on a typewriter well enough that your first draft is relatively clean, you owe it to your career to take a typing course.

The camera Photographs have been recognized as reliable and sometimes incomparable reporting instruments since Mathew Brady's Civil War pictures introduced a new brand of journalism. Today every print journalist should know how to handle a camera, even though larger papers with separate photo departments usually encourage reporters to stick to words. Help-wanted ads in *Editor & Publisher* for beginning reporters commonly ask for camera skills.

Motion pictures, picture magazines and the TV screen often justify the old adage, "one picture is worth a thousand words." But if the truism is stretched too far, it's no more dependable than its companion, "pictures don't lie." Pictures and words should complement each other for the best reporting.

The tape recorder Although radio reporters think of the tape recorder as their own special instrument, it is common throughout reporting. For radio and sometimes for TV it records live interviews and speeches down to accents and inflections; it captures the crackle of rifle fire or the blare of a marching band.

It is partly thanks to the miniaturization of tape recorders that "Q and A" interviews are becoming more popular. Bennett and Greeley used Q and A stories more than a century ago without electronics, but they probably didn't use them as well, for example, as two such different magazines as *Playboy* and the *Paris Review*.

There are problems with use of tape recorders beyond the time it takes to transcribe an interview. As they become more popular, "mike fright" is less often a problem; still, some sources freeze at the sight of a microphone. And mechanical failures can make reporters tear out their hair. One carefully checked recorder used in a

Hot and Cold

For the past 127 years, The New York Times's type has been hot, set like this paragraph, with each letter summoned to align itself beside the next until a whole line of words could be cast in molten lead. At the direction of a linotypist, the letters danced into place with the precision of the Rockettes, but to the discerning eye they were always individualists. Look closely and you can see one tilting left or right, or a wounded one with a nicked shoulder, or a drunken one refusing to toe the mark. This morning we say farewell on this page and the page opposite to these hot characters that so often seemed to have the printer's devil in them. Within a month they'll be gone from the rest of the paper as well.

•

We switch to cool electronic characters that look like this. They dance lightly into line, choreographed and disciplined, head to toe, by computer. When we write, they come before us as green images on a black screen, which is now our paper. To dismiss an ill-fitting character, we depress a button marked "Del Char," meaning delete that misfit. To bring a replacement to life, we simply tap another key. When whole groups of them need to be banished, our lordly fingers reach for other buttons marked "Del Word" or "Del Para," and poof! the words or paragraphs disappear. With these powers of instantaneous creation and destruction we begin to understand how censors and other tyrants can misjudge the swift execution of their commands to be confirmation of the wisdom of their thought.

We depress a few more buttons and our chorus of words runs off the screen to reappear in serried ranks, dressed left and right as the army says, and automatically sliced into hyphenated syllables where necessary. They are "printed" now, black on white, in cold type untouched by human hands. We are automated — every writer his own printer — from the neck down. But in the head, alas, we remain hotly fallible, like the old characters, condemned to a life without buttons that automatically delete error, misjudgment and other outrages. Until you hear otherwise, it is wise to assume that this technology does not relieve the reader of the obligation to exercise the customary caution.

Out with the hot . . . This editorial appeared in the New York *Times* on May 26, 1978—the day the *Times* began the final stage of its transition from letterpress printing to electronic, computerized technology. The new type, with slightly fewer lines to the inch and characters to the line, appears easier to read. The transition was completed when, on July 3, 1978, all news stories were set in cold type. (The *Times* of that date described the new technology in two long articles illustrated with 10 photographs.) *(Copyright © 1978 by The New York Times Company. Reproduced by permission)*

50-minute interview stopped recording after 10 minutes; backup notes and a phone call to the source saved the reporter's skin.

For a print reporter the tape recorder has two advantages: it provides copious and accurate quotes; and it makes it bad judgment for the interviewee to assert later that "I didn't say it."

The computer It won't be long before copy paper is gone from most newsrooms. "The System," as computer technology is known in many newsrooms, is taking over. Technology is advancing at such a startling rate and in so many directions that details become quickly dated; but a typical fairly sophisticated system works like this:

The reporter writes and electronically edits a story on a video display terminal (VDT)—essentially a television screen actuated by a typewriter keyboard. Electric impulses send it to the city desk screen. The city desk edits it and sends it along to news or copy desks for further editing, headline writing and so on. In many systems the copy desk provides the typesetting instructions and punches a button. A few minutes later a machine in the composing room spits out finished type—usually "cold type"—without any intervention by a printer. Wire services, too, feed their copy into the computer; from the news desk the finished wire stories go to the copy desk for the same kind of handling the local copy gets.

Old-timers at first feared "the system" and occasionally resisted it mightily. But the Detroit *News* reports that it took its reporters an average of about two hours to learn to switch from typewriters to terminals. (The reporter-author of *Reporting* made the switch quite smoothly within an hour; but for a year he was still learning wonderful things the system can do.)

Computers are emerging as valuable news tools in other ways, too. Two Wilmington *News* and *Journal* reporters, Ralph S. Moyed and Jay T. Harris, stored thousands of items of information on criminal drug traffic in a computer so that it could be sorted, combined and analyzed in a few seconds. The New York *Times*, among other newspapers, has stored the contents of newspapers and magazines in its computer. A visiting professor asked how many stories had been printed on Supreme Court decisions and how many had appeared on page one. The computer answered in seconds.

The telephone The telephone has been called the enemy of good reporting, but whoever said it probably didn't have to cover 26 suburbs and eight school districts spread out over 30 miles. Certainly reporters extract the most from an interview when they're face to face with the interviewees. Subtleties often get lost on the telephone wire. Most reporters use the phone only when they can't avoid it; but the requirements of speed, geography and work load make it indispensable.

Reporter Diane Slovut (page 191) used the telephone for routine calls on her beat. The calls saved both her time and that of her sources. But she also made a point of knowing everyone she talked to regularly. The long-distance interview has added a new dimension to reporting. Telephone-recorded interviews (some states require two-party consent), conference calls, two-way radio and telephone patches are becoming common in news practice. Sometimes a telephone call will bypass a closed door that no amount of knocking will open.

Reporters on deadline frequently telephone stories to their offices. There are two common patterns: dictating copy and dictating notes. Slovut dictated finished copy when she called in the story from the medical convention. Creating a story in your head is a high art, and it's most commonly used when a reporter is more familiar with the topic than the workers "on rewrite."

The other method resembles the casual manner you use to tell a

NOTES: Furst, Guenther off. Peterson in Brainerd. Brown travelling to look at zoos.

SMITH: Feature on new methods used in teaching severely retarded kids to talk. with art. ZONE COVER.

WHEREATT: Fifth district DFL convention Saturday appears to be split three ways and it will take more than one ballot to decide on a candidate to run for Don Fraser's seat.

STONE: Story on a new plan for redeveloping the Elliott Park area. with art.

Cockroach corners group demands that S & T repair the building.

PETERSON: State Crime Control board issues eport on sentencing. Unsure story will develop.

ALLEN: Story on NSP's profits increasing by about 30 percent, but they've written their financial report to hide it as much as possible. The company just had a rate increase and is asking for another one. Poss. P1A. Should key to agate table on biz pages.

Control Data agrees to pay $1.4 million fine in connection with charges that it bribed foreign officials. Poss. P1A.

GUENTHER: Alderman criticize 7-11 operations as being bad neighbors, mostly because some have pinball machines and are open 24 hours a day. Pix of 7-11 pinballers ordered.

G.JONES: Woman sues Hennepin County Medical Center for $1.2 million after having an abortion performed which proved unsuccessful. She wants money to raise the child. (Turns out the woman had a double uterus.)

80-year-old woman sues Daytons for $210,000 after her hip was broken when in an accident in one of the store's 58-year-old revolving doors.

Judge says Minneapolis does not have to provide sewer hookup for bank in St. Anthony. City wants bank to pay $2,400 the previous landowner owed on its sewer bill.

Out with the typewriter . . . This is the computer printout assignment sheet (reduced in size) for the afternoon Minneapolis *Star* of April 27, 1978. This sheet, put together the day before by the city desk, is primarily a working paper for editors, not distributed to reporters. In the day of typewriters, each reporter received a carbon of his or her section of the sheet; with the VDT-computer system, instructions to reporters are given orally or sometimes in a detailed memo. These assignments become the next day's principal local stories, supplemented by news that goes through the night news editor's hands and by stories that break the next morning. The first task for the city desk the next morning is a complete schedule of local stories, showing their length and where they are to go in the paper.

friend about the event. The reporter departs from pure conversation by weeding out facts that don't help the story, suggesting a lead and points of emphasis, and repeating facts, spellings and numbers. Such a conversation might go like this:

This is Williams from the police press room. This one's about a drowning this morning. I'll give you his name first: Felix Horsfelt. Felix: F for Frank, E for egg, L for Louisiana, I for independence, X for X-ray. Hors-

> felt: H for Hartford, O for Omaha, R for Richard, S for Sam, F for Frank, E for egg, L for Louisiana, T for Tennessee. He was 22 years old, according to his driver's license. Lived in Dayton, Ohio. . . . Here's the story: The cops say he was hitch-hiking westward—they found his clothes and a backpack with "Seattle" in big letters on it. Where? Mishpinish River, just south of where I-95 crosses it. Clothes lying on the bank. Squad car saw them as it crossed the bridge. Looks as though he stopped for a dip, and it got to be permanent. No sign of foul play or injury. . . . Yes, just happened—about 10:15. . . . No, I didn't go out. They brought the body to the morgue. . . . No—that's F, like Frank. Not S, like sank. Horsfelt.

Note how Williams reported the information:

1. He identified himself and the source of his information.
2. He summarized the substance and time in three words: "drowning this morning."
3. He pronounced the name and spelled it carefully.
4. He provided identifying information.
5. He summarized the facts briefly and repeated the source.
6. He gave the hour and location of the event.
7. Answering a question, he reported a final fact.
8. He answered questions and corrected a spelling error.

It's no accident that the example comes from the police beat. Many police reporters—though this practice seems to be declining—never write a story. They always call the rewrite desk. Such reporters are called "legmen"—they're fact gatherers, not writers. As Williams talked, the rewrite man took fast notes; he didn't take them verbatim. Williams talked at conversational speed, and the rewrite man jotted down names, numbers and hard facts, leaving the outline of the story to his memory. (Most reporters develop their own "shorthand," usually a collage of abbreviations and odd squiggles that are meaningless to any but their authors.)

STUDY SUGGESTIONS

1. Define the terms *news beat, A matter, futures book, news source, general assignment reporter.*
2. What are the two common guides to organization of news beats?
3. How might off-the-record methods of giving news information to a reporter create problems for the reporter?
4. How would examination of your paper's issues of a year ago be helpful in beat coverage?
5. Define the term *confidentiality* as applied to reporters' work.

PRACTICE ASSIGNMENTS

1. Pick a news center on your campus or in your school—an academic department, a sport, administrative offices, a religious center. Cover it as you think a beat reporter would, for two weeks or longer, and keep a record of all the news you think the campus paper ought to publish. Check your record against what the paper actually does publish.
2. Get a beat reporter's consent to interview one of the news sources on his beat and discuss the reporter's coverage with the source. Then talk with the reporter about the source's comments.
3. Go to the nearest county court house, acquaint yourself with it thoroughly, and make a list of all the news sources or news areas you think its beat reporter ought to cover.
4. Sign up as a reporter with your campus or school newspaper or radio station and get an assignment to cover a regular beat. Cover it for at least three months. Then write a self-criticism of what you've accomplished.
5. Find out what the "open records" laws of your state require (laws that define records open to the public). Interview reporters, lawyers, public officials, and others about observance of the laws (be sure to find out to what degree "keepers" of the records make access to them difficult). When you learn of problems, interview reporters about them.
6. Team up with another student, each of you gathering a set of facts suitable for a news story (different stories). Then practice exchanging the information by telephone, in the manner described on pages 207–208. Each of you, after having taken down the "phoned-in" facts, writes the story. Finally, check your stories with each other for comments and corrections.

RELATED READING

See Related Reading, page 109.

Meyer, Philip. *Precision Journalism.* Indiana University Press, 1973. Application of social science methods of newsgathering—how to use computers, statistics, surveys and polls, as adjuncts to public records and other aids and sources, to improve reporting.

12 Reporting 2: Bringing in the News

PREVIEW

Reporters' recognition of newsworthy material is a product of curiosity and imagination, backed by knowledge plus experience. Newsgathering itself depends on access to information; access can be impeded by the reluctance of newsmakers, government or private, to let the public see what they're up to. Closed doors are being opened—not always wide enough—by combined efforts of the press, some parts of the public and new laws; public relations agents sometimes aid, but sometimes block, journalists seeking legitimate information. Reporters are wary of off-the-record statements and news conferences because either can be used to dam up information about genuinely newsworthy actions or opinions.

Newsgathering methods are so various as to challenge description. On-the-job experience is the best teacher. The hope of beating the competition is an ever-present drive, but sometimes collaboration is the only road to covering an event. Reporters rarely resort to deceit in getting news, but in some cases desirable ends are cited to justify questionable means.

Accuracy is the overriding necessity in reporting. It requires a patient willingness to check and double-check, to resolve every doubt, to put emphases where they belong, and above all to report completely, to get all of the facts.

No book can illuminate all the problems reporters have in gathering news, and no reporter can experience them all. This chapter concentrates on three of the process's major challenges: recognizing news; getting to it; digging it loose.

RECOGNIZING NEWS

A reporter on a Kansas daily tells of his frustration trying to reach one of the paper's "country correspondents" to get information on a reported barn fire. Repeated telephone calls brought no answer. Later the correspondent explained. "I was out of the house all morning," she said, "watching our barn burn down." The lore of journalism is full of such tales: "No story on the speech—the speaker had a stroke just as he started"; or "I can't get anything on the new choir soprano. The minister eloped with her."

Reporters learn to recognize news when they meet it. Facts aren't news until they're reported. If no reporter's personal radar glows at contact with an event, the event never becomes news. News radar, however, can be cultivated, old-time reporters' views notwithstanding. Help comes from many directions.

Experience You learn more by baiting a fishhook then by reading about it. You learn how to report by reporting. So how do you get experience?

A common avenue for new reporters today runs through college journalism education, buttressed often—and significantly—by work on the college newspaper or part-time or summer work on commercial papers or in broadcasting newsrooms. Not all beginning reporters have that kind of background; some editors and station managers prefer to give their own brand of training to new employees with liberal arts rather than journalism degrees. Many major employers like to hire men and women with small-town or small-station experience. Reporters often work longer hours and write more stories in a day on a small daily than they would in a metropolitan city room, and they learn about a wider range of subjects. Many employers believe starting experience on small newspapers is more valuable than that in radio and TV stations because of the greater variety and depth a newspaper reporter encounters. In any case, beginning reporters need intellectual equipment to understand and make sense of society (or recognize its nonsense), and as much "amateur" experience and training as they can muster.

Curiosity A properly skeptical, inquisitive reporter is forever demanding, "Why? How? Who says so? Prove it." Good reporters always try to find out what makes today's event different from anything that's ever happened, not "just another sewer hearing." They demand proof. They want to see the broken switch that caused the train wreck, not just to be told about it. And they get more "dope" than they need. It's easy to discard nonessentials when you sit down to write, but impossible to invent answers to questions you forgot to ask.

Imagination Reporters, dealing with facts, use imagination as much as novelists, who deal with fiction. But reporters use their imagination in a different way. They take facts that may seem unrelated and put them into context to create a new reality. It's not only in the writing that reporters use imagination. It starts with the questions asked; "How will this event affect my readers and their families? Their jobs? Their community? Who can tell me what went wrong? How much will listeners understand? and, if 'not much,' how can I let light into it?"

A reporter's imagination needs a heavy dose of foresight. A principal complaint against the news media is that they allow major events to burst upon the public's consciousness without warning. Why did the subjugation of American blacks come so abruptly into focus? Why weren't the urban cancers that led to the riots of Watts, Detroit, New York, Newark and Chicato reported so that the disease could be treated? Surely there were hints of the "generation gap" that seemed to take everybody by surprise in the 1950s and 1960s. If the economists who warned in the 1960s that oil supplies might be limited hadn't been dismissed as professional viewers-with-alarm, perhaps schools and industries wouldn't have closed across the United States in the bitter winter of 1977.

Reporting *before* the event means watching political, social and technological trends and relating them to analogous sequences in the past. This kind of reporting is not clairvoyance; it is hardheaded inference that draws on knowledge and imagination. It is the most difficult of the reportorial arts, and the one practiced least successfully.

Knowledge Recognizing a newsworthy event takes knowledge, not of journalism alone but of society, science, technology, art . . . on and on. That's why many editors prize reporters with liberal arts de-

---

Are Reporters Cynics?

Cynic: One who believes that everyone is motivated by self-interest. Are reporters cynics?

A common "yes" to this question probably comes from confusing cynicism with skepticism, a different attribute entirely. "Being a cynic is so contemptibly easy," Molly Ivins wrote in the Houston *Journalism Review* before she left Texas for the New York *Times*. "If you're a cynic, you don't have to invest anything in your work. No effort, no pride, no compassion, no sense of excellence, nothing." Ivins goes on to suggest that it's "the kids who come staggering out of J-schools into city rooms pretending to be characters out of 'The Front Page' who assume the cloak of the unbeliever. A good reporter is skeptical: he questions facts and often motives; he wonders how the $500-a-month bookkeeper got that Cadillac. He doesn't put conclusions ahead of facts."

---

grees, why journalism curricula include strong liberal arts programs. Knowledge in relation to news can mean as little as a half-hour's homework—looking up the guy you're about to interview in the library and *Who's Who*. It can mean as much as having enough background in computer science to shed light on the computer failure that shut down the local power plant.

"It is impossible in today's society," wrote the managing editor of the Minneapolis *Tribune*, in a memo for his city room bulletin board, "to reduce our guidelines to a simple list of Dos and Don'ts. Thorough, reliable and responsible coverage of racial matters demands deep knowledge and understanding on the parts of the editor and the reporter—something 'rules' can't teach." This warning about work in one sensitive area, race troubles, applies to any complex field of news.

GETTING THE NEWS

Access The First Amendment seems to many to take access to information for granted. All Americans have an implied claim to the information they need to make their decisions and guide their actions. Government doesn't have the right to get in their way or the way of their agent, the reporter. But almost everyone agrees that some limits are needed. Few would argue that plans for the neutron bomb should be generally available. But few would hold that the name of a mass-murder suspect should be secret once he's arrested and booked.

There are many areas of dispute between the public's right to know and the individual's—or the government's—right to privacy. For example, it's frequently argued that the *victim* of a crime has a right to privacy, at least until the suspected criminal is brought to trial. But suppose the victim is, for example, the Lindbergh baby—a victim, but a famous one. Or suppose burglars make off with the entire contents of a house—the house belonging to the county sheriff, who ran for office pledging to stamp out burglary. It's long been a practice of reporters to call hospitals to learn patients' "condition," but some regard this an invasion of privacy. Suppose you live in a state where a hard-drinking governor is arrested for causing an accident while intoxicated. Do the accident victims' rights of privacy exceed the public's right to know about its governor?

News of government has been routinely suppressed since the founding of government in the United States. The Continental Congress met behind closed doors. It's not surprising that government agencies sometimes want to make their own decisions about what to reveal. But the American system opens many decisions to the public, and the news media, with their commitment not only to public service but also to the need to sell papers and draw au-

President Carter has often ended a news conference—as he did here—by chatting one-to-one with reporters. *(United Press International Photo)*

diences, have traditionally opposed governmental roadblocks to information.

The press itself helped establish "national security" as a barrier to the free flow of information during World War II. United States news media observed a wartime self-censorship system under which they voluntarily held back information whose dissemination was classified "of aid or comfort to the enemy." The phrase "national security" became the touchstone. The 99 percent success of the controls firmly established in the popular mind the principle of

---

What Does Cover-Up Protect?

Tom Wicker, distinguished reporter and commentator of the New York *Times,* says of "national security" as a justification of secrecy that almost every time it has been invoked—the Bay of Pigs and the Laos "incursion" are instances—it is to conceal a story that should have run. National security, he says somberly, usually means that somebody has made, or is about to make, a mistake.

Efforts to Open Doors

Press and civil liberties groups have protested secrecy in government (many think too timidly). "Freedom of information" efforts have been led by professional societies and a handful of newspapers, broadcasters and magazines, but rarely by elected representatives. In 1966 Congress adopted a "Freedom of Information Act" that somewhat restricted the authority of federal agencies to bottle up information, and in 1975—over a presidential veto—extended it to increase press and purlic access to government records. Reporters working with these laws have succeeded in prying loose important information.

State governments have been opening doors, too. (In one state capitol, old hands in the press corps have found that the fact has one painful drawback: the press room bridge game, they complain mournfully, is almost a thing of the past. Reporters who used to spend hours waiting for legislators to emerge from closed conference committees now cover meetings on the spot.)

blacking out news threatening to national security. It also established in many quarters an ominous tendency to look on withholding information as a way of life; it became all too easy, in peace or war, to decide that information was "sensitive" and, by labeling it secret, to bottle it up.

The tense years of the twin bogies, communism and nuclear catastrophe, along with a series of small wars that might have become big ones, helped strengthen official desire to close the curtains. "Security" was carried beyond common sense. After the public discovered the White House had lied about U-2 spying on the Soviet Union and the abortive Cuba invasion, a Defense Department information officer said that "management of the news" was a government responsibility. This meant, he said, that the government might withhold news, present news in what it considered an appropriate light, or even invent "facts" as it saw fit.

So the public was denied information about many kinds of governmental activities, and neither the news media nor many citizens liked it. "A secrecy system, with authority vested in file clerks as well as top officials, is as likely to be used to mask mismanagement, stupidity, or corruption as it is to protect national security," a critic said. "Moreover, harm from occasional unwise release of information is less menacing than not letting people know what government is doing."

Classification and the doctrine of "executive privilege" by every administration from Truman's on sprang in many cases from cynical or expedient motives. And cynicism and the government's increasing reliance on secret methods contributed to the bizarre willingness to eavesdrop, to steal documents and to cover up that came to light in the Watergate affair. There is no reason to think Watergate changed everybody's attitudes.

The systems of classifying data have not been eliminated; in some areas they have been extended. Private or nonofficial agencies—though they might arguably have a moral obligation to release some kinds of information—aren't covered by the "freedom of information laws." A good reporter faces a continual struggle to persuade or outwit news sources to pry loose information the public ought to have.

Cover-ups at work You don't have to look far to find a cover-up. Watergate didn't originate it—merely popularized a name for it.

Local officials such as city and county clerks, police, sheriffs, judges and other court officials frequently close their records to reporters—sometimes regardless of local or state laws. A county clerk, with more warmth than wisdom, refuses to let a reporter look at marriage-license records: "I'm not going to let it out that those kids got married just before the baby came." A desk sergeant denies access to local arrest records: "You might mess up our case against this guy with all your publicity. Besides, you'll get it all when he comes to trial." The motives for suppressing information often are laudable; the acts, however, often are illegal or at best violations of public policy. Newsmen can do more than just argue about such violations, as some examples show:

- When police refused to give a Connecticut newspaper information about a car theft, a reporter got it from other sources (and incidentally brought about recovery of the car).
- A Wisconsin police chief refused to give out information about allegations that his men had been "fixing" traffic tickets. A judge ordered release of the information under a state public records law.
- An Illinois judge ruled that information officially designated "of public record" could not be denied to news media.
- A Minnesota school board held private "agenda meetings" at which it made decisions on hiring, firing, building contracts, taxation levels. The news director of a TV station, protesting the violation of state law, obtained an injunction forbidding it. Later he learned of plans for a meeting a hundred miles away, at public expense; he arranged that the board members would be arrested if they held to the plan (they didn't).
- A state capitol reporter, observing the absence of leading legislators from their scheduled committee meetings, breezed past an open-mouthed secretary into a conference room and "joined" their unannounced session. "Sorry I'm late," she said, "but I just heard about

your meeting." The legislators, working on a bill that would double their pay, had no choice but to continue.

Stratagems like these, at all levels of government, are reported frequently. Reporting them has proved to be a serviceable method of limiting them.

Courts sometimes establish arbitrary limits ("gag rules," to unadmiring reporters) on release of information in criminal or highly charged cases to protect the rights of participants. Reporters often accept reasonable restrictions, but there's wide disagreement about what is "reasonable."

Public relations Every sophisticated news source knows that shrewd PR people can conceal information as well as make it public. The goal of a public relations operative is to nurture a favorable attitude toward the client—business, social cause, political party, baseball club, rock star. It may suit the client's cause to "forget" damaging information or to color it rosy.

Reporters and editors are wary of handouts and other controlled information that may give only part of the story or a slanted view of it. One alert editor thought a young reporter put too much trust in a senator's press release. His story said, "Sen. X will meet tomorrow with President Carter to explain his opposition to the B1 bomber." After the editor's questions and telephone calls to the senator's office, the story said, "Sen. X will be among about twelve senators who will meet with . . . ." The news release stated a literal fact. But the editor had remembered that Sen. X, in office only six months, wasn't likely to have private Oval Office audiences.

Newsworkers also watch for what social critic Daniel Boorstin calls "pseudo-events." Henry Ford once spent a million dollars to support a celebration in honor of his old friend, Thomas Alva Edison, only to find that the event was "manufactured news"—an event designed to promote the interests of the National Electric Light Association. Staged events become regularly more sophisticated. The native American occupation of a South Dakota reservation town, Wounded Knee, in the 1970s originated not in Indian desire to control the town but in the hope of drawing attention to attitudes and actions of the Bureau of Indian Affairs (it succeeded in spades). Comparable impulses lay behind black protest marches in the South, farmers' picketing the U.S. Capitol, student occupation of university presidents' offices, and many anti-war protests. (See Chapter 4 for a related kind of manufactured news, the "publicity crime.")

Journalists call such outbursts "media events"—in the jargon, *hype*—because, though they are staged, they must be reported. Thus the media become their inadvertent agents. Because they make exciting pictures, they are "better" news for TV than for newspapers. Newsworkers know that they are "used" by such events; but, says one city editor, "the press—like the rest of society—sometimes has to be punched in the nose by those who want its attention." The quandary is how to hold the attention within bounds.

PR workers, one of whose functions is to win attention, are often invaluable to reporters. They open doors reporters can't breach themselves, they dig out in minutes information reporters couldn't get in weeks. Responsible PR men and women have standards on a par with the best the newsrooms can offer. They know that when a client is in position to suffer from "bad publicity"—when a company's oil truck has made a big spill or one of its employees has falsified an expense statement—it's best to help reporters get the news fast, rather than drag it out bit by bit, thus making everybody, including headline writers, speculate about it. Some stories couldn't be covered at all without "inside help" from the PR department.

News releases "Handouts"—prepared news stories often marked for use at prescribed times—can be either slanted or dependable, useful tools. Typically, they come from professional public relations departments, and they're often factual, complete, well-timed. One release from a telephone company about a rate increase was so well-done that the reporter who "rewrote" it made one telephone call for verification and additional facts, penciled in a few changes, and got a page-one byline.

News media that depend heavily on releases, however, are suspect. A reporter should look on a handout as a news tip—a suggestion for a story—that requires a close look for accuracy and bias, for further information and completeness. Few releases are developed for particular audiences; a national union's release about a steel strike may not tell how many jobs in your city are affected. Local amplification makes stories more meaningful.

News release dates and times can cause headaches. The media generally observe stated release times; but reporters frequently complain about them and try to get their authors to agree to earlier release. "The governor's speech is marked for release at 1:30 p.m.," a reporter explains to the press secretary. "Our presses start rolling the home edition at 12:30. If I write an 'according to prepared remarks' story, we can give it good play in the home. If we have to wait until tomorrow, you'll see it on page 9E." The decision might rest on what the reporter has written recently about the governor or even the state of the secretary's ulcer, but more likely it will depend on the weight of immediate first-page play against what TV may do with it at 6 p.m.

Most news media honor release times. These are exceptions:

- The Milwaukee *Journal*, upbraided by the Chrysler Corporation for stories about the new Plymouths to be offered three weeks later, replied that the cars already were on the streets. The managing editor of the *Journal* said further: "We honor release dates on our paper. But we also follow the time-honored practice of considering a release date broken for all when it is broken by one."
- The Chicago *Tribune* broke what it thought an unreasonable time stipulation on a science convention release; the convention barred the *Tribune* reporter from future meetings. The *Tribune* sent several reporters who covered the sessions fully "from the outside."
- The Toronto *Globe and Mail* for a time refused to publish *any* hold-for-release news in the belief that controlling the time was a form of managing news.

Off-the-record The "off-the-record" stratagem—"I'm telling you this but you can't print it" or "you can't say I said it"—is sometimes properly used, sometimes abused. Often background information is dealt to reporters not for publication but to help them understand, evaluate and put into perspective the events they cover. Cagey news sources, however, knowing that most journalists honor promises of confidentiality, sometimes trap reporters into unwilling silence. The problem is both moral and tactical; reporters may escape it by refusing to listen, and their media may do so by office prohibitions.

Other variants of the off-the-record device and its not-for-attribution variant are common. A news source unwilling to bear responsibility for news he wants to "leak" may hide behind anonymity. So the "authoritative spokesman" is born. This shadowy individual makes it possible for a reporter to write stories on his own responsibility but avoid saying so—or to the unhappy frequency of trial balloons. Government officials, embarrassed when what they said

"Deep Throat" and Other Ploys

The term "off the record" has to many reporters a quaint sound among the lasting echoes of Watergate. The Woodward-Bernstein Deep Throat source will be remembered, long after Linda Lovelace has faded, as one of the farthest-off-record sources in journalistic history, and possibly one of the most significant. "Woodstein" used scores of off-the-record sources in their drive to get at the roots of Watergate, and administration complaints that it was asked to reply to will-o'-the-wisp allegations had some substance. Careful as the two reporters were, they were led from time to time down the garden path.

becomes public, can always deny they said it, knowing that reporters may be unable to prove they did. On the other hand, reporters using unattributed information—however authentic—may face, and fail to resist, the temptation to take credit for having "exclusive" inside sources. A Chicago city editor once told a convention of the American Society of Newspaper Editors that "a story can be given a kind of breathless quality if the reporter doesn't identify its source."

Off-the-record tactics Reporters who let news sources back off *after* they have made a statement may be asking for trouble. The agreement that information or source is to be withheld must come first. Norman Cousins, *Saturday Review* editor, once saw a newspaper publisher walk out when he announced midway through a speech that he was going off the record (he later apologized).

- A source who goes off the record can use you. When reporters accept unattributed material, they are saying they believe it to be reliable; if it turns out not to be, they and their paper or station lose credibility.
- At times it's necessary to let sources go off the record. But there must be complete agreement with the sources. Does it mean you won't use their names but will attribute information to "an informed source"? Will any sources object if you verify elsewhere the information they give you, before you use it? If they object, should you skip the whole thing? How much do you trust them?

The Washington *Post* has instructed reporters not to accept off-the-record or unattributable information offered by public officials in background briefing sessions that the officials have initiated. Reporters may walk out if officials refuse to talk on the record, or they may make it clear that the decision on use of information is theirs and their editors', not the officials'. (When a contact is initiated by a reporter, reporter and source can agree on conditions governing use of information.)

A tape recorder is a precaution against the I-didn't-say-it ploy.[1]

A final word: Reporters sometimes complain—with evidence—that they are just as well informed as the sources they are asked not to quote. It's the obligation of reporters to know the topic they are reporting, and sometimes they know it better than the banker, the council member, or the labor leader. Interviewees who don't know their stuff can distort by refusing to take responsibility for what they

[1] A searching discussion of the use of background briefings and unattributed sources appears in Chapter I of *Aspen Notebook on Government and the Media*. See Related Reading, Chapter 19.

Backgrounders: Use and Misuse

A federal appeals court took a searching look in 1977 at "backgrounders" based on off-the-record statements, and didn't like what it saw.

The court defined off-the-record backgrounders as stories "designed to permit dissemination of information to the public while avoiding the risks of direct quotation of government officials or official attribution of sensitive statements . . ." The case grew from a reporter's suit to obtain records of a 30-reporter news conference whose transcription the State Department declared "confidential" and not open to reporters. The appeals court, terming the department's conduct "almost incredible," went on to say that "in view of the deliberate, not to say daring, use the department had made of the backgrounder practice in the past, one would think it would have been alert" to whatever bearing such a device might have on "national security."

A critic of the backgrounder device said that "true background discussions in private between reporters and officials who prefer not to be quoted are useful if not abused. They can be protected by the usual confidential arrangement between reporters and sources." But, he added, "Officials who give mass backgrounders are not motivated by love of the press. They have a purpose, and almost always it is to manipulate public opinion through the press."

say; and they often have little regard for accuracy when they know they're not going to be called to account.

News conferences Theodore Roosevelt or Woodrow Wilson, depending on your choice of historian, is credited with inventing the press conference. Allowing one public official or sports, industrial or political figure to talk with many reporters saves time, multiplies the audience a source reaches, and provides news information to some reporters who might never be granted interviews. When broadcasting news became established, the word "press" was replaced by "news" (not without some newspaper squirming), and now television not only brings *what* the president said into millions of living rooms, but also shows *how* he presented it. Moreover, a news conference lets inexperienced or inept reporters take advantage of the skills of others, a fact that annoys seasoned reporters but undeniably serves the public.

On the other hand, there are severe problems with news conferences. First, the sources have control over the flow of news. They decide which reporters may ask questions and whether an answer is complete; there's rarely an opportunity for a "yes, but . . ." A newspaper editorialized in 1973 that a news conference "is usually staged by someone trying to make a score. And if he has any skill at all, he can manipulate the conference to his own ends—not really answering any questions he doesn't want to answer and phrasing the answers he wants to give in the most acceptable fashion." In 1974 a Washington correspondent writing about one of President Nixon's infrequent news conferences made the point more sharply:

> President Nixon's press conference Monday night demonstrated again how difficult it can be to pin down a president—even a troubled one—who does not wish to be pinned down . . .
>
> On the question of defining an impeachable offense, for example, Nixon did not hesitate to respond in a narrow way that would benefit his own self-interest and self-preservation. . . . He chose to ignore the very large body of opinion that says that the founding fathers intended that a president could be impeached not only for criminal acts but for political transgressions, such as the misuse of office. . . .

The same correspondent—Reston of the New York *Times*—wrote in 1977 that three recent presidents had "handled reporters" in news conferences in three ways:

- Telling as much of the truth as possible; being responsive to serious questions and lighthearted about silly ones.
- Telling as little as possible. "This infuriates reporters and doesn't work in the end, but at least it gives them the excitement of the chase."
- Fiddling with the reporters, giving the impression of openness and sincerity when actually evading or filibustering every question.

The first way, and the best, said Reston, was the Carter way (in his early conferences). The second, in the middle, was Johnson's. The third, and worst, was Nixon's.

Reporters have varying attitudes toward news conferences. An experienced woman reporter refuses to ask questions. "Why," she says, "should I let my questions get answered on TV before I can put them in print? I try to talk with the news source in advance, and make the first edition." She sometimes gets story tips, however. Once she heard a rival demand state revenue figures; the governor replied, "All that stuff is on my desk. C'mon in and get it." The questioner didn't get around to it; the woman did—and came up with a "play story" on page one.

International news If you think you have trouble getting arrest records in Hoboken, you should try it in Minsk, Addis Ababa or Peking. Many nations hold to the view that the people have the right to know what the government wants them to know, and nothing more. Gestures in the United Nations toward a code for exchange of news (most recently in the late 1970s) have foundered; many nations refuse to support free international movement of news or other types of information, but rather seek mandatory controls.

Broadcaster's access It took 20 years for radio correspondents to gain access to the White House and Capitol press galleries. Scorn or fear, or both, on the part of print journalists kept broadcasters at a disadvantage. This era has passed, and the public is more dependent for news on the broadcast media—especially the kind with living color—that it is on print. (Nevertheless, people seem more likely to "call the paper" than the broadcaster when they have news tips.)

Broadcasters' progress in their access battles has been significant. Restrictions on camera reporting of congressional hearings and such public functions as city council meetings began to break down in the 1950s; the nation was glued to TV sets for the Army-McCarthy hearings in 1954, the Senate Watergate hearings of 1973 and the impeachment proceedings that followed. Limited TV coverage of some congressional sessions (under restrictions that journalists think unreasonable) is now permitted; a number of states admit TV cameras to legislative sessions and many committee hearings. In Albany, New York, a weekly "Inside Albany" program has been a vehicle for state and court news. A prime obstacle to broadcasters (print photographers as well) has been the American Bar Association's potent Canon 35. This rule, without the force of law, has for nearly 50 years barred cameras from most courtrooms, based on the fear that their use may interfere with fair trial. But news organizations have been increasingly persuasive in the campaign to soften the rule; the ABA shows signs of relenting, as photographic procedures become more skillful and less intrusive. Six states, led by Colorado, have opened courtrooms to TV by statute (sometimes on an experimental basis). Telecasts of presidential news conferences have been common since John F. Kennedy permitted them. Senate debates—that over the Panama Canal treaties a notable example—are open to radio. The trend toward "sunshine laws" requiring open meetings of many government bodies has been a wholesome innovation.

Reporter-news source rapport Good relationships between reporters and news sources should be weighed on a jeweler's scale. A source who has doubts about a reporter is not likely to talk freely, and perhaps will refuse to grant an interview or the use of a tape recorder. And such sources won't come forth with the tips a beat reporter depends on.

Many news staffs have a "hammer"—a reporter who figuratively grabs a source by the throat and shakes until information comes tumbling out. There is a place for the "blunt instrument" interviewing technique. But reporters who use only that style have a limited range. Good manners and understanding of the topic at hand may work better than bludgeons. If you start your interview with a jazz musician by asking when he started playing country and western, you might as well go home.

In some areas productive relationships face built-in obstacles. Many policemen distrust reporters or photographers who, they fear, may be "spying." Cops who lose self-control and start swinging riot sticks are not likely to thank the cameraman who put them on the six-o'clock news. A study of police attitudes toward journalists in Bloomington, Indiana, showed police and reporters to be mutually distrustful; the policemen's hostility was slightly greater than the reporters'. Angry police chiefs often issue orders that only "authorized spokesmen" may talk to reporters. But the Bloomington study found that patrolmen involved in newsworthy events were likely to leak information to the news media even when ordered not to. Such leaks usually are the product of "good" personal relations, and good relations are rarely accidents.

Rapport with the tycoon, the cop or the congressman who knows the answers to your questions is essential. But there can be too much of it. The reporters who went all over the world with Henry Kissinger found him friendly and approachable. Some of them believed this made them less aggressive in questioning than they ought to be, overready to accept whatever Kissinger wanted them to believe. A Kissinger aide, Roger Morris, reported in the *Columbia Journalism Review* that half-truths and even falsehoods were accepted and became news.

One newspaper found that a reporter kept on the police beat too long tended to "go over to the police side" and make decisions as buddy rather than reporter. The brand of "good relations" that leaves skepticism and hard-nosed reporting behind is a liability.

DIGGING OUT NEWS

"Digging out" is a term too pretentious for most of what reporters do. You're assigned to cover a hockey match, a convention or a city water board meeting. You get background information; you attend the event and take notes; you ask questions; or you conduct an interview (see Chapter 14) and doublecheck statements that raise doubts; then you write the story.

It's not always that simple. (If it were, reporters' jobs would be

When there's a big crowd event, a TV camera operator needs the best view. This one is filming a Columbus Day parade in New York. *(Ray Ellis photo from Photo Researchers, Inc., New York)*

dull indeed.) Obstacles can pop up at any corner. Ways of dealing with some of the obstacles are discussed below.

Newsgathering methods If public sources are sometimes reluctant to provide information, private sources are more so. The law doesn't require businessmen, doctors, church officials or the operators of bowling alleys, brothels or boardinghouses to talk with reporters, even when they clearly have information of public significance. Every reporter has had trouble prying facts that ought to be public out of a source who wants to conceal them. A source may prefer silence for defensible reasons: Release of information might endanger business plans, cost money or invade privacy. On the other hand, the source just might not have authority to release it. There are reasons reporters might reject: embarrassment, the wish to cover unethical or illegal behavior, sometimes misguided diffidence. So reporters who want the information badly enough have to dig for it.

Sometimes there's nothing to do but try to persuade the source to open up. But sometimes other approaches work:

- A reporter usually can find alternate sources. It's rare that newsworthy facts are corked up in only one flask.
- The reporter may publish a "no comment" response—often an answer more damaging to the source than the information would have been, because readers tend to assume the worst. "City Manager Robert Putnam refused to comment yesterday on allegations that he embezzled $48,000" can hardly fail to suggest that he's hiding something. But maybe he's keeping mum to avoid blowing an investigation of the real thief. The "no comment" device may be strong-arming, and it is tricky; it is so effective a weapon that it must be used with scrupulous care.
- A young reporter, questioning two businessmen in a tête-à-tête that he believed might concern a rumored business deal, was turned away. He went to his city editor, a man of standing in the community, and the city editor got the answer.
- A reporter asked a city council member about his involvement in a shopping center deal. The council member said he wasn't involved; the reporter caught the lie through deeds in the county courthouse and corporate records filed with the secretary of state.

Every case is in one way or another unique. But imagination, ingenuity and persistence open a great many doors.

News by sleight-of-hand Fiction is full of reporters who disguise themselves as gardeners, grease monkeys or schoolmarms to get the news (Hollywood prefers "crack the case"). Like most fictional creations, they have prototypes in reality. A reporter borrows a white jacket and a tray to get into a senator's hotel room. Another grows a

---

Working Together

Bylines of two reporters on one story are increasingly common. When a major event breaks close to deadline, a well-staffed paper may put half a dozen reporters, several photographers and a crew from the copy and rewrite desks on it. Any complex story—a forest fire, the solution of a threatening international impasse, a spectacular crime—can be better reported by teamwork than by a lone hand. Sometimes geography dictates the joint byline: A new state budget may reach its fingers into city government, Washington and a small town in the farthest corner of the state. One reporter can't be in three places. So several channels move facts to an editor or rewrite person in the central office. Or two reporters may race to cover a brush fire threatening suburban homes; dividing the work, they cover the family at a burned-down home, fire and police officials, and the color and action of the scene. One may write the hard news story, another a color sidebar, each using information from the other. And both stories may carry both bylines.

"The Underhanded Means to an End"

Under the title above, four reporters argue (in the November 1977 *Quill*) the question of deceit as a reportorial tool—two on one side, two on the other. Two belong to the ends-justify-the-means school, two say that " 'the story at any cost' parallels too closely 'my country right or wrong.' " Wherever a reporter sets the level of personal behavior, the four articles are worth study.

ragged beard and puts on his dirtiest jeans before going to a hangout suspected of harboring dope dealers. Can deceit be defended?

No two cases have the same values. The white jacket and dirty jeans examples, both "real," may be as far apart in merit as they are in circumstance. The "waiter" got in by a deception; does he maintain the disguise? If he does, can he hope to conduct a meaningful interview, to ask acceptable questions, to get respectful answers? Is his action defensible? Is it a form of theft? Is it justifiable invasion of privacy? Is it mitigated by the fact that the senator "belongs" to the public? If the reporter gets something that is genuinely newsworthy, something the public is entitled to, does the result excuse the subterfuge? What if the senator had intended to release the information two hours later? What if the reporter, unidentified, overhears something damaging to the senator? What effect does the trick have on the senator's confidence in the press?

As for the seedy reporter in the junkie hangout: What if he gets information the police can't get? Does this justify the trickery? Is public concern about drug traffic an acceptable defense? Or its illegality? Most journalists would say "yes," and so would most readers.

Consider another case. A defeated political candidate appears before a small student group of party members to speculate on the party's future. Reporters from the campus daily and a city paper show up and are asked to leave because the meeting is private. The campus reporter leaves, but the other refuses to go until he is, in effect, thrown out. He "puts his ear to a keyhole" and listens.

In this actual case the campus paper published a two-and-a-half-inch story reporting the closed meeting and a later telephone interview in which the politico added comments. The city paper used a 14-inch story that detailed the meeting, adding that "the press was barred, but one reporter heard a portion of the remarks before he was persuaded to leave." This reporter held that any political meeting is an event the public should hear about. The campus reporter said that he considered the meeting nonpolitical, comparable to a classroom study group.

Payoff

A reporter hid in a closet off a city council chamber to listen in on an executive session on a proposed open-meeting ordinance. The reporter was discovered and thrown out; the council then rejected the open-meeting proposal.

That two reporters arrived at opposite conclusions isn't unusual. Some news executives demand unequivocally that their reporters never seek, take or accept information without the consent of the source; others ask hardheadedly only that the reporter come back with the story. Some journalists, either because they believe in getting the news at all costs or because they think outwitting news sources is a game, don't balk at trickery. Others refuse to countenance it.

Thanks in part to modern photographic expertise, the fine art of picture-stealing has become passé. (A retired reporter recalls soberly that he might not have made it years ago on a Chicago paper if he hadn't been so good at getting into houses through coal chutes. One veteran photographer remembers penitently that when a fire photo didn't measure up to a city editor's expectation, he was told, "Gimme some flames." Careful doctoring with old negatives made the picture "usable.")

That such tactics are less common today is to be explained in part by the decline in local newspaper competition. The trend is consistent with what a news executive of the 1960s said: "The occupation has changed from game to profession." In the mid-1970s a collumnist wrote of a competitor involved in a college-athlete-recruiting scandal, "He got into the newspaper business before ethics were invented."

But when the heat is on, the fine line between "good" and "bad" behavior may get trampled. More than one reporter boasts of the ability to read, upside down, a letter on the desk of an interviewee. Some, left alone in a news source's office, have been known to take quick notes on a report or a draft statement (perhaps from a wastebasket). Few go as far as the *National Enquirer* reporter who made news of the trash he lifted from Henry Kissinger's garbage can. Each station and newspaper, as well as each reporter, draws individual lines—some, happily, tighter than others.

Not as a footnote but as a credo, the authors of *Reporting* hold that deceit, trickery, theft, fraud in newsgathering are self-defeating. What such practices win for today is lost for all the tomorrows (and today's profit may be trivial). The reporter and the news medium that ask to be believed can't take holidays; information gained by sneakery is hard to legitimize.

A TV camera operator uses a portable camera to film a track meet. Her assistant carries audio equipment. *(HRW photo by Russell Dian)*

THE COMPETITION

The pressroom In the shared police pressroom in Seattle a *Times* reporter once discovered that a competitor was lifting news from carbon copies taken from the *Times* desk. The remedy: The *Times* reporter planted a phony carbon alleging threats against a Seattle clergyman. The rival bit; his paper used a banner line in its first edition. Its story dwindled to a "denial of the rumor" late in the day. The unhappy reporter gave up filching; but the trick, however successful, was as unfair to readers and the minister as the thefts were to the *Times* reporter.

Experience in the state capitol pressroom in St. Paul, Minnesota (in the 1977 legislative session the stamping ground of one of the authors of this book) suggests that laments over the death of competition are premature. This pressroom, a rabbit warren of eight small basement offices, was shared by nearly two dozen reporters every day during the legislative session: full-time reporters for the

St. Paul *Dispatch* and *Pioneer-Press* (three) and the Minneapolis *Star* (two) and *Tribune* (three); two AP and two UPI reporters; three for Minnesota Public Radio (MPR); four representing out-state dailies; one each for three network-affiliated TV stations; three others for other radio newsrooms. Sometimes the complement was swollen by special-assignment reporters—an environmental reporter when a power-line bill was in the works, or a medical writer when health legislation was up.

The competition for "beats" (the term *scoop* is nowadays employed chiefly by movie journalists) was heaviest among the big-city reporters. Those from St. Paul wrote for both papers and thus faced no local print competition. The other papers were represented by their own reporters, and internewspaper rivalry flourished (that between the two Minneapolis papers was perhaps the bloodiest). All reporters scored occasional beats; those of the MPR reporters were notable, and they left newspaper reporters muttering: "Beaten by a *radio* station?"

It is not unusual in the pressroom to hear reporters arguing the fine points of a bill before they sit down to write or collaborating on counting votes in a committee hearing. This is the routine news that everyone covers, and the way you beat the other guy, if it doesn't happen on your time instead of his, is by doing additional reporting to strengthen your story. The real bloodletting comes over stories that reporters develop on their own initiative—who's making what deal to get a bill passed, which legislator is out to get a state administrator fired, a report to the governor that suggests mismanagement in a state office. A reporter working on that kind of story becomes wary. Some competing reporters who share offices scrupulously avoid looking over other shoulders; but it is not unheard of to see reporters quietly covering notes or turning off VDT screens when rivals known for wandering eyes come in for coffee or a "chat."

"Rules for Himself"

When Eric Sevareid closed nearly 40 years as a CBS newsman in 1977, he told his listeners his personal guidelines as a reporter:

Not to underestimate the intelligence of the audience and not to overestimate its information

To elucidate when one can, more than to advocate

To retain the courage of one's doubts as well as one's convictions, in this world of dangerously passionate certainties

To comfort oneself, in times of error, with the knowledge that the saving grace of the press, print or broadcast, is its self-correcting nature

And to remember that ignorant and biased reporting has its counterpart in ignorant and biased reading and listening

---

In this pressroom there's little of the kind of "syndicating" found in some news settings, particularly in towns with one newspaper and one TV or radio outlet. Here the reporter for the *Graphic* may cover the first and second floors of the city hall for routine news, while the woman from WWWW covers the third and fourth. They swap routine news but keep jealous control of their own "exclusives."

Some news media forbid syndicating or any kind of cooperation with the competition. It dulls initiative, they say; it makes reporters lazy and their coverage routine. Syndication is nevertheless in some cases impossible to avoid. When an important news source is willing or able to talk to one reporter but not a roomful, a pool arrangement is necessary. When President Kennedy's body was flown to Washington after his assassination, one reporter represented all wire services and another all other media; no others were permitted on the plane. A pool was on Air Force One when President Carter swung around Europe late in 1977 (such a pool normally includes two wire-service reporters, one each from the networks and the newspapers, several photographers, and a TV camera crew). This group served up the news to the two planefuls of newspeople—about 175 of them—representing individual publications and broadcasters.

ACCURACY

Being in favor of accuracy is like being for apple pie. Achieving it is not so straightforward. A reporter can depend on facts only when he *knows* they are facts. That means first of all a stubborn insistence on seeing them as they are. It means working for the unachievable ideal—objectivity: distinguishing between what the facts *really* are and what his prejudices might make him *wish* they were, what biased witnesses *say* they are, or what public relations efforts might try to *make* them. It means lightning-fast observation and mental recording of fast-breaking events. A time-honored classroom device is the staged surprise brawl before a group of students, followed by a "write-the-story" assignment. Students see pistols that weren't there; they make mistakes in the colors of hair, clothes, skin and eyes; they report remarks that weren't made.

The problem isn't limited to students. About 50 journalists—reporters, copy editors, editorial writers and news executives—looked out of the windows of the Detroit *News* building one rainy spring morning when they heard gunfire in the street. The reporter who handled the story, interviewing all the witnesses he could find, got broad agreement that the payroll bandits had run from the *News* front entrance toward a waiting car, that nearby policemen had fired at them, that one policeman was shot, and that the bandits fled in the car. But no two observers' stories checked in all details. There had been from four to eight bandits, one to three policemen. Some of the bandits had carried sawed-off shotguns or rifles; all had carried handguns; only two had been armed. The policemen had been wearing white raincoats, black raincoats, no raincoats. A wounded bandit had been dragged into the car by his mates; nobody (not even the policeman found dead on the sidewalk) had been shot. Even experienced newsworkers can make errors when action is fast and unexpected.

How can reporters hope to approach accuracy? First, they pay scrupulous attention to detail and impose a self-discipline that most people don't have. Second, they are compulsive notetakers—memory rarely is good enough. Third, they check and recheck, ask questions relentlessly. One of the Washington *Post* reporters who developed the Watergate story said, "We never accepted a statement of fact as true until we had at least two sources we could trust without vestige of doubt."

SOME SPECIFICS OF ACCURACY

Patience As the "Woodstein" quotation implies, a prime quality in the search for accuracy is the patience it takes to make sure: dogged persistence in running down the little facts, such as titles, addresses, names, times, dates; double-checking notes, referring to telephone books, directories, almanacs, government manuals and the like. And it asks for that extra phone call, knocking on that extra door.

Slow down One thing harder than telling an editor "I couldn't pin it down for today's paper" is "I got it wrong yesterday." News deadlines are such that some stories have to go to composing (or the microphone) *now*. Experienced deadline reporters learn to "write around holes"—to avoid flat statements they can't prove, sometimes to fall back on the "it could not be determined" crutch. Sometimes spot stories leave no alternative. A tornado warning has to go on the air the instant it comes in—but every circumstance about it, including doubts, if there are any, must be attached. A feature on a new school tax proposal will be more useful tomorrow, confirmed, than it is today, unconfirmed.

Emphasis Select the key facts and subordinate or throw out the others. Get rid of the irrelevant or the distracting. Distinguish between the meaningful and the merely interesting in order to put the weight where it belongs.

Emphasis may go wrong in obvious ways, such as overplay of secondary aspects of an event at the expense of the primary. But it is also possible to emphasize incorrectly in subtle ways. One example: A story reporting a legislative investigation into university faculty moonlighting said that the inquiry was looking at "faculty members shirking their teaching responsibilities." Actually, the legislators wanted to know whether the faculty in general was delinquent; the story made it appear that specific teachers were suspected—a delicate but misleading difference.

Get all of the story A good-natured multiracial crowd gathered to watch a fire in a Washington, D.C., warehouse. As the spectators chatted and joked, the firemen arrived, the TV cameras just behind them. Some of the crowd, according to a reporter who saw the entire event, "grabbed a grinning black fireman" and demanded "that he be made fire chief. The fireman laughed, shook them off, and went on about his work." But the camera kept grinding, and the crowd kept playing to it. "In minutes the police were there, brandishing billy clubs and advancing with swift efficiency toward the crowd." The police threw some tear gas, and the crowd, with mocking laughter, retreated. The reporter commented: "You could tell it any way you like. Your headline could have been 'POLICE ROUT ANGRY MOB.' Or you could have told it like it was—a piece of theater staged for TV. But to get it right you had to get there early and see it all. If only a few feet of film were shown, with what looked like angry, shouting blacks, you sent a message. But it was a false message."

Add and multiply right A story says that $653 50 is "1,500 percent of the original 98 cents price." But 100 percent of 98 cents is 98 cents; 1,500 percent is 15 times 98, or $14.70. The sum $653 50 is not quite 640 times 98—about 64,000 percent.

"Five local citizens, three men and two women, will head the Swarthmore PTA next year," says a lead. "They are Arthur Morrison, Ted Walpuski, Bob Gilmore, Henry Stebbins, Jane Quayle, and Mrs. Felix Simons. . . " Count.

Watch for the Phonies

The president of CBS News once told his staff, "If you have any feeling that the thing is being staged for you, don't film it." Staged events may at times be news—if Liza Minnelli were to sing Christmas carols in Times Square to promote a movie called "Santa Claus," and the event tied up Manhattan traffic so that nobody could get home for Christmas Eve, the media would be wrong not to report it. But their reports should show that the event was staged, and for what purpose. (And it might be even more reportable if nobody came to hear.)

The Bigger the Better?

Press critic Timothy Crouse tells this story in his book *The Boys on the Bus:* After President Nixon made a visit to Atlanta, his press secretary assured the press that at least 700,000 people had been on hand. Most reporters used the figure. Jim Perry of the *National Observer* did his homework: At 4,000 spectators a block for fifteen blocks, 60,000 could have seen the president. Throw in 15,000 for neck-craners on side streets: 75,000 Perry wrote, "In an act of charity I'm willing to say that 75,000 people turned out . . ."

The formula: Find out how many people can fit into a given space; make your own estimate of how full it is. If a room holds 600 and you think it's half full, you have your number.

Watch your estimates The Department of Justice and Washington police estimated a "Victory Rally" in Washington at 15,000 to 20,000 people; the Washington *Post* counted part of the crowd at 7,500 (who "were joined by 7,500 others.") The *Christian Beacon,* whose editor had inspired the rally, put the number at 200,000 to 250,000.

Estimating is a hazardous business—whether you're counting people or dead fish in a poisoned stream. There's no easy guide to the art. An article on estimating (*Society,* April, 1972) ends: "When in doubt, discount." A relief worker in Honduras after the 1974 hurricane answered a reporter's question about the number of deaths: "Pick a number. Pick any number you want. The bottom figure is 5,000; the government puts it at 20,000." (A careful reporter used "5,000 or more.")

Hearsay "They just found a kid dead in the administration building," a secretary told coworkers. "How do you know?" "Somebody just came in and told me." "Who?" "I don't know him—a guy." "Did he see it?" "No, he got it from his wife." "How did she know?" "Well, this guy says she overheard it at the grocery . . ." The fact: A man had fainted, recovered and walked away.

Deceit The outgoing administrative assistant to the mayor says he quit to go into business for himself. The next week it's revealed that he was fired for giving inside information to one of the bidders on the contract to build the new auditorium.

The owner of the roofing-paper plant tells you that neighbors' complaints about air pollution from his chimneys are hogwash. "Why, we've got laboratory tests to show there's nothing bad in the air." You check and discover that no laboratory tests have ever been made.

There's a great deal more to accurate reporting than this book and

Check, Double-check, Triple-check

The New Yorker magazine has been called "the most accurate publication in America." It earned the reputation by rigorous checking of facts. A full-time staff does nothing but ferret out mistakes. *The New Yorker* comes so close to absolute accuracy as to be a publishing miracle. Telephones, references, interviews, library research and long investigative journeys are all regular parts of the checking process. Sometimes an article is held up for weeks to make sure that a date in it is right.

all the teachers and city editors since Moses can tell you It is a matter of a reporter's self-respect and dedication. Curiosity and imagination, advance preparation and realistic skepticism, patience, and the careful second look all are weapons in a reporter's arsenal.

THE REPORTER AS PARTICIPANT

When is it appropriate for a reporter to put himself into the story he is writing? When may he frankly abandon objectivity and say "I"? One editor suggests that it's permissible about one time in 10 that it's tried—"it just doesn't work most of the time."

What should a reporter write, for example, after plunging into the ocean and saving a screaming child? That's an easy example. A reporter who actually did it wrote a first-person story, covering not only what happened and who was involved, but what he felt and thought about it. A byline protected him. But he could have written it straight, objectively, without showing that he was both writer and rescuer. Either method would be acceptable, though it's likely that the first, with its added human interest, would be preferred by most media.

In general, participation by reporters in a news event seems permissible if it's necessary to gather information, or if they are thrown into the middle of the event by chance. In addition, more and more papers are carrying first-person features: "how I climbed Mount Fizzletop" or "reporter goes hang-gliding." There's more possibility of producing interesting color if you're in the middle of a story, as was the reporter who crawled from the bridge just before it fell into Puget Sound. His "I" story was more dramatic than a "he" story could have been.

A development of the mid-'70s, however, has drawn frowns from both journalists and critics of the press: the practice of gratuitous participation by reporters in news events. A reporter manages to get on the phone with the gunman holding a family hostage and keeps him there while police are trying to negotiate. Reporters follow a squad car attempting to stake out a ransom pick-up and frustrate the ambush. In the first case the reporter is trying to make news rather than cover it; in the second newsgathering gets in the way of police work. Reporters are free to gather news, but not to make it or to interfere with the processes of law or law enforcement. The reporter on the bridge neither put himself there to get a story nor caused the bridge to fall.

STUDY SUGGESTIONS

1. Explain the occasional conflict between the reporter's need for access to information and the citizen's right to privacy.
2. Comment on the validity of the journalistic view that in some cases access to information takes priority over the right to privacy.
3. Cite several instances, actual or speculative, in which the right to access should override private right and several in which privacy should take precedence.
4. Why may the purposes of a public relations agent and those of a reporter sometimes be at odds?
5. How are public relations agents a help to reporters?
6. Define the terms *news release, off the record, news conference, backgrounder.*
7. What do you see as the plus and the minus values of "cooperation" among reporters for competing media?
8. How many times as large as 100 is a figure 200 percent larger?

PRACTICE ASSIGNMENTS

1. Ask 10 or more people at a "crowd event" to estimate the size of the crowd. Make your own estimate. Then get a dependable estimate or an exact figure from an official or sponsor of the event. Comment on differences, if any.
2. Interview for news facts somebody who attended a prize fight, a club meeting, a political rally, or some other news event, taking careful notes. Then go to official records, responsible officials, and other dependable sources for the same facts. If the two sets of "facts" differ, explain the causes of the differences, and what you would do to reconcile them.
3. Under what circumstances would you justify a reporter's examining papers or records on an unattended desk and, without informing the person in charge, using the materials thus gained as basis for a news story?
4. Select a print or broadcast news story that seems to you not to contain enough information. List the questions you think should have been asked and the details that should have been sought. If possible, continue the process by going yourself to appropriate sources for the information. Then write your own story.
5. Find out from public records and laws, reporters, public officials and other sources what kinds of local government business are by statute open to the public and what kinds may be closed. Study current news relating to or coming from (or prevented coming from) the agencies you have identified. If you find evidence that "open" agencies are being closed, or vice versa, investigate and write a report.

RELATED READING

Archibald, S. J. "The Revised Freedom of Information Law and How to Use It." *Columbia Journalism Review,* July–August 1977.

Bernstein, Carl, and Bob Woodward. *All the President's Men.* Simon & Schuster, 1974. The two Washington *Post* reporters who broke the Watergate story tell practically all. A fascinating and revealing account of the reportorial feat that every journalist ought to study, analyze and criticize. (Available in paperback.)

Bernstein, Carl, and Bob Woodward. *The Final Days.* Simon & Schuster, 1976. The same reporters' follow-up. This book is not so much about the reporting process as their first one; rather it *is* investigative reporting, much of it original, about the downfall of the Nixon administration. (Available in paperback.)

Blanchard, Robert O. "First, the Good News." *Quill,* January 1977. A "status report" on the effects of federal freedom of information legislation.

Crouse, Timothy. *The Boys on the Bus.* Random House, 1974. Detailed critique of news coverage of the 1972 presidential campaign and election. It raises profound questions about the information the American people get about the nation's most important political event. (Available in paperback.)

Rivers, William L. *The Mass Media.* Harper & Row, 1975. Subtitled *Reporting, Writing, Editing,* this 600-page book seeks to tell the beginner just about everything about the reporting craft.

Ryan, Michael, and James W. Tankard, Jr. *Basic News Reporting.* Mayfield, 1977. An exceedingly complete reporting textbook, with a long list of information sources in its useful appendix. Illustrated.

UPI

PART FOUR

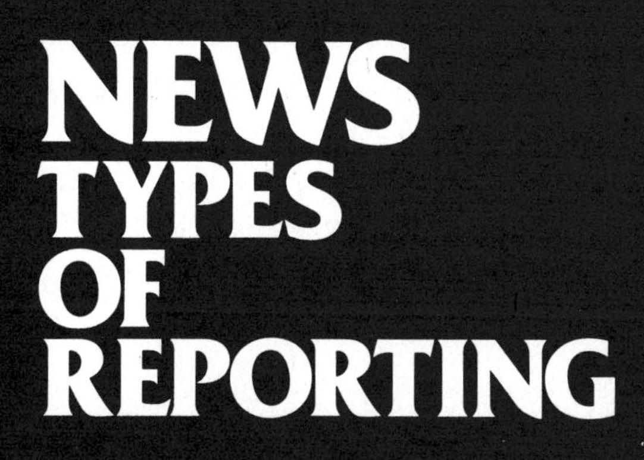
NEWS
TYPES
OF
REPORTING

13 News of the Spoken Word 1: Speech and Meeting Stories

PREVIEW

Most news depends in some part on spoken words. Stories about speeches are obvious examples. Covering a speech, a task constantly repeated in a reporter's work, usually involves:

- Advance preparation to gain understanding of the substance and context of the speech and often to evaluate the speaker's dependability
- Use of an advance copy of the speech when possible and checking minutely as the talk is given to observe departures from it
- Scrupulous note-taking, about what is said and about the setting in which it occurs
- Decision on the story's theme and on what parts of the talk can fairly be omitted
- Care that misplaced emphasis does not misrepresent speech or speaker
- Competent use of the alternation of direct and indirect quotation

Meeting stories involve spoken words—formal or informal talks, transaction of business, discussion of policies, proposals or decisions on actions. They involve careful notes, decision on central theme or emphasis, choice as to rejectable materials, and usually use of quotations.

People are always talking . . . and a good many of the things they say make news.

Spoken words make news at public audiences, in speeches and meetings, or on the air, when they are answering reporters' questions, when they are addressed to legislative or other governmental bodies, or at news conferences. Sometimes things said in private become news when reporters hear about them (though hearsay talk, like hearsay testimony in court, is suspect and must be authenticated).

More than half of all news stories are directly or indirectly drawn from spoken or attributed words. Some stories do not come from oral sources—the report of a hockey game, the vote of a house of Congress, an account of a prison riot filtered through a police or official document—but such stories are often fleshed out through interviews. News of observed or officially reported activity is usually *what* news, and may not require supporting authority. You can safely write that "107 passengers were on the hijacked plane." But even this kind of news often shows its source—a witness of an event or the representative of a committee—and it is often amplified by spoken words. Members of Congress may explain why they voted the way they did, a prison official may comment on how the riot was quelled. And much news that reaches a reporter by publicity release or from an unsolicited source has to be orally checked or amplified before publication.

This chapter covers the reporting of speeches and meetings; the next, interviews. Both kinds of news rely on the spoken word.

SPEECH STORIES

Civilized men appear always to have liked speeches. From Cicero to Fidel Castro, from Savonarola to Hitler, Billy Graham and Eugene McCarthy, orators have drawn audiences to listen and to cheer or jeer.

Though the 20th-century network of communications lets you read, see or hear what speakers say as soon as they say it, the formally spoken word remains an American passion. Luncheon clubs, stadium dedications, queen coronations, commencements, churches offer speeches—scores and hundreds a day. The news media cover them for good reasons:

- As group events they concern community interests that merit notice if not always detailed report.

Stories Without Attribution

News that shows no source of information nevertheless is pretty sure to have spoken words behind it. A routine business story about a stock dividend may contain no attribution—no "according to" or "he said"—yet a reporter may have spent 10 minutes on the telephone checking the mailed publicity release. A story announcing tersely that "The North Shore Clambake Guild will hold . . . ," without saying where the information came from, may be the result of an unsolicited phone call. When stories like these don't name sources, a reporter has decided they're so straightforward that no credit is needed. Some reporters and editors, however, insist on attribution, if only "the Clambake Guild announced today"; others think it often a waste of space.

- Usually a speech is arranged in hope that it will illuminate a topic of current concern, one that involves identifiable groups of citizens.
- The speaker may have something to contribute to general knowledge.
- Some speakers themselves are newsworthy, so that their words deserve public notice even if what they say is piffle.
- Lightning, of one kind or another, may strike.

Journalists are often bored with covering speeches, many of which are banal, many better unheard. But it may be important to let the public know that a speaker has said nothing, or that he played a familiar tune. Reporters find it hard to accept the apparently reliable statistic that only 7 percent of news space goes to speech reporting. (On a given day, when a speech merits publishing the full text, or when a president preempts time, the percentage is higher.)

However onerous the chore, covering speeches involves a number of primary reporting skills. The number is shown by a case history (fiction only in identifying details):

A woman reporter is told on Tuesday that on Friday she is to cover a luncheon talk before the State Chamber of Commerce convention. Dr. Wilfred Guntzlin, industrial psychologist, is to address the topic "Freud Couldn't Sell Automobiles." "Sounds silly," says the city editor, "but it might make a yarn. Write a piece that even *I* can understand." The reporter casts back into undergraduate psychology to recall what she learned about Freud. Hypnotism . . . the Oedipus complex . . . sex as a life force. Selling autos? She needs updating.

She calls the Chamber of Commerce secretary and learns about the kind of talk Guntzlin has been asked to give. At the public library she finds a popular treatment of Freudian concepts and a nontechnical work on psychology in business. She digs hard into the Freud book, skims the other; she comes up with what she thinks is a working understanding of the Freudian approach and some questions about its relation to business.

She calls a psychologist at the local college; he refers her to a psychiatrist. "I knew Bill Guntzlin in med school," the psychiatrist says. "He'll make sense. But watch out when he gets to free association. Bill outFreuds Freud on that."

The reporter needs to know more about Guntzlin. *Who's Who* gives her biographical data; two book titles sound like his speech topic. Married, two sons. Belongs to a yacht club, two golf clubs, a handful of professional societies.

All of this, with what the psychiatrist told her, lets her feel reasonably prepared for the assignment.

How Many Notes?

There are the tons-of-notes school of reporting, the I-don't need-'em school, and the in-between. Beware the second, of which we shall say no more.

Some reporters record furiously, a few in shorthand and many with their own brand of speed-writing. Others prefer reminder notes, jotted phrases to recall points of emphasis, witticisms, colorful illustrations, structural outline; they depend on memory for the fill-in. Reporters debate this problem over post-deadline coffee:

"You take enough notes to choke a camel," says one reporter. "I'd miss half the speech if I took that many. I'm not a stenographer, I'm a reporter."

The other responds. "I start a lot of sentences I don't finish; I get the main points. I have a view of the whole speech. I can throw out stuff I don't want, but go back and fill in where it's needed."

They don't argue taking down names, statistics and dates, and other specifics. And they agree on gathering more material than they expect to use.

She tries another step: an interview with Guntzlin. And she asks for an advance copy of the talk. She learns by telephone that Guntzlin won't be available before the luncheon; he will grant an interview later. And she can pick up a copy of the talk at the Chamber.

Before the speech, the reporter runs through the advance copy, marking possible points of emphasis. As she settles herself for the talk, she has the script open before her. She underlines here and there, jotting reminders in margins when Guntzlin leaves the text, striking out what he omits. She notes bursts of applause.

(The advance copy doesn't always match what comes over the lectern. On formal occasions a talk is likely to follow the script literally; when the secretary of state makes a foreign policy pronouncement, the words he utters must be precisely those he and his advisers have put together. Some speakers throw the book out the window.)

Guntzlin sticks to his text. The reporter interviews him to clarify a couple of points, then heads back to the newsroom. By the time she gets there, she is primed to write tomorrow's story—she has reviewed her materials mentally and decided on lead emphasis and story structure. What are her guides?

She starts with the assumption that underlies all reporting; that the reporter is the representative of an absent audience. Her obligation is to write a story that will let readers (particularly those interested in psychology or business) take from it substantially what they would have gained had they been present. This means objective reporting—reporting, not comment; it means scrupulous accuracy and balanced summary, fastidious selection and rejection. And it means decision as to what accompanying incidents are to be reported, and with what emphasis. The reporter's thinking, on her way to her desk, might go like this:

"A serious talk, and a sober, attentive audience. Of concern to all kinds of business. I'll put the lead on the three kinds of sales tactics Guntzlin listed. . . . The Freud angle? He didn't give it more than a nod. A trick to furnish a title. I'll ignore it. . . . Not much incidental color, except that he had such a tight grip on his audience. Made them laugh—maybe a couple jokes. . . . Should I mention that he's the matinee idol type? How big he looked behind the lectern?"

She starts typing. First a brief report to the city desk: "I can do two and a half pages on Guntzlin. And I've got stuff for an interview next day—how he thinks business psychology ought to be taught in high schools. We could get a piece later on what the high schools think."

Not every speech assignment gets this much care. A good many public talks are routine, and routine reporting (as much to record their occurrence as their content) may be all they demand.

Speech story form American news media have developed a functional pattern for speech stories, one that prescribes direct quotation where it is needed and summary passages for parts that don't demand detail. The pattern belongs to the straight-news form: summary lead followed by development of significant detail, usually in order of decreasing importance (a speech story that follows the speech pattern religiously is usually a bad story. Full-text reproductions do that.) Specifically, the form involves:

1. A lead of one or more paragraphs, usually in indirect (paraphrased) discourse;
2. Passages of direct quotation for major points that justify elaboration.

When Minor Becomes Major

Secondary incidents sometimes overshadow the main event. If the speaker stalks to stage front to blast at a questioner, if some of the audience walks out on him or if he keeps his audience in stitches, the secondary fact may get major billing.

Making a sidelight the lead, however, can dilute a talk's substance. A city councilman got a big laugh when, in a sober council meeting, he proposed—just after a visiting outfielder's home run had taken a pennant from the local team—"let's arrest that guy for larceny." The reporter wrote a "bright" that his paper front-paged; a serious story on the meeting ran next to the want ads. Was either the council or the public well served?

These passages alternate with:

3. Passages in indirect discourse, usually summaries of sections of the talk;
4. Circumstantial detail: time, place, pedigree of the speaker, sponsorship, other tangential matter;
5. Secondary incidents (which might be presented in sidebars).

DIFFERING TREATMENTS OF A SPEECH

Six months after President Carter sent to the Capitol a plan to stimulate the nation's oil-and-gas energy program, the President went to the nation on TV to goad Congress and arouse the people to the gravity of the problem. He emphasized six points:

1. We are using gas and oil faster than ever. "If we fail to act boldly today, then we will surely face a greater series of crises tomorrow."
2. The problem arises because "we use too much—and waste too much—energy."
3. We must consume less, shift to other energy sources and encourage domestic energy production.
4. Congress and the people must take specific action to meet the problem.
5. "I will sign the energy bills" only if they are economically fair and sound, if they meet conservation and production needs, and if they protect the federal budget.
6. Everybody—government and the people—must work and sacrifice if the goal is to be met.

The speech was the biggest national news that evening and the next day to virtually every news medium (it was election day, and political news dominated the media). Most front-paged or stressed the talk. What did the stories emphasize?

The nearly unanimous choice was the warning that Carter would not sign unsatisfactory bills (most stories used the word "veto," which Carter sidestepped). The Associated Press lead, used by hundreds of papers and newscasts that did not have their own correspondents, said:

> President Carter, saying Congress must "resist pressures from a few for special favors," threatened Tuesday night to veto any energy legislation that fails to meet his test for fairness.

Variant leads on the same theme:

> President Carter last night threatened to veto any energy package that does not support the main objectives of his initial energy program.—Chicago *Sun-Times*

> Saying that the nation cannot solve its economic problems until it has first dealt with its growing energy problem, President Carter warned Tuesday night that he would veto any energy bills passed by Congress that were not "well balanced" and "fair."—Los Angeles *Times*.

> President Carter said tonight that he would sign energy legislation only if it meets the basic criteria for equity and effectiveness on which he based his initial energy proposals to Congress last April.—New York *Times*

One other theme, the plea for popular support, appeared in a few stories:

> President Carter, seeking support for his energy plan now undergoing crucial congressional action, called Tuesday for a spirit of national sacrifice to meet a serious challenge.—Minneapolis *Tribune*

> President Carter asked the American people last night for "your support and understanding" as Congress nears its climactic votes on his national energy plan that would dramatically increase the price of energy to all consumers.—Washington *Post*

Secondary stories Afternoon papers, instead of reporting the talk itself, often depended on sidebars or folos. Two widely used stories—both from wire services—reported Congressional reaction. Their leads:

> President Carter probably swayed few votes in Congress with his bid for public support for his embryo plan, administration supporters and critics agree.

> Republican Sen. Ted Stevens of Alaska grumped that President Carter invited only Democrats to the White House to witness his energy speech, proving that he was partisan. But the Democratic chairman of the Senate Energy Committee, Sen. Henry Jackson of Washington, said Carter was "telling it like it is."

Story form and organization Organization patterns of the stories were similar, whatever the leads. All provided at least passing attention to the president's major points; all used paraphrased leads, followed by alternating direct and indirect quotation. The Associated Press story held rigorously to the speech text; some of the others (all byline stories) added supporting matter. The New York *Times* gave half a column, once the speech was reported, to the fact that congressmen invited to listen did so in a separate room and to the meticulous processes of research and writing that produced the speech. The Los Angeles *Times* tied in more than a column of material on congressional reaction and the concurrent efforts of House and Senate to reconcile differences in their energy bills. Two stories speculated about relationships between the speech and the President's abrupt decision to postpone a long-planned foreign trip. Byline writers, it was clear, enjoyed greater freedom to weave in background and contextual matter than did wire-service reporters.

Only one of the speech stories failed to open with the words "President Carter." (See pages 246–247.)

QUOTATIONS—QUOTATION MARKS

Verbatim? Quotation marks mean literally that the words they enclose are exactly as the source gave them—verbatim. In a quotation attributed to a president, by common consent, they mean just that. But there is professional disagreement about whether the rule is unbreakable. One argument goes:

"You have no license to use quotes unless they mean what a literate reader expects them to mean—that they enclose exact quotations. If you put into quotes anything but verbatim material, you're deceiving, and you forfeit reader confidence."

The opposition responds: "The important thing is to give the right impression, and to do it without wasting space. As long as your paraphrase gives the reader accurate meaning and flavor, you have tacit permission to depart from strict wording. You can often help speakers to say what they mean better than they have said it—a favor to them and to the readers. And you keep your story from getting too long."

Writers who follow the second principle are aware that it is hazardous. Some publications fear its risks enough to prohibit alteration of a speaker's words. *Editor & Publisher* once commented that a story written word-for-word "contains a lot of the verbiage, bypasses, and repetitious figures of speech with which most of us adorn our spoken words. No man can impugn its accuracy; the question is, will anybody except the hero of the speech read it?"

A related puzzle is that verbatim quotation, though literally accurate, may give a false impression. A speaker who lightens a windy speech with throwaways and gestures won't be fairly served by

A reporter phones in her story as soon as possible after an important meeting. *(Chester Higgins photo from Photo Researchers, Inc., New York)*

endless dull quotation. Suppose he mumbles, mangles grammar or gets his foreign phrases wrong, but still makes his points strongly: Will simon-pure reporting be as accurate as paraphrase that helps him say what he intends to say? A politician once told a reporter, "Those weren't my words, but they gave my meaning better than I could." On the other hand, a reporter who quoted with painful fidelity did this to a football cornerback:

> I think the secondary is closer with each other than probably any other place on the team. We have to talk to each other. We all know that if we don't and we make a mistake it's going to be us standing there looking embarrassed and the other team will have scored.

Editing would have saved embarrassment and helped the reader to understand what the player meant. The questions are: Is it accurate reporting? Should the reporter be concerned about making the athlete look foolish? There are arguments on each side.

Verbatim reporting cannot by itself take account of gestures, inflections or interruptions—they require a reporter's description. Some listeners, including other reporters, may see or interpret them differently. Moreover, the wisest pro may make errors in judgment.

When not to use quotes One guide to punctuation says that quotation marks may be used for "words used in an unusual sense; or for coined words for which the author offers apology." True. But if the usage is so far out that you have to use quotation marks as crutches to tell the reader, "I really know better," or—worse—to call attention to your wit, you'd do better to rewrite. Sportswriters who saddle conventional sports terms with quotes—"hash mark," or "dunk," or "sleeper"—show their insecurity and their disrespect for readers. If you write that "she had a 'gypsy' air" or "he is a religious 'freak,' " you're saying, "Hey, reader, look out—I'm going to say something you might not catch unless I warn you."

Another quotation-mark misdemeanor is inserting explanatory words inside quotes to help a quotation along with instant clarification. Examples show the wrong way:

> "We'll take a vote on Thursday (Feb. 25)," the chairman said.
>
> "We can always lick the Crimson and White (Goshen High)," the Elkhart coach said.
>
> "There are many (students) who are likely to say, "Well, I can't see the difference (between my educational facilities last year and those this year),' " Snoke said. "If we demonstrate (through the pursuit of excellence) that we are going to make this place a great place, I think it (increased tuition) will be worth it to the students."

The parenthesized passages are not quotations, but reporter's additions. A better way to do it: "We'll take a vote on Thursday," the chairman said (Thursday will be Feb. 25).

Quotation use is discussed further in Chapter 14.

CREDIT LINES—ATTRIBUTIONS

A credit line or attribution is a phrase that explains who said what—"he said" or "Winslow added." Its skillful use is a mark of the professional. Here are some guidelines:

1. Every sentence of indirect quotation ordinarily requires a

credit line. Without either attribution or quotation marks, a sentence is to be attributed to the reporter. This means that a long passage of indirect quotation may be made monotonous by "he said" lines. When you write two or three sentences of indirect quotation, it's wise to move to a passage of direct quotation.

There is an exception to the one-attribution-per-sentence mode: If a first sentence is properly tied to the speaker, a second that is obviously coupled to it may be able to get along on its own (when it's followed by another credited sentence, there's little doubt). For example, the following passage appeared in the New York *Times's* report of the Carter speech:

> "It is crucial that you understand how serious this challenge is," he said, perhaps directing his language as much to Congress as to the American people.
>
> Not only do energy problems exacerbate present weaknesses in the country's economic system, but they also threaten its national security.
>
> "Our national security depends on more than our armed forces," he explained. "It also rests on the strength of our economy . . ."

That one sentence of uncredited quotation, however, was the lone example in the reports of the *Times,* the Los Angeles *Times,* the Chicago *Sun-Times,* the Minneapolis *Tribune,* the Washington *Post* and the Associated Press on the speech.

2. One credit line does the job for any continuous direct quotation within quotation marks, whether its length is one paragraph or 20. In a continuous quotation of several paragraphs, however, you may find meaning clearer or rhetoric smoother if you insert additional attributions, such as "she went on" or "the speaker concluded."

3. In direct quotations the credit line must always be attached to the first sentence of quoted matter, usually in its body or at its close. You confuse a reader when you ask him to read more of what is said before you tell him who said it.

Opening a quoted passage with the credit line is often clumsy. Perhaps because of the speaker's prominence, this device occurs seven times in the AP Carter speech story. The credit line is a part of the mechanics of a speech story, however, not of its substance, and it should be kept unobtrusive. Putting it at the middle or end of the sentence plays it down.

4. Few words of attribution are as effective and as invisible as "said." Inexperienced advisers sometimes urge pupils to seek elegance by substituting *stated, declared, averred* and the like, but careful writers think them pretentious and distracting. On occasion

an *added, continued, shouted* or *went on* may fit a passage's rhythm as well as its sense. But ornate substitutes like *revealed* ("Jones revealed that he will have turkey for Thanksgiving dinner") or *announced* ("Mary announced that she goes to bed at 11 every night") should be avoided unless a genuine revelation or announcement takes place. Misused, such words are at best pompous and at worst a form of sensationalizing. Communication researchers have produced evidence of higher reader confidence in *said* than in other attributive words.

Most of these guides apply to writing for broadcast. The listener's ear can't check back as the reader's eye can. For radio and TV, however, the credit line must almost always precede rather than interrupt or follow the quotation. Listeners don't know that somebody other than the announcer is talking to them if they aren't told at the start.

SPEECH STORIES FOR ANALYSIS

From the Washington *Post* comes a speech story that observes some of these guidelines and ignores or shatters others. It is a well-constructed story, setting its theme in the lead paragraph—what America lost when it "lost reticence"—and developing it in later paragraphs. About half of the story is devoted to the talk; most of the remainder goes to portrayal of the speaker's expertise to show his authority. The annotations point out these and other characteristics.

Louis Booker Wright, a self-confessed Victorian who talks about Colonial times as if they were his times and 17th-century England as if he were an Elizabethan, believes that modern society "lost a great deal when it lost reticence."

Present-tense verbs say "what he believed when he spoke he believes today"—justifiable reportorial assumption. They give the story currency.

Wright, 77, was not talking about a simple disposition to silence, which he clearly lacks, but rather what he calls "moral and linguistic" reticence.

Past tense introduced, but present tense continues sense of lead paragraph.

"It doesn't seem to me hypocritical to be reticent," said the former director of the Folger Shakespeare Library here, who received Phi Beta Kappa's award for distinguished service to the humanities at the society's convention in Williamsburg recently.

Time element introduced (should it be given earlier?) Recently *suggests that this may be a relatively old event. Is this an acceptable practice, or must the time be precise—"last week," "in August"?*

"When frankness is necessary, that's one thing, but frankness for the sake of shock is evidence of lack of judgment. The thought of using any obscenity in any

No credit line, but in context it seems unnecessary.

company is deplorable evidence of a lack of taste, if nothing else."

Wright, a homespun gentleman from the up-country farm—as opposed to low-country plantation—society of South Carolina, speaks for a set of values that disappeared as cornfields were paved over for shopping centers.

Subjective description by the reporter. Would the reader question it?

"It has followed the Renaissance tradition," he said in his acceptance speech at the College of William and Mary, "that the learned man would be a gentleman, a status that had special meaning in an earlier age before we lost both the concept of the gentleman and respect for tradition."

Wright is of that age. Tradition came early in the form of Caesar's "Gallic Wars," which his mother read to him as a child. "I wondered why she chose Caesar," he said, "but I guess it was because she spent so much time learning Latin."

"My father (a schoolmaster) never forbade me to read anything," said the small, white-haired, brown-eyed scholar. "I read Rabelais early on. And once I had Taine's 'History of English Literature.' My father asked, 'Are you getting anything out of that?' 'A little, as far as I can understand it,' I answered. 'Then read on,' he said, 'read on.' "

The words a schoolmaster *that don't belong to the speaker have been forced into the quotation. Would you approve replacing parentheses with commas, thus giving the speaker credit for them, on the defense that the phrase is accurate? Note that the preceding paragraph ends a quotation and this one begins a new one. Use of quotation marks in both places says to the reader that the two quotations are not continuous.*

Wright did. And has done so ever since. Reading on, that is, largely in the fields of American history, Renaissance history, and Shakespeare and Shakespearean scholarship.

In 1926 Wright received a Ph.D. from the University of North Carolina and by 1935 published "Middle Class Culture in Elizabethan England."

Should the four paragraphs of background information beginning "Wright did" be placed elsewhere—perhaps before the two final paragraphs?

More than 20 books have followed, exploring such diverse subjects as "Puritans in the South Seas," "Everyday Life in Colonial America," and "On Books and Men," which Wright said was "on my growing up years in South Carolina."

Out of all this came an enormous respect for the English language which, he believes, is in need of a renaissance similar to

Is the "belief" here attributed to the speaker drawn from the speech, or another source? You can't tell.

the one that has brought Hebrew into the modern world.

"Communications has now become a rumbling babble of jargon, clichés, patois, slang, and inexact expressions of dubious meaning," he told the Phi Beta Kappans.

He went on to say that "the deterioration of the ability to communicate with exactness—or even intelligence—is only one of the symptoms of an epidemic of permissiveness that has brought disasters—social, intellectual, and moral—upon us.

Direct quotation is introduced by the "He went on" credit line that serves for three paragraphs.

"The depreciation of standard speech is evidence of sentimental and superficial thinking that has done great harm to minorities whom some educationists thought they were helping.

The word educationist, *shown in dictionaries as "chiefly British," is unfamiliar to Americans, and may be ambiguous. But the speaker said it, and it fits the character of his talk. Would you consider changing it, if you could learn from the speaker what American word he would substitute?*

"These educational sociologists, for example, have encouraged children of the ghetto to believe that their patois is just as good as the standard language and requires no improvement."

Wright is a conservative. When asked what modern play he liked, he named "A Man for All Seasons," a very traditional drama about Sir Thomas More, the late-15th- and early-16th-century churchman and statesman who served Henry VIII.

". . . is a conservative" is the reporter's comment. Acceptable?

His favorite dramatist, of course, is Shakespeare, and Wright and his assistant, Elaine W. Fowler, are now working on a television series on such questions as how Shakespeare chose his themes and how he was inspired by certain events in his youth. The programs are intended for presentation on public television at the end of this year or the beginning of next.

Of course?

Another speech story (excerpts follow) reports a sermon at the National Cathedral. It departs from the strict pattern by inserting interview material and a paragraph of background between its opening section and the speaker's development of the "increased racial tension" topic suggested in the lead.

Axiom

During a speech, the emphasis belongs to the speaker. Afterward, it belongs to the reporter.

City Council Chairman Sterling Tucker warned yesterday, in a National Cathedral sermon, that revelations of alleged conflict of interest, cronyism, and other irregularities in city government have increased racial tension in Washington.

"For any who care about the future of the District of Columbia," Tucker said, there have been "no pluses, no heroes, no victors, and no victories" in the news of the last several weeks.

Although Tucker mentioned no names, he left no doubt that he was referring to Joseph P. Yeldell, the suspended director of the Department of Human Resources, and more generally to the administration of Mayor Walter E. Washington.

[*Two paragraphs express Tucker's "rejection" of insinuations that Washington, "a black-ruled city, is unfit for home rule." The story then continues:*]

Asked by a reporter after his sermon who was asserting that the District was "unfit for home rule," Tucker replied that sentiment "is implicit in a great many comments that the Congress is going to take it back."

Pressed to name someone who had made such comments, Tucker said he "hears them at parties" from both blacks and whites. "Blacks fear it and some whites say it with anticipation," Tucker said.

In the last several weeks, charges have been reported that Yeldell had relatives put on the city payroll, used his position to benefit D.C. parking magnate Dominic Antonelli, and cut services to the poor while aiding business interests. More recently, articles in the Washington *Post* have disclosed alleged irregularities in the financing of Mayor Washington's 1974 campaign. . . .[1]

[*The story now returns to the speech and concludes with Tucker's remarks about "increased racial tension."*]

Unusual leads or story structures sometimes give routine speech reports flare or interest that routine treatment would lack. A story in the Minneapolis *Star* used a five-paragraph lead that not only catches attention but also plants the speaker's rhetorical device:

Take a drive to Becker in Sherburne County and look at a power plant. Then zip over to Burnsville and look at a landfill. Finally, stop anywhere in Minneapolis and look at the IDS Tower.

Remember that the plant at Becker is to double its production next year and that about 19 more such plants would be needed to meet Minnesota's projected power needs by the year 2000.

At the landfill, reflect that for you and everyone else in Minnesota 3.5 pounds of trash are generated each day and that 65 percent of that is packaging—single-use, disposable, and often made from non-renewable resources.

Imagine that the IDS Tower is 8,000 feet tall, instead of about 600 feet, and that it's made of dry taconite tailings—that's the amount of tailings that Reserve Mining Co. has dumped into Lake Superior each year since 1955.

That tour was the answer given yesterday by Peter Gove when he was asked to tell the Citizens League what major unresolved environmental questions face Minnesota.

Gove has resigned his post as director of the Minnesota Pollution Control Agency to join Wendell Anderson's Senate staff. Gove's tour . . .

The lead on the last story suggests the flavor of the event as well as its substance.

In the story that follows, the writer—a university-daily reporter—combined coverage of the speech with interview material and a considerable amount of his own comment. This perilous practice sometimes becomes an exercise in virtuosity. In this case, you sense that the writer knows what he is talking about; he gives the story unity, in spite of its irregular structure, by making the speaker's personality the theme.

High priest poet visionary chanting madman Allen Ginsberg blew through the university Friday like a fresh wind down from the mountain.

He came to meditate, discuss his theory of poetry, share old, new, and borrowed poems, and belt out some gravel-throated dirty sad street corner blues.

Ginsberg began his howl at the American dream as a member of the San Francisco "Beat Generation" of the mid-1950s. Since then he has bummed and thundered through the literature and cities of this country like a space-age Siddhartha. To say he is a major figure in Western poetry is both hyperbole and understatement. Ginsberg can't be classified easily.

His poetic vision, always tinted with politics, has led him from Berkeley flower power marchings against the Vietnam war and riding highways of psychedelic drugs with Timothy Leary in the early 1960s, to chanting "Aum" amid a teargas blitz at the Yippie Life-Festival during the 1968 Chicago Democratic convention, to founding the Jack Kerouac School of Disembodied Poetics in Boulder, Colo., in 1974, to touring the nation with Bob Dylan's Rolling Thunder Revue in 1975 as poet-percussionist.

And where is Ginsberg's vision directed in 1977? He's no longer as much the beatnik peace warrior fueled by mystic frenzy. He's a gentle man who comes with a pitch as well as a song He has immersed himself in Buddhist meditation for five years, and his recent poems radiate both the practice and the perceptions of meditative discipline. His afternoon lecture in the Union and evening reading in the West Bank Auditorium revolved around the theme of poetry as intimate companion of meditation.

"I'm writing about matters close to the nose," he said in an interview, "microscopic acute perceptions, like snowy mountain fields seen through the transparent wings of a fly on a windowpane.

"Ninety-nine out of 100 poets I see are writing—it's actually bullshit. There's very little attempt to focus on anything that's there. They are at the mercy of the winds of passion and ignorance."

[*A dozen paragraphs—some from the interview, some from the speech, some contributed by the reporter—describe Ginsberg's theories of poetry and his opinions about other American poets. The story then concludes:*]

Both poetry and meditation begin with inspiration, breathing in, Ginsberg observed. He included a five-minute session of meditative silence in both lecture and reading, each starting and ending on the note of a bell.

He gave the audience his formula for "meditation poetics," including instructions to sit erect with mouth closed, eyes open but not staring, and breathing through nostrils. "Be mindful of the outbreathing, flowing out with the breath until it dissolves in space; pay no particular attention to the in-breath."

After the lecture's meditation session Ginsberg said he always approaches group participation exercises "with some amount of terror."

Ginsberg said William Carlos Williams' poems provided the point at which American poetry grew into "supreme reality of real mind," leaving the "stereotyped national Boy Scout Reader's Digest poetry of the past decades." Williams led the way to "a more direct appreciation of things as they really are."

Like Williams, Ginsberg says, he has planted his feet firmly on the ground and resolves to dream no more.

"Flies do all my talking for me," he said. With flies for his spokesmen and their wings for his lenses, Allen Ginsberg goes spacetrucking through the Buddha blues Kerouaced-out politic Dharma incantation galaxy of "ordinary mind."[2]

How to misuse an advance script Speeches are often composed in language that is wooden, stuffy or bombastic. Reporters working from an advance copy need to keep up a guard to prevent dullness from sabotaging their stories. The writer of the story below wasn't wary enough; his managing editor provided pungent comments:

The Story as Published

Wilmer Dodge, state budget administrator, told the state education commission today that the state has "ample financial resources for an orderly and effective attack on its many serious problems."

Because of this, he said, "Our educators have a clear and challenging mandate to expand and improve the system at all levels."

The committee held its first fall meeting today at the state capitol. High on its agenda was a report from a subcommittee assigned to evaluate the objectives and structure of the full group.

Dodge praised the governor for what he called "courageous" insistence on refusing to be deterred by financial problems in improving the standards and services of the state's schools.

He said "it would have been easy for the governor to turn away from the full reality of the educational problem because the scope of the need obviously meant that appropriations would have to be greatly increased."

Dodge pointed out that the program approved by the legislature provided 59 million dollars more for the current biennium than was appropriated for the preceding two years, an increase of 32 percent.

The M.E.'s Comments

Here is the type of news copy this paper can do without.

Note the pattern of linking high-sounding phrases into a chain.

Note how removed those quoted phrases, and some of the others, are from common language.

You may conclude that the only hard news is in the last graf. (And even that news is not fresh news.)

What can we do with such stories?

A copy editor can point out to the copy chief that a story is all wind.

A copy chief can ask the news desk whether the story should be spiked.

The news editor may consult with the city desk regarding the importance of the story. (They may decide to run the story despite its faults.)

The city desk may discuss the story with the reporter who prepared it.

If the story came from the wire services, the city editor may address his remarks to the wire services.

[2] Copyright © 1977 by the *Minnesota Daily.* Reprinted by permission.

Sidelights shouldn't become spotlights An unwary reporter can be misled by a striking secondary issue. For example: A mayoral candidate talked about campaign themes for 45 minutes before a luncheon club, then asked for questions. "What about those chiselers on relief?" somebody demanded. The speaker warned his listeners that he had not studied the problem and considered himself ill-informed; he added that "reports that hundreds of families on relief are getting relief money fraudulently" should be examined rigorously, and that he would do so if he were elected. A reporter wrote this lead:

> Hundreds of chiseling families in this city getting relief illegally will be cracked down on if John B. Candidate is elected.

Some of the errors in that lead:

1. It gives an initial impression that the talk was devoted largely to the chiseling theme.
2. It presents the speaker as claiming knowledge he said he did not have.
3. It presents the problem in what may not have been a fair light.
4. It makes the reporter suspect, since the city's relief rolls at that time carried only 200 families.

In some cases, however, a "minor" element clearly commands elevation. When a man speaking on "The Future of Fossil Fuels" tells an audience that "the largest atomic reactor in the world will help us produce this community's light, heat and power within five years," the reporter would be delinquent not to consider the assertion for the lead. But a competent reporter must make it clear that the remark was a throwaway (and must also persuade the speaker, after the talk, to develop the tip.)

STORIES ABOUT MEETINGS

Recall the assertion at the opening of this chapter that a high proportion of news stories derive from the spoken word.

Formal or informal meetings provide many such stories—meetings of committees, clubs, PTAs, neighborhood associations, civic groups and others. In a metropolitan area most such meetings go unreported. There are hundreds of them, and they carry interest for only a smattering of a big medium's audience. But in a small community—small town or city neighborhood—local media give them faithful attention. Lots of them are tiresome stories. It's hard to write a sprightly account of an event you feel you've covered a dozen times before. But almost every event worth reporting at all has one element of novelty or one peak of interest, and the challenge to the reporter is to unearth it.

Meetings—unless they break up in brawls—provide one of two kinds of news material: either business or group action, or formal or informal talks. Thus the reporting problem is one of emphasis. Is the business transacted—election of officers, decision to stage a fund drive, a resolution of support for an aldermanic candidate (or the fact that there was no business)—the heart of the story? Or is it the outraged speech by the director of the state grange blasting the chamber of commerce?

If the decision is to leave out one element or the other, construction of the story is easy. If it is to include both, a two-part lead may be the answer. Here are two examples:

> Local business interests are giving the farmer the run-around, Grange Director Wilfred Oelstein told the Kiwanis Club yesterday noon.
>
> His talk followed the reelection of all current Club officers for another year's service.
>
> "We can't have farm prosperity without help from you bankers and retailers," Oelstein said . . .

> A decision to stage a drive for funds followed adoption of a new constitution at the Improvement Association meeting last night.
>
> The two actions came after a talk by Prof. George F. Pierrot on the fight against Dutch elm disease . . .

Either approach, with essential elements in a multiple-paragraph lead, makes for orderly development of the story.

The meeting story that follows is one in which the reporter found no formal action to report. He concentrated on the response to the speech, which had been the meeting's chief purpose. It presents an unorthodox but imaginative and easy-to-follow structural pattern:

A shouting match ended last night's Mayor's Human Relations Commission meeting after a black woman member said that most whites don't know what integration means.

"It does not mean one group 'rising up' to the other group," said Mrs. Hannah Minster, 2417 Index Avenue.

"It means two groups coming together into something new."

"Until human rights bodies learn this, we are going to keep talking at each other, instead of to each other," said Mrs. Minster, a social service worker at Neighborhood House.

Mrs. Minster had been set off by three assertions:

That by the evening's speaker, Alexander F. Milles, an official of the Anti-Defamation League of B'nai B'rith, that blacks were left without a culture by slavery.

That of Stephen Korsov, president of the Council for Civil and Human Rights, that minority groups need special treatment in employment but that it is offensive to the white community to say so.

That of Walter Meyer, executive director of the Jewish Community Relations Council, that newspapers should run news of successful blacks to "improve the black image."

To Milles, Mrs. Minster said: blacks have put together a culture combining their African heritage and "our European ancestors, the slave-masters."

"It's not a white man's culture," she said. "Not even the integrationists have taken the time to understand that."

To Korsov she said: "We don't want special treatment like you give your children. I don't want your help. Just get out of my way."

She said Meyer exhibited a patronizing attitude about black culture in claiming he wanted a "better life" for minority groups.

"YOU want it," she snapped. "What about what WE want?"

The discussion flared after the lunch meeting at the Protestant Center as Meyer and Korsov sought to explain their positions to Mrs. Minster.

To a comment about law and order, Mrs. Minster cried, "Whose law and order? Your law and order." Discrimination hides in Northern law and order, she said.

"I'm out of Alabama, and if I had the choice, I'd go back. I can see it there. I can fight it."

"Did you lose six million Jews in concentration camps?" Meyer demanded.

"Comparatively, I lost that many hanging down there," Mrs. Minster snapped.

Later Mrs. Minster said she had seen six blacks hanged, among them her 14-year-old cousin, when she was 12. He had looked at a white woman in a bathing suit in Prichard, Ala., she said. "And they hung him then. Not later—then."

The reporter later interviewed Mrs. Minster, to let her develop her position more fully—and more calmly.

STUDY SUGGESTIONS

1. Cite examples of news stories that do not depend on "spoken words"—on materials gained by ear.
2. Cite advantages and disadvantages of the alternation of direct and indirect quotation usually employed in writing speech stories.
3. Examine the six Carter speech story leads (pages 246–247). Rate them in what you consider the order of their effectiveness. Explain your choices.
4. Give several examples of news events in which you think secondary incidents should take precedence over the speech content in the stories.
5. Present your opinion about the problem of departure from verbatim quotation within quotation marks. Explain your reasoning.
6. Note that the speech story lead on page 255 says nothing about the speech until its fifth paragraph. Do you defend this structure?
7. Do you think the mixture of interview, speech and reporter-added material in the Ginsberg story (page 256) is defensible?
8. Criticize—pro or con—the managing editor's comments on page 257. Do you agree that "the only hard news is in the last graf"?

9. Do you think "a shouting match" the best opening words for the meeting story on page 259? If you don't, how would you write the lead?

PRACTICE ASSIGNMENTS

1. British newspapers commonly report speeches without attribution or credit lines, except for one at the beginning, but depend on past-tense verbs to indicate attribution. Thus (after a lead with housekeeping information—time, place, speaker, and so on):

   The city was not able to afford 30-minute bus service to all areas. The buses in service were not paying their way. They were less than half full most of the time. Bus riders in the suburbs did not especially want better service. The cost of new buses to speed up service was 18 million pounds.

   First, comment on the effectiveness of the British manner. Second, if you think it could be bettered, write it the way you'd like to see it.
2. Check five or more speech, interview or meeting stories in your local paper against the guides to credit-line usage on page 250.
3. Read a story on a major speech in your local paper and listen to a radio report on it (not to the speech itself). Compare leads, content, story structure and other characteristics that strike you.
4. Attend a group or club meeting in which the program is to include both a talk and group business. Write two stories, one of 75 to 100 words, the other of 500. How do they differ? Which is the harder to write?
5. Write two radio stories about the meeting you used in Assignment 3, a one-minute story and a three-minute story. How do they differ?
6. Attend a major speech on your campus or in your city. Write a story of at least 1,000 words (about three typewritten pages) for an appropriate newspaper. Then rewrite the story for local broadcast.

14 News of the Spoken Word 2: Interview Stories

PREVIEW

Interviewing is a part of almost all reporting; but stories are termed interviews only when their meaning grows from *what* is said and *who* says it. Interview stories are commonly of three types: news interviews (development of a theme drawn from current news); symposium interviews (stories based on a collection of interviews); personality interviews (revelation of an interviewee's personality through his own words).

Characteristics of the news interview:

- A topic growing from current news
- An interviewee whose views on the topic or explanation of it can be looked on as authoritative or worth hearing
- Illumination of the topic beyond the point to which factual reporting takes it

Like speech stories, interviews usually demand advance preparation. They require that a reporter steer the interview, keep it on track and ask for elaboration as needed. Some settings are "good" for interviewing, some not; sometimes presence of a witness or use of a tape recorder is desirable. Note-taking is crucial: the reporter must be certain of the interviewee's words and meanings.

Interview story form is much like that of speech stories. It requires theme selection, rejection of extraneous material, and alternation of direct and indirect quotation.

Guides to sources of error in interview stories are available (see Related Reading, page 297). Errors can arise from either the reporter's or the interviewee's side of the table. Interviewees may inject error purposely or without intent.

Symposium interviews impose the caution to avoid making them say more than they should. Often based on random-sample questioning, they do not assure representative views. They are often more entertaining than illuminating. (Harris, Gallup, and other public opinion surveys—refined forms of symposium interviewing—base their credibility on the careful selection of their respondents and the technical excellence of the interviewing methods.)

Personality interviews, whose subjects are selected either for prominence or unusualness, seek to reveal personal attitudes and idiosyncracies by letting people talk about themselves. They differ from biographical sketches, which tell *about* their subjects rather than explore their views of themselves.

Newsworkers distinguish between "interview stories" and stories that are all or in part based on interviewing.

Stories based on interviewing are the nuts and bolts of reporting: a reporter asks for information, a news source responds. The facts from the interview help make up the story. The reader's interest is in the information rather than the source.

An interview story, by contrast, draws much of its authority and interest from the person who has been interviewed. The statements in the story—often opinions rather than facts—have weight because of their source. The source's authority, special knowledge, fame or personal circumstances give them their distinction.

To illustrate: Your assignment is to get a story on the nonpolluting sewage-disposal plant your county commissioners have decided to install. You go to the commission secretary with questions: Where will the plant be built? When will it start operating? Cost? Employment plans? Management personnel? Types of equipment? Advantages over the old system? You come up with an orderly body of facts. It is a story you might have elicited from the county engineer, the chairman of the planning committee or the contractor, with virtually no substantial differences. Its emphasis, though it is based on an interview, is on the *what* rather than the *who*.

This is the first kind of story, a story based on interviewing.

Two days later you are told to ask the president of the local Citizens Against Pollution (known, naturally, as CAP) why he opposes the plan. Why does he think it will not reduce local water pollution? Why does he expect the plan advocated by CAP to work better than the commission plan? Will he urge CAP not to support the program?

The resulting story is, in journalistic jargon, an interview story. Its content may overlap that of the first story, but its essence will be different. It will be an opinion story. As a reporter you will have sought opinion from somebody qualified to make informed comment; your emphasis will be on the judgment and attitudes expressed by the source, not on the already-reported facts. (Combination of the two approaches will receive attention in Chapter 18, Interpretive Reporting.)

Interview stories take many shapes; the three common types are:

1. The news interview, a form that provides competent illumination (background fact or expert or qualified opinion) on a topic current in the news
2. The personality interview, whose purpose is to let the interviewees reveal their individuality through their own words
3. The symposium interview, in which the views, attitudes or knowledge of a number of people—sometimes a large number—are reported

NEWS INTERVIEWS

The CAP interview suggested above has the three essential characteristics of the news interview:

1. It deals with a topic in current news.
2. Its source, the interviewee, is qualified to explain, amplify or throw light that facts so far reported don't shed. The source should be—by expertise, training, position or status—one in whom the audience will have confidence.
3. It adds significantly to public knowledge or understanding of the subject. It enlightens, expands, debunks, views with alarm or hope. It offers depth or context not before made available.

The importance of this kind of news is clear. No one in the complex 20th century, as Chapter 1 pointed out, is well enough informed to evaluate, explain or even digest more than a few of the facts in the news. More and more it has become news media responsibility to provide background for public understanding (as Joseph P.

Whence the Interview?

The interview is an essential tool of journalism today. It was not always so. Soon after James Gordon Bennett "invented" it in 1836, a London newspaper called it "degrading to the interviewer, disgusting to the interviewee, and tiresome to the public." The intellectual magazine *Nation* said that it generally comes from "two humbugs, a hack politician and a reporter." Much great journalism of the 20th century, however, is interview journalism. Outstanding reporters like Henry W. Grady, Lincoln Steffens, Eric Sevareid, James B. Reston, William Safire, Woodward and Bernstein, and many others have depended on it. Studs Terkel and Charles Kuralt have made it a tool to take readers to places and minds they could never reach otherwise.

Lyford puts it, "to write about the subliminal influences that are powerfully conditioning society but that do not fall within conventional definitions of news").

When war breaks out between Arabs and Israelis, a reporter goes to a recognized authority on Mideast affairs for a competent interpretation. When the home-town baseball franchise is sold down the river, leading sports promoters, perhaps along with local bankers, retailers, motelkeepers and fans, are asked for comment. When a fire kills elderly residents of a nursing home in the next county, views and facts about comparable dangers locally are sought from county, city, arson, welfare and health authorities.

Such reportorial efforts develop news interviews. The three characteristics are present: a topic in the current news; interviewees whose competence will be generally accepted; the search for light that throws clouded facts into understandable relief.

Step by step through a news interview A reporter finds this assignment on the daily run sheet:

> Dr. Ivan Meyer, the urban sociologist from the U of California, is visiting here next week. See whether he'll talk about the effect of moving 300 new paper mill families into town. Will it dislocate our business patterns? our social balance? Since housing is so tight, what would Meyer advise—suburban development, condominiums, scattered apartments? Do nothing?

Preparation for an interview is much like that for covering a speech. But knowing the subject is a more pressing need than it is in speech reporting. In speech reporting you can go to the library or to an authority if you haven't understood the talk or some of its references. Sometimes this kind of second look is possible after an interview; but there is a compelling difference: You have to steer the interview, and do it with questions that will neither make you look feebleminded nor turn off your interviewee. What you get will depend on what you ask. You're on your own.

The reporter in this case knows something about urban housing from college sociology; he may learn more at a library. He knows from advance stories the incoming industry's plans for housing its workers. The newspaper's reference library yields information about the city's recent housing problems. Calls to real estate dealers and contractors update the information (and perhaps provide tips for later stories). Periodical and book references on suburbia, social movement and urban problems may help. The reporter ends with an understanding of the problem in broad and local implications.

Obit

Obit is short for "obituary." In newsrooms it means not only the published biography of one who has died but also any detailed account of a career, prepared in advance ready for instant use. The Associated Press maintains a "live" file of some 500 obits.

An interview is sharply personal, one-to-one; its success may depend on establishment of rapport. Rapport in turn usually depends heavily on what the reporters know about the individuals they are to meet.

The reporter uses the newspaper's library, the public library, telephone chats with Meyer's host and other local contacts to provide a thorough "obit." Meyer, it develops, is 47 years old; born in Poland, educated at MIT. He has traveled widely, has several honorary degrees and has written half a dozen books. The reporter runs quickly through one titled *The Doom of the City.* Meyer is on leave from his teaching post to serve as a consultant on housing projects. He has sometimes shown annoyance at reporters who, he asserts, "never quote me accurately." He was New England golf champion for two years during college. He has exacted from his host a promise that there will be "no cocktail brawls with more than six brawlers."

The reporter finds his questions taking shape. How does the hypothesis of *The Doom of the City* fit this city and its recent population trends? Can instant growth be absorbed by normal school, business and social facilities? How have similar cities met similar problems? What about the Realtors Institute proposal that new families be scattered throughout the city and suburbs rather than concentrated in a new subdivision? Are there transportation problems? How long does it take a community to assimilate this large an influx?

These questions ought to lead to a meaty story or suggest other approaches. But there remains the problem of persuading Meyer, known to be less than cordial to reporters, to grant the interview. The reporter decides on the direct approach. He telephones Meyer's prospective host:

> This is Salerno of the *Herald.* I'd like to talk with Dr. Meyer about what the new paper mill families will do to the city. . . . Yes, a real problem. We think Dr. Meyer may have some of the answers. . . . Yes, I know it's a social visit. But if he could give us about an hour . . . I've heard that. What I'm hoping is that I'll be one of the reporters he thinks he can trust. . . . Perhaps an hour before he goes to the golf club?

Thus the groundwork is laid.

The Smaller the Tougher

A paradox well known to journalists is that it's often the little man rather than the big who makes interviews hard. Public figures of stature are accustomed to reporters; they usually understand public relations and are confident that the more they help a reporter the better the results. The man who has never been interviewed may be overcautious or self-important. So may the one who has just been kicked upstairs, whether to a carpeted corner office or as principal dogcatcher.

A matter to which every reporter has to give thought is the setting of the interview. Where should it be staged? Experience has evolved some road signs:

- It's usually best to make the interview a twosome. If more are present, there may be distractions, and the interviewee may not be as relaxed and responsive as he would without observers. He also might be less honest and direct in his comments.
- In delicate cases it's a good thing to have witnesses (perhaps the photographer who goes along on the assignment). Sometimes people don't like what they've said when they see it in print; sometimes they deny that they said it. A tape recorder may come in handy.
- Interviews over a cup of coffee or a mug of beer, in a restaurant or cafe, have advantages but also hazards. It's usually easy to get into relaxed conversation in such a setting. On the other hand, you're subject to interruptions: the waiter, friends, Muzak, noisy kids at the next table.
- A home or hotel room may be best. The golf club is relaxing, but the interviewee isn't there to be interviewed—he's there to play golf. He may cut you short to get to the tee.

The reporter decides to try for a meeting at the home of the host. Normally he would telephone for an appointment, but this time he decides on a note as an ice-breaker:

> We're going to have 300 new families in our city next year, and the *Herald* would like to give its readers a preview of what this may mean—both to the new families and to those here now. *The Doom of the City* suggests that we may be in for a hard time if we don't plan things right.
>
> I'm doing a story for the *Herald* on this, and I'd like very much to include your views. I'll telephone Tuesday about an appointment.

This approach, the reporter hopes, will indicate that he knows something about the subject. His stratagem works. On the phone

"I Said It—But . . ."

News sources sometimes don't know (or pretend they didn't) when they're talking for publication. Even when reporters identify themselves carefully (the risk is most acute in a telephone interview), an interviewee may not be fully aware that he's talking on the record. "Certainly I said it," such a source may complain. "But I didn't know it would be printed."

The remedy is simple. Sharp and clear identification as the interview starts; repetition if there's doubt; and direct request for permission to use quotations. Open diplomacy is a prime reportorial weapon.

Meyer says, "Come over at 9:30 tomorrow morning—we'll have an hour to ourselves . . ."

At 9:30 the reporter is seated in a comfortable living room, facing a tanned man in casual slacks. The initial lead comes from the costume. "You've kept up your golf, I see."

Meyer responds warmly: "Yes indeed—heart attack insurance, my doctor calls it."

The reporter follows the theme for a minute. The easy mood confirmed, he shifts to business.

"Dr. Meyer, I've noticed that you're retained by a number of cities as a consultant on housing and city planning. We were wondering at the paper whether anything like that might happen here."

"Strictly a personal visit," Meyer says. "Fact is, I don't know much about the local situation."

This is a cue for the reporter. He talks for several minutes, answering occasional queries; he pulls a city map from his pocket and refers to it, to Meyer's evident satisfaction. Finally:

"I see some problems," Meyer says. "But they don't look insuperable to me, if the city council . . .

The interview is launched, and the reporter may already have the theme for his story: Problems not too tough. Exploratory questions confirm the theme; Meyer develops it, under the reporter's lead, so as to tie it to local circumstance. The reporter's task now is to sustain the flow of information and comment, to hold it on course should it begin to stray, to design questions that will draw understandable and quotable answers. He doesn't refer to the list of prepared questions in his pocket—to do so might dam the stream.

The interview well under way, the reporter starts to jot down notes. He watches closely to find whether his moving pencil is a distraction; he notices that, as Meyer goes into statistics, he slows up to watch the notetaking. The reporter employs a time-tested device: Handing his pad to Meyer, he says, "Would you check the figures?" Meyer examines them, hands them back; now he ignores the pencil.

The reporter keeps an eye on his watch. When his hour is end-

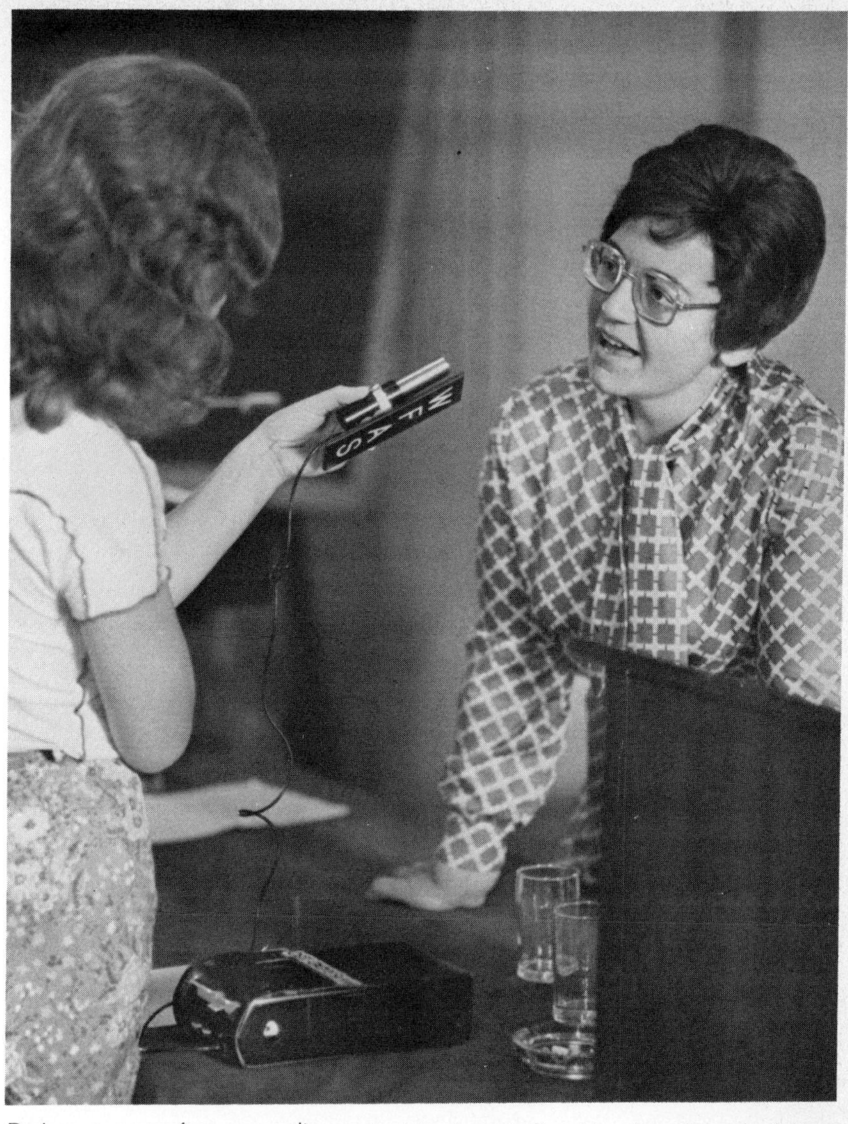

During a news conference, a radio reporter interviews Lt. Gov. Mary Anne Krupsak of New York. *(Mimi Forsyth photo from Monkmeyer Press Photo Service)*

ing, he prepares to close the interview. Would Meyer say that such-and-such subtopics are the ones to emphasize? Are there significant angles they haven't touched? Would Meyer be willing to check the story by telephone if the reporter finds himself in doubt?

Promptly at 10:30 he leaves. "Thanks again," he says. "I hope you shatter par."

Characteristics of interview stories This case history presents no out-of-the-ordinary problems, either in conduct of the interview or in writing the story. Thanks to preparation and getting Meyer's

When the Interviewee Don't Talk Good . . .

What does a writer do when his news sources dot their English with "at this point in time," "not to worry," "viable," "run it up the flagpole," and "thankfully it didn't rain"? Or when they say "of he and I," "the media is," "the varsity shot their bolt," or "disagreement as to whom is invited"? A quotation is not literally accurate unless it is precise (see page 248). But it is good judgment to ask whether verbatim language—incorrect syntax, precise word choice, vulgarism, diction that doesn't say what the speaker intends—is always good reporting.

Precise quotation becomes of special importance in a personality story. You don't paint a true picture of hillbilly or ambassador if you don't portray the way he or she talks.

counsel, the reporter can guide the elements of the story smoothly into place. Not many interviews in a reporter's daily round are so thoroughly planned as this one—time may not permit that. Often an interview has to be handled on the fly, which is one reason that errors occur and that questions go unasked. The more work you can do in advance, the farther you'll go with your story.

The form of the interview story is substantially that of the speech story: summary lead, usually in indirect discourse; development of individual subtopics, in order of decreasing importance; alternation of direct quotation and paraphrase, the direct for elaboration and detail of major subtopics or for forceful or colorful language, the indirect for summarizing passages. In her small book *Some Observations on the Art of Narrative* the British novelist Phyllis Bentley describes similar alternation. She calls it "scene and summary" as applied to fiction. (A half-hour with this book would profit any writer.)

Even more than in the speech story, the personal mannerisms and appearance of the central figure deserve attention. In the interview example above the reporter had to decide whether to describe Meyer's athletic air, his easy manner, the way he fingered a golf club as he talked. Would such details add meaning or readability to the story? Would they distract?

The gain in readability is likely to be considerable (in a personality interview the gain is doubled). Most reporters writing major interviews think such detail worth more than the space it costs. In routine interviews, and in stories "based on interviewing," its use is small.

If a reporter were to record the lessons learned from interviewing experience, the notes might run something like this:

- Always ask specific questions. Don't generalize. An open-end question is likely to get an answer that takes off in all directions. Rather than ask "Does a sudden influx of population hurt a city?" try something like "Can a city of this size—about 80,000—come up with housing for 300 new families?".

- The interviewer's job is to lead the conversation, but not to monopolize it.
- Hold it on course. Don't let the interviewee spend too much time on his trip to the Canary Islands.
- Remember that nobody *has* to give you an interview. You and your audience are more in his debt than he is in yours. Impose on his time only as much as you must. Usually a news source with anything to say is one on whom there are plenty of other demands.
- Be suspicious of the people who are begging to be interviewed. They may have horses they'd like to trade. Watch for their interests and prejudices; make sure you know what they have to gain from public attention. It's good journalism to give your readers this perspective, whether it's to the interviewee's advantage or not.
- You can ask "good" questions, you can ask "bad." Good questions are those you've thought out, those that follow the subject, those that help the interviewee to develop a thread or theme. Bad questions are those that waste time, that wander, that don't relate to your interviewee's topic. Too often sportswriters ask a pitcher who gave up one hit in the ninth after two were out: "How did it feel to lose the no-hitter?" (The usual answer: "I'd have liked to make it, but the important thing is winning for the team.") Banal answers follow banal questions.

A psychologist-columnist for the Gannett string of newspapers warns against questions that antagonize the interviewee—a tactic that doesn't win prizes. But once in a while, when interviewees are being cagy or stubborn or unnecessarily close-lipped, questions that raise their blood pressure may detonate precisely the answers the reporter wants.

SOURCES OF INTERVIEW ERROR

A Stanford University journalism teacher, David L. Grey, several years ago asked reporters and their news sources to identify causes of error in news stories. All agreed that failure by reporters to get advance information led the list. But Grey's report points to other causes of error:

> After lack of background information, reporters and news sources agreed, come news desk and editing practices . . . The news sources cited "sensationalism, overdramatization, and overemphasis in phrasing" and lack of personal contact with reporters; the reporters added lack of time and, with considerable candor, a certain amount of reportorial "laziness and incompetence."

Dr. Grey comments:

> . . . it is significant that news sources cite "sensationalism" and lack of content, and that reporters emphasize lack of time . . . Reporters might well give the lack of contact factor more attention, if for no other reason than that news sources consider it important.

The Grey study suggests three remedies: that reporters ask news source advice about appropriate emphases (whether they accept the advice or not); that they take time to prepare for interviews; and that they work closely with editors, to guard against headline inaccuracies.

A helpful study of the techniques and products of interviews is reported in *The Interview, or The Only Wheel in Town* by Webb and Salanik (see Related Reading, page 297). It gives suggestions for reportorial behavior in interviews and tips on question formation, the values and dangers of leading questions, the influence of "interviewer expectation" on interviewee responses, and even the salutary effect of well-placed "mm-hmms" as the interviewer talks. The reprint of Allen Barton's tongue-in-cheek analysis of the different ways to ask "Did you kill your wife?" is both constructive and entertaining.

Another kind of approach to interviewing practice comes from studies by psychologists and sociologists. Designed to aid social workers in interviews, Annette Garrett's slim volume (see Related Reading) applies aptly to what reporters do.

Other causes of interview error are suggested by reporters' experience as well as by sources like those above:

Intentional falsehood For hundreds of reasons—most commonly self-interest—interviewees may lie. For instance:

- Falsification to cover complicity in shameful or criminal behavior
- Reluctance to admit having been on relief
- Fear that the truth will "look bad" to family, friends, or employer
- Hope of looking wealthy, well-traveled, or well-educated
- Desire to get public attention, "free publicity"
- Distrust of the reporter or of the use to which the story is to be put
- Attempt to tell the reporter what "the reporter wants to hear"

Faulty memory Passage of time may dim interviewees' recollections. They may have had little interest in the topic or event; or wishful thinking may disrupt memory.

Lack of information Respondents may have little information, or less than they think they have.

Misunderstanding Interviewees may not grasp the questions (which may be the fault of cloudy questioning). They may not perceive the questions in the right context (the reporter's responsibility).

Other interviewer missteps Reporters may use jargon or terminology that confuses their respondents. They may let personal bias misinterpret answers; they may antagonize interviewees. They may not be persistent enough; they may try to force an interview into a preconceived mold; they may close it before it is finished.

Experience teaches a reporter that people sometimes find it distasteful or difficult to talk on some topics but easy and congenial on others. Few people like to say how much money they make; they often conceal facts in personal history that they consider shameful. They are often shaky on dates: Was it in 1975 that the family went to San Diego, or 1974 (it may have been neither)?

On the other hand, people usually respond accurately to questions about their ages, education, nationality and professional or business careers. They can tell you the names of their children, if not always the ages. They know the make of the cars they drive (but not always the models or whether they use lead-free gas). They are usually able, if not always willing, to be accurate in talking about matters of constant or personal interest to them.

Checking back Reporters sometimes ask news sources to review stories for which they have given information. Is this "good" practice?

The answer is "yes" when a reporter has promised to permit review (which does not imply permission to alter the story). It is "yes" when the reporter has doubts about accuracy of fact or meaning. Often a telephone query will clear up questions.

Checking back may raise problems. Some news sources make demands reporters cannot accept. A source may dislike the wording of a story (note the criticism of phrasing reported in the Grey study), or may ask that one element be emphasized, another played down or omitted. A scientist may want a story written in jargon instead of language a lay audience can understand.

The newswriter's obligation is to assure accuracy and the likelihood that a story will carry a balanced impression. Beyond this there is no compulsion to accept a news source's comments. If reportorial or desk judgment differs from the interviewee's, qualified journalistic judgment should usually prevail. Reporters and editors are representatives of the public, not of the news source; their expertise, in contrast to that of the people they have interviewed, is in effective ways to reach their audiences. Their concern is to inform and explain, whereas the source may be driven by self-centered interest. Often news sources look on a news story not as an instrument to inform a broad audience but rather as a self-mirror; they may be more concerned with the opinion of fellow professionals than they are with communication to a wide public. Or they may have an impulse less acceptable (to journalists), such as self-promotion.

There is also the matter of tactics. When reporter and source cannot agree, some reporters may choose to risk the source's anger, even though it may block an information channel they'd like to use again. Factors in the decision are how important the story is to the public; how much the source's demands would weaken it; and the fact that the pace of reporting often allows little time for back-checking. Reporters meet the problem variously. Some fear that checking back, once permitted, may become expected practice. Others believe that its advantages outweigh its hazards. Circumstances determine procedures, they say.

INTERVIEW STORIES FOR STUDY

The excerpts that follow, above average in competence, have been chosen not for excellence but as demonstrations of different news interview patterns. The first, from a wire-service story, appeared at the time President Ford faced the problem of amnesty for draft dodgers and deserters.

VAIL, Colo. (AP)—President Ford said again yesterday he will take another look at the question of amnesty for Vietnam-era deserters and draft dodgers, but it was not clear whether he would take any action.

White House aides said they could give no guidance on what Ford plans to do.

As the President took off on his daily ski run yesterday, a reporter asked him to dispel the confusion that has arisen over his promise to the widow of Michigan Sen. Philip Hart to look into her request that he grant blanket amnesty before leaving office.

"There's no confusion whatsoever," Ford replied. "I said at her request that I would take a look at it and that's what I'm going to do."

He was asked if it was just a courtesy gesture to Mrs. Hart, who was a vehement Vietnam War protester, or if he really meant to make a thorough review of the issue. Ford replied: "The words speak for themselves."

When he returned from two and a half hours on the ski slopes, reporters asked Ford again about amnesty. He told them, "You don't have to make stories about something that is very plain and very direct."

He said he had promised to take a look at it and that was that.

Questioned whether he has asked the Justice Department to start work on it, Ford said, "We have started the process."[1]

[*The story continues with recap of Mrs. Hart's views and a brief account of the President's day.*]

The first two paragraphs summarize all of the story except the background and secondary materials with which it ends. Note the persistence of the reporters and of the President. Ford makes only one informative concession, "We have started the process." The story illustrates the alternation of direct and indirect discourse. Its repetition of the reporters' questions is unusual, but effective.

The next story employs a different pattern. Statement of the reason for the interview, which is personalized in the leisurely fashion of sportswriting, precedes the interview itself. This is followed by what might be called a second news interview on a second subject; thus the story breaks in two in the middle.

MANKATO, Minn.—When last we left Fran Tarkenton he was in a crowded locker room at the Rose Bowl in Pasadena, Calif., chatting with reporters about the highlights of the Minnesota Vikings' last football game.

It seems like only yesterday, but then time, like Tark, is not prone to stand still. Already the Vikings and a number of young men who would like to be Vikings are engrossed in their annual summer festival at Mankato State University.

Tarkenton, as usual, kept himself busy while waiting for the action to start in Mankato, but apparently some of the reports of what he has been doing or saying have not been entirely accurate.

It was good, then, to sit down with the old (for a football player) passing champ and sort out some of the half truths that complicate the public's image of any celebrity.

The thing that seemed to trouble fans most was a midwinter report that Tarkenton, in his final couple of years with the team, did not intend to be of much help in breaking in the new rookie quarterback, Tommy Kramer.

"Training quarterbacks ain't my job" was the way a dispatch from somewhere in Texas quoted Tarkenton back in May.

"That's not what I said," said Tarkenton, "and I'm not concerned with it anyway. The credibility of the written press is well known to most people. Local press excepted, of course. We've got good reporters here."

So, apparently, while Tarkenton does not plan to hold master classes for young Kramer, he will not object if some of his finesse and skill rub off on the eager student.

"He's a nice kid and he's got a good football background and that's good," said Tarkenton. "I think he'll come along just fine if we can keep too many people from trying to tell him how to do things.

"He's in a good situation here. He's got two veteran quarterbacks to look at, observe every day. Bobby Lee and I aren't going to keep any secrets from him. There are certain things you can't explain unless you've been there yourself.

"But it ain't gonna be what I tell him or what Burns (Jerry, offensive coordinator) or Bud (Grant, head coach) tells him. It's got to come from Kramer himself, and what he learns won't be seen the first day or the first week or maybe the first year."

Which brings up the question of just how long Tarkenton will be around to set an example.[2]

[*The second half of the story goes into Tarkenton's plans for post-football years.*]

[2] Copyright © 1977 by the Minneapolis *Tribune*. Reprinted by permission.

On election day in New York, a reporter catches candidate Edward I. Koch (he later became mayor) on the sidewalk for an on-the-spot interview. *(Hilda Bijur photo from Monkmeyer Press Photo Service)*

The story leaves questions:

- You do not learn the major theme until paragraph 5. What follows is in standard news interview form. Does the topic statement come too late?
- Is the attention the writer draws to himself before getting down to business justified? Does it add or detract?
- Could the clumsy use of parenthetical material (paragraphs 4, 12) be avoided? How?
- The second clause of the third paragraph is unrelated (though linked by a conjunction) to the first. Can you repair this non sequitur?

The gasoline shortage in the United States was at a peak of public interest at the time the story below was published. The first nine paragraphs constitute a news interview with authoritative comments. Then, like the Ford story above, the writer moves to background and supporting material—facts and opinion related to the lead topic but not presented by the interviewee:

WASHINGTON, Dec. 31 (AP)—Motorists soon will face longer lines for less gasoline at service stations than they experienced over the Christmas-New Year's holiday, an administration source said today. He said the gasoline shortage would really make itself felt by the last part of January.

"It's going to get a lot worse because we're going to make less gasoline. We're getting down to where we're talking about eight to 10 gallons of gasoline per week per driver.

"We're still riding off Arab oil, and we've been drawing on our stocks, but we can't continue it," the source continued. "No more ships are coming and we can't draw down on our stocks any further."

His comments were made as motorists experienced their second consecutive holiday weekend of long lines and empty pumps. Fewer automobiles than usual for a New Year's weekend took to the highways and there were reports in Washington that turnpike traffic was down sharply.

An investigation was started by the Federal Energy Office and four East Coast states. It concerned reports that oil tankers were waiting offshore for oil prices to rise before unloading their cargoes.

New York, New Jersey, Pennsylvania, and Connecticut had begun or were preparing to begin investigations. However, the administration spokesman and spokesmen for the ports of Boston, New York, Philadelphia and New Haven said they did not think there was much to the reports.

The administration source put current gasoline stocks at about 200,000,000 barrels, enough for about 30 days at the current rate of consumption, 6,700,000 barrels a day.

He said that if stocks drop below 180,000,000 barrels the result would be shortages more severe than those that have occurred—"spot shortages, where a city is out of gasoline," he said.

"People still don't believe there's a shortage. They feel it's a conspiracy, a way to raise prices and so forth. We're trying to tell them that come January or February it's going to be rough and that's all there is to it unless driving is cut back."

Demand for gasoline this weekend resulted in the closing of numerous stations that had planned to be open today.

Before the weekend began, service station associations and motor clubs had predicted that 75 percent or more of the stations would be open today and closed tomorrow, New Year's Day. High demand emptied pumps on Saturday at many stations, and new supplies will not arrive before Wednesday.

Reports of price gouging kept local and federal officials on the lookout. The extent of illegal prices was not determined, although dozens of complaints were found to be valid.

In Philadelphia, Internal Revenue Service agents said they had found 23 stations overcharging and that all agreed to roll back prices.

Distributors gave service stations in Arizona and Oregon their January fuel allocations only to ease shortages.

Twenty-three business and industry trade associations announced the formation of an Energy Users Council. Its purpose is to keep business and industry informed on energy policies and to bring business problems to the attention of Government officials. . . .[3]

Does the anonymity of the interviewee, "an administration source," weaken the story?

In the next story an angry political candidate lets off steam (names have been changed). The interview illuminates an aspect of current news:

Black activist Tony Sharpness strongly criticized City Council President Robert Hoover Thursday and said he plans to challenge Hoover for the right to run as the Democratic council candidate from the 5th Ward.

Sharpness, joined by representatives of the Urban League, the NAACP and several other black community organizations, said he intends to test Hoover's electoral strength at the party nominating convention Saturday and in the September primary.

Hoover told supporters last month that he would not seek a fourth term because his heart wasn't in the council anymore. He announced Wednesday, however, that he had changed his mind and decided to run after "many, many good people in my ward, in my party, and in the community at large" had begged him not to step down.

But there is suspicion among 5th Ward black leaders that Hoover reentered the race because the party leadership feared a Republican victory if a black candidate were to run in his place.

"I waited patiently until Mr. Hoover said he had no interest in serving for another term before announcing myself as a candidate," Sharpness said, "and I find it somewhat suspicious that less than 48 hours after I made my decision to run he should announce that he's changed his mind."

Sharpness said he feels betrayed by the council president, and said Hoover's indecision shows "shallow concern for the interests of the voters of the 5th Ward" and a lack of sincerity.

"I think we must ask ourselves," he said, "is this man for real, and is his candidacy for real?"

Sharpness also criticized some "national politicians" who, he said, are "dabbling in 5th Ward politics as they've dabbled in the politics of the 7th Congressional District in the past." It had been reported that both of the state's U.S. senators were involved in the move to persuade Hoover to run.

Most of the other candidates have withdrawn from consideration in the wake of Hoover's announcement, but Sharpness said he intends to stand firm despite some private doubts "whether the democratic process is going to be observed" at Saturday's endorsement convention.

"I have never been a quitter," he said. "And I have not grown tired."

Q-AND-A INTERVIEWS

The direct question-and-answer interview is no longer a rarity, partly because the tape recorder makes it easy and accurate (and sometimes long-winded). A tape must be edited to cut verbosity, take out "ums" and "y'knows," and delete passages that do not sup-

[3] Copyright © 1974 by the Associated Press. Reprinted by permission.

port the story theme. But literal fidelity can be guaranteed, as Watergate showed.

Patterns for Q-and-A interviews have no set rules. Eight introductory paragraphs preceding the Q-and-A passage below are followed by two columns of verbatim material. A tape recorder was used. The story is distinguished by literal reproduction of conversational mannerisms—repetitions, short sentences, sentence fragments, even the loose "like" of vernacular speech. Here are the opening paragraphs of the Q-and A section:

> Q. What do you think bothers adolescent girls the most?
> A. What I hear over and over is that people do not like to listen to them. I do not say that it is only the girls. But I have heard a lot of this from the girls. They say people do not listen to them, especially the adults. It is not just listening, but also understanding.
> Q. Is it the parents who are not listening or just adults in general?
> A. It is a general complaint against the adult world. Most adults don't take them seriously. There is rarely a serious discussion. I was working with some people in youth organizations one time and I said, why don't you just sit down with the young people and ask them some serious questions. Like, if you were going to change the world, what would you do to change it? These people said later it was an absolute revelation to them. The young people were so delighted that someone asked.

Three hours' conversation, in two sittings, produced this story. The interviewee called it "totally accurate and understanding."

In the interview from which the following excerpt is taken, questions and answers were dry-cleaned before publication, either by ellipses or by clearing away conversational idiosyncracies:

"Literary" Interviews

Interviews with contemporary literary figures have been used skillfully by the *Paris Review,* a magazine of arts and letters. Members of the *Review* staff or invited writers, often in teams of two, have conducted thoughtful but sprightly and entertaining interviews. Intensive preparation is characteristic of the interviewers' approach. Many of these interviews are published in *Writers at Work,* edited by Malcolm Cowley.

A variant—an interview with Vladimir Nabokov shortly after the appearance of one of his novels—used questions submitted to Nabokov in advance. A report of the questions and written answers, supplemented by comments by George Feifer, the novelist-interviewer, appeared in the *Saturday Review* of Nov. 11, 1976.

John Gilbert Graham flatly denies planting a bomb on an airliner which killed 44 persons, including his mother. He hints his mother herself might have planted the explosive.

My questions were direct and straightforward. Graham looked straight at me with his penetrating gray-green eyes when answering many of the questions.

But when it came to such questions as whether he had experience in handling explosives, Graham would turn away or look down in his lap, his heavy lips pursing in annoyance.

Graham, dressed in the gray denim coveralls of the jail, sat with his hands folded in his lap in the office of Warden Gorden Dolliver.

Q. Jack, I understand the FBI obtained a signed statement from you, admitting you placed a bomb on that plane . . .

A. Yes, I signed a statement. But it's not true. They told me they were going to put my wife in jail, and I'd better get it straightened out myself.

Q. You mean, they used duress—they kept questioning you until you confessed?

A. Well, they started about noon that Sunday and didn't stop until I signed a confession about 4 a.m., the next morning. Oh, they took me out for dinner once and gave me drinks of water and milk . . .

Q. They say you forged the insurance policies on your mother that night when the plane crashed. Can you straighten that out?

A. I didn't. My mother signed them. I made out three—one for myself, one for my sister and one for my aunt.

Q. How much were they for?

A. I don't remember. There was a foul-up on the machine . . .

Q. Did you put a present—or a bundle of dynamite—in your mother's luggage?

A. I didn't put anything in her luggage. I only bought some straps to put around the luggage . . . I don't want to discuss the present.

Q. Did you have a premonition of your mother's death before you had been formally notified of it?

A. I didn't—she had. She called everybody she could think of before she left . . .

Q. Do you mean your mother might have planted the dynamite in her own suitcase to take her own life? Has your mother ever mentioned taking her life?

A. I won't answer that . . .

Q. How do you think that dynamite got on the plane—in your mother's suitcase?

A. I don't remember.

A different method of presenting questions, without intrusion of Qs and As or the reporter, is this one:

> The man stood looking at a rubble-filled hole in the ground. He stooped to pick up a crumpled mailbox. As he turned to his visitor, he spoke.
>
> "That was on the road—100 rods away," he said. "How it got here . . ." You could make out a name on the box: George B. Linsson, Route 7.
>
> "Did the tornado leave you anything else, Mr. Linsson?"
>
> "Just what you see. We weren't at home. When we got back, we didn't have any house . . . didn't have anything."
>
> "How about your neighbors?"
>
> "We were right in the path. Seems as if we got it harder than almost anybody . . ."

"Ever had any previous experience with tornadoes?"
"Not in this part of the country. But we used to live in Kansas, and . . ."

Conference interviews News conferences are interviews with a group of reporters present, sometimes a hundred or more (see Chapter 10). They are more formal than one-to-one interviews, and usually less productive. Reporters dislike working with precisely the same clay that their competitors are using, and they ask questions less freely. But the products, commonly of the news interview type, follow the pattern of the one-to-one story. Here are the opening paragraphs of one such story:

WASHINGTON, D.C. (AP)—With the House set to tackle his energy program this week, President Carter is warning that voluntary energy conservation efforts are probably inadequate.

"The public is not paying attention" to the need to save fuel because there are no visible signs of any impending oil shortage, Carter said.

"I am afraid that a series of crises is going to be a prerequisite to a sincere desire on the part of the American people to quit wasting so much fuel," Carter said.

He said the 1973 oil embargo, the subsequent escalation in petroleum prices, last winter's natural gas shortage, and the current U.S. trade imbalance "are just predictions of what is to come."

The president's remarks were made Friday during a discussion with 26 journalists. A transcript of his comments was made available by the White House on Saturday.

Carter also said:

- He saw no possibility of normalizing U.S. relations with Cuba soon.
- Although he is from the Sunbelt, he believes that too much federal money has been channeled into that area in comparison with other areas of the United States. Suburbs, compared with ghetto areas, have gotten more than their share of federal funds, too, he said.
- He has found the Soviet Union, in "private attitudes toward us, to be very forthcoming and cooperative."

Referring to pleas for voluntary energy conservation, the president said. . . .[4]

Reporting with a capital I A news story may be reduced in effectiveness if its writer injects himself into it. Reporters usually try not to get between the consumer and the news. When a story says "the reporter asked" or "the banker told this writer," attention is drawn to newsgathering mechanics and away from substance. A trademark of the beginning high school journalist is writing about himself: "I really thought I would have a ball when I was assigned to interview Farah Fawcett-Majors."

Letting the reporter into the story may, however, be justified in two circumstances:

[4] Copyright © 1977 by the Associated Press. Reprinted by permission.

1. *When he becomes part of the news.* He delivers the ransom money to the kidnapper; he finds the starving trapper lost in the woods. Even then, he focuses attention on the event rather than on his participation in it.

   Sometimes, it's true, a reporter can't tell the whole story without describing in first-person terms the things seen, heard, felt. The *Twin Cities Journalism Review* was sharply critical of a newspaper whose keep-yourself-out-of-it policy barred one of its writers from revealing that he had sat in on "hostage negotiations" with the jailbreak captors of a farm family. The policy, the *Review* said, "got in the way of coverage of the story." The reporter's suspenseful account of deal-making and the hostages' terrors, showing that he had been on the scene, had been jettisoned in favor of an "objective" but less revealing account. Such a rule is made to be broken once in a while.
2. *When the reporter is a personality of audience interest.* Feature and human-interest writers who have built individual audiences are often privileged to write in first person. Readers of the New York *Daily News* are interested in Jimmy Breslin, its premier columnist, as well as in the events he writes about. Bob Krauss of the Honolulu *Advertiser,* touted by his paper accurately as the "best-known columnist in Hawaii," tells his devoted audience what he sees, thinks, hears as he reports. But neither of these writers used "I" when he was a new reporter. Their skills, their wit, their fresh and perceptive points of view had to be established first.

Some journalists—especially the New Journalists of the 1960s and 1970s, writers like Gay Talese, David Halberstam, Gail Sheehy—call third-person journalism "sterile," "stultifying," "degrading." Dan Wakefield, an accomplished magazine journalist, devotes pages of his book *Between the Lines* to a defense of his decision to "break out of the formulas of the trade." Wakefield is bored, he says, with writing "in lofty omniscience" from the shadows behind the scenes. But Wakefield, like Krauss and Breslin, has proved that he has something to say and the capacity to say it well. That makes a difference.

Wakefield states a personal attitude that should be required of every reporter: impatience with the disguises for the first-person pronoun that are "silly at best and pompously misleading at worst." These are the self-conscious "we," "this paper," "your reporter," such labored circumlocutions as "this scribe," "the author," and—worst of all—"yours truly." The usage "a reporter" is moderately

As a street demonstration goes on, a radio reporter interviews one of the leaders. *(Les Mahon photo from Monkmeyer Press Photo Service)*

successful—no more than moderately because it doesn't really conceal. Usually no such subterfuge is needed.

Interview hazards One interview in a university newspaper opened thus:

> In Israel everyone starves equally. In Iran, 99 percent of the people starve while the rest drive Cadillacs.

A prompt letter from the interviewee complained that the paragraph "conveyed a false impression." It added that "in Israel no one lacks the food essentials" and that in Iran "no one is really starving." The reporter made this comment:

> I had a rough time getting an angle for this story because I thought the interviewee had nothing new to offer—his stuff was largely familiar.

> But he did use the precise words I wrote (I have them in my notes, in quotes, which means that they are verbatim). The story would have protected him if its second paragraph had added, "That was the figurative impression . . ."
>
> I think his complaint legitimate, for he did not intend the words to be taken literally.

A story contrasting the tasks of Democratic and Republican national party chairmen, just after an election, talked convincingly about their views of their responsibilities—convincingly until you became aware that at no point did it appear that the reporter directly interviewed the sources. The story used phrases like "his immediate worry is," "his political judgment is," and "he readily admits that . . ." But it doesn't show how the reporter knew. From an interview? From outside sources? What sources? Background knowledge? Speculation? Though the story says several times "he said" or "he added," it fails to show when the statements were made, or to whom or under what circumstances. And it builds confusion by using present- and past-tense attributions.

These two cases emphasize the imperative that a reporter take nothing for granted. Both reporters went only halfway toward putting readers in their own shoes; both made assumptions of reader knowledge that did not stand up.

Another interviewer mistake—cited elsewhere in this book—is dependence on questions that are worn out, irrelevant or answerable only in timeworn phrases. Examples:

> Did you feel good when you won the lottery?
>
> Is it hot enough for you?
>
> Did you expect to break the record?
>
> Do you think women should smoke?
>
> Would you want to go through a tornado again?

Answers to such questions are rarely worth recording.

"An authoritative source" Reporters learn to put up their guards when news sources ask for anonymity. Disguises like "informed sources," "a department spokesman," "a senior official" or "authoritative circles" say little and occasionally are dishonest. Among the reasons they are in disrepute are these:

1. They are vague and uninformative, even when they are accurate.
2. They can be misused by news sources. A "Defense Department source" who asks that a reporter conceal his identity may

be floating a trial balloon—suggesting a policy move only to test public reaction (if reaction is negative, he can deny saying it). A "highly placed authority" can issue information without taking responsibility for it, and often this kind of information is no better than gossip. Behind every "news leak" there is a source, and when the source is anonymous, the purpose is suspect.

3. They can be misused by reporters. Fiction can masquerade as fact under nonexistent "unnamed sources." Writers who use them may be eager to get to the beach; they may be protecting themselves or others; they may be in the wrong business.
4. Often they fool only the unsophisticated. Benjamin C. Bradlee, executive editor of the Washington *Post*, once complained that "everyone in Washington," including the Soviet ambassador and Red Chinese spies, "knew that a certain reporter"—Bradlee named him—"was quoting Dean Rusk. Everyone, that is, but the readers. Who is conning whom?"
5. They diminish the none-too-robust credibility of the news media.

Columnist Art Buchwald satirized the unnamed-source syndrome at the time the Agnew vice presidency was under attack:

> A highly placed source close to an unidentified attorney general who formerly was secretary of HEW and defense denied that any leaks came from the Justice Department. "We are not the only people in Washington who have unnamed sources."

Sometimes sources "who prefer to remain anonymous" may be protected with justification—for personal safety or as a shield from innocent humiliation or embarrassment. But the device dilutes the impact and meaning of news.

SYMPOSIUM INTERVIEWS

The "symposium interview," which involves not one or two sources but a dozen, a score or a hundred, is an associate member of the interview family. Normally its topic is of enough current concern that interviewees can be found literally on any busy corner. The topic may be serious or frivolous; it may affect peoples' pocketbooks, personal comfort, general security or funny bones. Typical topics are the proposed gasoline tax: Do you approve? Or the hottest week in thirty years: How do you keep cool? Or the collapse of a threat of a general strike: Would you have struck had it been called?

Interviewees for a symposium story are chosen not as authorities but as people who have "typical" views; their opinions, added together, may suggest how a news situation is affecting a community or group. The opinion of one of them alone wouldn't be worth reporting; cumulative weight makes the story. The story may be fluff: The purpose of the "how do you keep cool?" question is not to develop studied generalizations about lowering body heat but rather to laugh a little at summer discomfort.

Some symposiums, however, bring together views that carry weight. The New York *Times* once assigned correspondents throughout the United States to ask Teamsters Union members their opinions of alleged misconduct by key union officers; the reporters talked with truckers in New York, Denver, Jersey City, Minneapolis, Chicago and a dozen other cities. The comments justified a lead saying that "sentiment for the ouster of key officers . . . is growing among the rank and file of the giant truck union." Sometimes responses from a representative group of average citizens tell more than many pages of speeches in the *Congressional Record*. (Notice that the *Times* offered a trend rather than a precise measure of opinion.)

The distinction between authoritative response and average response is commonly a difference between news interviews and symposium interviews. Though most news interviews report the contributions of only one interviewee, some may draw material from multiple sources. In a campus newspaper's story about liquor in the stands at a football game (drinking at a game violated several laws), comments were collected from three student drinkers, a ticket taker, the ticket manager and the chief of campus police. All were "expert" on one phase of the subject or another.

Some observations on developing symposium interviews are in order:

1. Finding interviewees is rarely a problem, though none are identified in advance. If you're working on the how-to-keep-cool or the gas tax story, you station yourself at a busy street corner and query the first 25 passersby you can buttonhole. The general strike story demands a different approach—attending a labor mass meeting, visiting a big factory as the shifts change, or finding some other locale where you won't waste time on irrelevant responses.
2. There's no rule about number of responses. If your purpose is only to report what a few people say, without drawing a conclusion (as in the familiar "inquiring reporter" features), you can stop with half a dozen. But if you propose to develop a story that will reflect a general attitude, you may need to question a hundred. If your purpose is to entertain, you continue asking ques-

tions until you have enough "good" answers to flesh out an amusing yarn.

Whatever the number, it's always necessary to let your reader know how big it is and of what composition. If you assert that "four-fifths of the city's taxpayers believe property assessments are too high" on the basis of interviews with 10 citizens, you're writing nonsense. But if you've interviewed 100 passersby at a street corner and find 80 holding one opinion, you have a basis for writing that "most of 100 local residents interviewed at Main and Fourth streets yesterday said that . . ." or "many local people say that . . ." And haphazard surveys on Wall Street and in Harlem may produce wildly different results.

3. If generalization is to be justifiable, you must ask each person substantially the same question in substantially the same words and manner so as to get classifiable and comparable answers. If you approach interviewees in different ways, you'll get responses to different concepts, and you'll end with an amorphous collection of comments adding up to nothing.

   You not only ask the same questions, but you make them simple. You don't say, "If the authorized agents of your horizontally organized fellow workers, by the legal right they possess, issue an order directing all members of affiliated associations to absent themselves from their places of employment, would you probably have the inclination to conform?" You ask, "Would you strike if the union orders it?"

   You design questions that don't suggest answers. The question above may be answered either "yes" or "no." But if you say,

---

Symposiums on a Big Scale

The public opinion polls and surveys that have become fixtures of modern journalism—Gallup, Harris and others—are symposium interviews refined by social science methods. Knowledge of their procedures, though they cannot be duplicated in day-by-day journalism, ought to be part of every reporter's equipment. Philip Meyer's *Precision Journalism,* written for both working press and journalism students, contains information and counsel on this and other forms of modern "quantitative" reporting.

A caution: Symposium interviews, which are carried out by one or two reporters in an hour or an afternoon, are not scientific measurements of public opinion. Some newspapers carefully reserve the word "poll" for such studies as those of Gallup, Quayle and Harris. Lesser attempts to gather collective opinions are commonly called "surveys," and stories about them should make clear what they are or aren't. One reporter assigned to write a story on what he considered a flimsy body of information proposed this lead for it: "Not that it means anything, but 57 percent of the 36 people interviewed in an utterly unscientific telephone survey last night said . . ." The lead did not appear in just that form.

"When you became a union member, you agreed to obey a properly issued strike call. If such a call were issued today, would you obey?" It might be hard for some respondents to answer negatively.

4. A simple summary lead is often the best choice for a symposium story. When interviewees show substantial agreement, the lead is easy and obvious. It's not much more difficult when they disagree, for disagreement may be as newsy as consensus.

The lead of a frothy story usually reflects its character:

> A week of sizzling sun has driven local citizens to drink (usually lemonade) or to six baths a day.

Near the lead, if not in it, should appear the news peg that justifies the story (this is news interview technique as well):

> And there's no letup in sight. Yesterday's 98-degree peak will be repeated today and tomorrow.

Someplace soon in the story should appear a brief explanation of how the facts were gathered:

> The things people are doing to forget the heat were described by 20 local residents asked this morning by a Herald reporter, "How do you keep cool?"

5. One of the virtues of the symposium interview is that it's specific. It reports what men and women think or feel or do, and you can bring the people to life by telling who they are. This means that you:

   a. Identify them precisely whenever you can. Names are often used, especially names of those you quote exactly. Or you can make them come alive by writing that "a redheaded workman who had shed his shirt said . . ."
   b. Use direct quotations freely.
   c. Support your generalizations with specific evidence.

6. Try to follow one pattern throughout a story. If you start with a name, continue doing it:

> Joe Antonio, 2179 Robisdaile Ave.—I wouldn't strike if they gave me the plant.
> Melissa Trapp, 433 S. Pittern St.—I'm ready to strike any time they tell me to.

But if you start with a different pattern, stick to it:

> "I wouldn't strike if they gave me the plant," said Joe Antonio, 2179 Robisdaile Ave.
> But Melissa Trapp, 433 S. Pittern St., said she is "ready to strike any time" they tell her to.

The following symposium interview, from an enterprising high school paper, illustrates some of these suggestions.

Students in the three local high schools appear to have no doubts as to whom to blame for teen-age "delinquency."

"Blame the teen-agers themselves," they say.

At least that's the opinion of 72 out of 100 of them queried this week by the Schoolmate.

But they'd don't think it's a black-and-white matter. Here are some of the differing views they offer:

- Most teen-agers are "all right." They shouldn't all be held responsible for the misbehavior of a few.
- Parents have to share some of the burden of their children's misconduct.
- More understanding policemen could help to cut down on violence.
- There isn't nearly as much drinking or pot-smoking among teen-agers "as people seem to think."

The "blame-the-teen-agers" theme, expressed in one way or another by nearly three fourths of the students interviewed by Schoolmate reporters, was well summarized by a senior girl at Foster High:

"You can't tell me that the kids who get themselves into trouble don't know better," said Caryl Pitson, senior, president of her school's Student Council.

"Most of us come from good homes, and our parents have told us the score," she went on. "I've never seen a teen-ager who was misbehaving—maybe drinking, maybe driving too fast—who didn't know he was acting foolish."

Why do they "act foolish"? Junior Fritz Apfchen of Worthington High has some answers.

"They like to look big," said Fritz. "They think it makes an impression on the girls."

Tony Karnak, junior, also from Worthington, offered a qualification. "Girls like to make impressions on boys, too," he said. "I don't think we're much different from older people, as a matter of fact. Don't adults ever do things they're sorry for?"

From Fannie Fergus, senior in our own school, came this answer: "Our speech class had a debate on this last week, and we all thought the affirmative won." The question was "Resolved, that juvenile delinquency must be controlled by juveniles rather than by school, church or city."

But Fannie expressed a second theme that was common:

"I think the kids who have the best home life—the ones who get along best with their parents and don't see them drunk every weekend—are the ones who get into the least trouble."

About a third of the students interviewed supported variants of this view. Another third asked that the city's policemen "try to help high school kids keep out of trouble, rather than just show how tough they can get."

Drinking, it seemed generally agreed, is not a major problem.

"Sure some of the kids do it," said one Horace Mann sophomore. "I've done it myself a couple times—not that I'm very proud of it. But I don't think I'll do it again very soon. And neither will the gang I go with. We've talked about it, and we know it gets us no place."

Another Horace Mann senior pointed out that there have been no local charges of marijuana possession or use by minors in the last few months. "That's really kid stuff," he said.

But a few older students—mostly boys, a few girls—aren't so sure. One told a Schoolmate reporter that "I really get a bang out of getting smashed, and so does my girl. Don't bet anything on our cutting it out."

The questions were asked of a random sample of students at three schools—33 each at Foster and Worthington, 34 at Horace Mann. Three Schoolmate reporters conducted the survey, with the approval of the three principals.

PERSONALITY INTERVIEWS

Personality interviews offer two benefits:

1. As a tool for revealing who and what people are, no form of journalism is superior. In addition, such stories give a "human touch" to the news, a leaven for the tales of crime, unhappiness and disaster that make up so much of every day's news budget.
2. They are fun for the reporter; they offer opportunity for use of reportorial insights and skills not regularly used in "straight" reporting. And they are demanding. It is not always easy to help subjects—some of them less than willing—reveal by what they say what kind of men and women they are.

Such stories are high in audience interest. To let news figures or people with unique characteristics discuss likes and dislikes, attitudes about diets and dictatorships and doodling, in their own words and manner, is to place the news consumer squarely where the reporter sits.

This virtue underlines the distinction between the personality interview and the biographical sketch. The sketch, written at a careful distance from its subject, tells facts about the people—date and place of birth, number of children, date of approval as ambassador,

---

Statements as Questions

An ingenious departure from the direct-question technique was used by a reporter trying to find out, as the Vietnam war was winding down, what the job market held for returning veterans. He wrote his questions as statements on which he asked comment, thus:

Job fairs and job marts have been tried across the country. They generally have been failures.

The manpower expert in the governor's office: "The results are not all good . . . It's one thing to get pledges, another to get actual jobs."

Many veterans come back dead set against assembly-line work, even when it pays well.

A veteran: "Those jobs are for robots . . . you know, where it's up, down, right, left . . . just punching a button . . . I'm not going to start that because I'd be doing it the rest of my life."

---

and the like. One of its uses is that, prepared and filed in advance, it may serve as an obit. It is a readable substitute for *Who's Who.* But it rarely achieves the warmth and intimacy of the interview, in which a skillful reporter lets the subject's words and mannerisms turn name-and-address journalism into flesh and blood. The comments on a biographical sketch on page 294, however, show that this form too can come to life.

Two principal clues help decide whether a subject is worth the effort:

1. The subject, male or female, is a news personality, one who has gained a place in the stream of current events. He has been elected district judge, made his fifth hole in one, or refused to accept a million-dollar bequest from a detested uncle. She is managing the Christmas Seal campaign again this year, has been sent to Congress, or is looking happily on the booming sales of her first novel. Public attention is already centered; the public wants to know more.
2. Though outside the news orbits, an individual becomes newsworthy through a trait of personality or a distinction of life, habit or work. Such a person would be the teen-ager whose tree bark collection contains 400 specimens; the professional foster mother who has given homes to a battalion of children; the old man who, having read every book about the sea in the local library, is starting over again; the World War II soldier who hasn't been out of Veterans Hospital for 30 years. None of these is involved in the news; an out-of-the-ordinary characteristic is what assures audience interest.

Development of the personality interview differs little from that of the news interview. Advance preparation is necessary, especially when subjects are aware of their eminence. It's perilously easy to offend newly newsworthy people by not knowing they were born in Yuma, Muncie or Flatbush. Moreover, a news figure is likely to be a busy figure, and reporters win points by saving time.

The techniques used in the news interview can be applied almost intact to personality interviews. But there are additional guides:

1. It is a sound tactic to steer the interviewee, as soon as an easy relationship has been established, to the topic that has led to the interview.
2. More than in the news interview, the spoken and physical mannerisms of the interviewee deserve attention. A news interview's emphasis is on *what* is said; in the personality story emphasis is

on the *how* as well. That a medical researcher constantly repeats "know what I mean?" is of no significance if the story is about his new theory of cancer identification, nor is the fact that he finds any Scotch but Chivas Regal abhorrent. But either aids the reader of a personality story to learn something about him.

3. A personality story increases understanding, letting the reader *see* the subject. Artfully interpolated description belongs in personality stories. Injected with a heavy hand—"here is a paragraph about how she looks"—it is a liability. But it helps a reader to be told that there are knife-edge creases in a man's trousers, or that a woman talks with her hands as much as with her mouth.

   Details of the interview's setting—particularly if it is the interviewee's habitual environment—also add vitality.

   But observe these cautions: Don't load the story with excess detail: use color not for the sake of color but rather for what it adds to the effect you want; sneak touches of setting and of personal description into the story in small doses: don't overwork descriptive bromides (*pretty coed, sparkling blue eyes, pearly teeth, snowy hair, vine-covered cottage, fair sex, acid test, comfortable as an old shoe*).
4. Remember that, even though your purpose is to reveal personality, you are rarely justified in ignoring feelings. Reproducing earthy or sloppy language, down to the last "he don't," is honest reporting and likely to say something about the interviewee. But if the interviewee is a high school English teacher, this kind of reporting would be embarrassing and might bring incommensurate penalty (presidents of the United States sometimes say "of him and I"). A careful reporter questions, "Is the gain from literal reporting sufficient to offset potential damage? When public obligation and personal values collide, which do I protect?" Sometimes the question is more drastic: "If I cut out the bad grammar and the bad manners, the story will be a lie. Is it worth using if I omit them?"
5. "Newspaper reporters have a lot to learn from magazine writers," a magazine journalist once said. "The real pros know that merely talking with a man or woman is not the beginning and the end of research for this kind of story. But lots of reporters—especially if they are pressed for time—fail to carry research beyond the interview itself. No competent magazine writer would let himself become the prisoner of the subject's personal views alone. Some interviewees must be checked and double-checked."

   The man gives good advice. Magazine writers may spend

weeks or months gathering material for personality articles—profiles, as *The New Yorker* calls them. One such writer, unable to persuade the reclusive Greta Garbo to see him, went to more than 30 people who knew things about her, and ended with an illuminating biographical sketch. Another interviewed a Big Leaguer five times before starting to write.

A personality story from the Minneapolis *Tribune*—a combination of interview and background reporting—expresses its theme in the fourth paragraph: "I always felt when a man retired he should retire *to* something, not *from* something." The theme dominates the long story (parts of it are omitted here). A word-picture of the subject's appearance and perhaps the scene of the interview would improve it. But a reader ends up with a clear idea of the man's drive and motivations. Details like his Rolls-Royce, $1-a-year-salary and public service activities are revealing.

Once a week, John H. Myers gets into his black Rolls-Royce and drives to St. John's University at Collegeville.

He climbs the steps, walks into the development office, and is on the job as assistant to the president, the Rev. Michael Blecker.

Meyers, 67, is a $1-a-year man for the Benedictine college. He took on the post last fall when he retired as chairman and chief executive officer of Hoerner Waldorf Corp., St. Paul packaging firm.

"I told my friends at St. John's they needed a good Episcopalian to keep things in order with the Man Upstairs," Meyers said recently. "I always felt when a man retired he should retire to something, not from something. I felt I wanted to go into an educational field to give support to business and the free enterprise system."

Myers won't draw his $1 salary until the 365th day of the year. He said he is helping to organize the first full-fledged fund drive that the Benedictines have conducted since they founded the university in 1857.

"The monks never have asked the public for money. They felt solicitation wasn't a humble task. The Benedictine credo is self-sufficiency in all circumstances. They till the soil to raise their food, tap their own maple trees, bake their own bread. They have 2,000 acres that they use to sustain their way of life."

He said the monks "allow" him to lecture on economics and business "to set the students right about the free enterprise system." The lectures are not in the regular curriculum.

"More recently, I have been helping juniors and seniors with how to put their best foot forward in applying for jobs in the business world," he said. "Kids are so serious about looking for jobs today."

Myers, best known to the public for his role in business, functions as a senior statesman of cultural activities for the Twin Cities.

He comes from a socially prominent background. Member of an old St. Paul family, his schools include St. Paul Academy, Deerfield Academy, Williams College, Carleton and Stanford University; his clubs include the Minneapolis and the Minnesota and the St. Paul Chamber of Commerce.

He helped last week with the 33rd annual spring visit of the Metropolitan Opera Company, as chairman of the Upper Midwest Metropolitan Opera Association, which embraces seven states and the Canadian provinces Saskatchewan and Manitoba. He inherited the position from the late Stanley Hawks, of whom he told this story:

"Stan called and said, 'Johnny, come to my house for cocktails at 4:30.' When I got there, he said 'Johnny, we've got to get a successor for me on the Met. I've been on the job too long. You take it. Thank you for accepting. Now let's have a drink.' "

[The story continues for 10 paragraphs that develop his activities in support of musical and other civic activities and his reputation as a "quintessential fund-raiser." The concluding paragraph:]

The man who said he wanted "to retire into something" keeps in trim playing tennis on courts in the back yard of his home in St. Paul. He usually gets in a couple of hours a week playing the piano.[5]

The biographical sketch Six months after Rudy Perpich unexpectedly became governor of Minnesota, the Washington *Post* sent a reporter to find out how the little-known Croatian was doing in a state where governors usually have names like Anderson, Olson, Peterson and Youngdahl. The reporter (also, by chance, a Peterson—Bill) says of the story, for which he went to St. Paul:

> I talked at length with Governor Perpich. I suppose it would have been possible to write a story without an interview, but for a number of reasons I decided against it. I was fascinated with the guy, and wanted to meet him to find out whether what people said about him—particularly his unpretentious manner—was true. I needed to hear him talk about his administration, his background and his critics. I also wanted some fresh quotes. And of course direct interview is the only way to be fair to a man.
>
> I spent four or five hours on the phone talking to friends and foes of the governor, before the interview. I read 100 or so newsclips about him, interviewed him for 90 minutes, and later spent another couple of hours on the phone interviewing people about him.

Peterson's story, two columns long, uses only five sentences of direct quotation, and for this reason is defined as a biographical sketch rather than an interview. It depends heavily on reports from others to let the reader see Perpich as Peterson pictured him. Here are excerpts:

The state that gave the nation effusive Hubert Humphrey, quixotic Eugene McCarthy and earnest Walter Mondale has come up with a hot new political commodity. He is a 49-year-old dentist with the unlikely Minnesota name Rudy Perpich.

In a place where governors almost invariably have blue eyes and Scandinavian names and senators routinely consider themselves presidential timber, Perpich is an oddity.

He is dark. He is Catholic. And he says he has no national ambitions. In fact, he

[5] Copyright © 1977 by the Minneapolis *Tribune*. Reprinted by permission.

has yet to move his family from his home in Hibbing to the governor's mansion. "The difference between me and those other guys," he declares, "is that I'm going home when it's all over, and I don't think my family will shed a tear."

In his seven months as governor, Perpich has been unpredictable, open almost to a fault and, at times, outrageous.

At various points, he's banned the pickup of litter along state highways, ordered that a $17,500 increase in his salary be used to buy Italian bocce balls, thrown away a prepared speech when he found the crowd would rather see him polka, dined with Minneapolis's best-known madam, and slipped away from his office alone and unannounced to mingle with farmers and small-town businessmen. . . .

There's a touch of the new politics of Georgian Jimmy Carter and Californian Jerry Brown in Perpich. He travels coach and carries his own suitcase. He avoids national meetings of governors, he has set up a task force to find waste in government, and claims one of the best ways to make government more efficient is to keep bureaucrats from buying any more filing cabinets.

His style is strictly midwestern. It is Main Street populism, a combination of small-town naivete and openness, sprinkled with an affinity for the underdog.

He spends days visiting county fairs[6] and shopping centers, getting what he claims is a cross section of public opinion.

He plunges impulsively into issues some politicians wouldn't touch.

When a controversy developed over a stop light in an Indian neighborhood in Minneapolis, Perpich visited the site, met with community leaders and pushed for a light. When tensions over a controversial power line in central Minnesota flared to fever pitch last winter, he slipped quietly out of his office and spent two days visiting upset farmers.

"You have to be out there talking to people to know what's going on," Perpich says. "Something that might sound like a Mickey Mouse issue to big shots in Minneapolis may mean the world to someone else. So I just take off and go."

[*Several background paragraphs describe Perpich's appointment as governor and his frank satisfaction in it. The story continues:*]

Perpich is the first Minnesota governor who is a Roman Catholic. He's also the first from the Mesabi Iron Range in the northeastern part of the state, a fact that shaped his personality and politics.

He is the oldest son of a Croatian immigrant iron ore miner and grew up poor, hating the steel companies that dominated the area. He entered school without knowing English or the fine points of indoor plumbing. When he heard a toilet flush on his first visit to the school restroom he was terrified and ran home, informing his mother that a water pipe had burst. "I told her, 'I got out but I'm not sure if the rest of the kids made it,' " he recalls.

His father, Anton Perpich, didn't want his sons to work in the mines. He saw education as the way out. Rudy and two of his brothers became dentists, then state legislators. The fourth became a lawyer and psychiatrist.

[*A paragraph compares Perpich to his handsome, well-organized predecessor. Then:*]

To almost everyone's surprise, he quickly captured the public imagination after his appointment. By midspring a newspaper poll reported 63 percent of those surveyed felt he was doing an excellent job; only 4 percent gave him a poor rating . . . .

He is not without his critics. He has an-

[6] See page 311.

gered labor leaders with several appointments, made party leaders uneasy over his shoot-from-the-hip manner, and worried friends by failure to delegate authority. Republicans charge he really hasn't accomplished anything in office.

And there is the possibility that his "plain folks" image may wear thin. The St. Paul Dispatch called him "Mortimer Snerd" after he had trouble getting into a meeting with President Carter because he had no identification to show White House guards. Perpich's explanation to reporters: "Why should I carry a wallet? Everyone knows me back home on the range."[7]

The biographical sketch thus accomplishes much of what the personal interview does. It lacks, however, the intimate contact with its subject. And typically—like this one—it skips the time element.

STUDY SUGGESTIONS

1. Define the *interview story*, in journalists' terms.
2. Distinguish among the three common types of interview story.
3. Cite some factors that you think support the statement that the news interview is one of the most valuable of reportorial tools.
4. Among the sources of error cited in this chapter, are there any that have affected your own work? If there are, can you plan what to do about it?
5. Have you run across other sources of error?
6. Are you critical or approving of the persistence of reporters interviewing President Ford (page 274)? Do you think their repeated questions added to the information they gained? Can you suggest other methods of developing information beyond those the story reveals?
7. Q-and-A interviews have both strengths and weaknesses. Cite all of either that you can identify.
8. In the Graham interview (page 280) the reporter uses the first-person approach. Would the straight reportorial manner, leaving the reporter invisible, improve the story? Is there justification for first person in this kind of reporting?
9. Suggest some of the hazards a reporter may experience in gathering information for a symposium interview and in writing it.
10. Would the personality sketch (page 294) be stronger if its writer brought its subject to the foreground with more direct quotation?

PRACTICE ASSIGNMENTS

1. From current news events, select five or more local news topics to which the news interview process might add understanding or illumination. For each one, decide on an appropriate interviewee and write a series of leading questions. Carry out one of the interviews and write the story.

2. Select a man or woman newly in a position of influence in your community—preferably one not well-known. After preparatory study, interview the person to bring out personality characteristics. Write the story for a local publication.
3. Choose a second individual on the basis of distinctive personal habit, occupation or point of view: a collector of pornographic books, a man or woman who walks 12 miles to work and 12 miles back every day, one who has a record better than the Weather Bureau's for forecasting storms. Conduct an interview and write a personality story.
4. Think up a topic of local interest for a symposium interview: Do we need a local bus system? Has the school integration program worked? What name would you give the new polar bear cub at the zoo? What do you think of the four-day work week? Station yourself at a strategic spot—bus station, airport, PTA meeting, football game. Ask your question of at least 20 people; with their answers, write the story (observing the cautions given in this chapter).

RELATED READING

Bentley, Phyllis. *Some Observations on the Art of Narrative.* Macmillan, 1947. See page 270.

Frankel, Charles E., and others. "Obituaries: With Care, Love." *Gannetteer,* June 1976. Observations about writing obits from six Gannett newspaper editors and reporters.

Garrett, Annette. *Interviewing: Its Principles and Practices.* Family Welfare Association of America, 1942. Prepared for social workers, this manual has many suggestions for journalistic interviewers.

Grey, David L., and Gary C. Lawrence. "Main Causes of Subjective Error in News Stories." American Association of Newspaper Publishers *News Research Bulletin,* Dec. 11, 1968. Report of a study.

Interviewer's Manual, rev. ed. Institute for Social Research, University of Michigan, 1976. Suggestions on telephone interviewing and evaluating interviewer performance, as well as technical material on sampling and coding.

Lyford, Joseph P. "Forming Journalists." *Center Magazine,* July–August 1975. Helpful comments on interviewing and other reportorial techniques.

Meyer, Philip. *Precision Journalism.* Indiana University Press, 1973. Chapter IX deals with interviewing and survey techniques. Other chapters have help for journalists using statistical, scientific and precision data.

Ringle, William M., and others. "Get the Interview as Reader's Surrogate." *Editorially Speaking,* Gannett Newspapers, Vol. 30, No. 6, 1974. Practical advice from the pros on interviewing problems and techniques.

Webb, Eugene J., and Jerry R. Salanik. *The Interview, or The Only Wheel in Town.* Journalism Monographs, Association for Education in Journalism, School of Journalism and Mass Communication, University of Minnesota, 1966. Tips on the newspaper interview. Good bibliography.

15 Feature and Human-Interest Stories

PREVIEW

The term *feature,* a catchall with many meanings, is here defined as a story that is strong primarily in elements other than timeliness. This definition includes human-interest stories, sidebars and "second-day features," news features, and background, interpretive and color stories, as well as many interviews. It includes such non-news material as special columns—health, gardening . . . even comic strips.

Human-interest stories are those that make people laugh, weep, get red in the face or twang other emotional chords. They are more often accidental than planned—they crop up unexpectedly. Human-interest stories frequently appear in suspended-interest pattern, the narrative pattern that holds back major facts rather than trumpet them in leads. As the label suggests, they are usually about people, and more commonly about individuals than groups. Some news media have human-interest specialists, but since many news events offer both straight and emotive elements, every reporter needs the ability to recognize and report both kinds.

Common types of features are:

- News features, those that emphasize human or "soft" values in events that also yield hard news
- Color stories, whose purpose is to paint word-pictures—to help audiences hear, see and sensually experience events
- Straight news stories with color added to make them more effective. But color must not be discoloration.

WHAT IS A "FEATURE"?

The term *feature,* on every newsworker's lips a dozen times a day, has at least a dozen meanings. It is a newsroom catchall. In contests for news story excellence, you find categories called *news feature, spot feature, short feature, long feature, sports feature, personality*

CBS's Walter Cronkite talks with an industrialist inside the hull of Howard Hughes' flying boat, the Spruce Goose, in 1978. This was the first news photo of the aircraft since its only flight 30 years earlier. *(United Press International Photo)*

feature, something-else feature. Rarely are there definitions, and the wide range of the entries shows little consensus.

Asked frequently to judge such contests, a publisher of the Denver *Post* asked help from Alexis McKinney, a veteran of 30 years in the newsroom. McKinney came up with a definition that said in part:

> A feature finds its impact outside or beyond the realm of the straight news story's basic and unvarnished who-what-when-where-why and how.
>
> The justification, strength and very identity of the feature is in its penetration of the imagination—not in departing from or stretching truth but in piercing the peculiar and particular truths that strike people's curiosity, sympathy, skepticism, consternation or amazement.
>
> Writing a feature story is not just recitation of facts . . . but rather adroit presentation of facts and ideas so as to spotlight those that may not be apparent to the casual observer.

The McKinney definition is a familiar one, but it stops too soon. The term *feature* also covers stories that depend little on imaginative (whatever that may mean) or emotional content. It is accurate to say that features present material *selected primarily because of elements other than timeliness.* Sidebars (see Chapter 6) are usually, in this sense, features. This definition does not quarrel with the McKinney emphasis on emotional values or with the claims of timeliness, the *when* element. It says rather that timeliness is not the dominant characteristic in the story, for either the reporter or the reader-listener. Its interest peaks in one or more of its other elements.

Newsworkers refer to all of the following types of stories—some strongly newsworthy, some not—as features:

Simple human-interest stories

- A man eats 15 pies on a bet and ends up in the hospital.
- A woman forgets to attend her own wedding because of a conflict with her weekly bowling date.
- An ambulance attendant discovers that the boy in the bicycle accident is his son.

These stories fit the McKinney definition. They get into the news because of their oddity, pathos or emotional or entertainment value rather than their contribution to knowledge or understanding. Some would be reported (with different emphases) because they are spot news—the bike accident, for instance; others wouldn't get a nod were it not for their oddity or amusement value. In any of them the *when* element would appear, but not as a primary.

Sidebars or "second-day" features

- During the big fire downtown, nobody could get water pressure for lawn sprinkling.
- A young man grumbles because his fiancee, just chosen Miss Jaycee, can give him only one date a week.
- A defensive tackle is glum—or laughs it off—after he scoops up a fumble and runs it for a wrong-way touchdown.
- This year's earlier rains make yesterday's downpour doubly disastrous.

Stories like these add something to audience understanding of an event reported elsewhere. Often they are high in human interest;

but their prime value is in illuminating or supplementing stories about weightier matters.

News features

Another term for these stories is *featurized news.* Like sidebars, they are timely in their dependence on current events. But they treat the events—often events of importance—with emphasis on human-interest or secondary elements. Sidebars and "simple" features are usually brief; news features are often long. Examples:

- The story about the pistol-packin' Secretary of State (page 98)
- The horrors of two elderly women who, trapped in a burning house, feared they couldn't escape—and how they did
- A little girl's experiences, in her own words, as she wandered for 48 hours in dense woods

Background or interpretive stories

- A reporter's survey shows that repeaters have been more common visitors to traffic court than first-timers.
- A psychologist says in an interview that personality tests are more often misused and misunderstood than put to legitimate purpose.
- Local housing problems, say several city councilmen, are going to escalate when the new steel-processing plant moves into town.

These stories might not be reported at all if journalists were concerned only with spot news. They add meaning to public understanding of current affairs.

Color stories

- A description of the scene in a flood-ravaged section of a city as looters have themselves a holiday
- The goings-on in a stadium parking lot during a tailgate party as participants start to have too good a time
- Sights, sounds and smells in the heating tunnels under a college campus, observed by a reporter accompanying a night watchman on his rounds

The color story's assignment is to put the reader squarely into the setting it describes (radio rarely uses it; TV does it with pictures). It paints a scene and the circumstances that give individual character to a place or event. Usually it grows out of a current event, but it may be based on scenes—like the heating tunnels—entirely unfamiliar to the audience.

Non-news features

- Household hints, child-care columns, horoscopes, health columns, how-to-win-at-bridge columns, gardening advice, movie gossip, comic strips, do-it-yourself tips—all are known as "features," though they rarely are news. They are often syndicated, prepared by a wire service or some other distant agency, and sold on contract to media that don't have the staff to do it themselves.

All of these are features. Many, in news jargon, are time copy. This chapter is devoted to those that reporters face often: human-interest stories, news features, color stories.

HUMAN-INTEREST STORIES

A human-interest story is one that strikes an emotional chord. It is one that makes you say "for gosh sakes," "what a shame!" "I'd have loved that," "it scares me." Hard news often has strong human interest—the shooting or resignation of a president, a disastrous flood, a World Series or a Wimbledon tournament. But a "pure" human-interest story doesn't need significance. Reaching emotions quickly, it provides sensuous rather than intellectual experience. When a story horrifies readers or makes them laugh, saddens or angers

---

The Kathy Fiscus Story

A generation ago America was stirred to its bones by the tragedy of a little girl, Kathy Fiscus, who fell into a California well shaft and died there. "For two days the great affairs of a nation took second place in the minds and hearts of the people," commented an editorial. Its last paragraph helps to define the power of emotion in human lives:

> The tragedy of a little girl in the shaft of a well is one that the human heart comprehends at once, and to which it responds with all the nobility that distinguishes it from the base and the brutal. But the tragedy of a million people in China or India in the grip of a famine, or of a city wiped out in a flash of a bomb, or of an army cut to pieces on the steppes of Russia—this kind of mass calamity becomes as something read about abstractly in a book. The fate of individuals is swallowed up in the vastness of the event. It is only when human suffering is broken down into the terms of one particular human being that it can be directly felt by the heart and comprehended by the mind.

The editorial defines the affective impact of such an event, but it does not touch another factor in news appeal: the acceleration of reader interest as suspense hangs on. The suspense factor explains why the media sometimes let continuing stories that are high in human interest get out of hand.

---

them, appeals to their self-interest, they become vicarious participants. Such a story excites *feelings,* and it demands less concentration than hard news. A story about saving a drowning child gets better attention than one about the new bank discount rate.

Newsworkers look for human interest as they decide what news events are worth space and time. It is the factor in news that gives "immediate reward"—the element that one of Hearst's brilliant editors meant when he said, "We want news that makes people say, 'Gee whiz!' "

Recognition, understanding and evaluation of human interest as a constituent in news appeal runs through any thinking about news. You take it into account when you examine the character of news audiences, when you talk about news style, when you consider the functional patterns in which you package news, when you plan and execute a newsgathering assignment. Appreciation of emotional and sensuous values is basic to every day of a reporter's work.

Developing human-interest news Though some reporters with deft touches tend to get human-interest assignments, a city editor usually doesn't assign one to a human-interest beat as he does to city hall or a police station. Human-interest news is not found only in defined areas. Much police news is alive with human interest. But police reporters learn to think of human interest as a kind of bonus—something to be looked for but not always found. City editors do not ask reporters to "go out and get human-interest stories." They talk in specific terms: "how does the man's wife like his being an auto racer?"; "find out how the fellow felt when he saw his home floating down the river"; "don't tell me how many people watched the fire—tell me what they said about it." Human interest shows itself in "people situations"—situations that draw emotional responses.

The human-interest story results from application of news imagination to an event or a concept. A reporter observing an event thinks—or intuits—"If I ask such-and-such questions, I'll come up with a human-interest story." Sometimes that's the only kind of story to be found in the event. And sometimes a news situation can be shown in true light only by integrating emotive values into a major feature (as in the Dakota blizzard story, page 147). Another example: A little girl in Ohio wrote a plaintive letter to the state Department of Education asking whether her school was to be shut down. A reporter, learning of the letter, suggested that the response be not in terms of three-mill levies and tax rates, but rather one written "so that a 12-year-old could understand it" (he actually drafted the letter). Then he wrote a story that had meaning for the whole state, in terms everybody would read (a story that confessed its debt to the famous New York *Sun* "Yes, Virginia, there is a Santa Claus" editorial).

Such a story depends not only on its facts but also on what its writer does with them. Without the writer's perceptiveness and sensitive approach, human-interest news would be rare, and it would be less compelling than many stories cited in this book. Had Weller written the appendectomy-under-the-sea story (page 145) as straight news, he could have done it in two paragraphs; but his paper gave it 65.

The suspended-interest form A distinctive news story form—one that grows out of the oldest pattern of story telling, the narrative—is the suspended-interest form. (You were introduced to the suspended-interest lead on page 133.) This is a rhetorical package that takes advantage of the nature of the materials.

Like straight news stories, suspended-interest stories are contrived—structured to gain effect. A straight news story gets its customer to the heart of the matter at once. A suspended-interest story moves in the opposite direction. It compels readers to stay with the story to learn its point. It deliberately holds back principal facts so as to inveigle them into staying with it. Like the plot structure of short stories, it keeps its audience in doubt.

Were it not for the suspended-interest story form, a great many trivial events that find space in crowded news columns or air time would go unrecorded. A sober face would make it ludicrous to bother with news such as that of the ambulatory fire that goes looking for help.

These are its facts: Two policemen in Denver stop auto driver John Marselle on a crowded viaduct, their siren halting traffic. Marselle, puzzled, asks, "Why?" "Your car's on fire," he is told. The police radio their dispatcher, who tells them to take the car to a fire station two blocks away. The dispatcher notifies the station. When the car gets there, firemen put out the blaze.

If this story were written as straight news, it would go something like this:

> Firemen at Northeast Station extinguished a flame this morning in a car owned and driven by John Marselle, 689 Elm Street. Police who halted Marselle on Midtown Viaduct told him his car was on fire and directed him to the fire station.

In this form the story would interest few outside the Marselle family. It is clearly not worth time on press-service trunk wires. But the

Question of Tactics

In the AP story Marselle is credited with asking, "What in blazes are you stopping me for?" The play on words has the odor of reportorial invention—gratuitous embroidery by a writer who likes to write cute.

It can be argued that "bright" writing sharpens a story, and that its phony tone in a trivial story misleads nobody.

But an astute reader, spotting the play on words as fiction, can hardly be blamed if, seeing one piece of fiction, he asks what others the reporter (and perhaps the paper, perhaps all news media) may have invented. It is one thing to hang an invention on a participant in an event, as apparently has been done here. It is a defensible variation to write it so that it is indisputably invention, not reporting. Art Buchwald writes as though he's reporting facts, but his manner quickly tells you that he isn't.

Associated Press sent it, in suspended-interest treatment, across the nation:

> DENVER, March 25 (AP)—"What in blazes are you stopping me for?" asked John Marselle when two policemen sirened his car to a stop on a crowded viaduct today. "Your car's on fire," they replied, radioing the police dispatcher for instructions. They were told to take the car to a fire station two blocks away. Firemen waiting there quickly extinguished the blaze.

This story has the principal characteristics of the suspended-interest form. Its facts are marked by a familiar human-interest characteristic—amusing oddity. Its lead "holds back," to arouse the reader's curiosity. The reader has to read the last line to get the denouement (which opens the straight story).

Look back at the facts from which the story is made and you see that it makes a pretty good suspended-interest story as it stands. That's because it's a narrative—beginning at the beginning, ending at the end (the chronological form). The following story and others later in this chapter illustrate this pattern. The story below is notable for its stylistic economy: its short sentences, lack of adornment and exclusion of unneeded detail make it move as fast as the event itself.

> "My sister's in the hole . . . my sister's in the hole . . ."
>
> This alarm, sounded quick and loud by 5-year-old Judy Johnston, 8308 Fouquet Ave. S., Renton, produced a chain reaction about 8 p.m. Monday.
>
> Tony Case, 45, 8313 Fouquet Ave. S., who was fixing his fence, saw the girl running across the street from a storm sewer excavation.
>
> Case understood. He dropped his hammer and ran toward the excavation, shouting for help.

> Raymond C. Manders, 8301 Fouquet Ave. S., dropped his newspaper and raced through his front door. Bruce O'Brien, 8337 Fouquet Ave. S., was talking to Marvin Hanick, 580 Holly St., a contractor's man keeping an eye on a pump.
>
> The two men broke into a sprint. By the time they and Manders reached the spot, Case had discovered a speck of Jeanmarie Johnston, 8, almost completely buried by an earth cave-in.
>
> "First, I saw a hand, then I could see her eyes," Case said.
>
> The four men got down on their knees and dug with their hands "like gophers," releasing the girl before emergency equipment arrived.
>
> Jeanmarie, flustered and frightened, ran home unhurt.

A modified suspended-interest pattern holds back the climactic fact only part way through the story. The Marselle story, for example, could have gone this way:

> John Marselle took a fire to the firemen today.
>
> Stopped by policemen on Midtown Viaduct with a warning that his car was on fire, Marselle drove to the Northeast Fire Station, two blocks away. There the fire was put out.
>
> Firemen at Northeast had been alerted by the police dispatcher, whom the police had radioed.

This version reveals the key fact at the end of the second paragraph; the third paragraph, secondary material, could be omitted. This compromise between the straight news form and the form that holds back until the end is a common practice.

In the following story the headline became the lead (most writers would have opened with the name of the principal actor):

> THREE TICKETS TO L.A., THE MAN SAID
>
> The man from Washington, making a holiday trip with his wife and daughter, bought three tickets to Los Angeles on a jumbo jet for $652.92 and finished the trip at a sedate 55 miles an hour, thus saving the nation about 40,000 gallons of fuel.
>
> President Nixon figured "he ought to set an example," an aide said.
>
> So Nixon made a surprise trip to the Western White House by commercial airliner yesterday. It was one of the few such trips by a president in office . . ." [1]

Some news bulging with human interest—the release of hostages from a train in Holland, 12 inches of rain in Kansas City, the crowning of a Miss America—is initially reported soberly, though its emotional impact may be developed in later stories. Even in the straight news report the human-interest aspects are implicit. If you open a story, "Shouting union members fought police with stones and clubs as they tried to break into the factory offices," you don't have to tell a reader there's emotion in the event.

Inventiveness and a seeing eye may turn routine into something novel. A court reporter found himself with notes about a woman juror whose stocking had been snagged on a jury chair. The lady wrote some lines of doggerel to the judge, claiming damages. This is the way the reporter wrote the story:

> A letter terse but rhythmic, and framed in phrases gay, arrived upon Judge Leary's bench in court the other day. The judge saw no one bring it and can't remember, now, the incident described therein—not when, nor why, nor how.
>
> But ever since the letter came the judge has tried to find a way to solve the issue and to get it off his mind. He's thumbed his tomes, he's scratched his head, he's racked his aching brain to reach a just decision that the high court might sustain . . .

Examples later in this chapter illustrate fitting pattern to material.

Chronological stories This story form is simple narrative. It begins at the beginning and ends at the end. It is the simplest suspended-interest pattern; it is usually reserved for human-interest news (news strong in comedy or pathos and light in the significance that demands a summary lead). Among examples in this book are the stories about the undersea appendectomy (page 145), the Brazilian doctor (page 150) and Satchel Paige (page 151). A variant, telling several parallel stories, is the Dakota blizzard story (page 147).

The story below is narrative halfway through; its second half brings together facts that would have slowed the narrative.

> Some people don't have any trouble getting a cab.
>
> When Max Artkins needed one Wednesday night to catch a thief, there it was at the corner. So he hopped right in with the passenger.
>
> Artkins, 24, is manager of Arnold's Market, 1229 Williams St. He was walking back into the store Wednesday evening when he saw someone walk out with groceries that weren't in a bag.
>
> He opened the door and asked a fellow employee if the groceries had been paid for. The worker said no, so Artkins ran to the red Cadillac the shoplifting suspect had entered and tried to open the car's

door. It was locked. The Cadillac took off.

"There was a cab at the stoplight going toward downtown," Artkins explained yesterday. "I flagged him over and got in. I had my apron on so the driver must have known I worked in the store.

"I told him, 'They just stole a bunch of groceries' and told him to follow the car and tell the dispatcher to call the police."

Artkins said the Cadillac, with two men in it, spun around on the icy road and ended up on a sidewalk at 12th and Williams.

"I pulled up behind in the cab and started to get out," he said. "They backed into the cab. Then they took off again and went down Williams and ran a couple of lights. They took a left on Correy, going the wrong way on a one-way street."

By that time, Artkins said, he spotted a police car on 1st Ave. and flagged it on toward the red Cadillac.

About that time, Artkins said, a Yellow Cab supervisor who was in the neighborhood and heard the commotion on the radio blocked off Correy with his cab.

Police said the Cadillac, headed west, went out of control at 11th and Correy and hit a sign. The passenger was caught about half a block away by policemen, the driver as he tried to get out of the car.

Police said the Cadillac had been reported stolen Wednesday from Short Cadillac, Hartsville. They said Halsey Wedge, 19, 1789 Fairmont Ave., was charged with careless driving, driving while intoxicated, possession of an open bottle in the car, hit and run, and failing to stop for a stop sign. They said he also probably would be charged with auto theft.

Officers said Mark Anderson, 19, address unknown, was charged with shoplifting.

Artkins said the cabbie didn't have much to say about the chase, because "it all happened so fast." It was the cabbie's fourth night on the job, Artkins said.

The man riding in the cab had little more to say than the driver, Artkins said. Yellow sent another cab to pick up the passenger after the chase.

"I paid for his fare," Artkins said. "The meter showed $2 at 11th and Correy. And I gave the cabbie a $3 tip."[2]

Human interest in broadcast news Human-interest stories on radio are usually brief—often the "kickers" or "brights" with which folksy newscasters like to close their programs. Their form is much like that of comparable print stories. Radio rarely has time to develop long stories of any kind, depending as it does on bulletin board format. A handful of stations, looking on news as entertainment to get audience ratings, direct news announcers to "be sure to get the X-rated stories on."

Informal writing and announcer personality help give radio news a *feeling* of human interest, whatever the type of news.

News on TV, in contrast, depends heavily on human interest. TV's need to take advantage of its distinctive vehicle, the picture tube, demands news that can be illustrated; and illustration usually means pictures of people or of events that involve people—parades, accidents, disasters, sports, policemen's clambakes—people doing things that other people in their living rooms like to see. A TV re-

[2] Copyright © 1977 by the Minneapolis *Tribune*. Reprinted by permission.

port of a Senate hearing, showing a gavel-pounding chairman or an angry witness, is more exciting than a printed story about it. A bigger share of television news time than of newspaper space goes to picnics in the park, sports and spectacular events like floods and hurricanes. Features like the human-interest adventures of Charles Kuralt on CBS add variety and sometimes comic relief. And certainly the human interest of television's reporting of the Vietnam War gave it an unparalleled dimension. The viewers could see the blood, the swamps, the explosions.

Short suspended-interest and human-interest stories The use of short stories in these categories in print and broadcast—for what reason the authors of this book don't know—has declined in recent years. The papers don't publish as many, the wire services don't provide as many, and radio and TV want more of them than they can get. Whatever causes the shortage, they are still in demand. Some examples illustrate their virtues and frailties:

> The editor's telephone rang. "Exactly when is that wedding for Patricia Sentry and Joe Arnott?" the caller asked.
> The editor checked. "This afternoon. Four o'clock," she responded.
> "Thanks," said the caller. "And where?"
> The editor told him. Then she got curious.
> "Who's this calling," she asked.
> "Joe Arnott," was the answer.

> CLARKSBURG, W.Va.—Smith Schuneman got a letter this week that made it through the mail with a two-cent stamp.
> And only 41 years late.
> The letter was mailed by the Clarksburg Community Chest Nov. 29, 1936, and found during the renovation of the post office last week.

The punch line comes at the end of the first story. In the second it is placed in the middle. In the story below the lead comes close to the summary pattern, but the elaboration is needed for full understanding:

> NORWALK, Conn. (AP)—A fire at the Edwards Co. yesterday had little chance of success. The firm makes smoke detectors.
> Dozens of stockpiled detectors began blaring when a soldering machine used to assemble them accidentally ignited a small vat of oil. A security guard called the fire department and workers at the factory got the day off.

Stop Me if You've Heard This One

The banality of some "brights" or "briefs" may be one reason their use seems to decline. A writer in an Arizona paper satirized their predictability with inventions like this one:

BROOKLYN—The customers of Lily Liefgreen, who dressed in rags and sold flowers in the streets, always assumed she was penniless.

Yesterday she died. Police searched her humble apartment. Sure enough, she was penniless.

"Briefs" like these are not always brief enough. The shorter such a story, the sharper its point (and usually the harder to write). The story as published below contains 176 words; the rewrite 69. The first tells its tale twice. The second asks the reader to supply some imagination and a little knowledge of history.

Original

BRIGHTON, England—A 22-year-old student brought a touch of Elizabethan England to the 20th century today.

As Queen Elizabeth II walked among the puddles on a visit to the new University of Sussex near Brighton the student, Peter Horne, threw down his black plastic raincoat for her to step on.

The queen smiled at the gallant gesture, as her namesake, Elizabeth I, had done four centuries earlier when Sir Walter Raleigh, so legend has it, threw down his cloak for her.

The queen walked across one corner of the raincoat and turned a handsome royal smile on Horne.

Crowds had waited in continuous rain for a glimpse of the queen as she drove from Brighton to the University, Britain's newest.

It was as she walked from her car to open a new 400,000-pound ($1.1 million) library that the modern-day Raleigh act took place.

As she picked her way among the puddles, student Horne dashed forward and threw down his plastic coat—price, when new: 30 shillings ($3.50). Horne is a post-graduate student of politics. [176 words]

Short version

The day of Queen Elizabeth I and Sir Walter Raleigh was relived here Friday, 400 years late.

As Elizabeth II picked her way among puddles, on her way to open the University of Sussex's new library, 22-year-old Peter Horne, a student, dashed out to throw down his raincoat before her.

The queen stepped on a corner of the coat, and Horne got a royal smile for his trouble. [69 words]

The story below sounds like a publicity handout ("wood," such filler is called in some news offices). A number of papers considered it worth publishing because of its oddity, good humor and closing fillip.

If you are flying Northwest Orient Airlines and the man in the next seat starts riffling a deck of playing cards, don't jump to the conclusion that he's a gambler planning to relieve you of your money.

He may be preparing for his arrival in the Orient by selecting a card that says "where can I get a taxi?" in English at the top and in Japanese, Korean and Chinese underneath. That card, incidentally, is the queen of diamonds. "May I see the manager?" is the jack of diamonds; "where is the nearest doctor?" the seven of spades; and "please bring the check'" the jack of clubs.

Northwest Orient, which serves 38 domestic and seven Oriental cities, offers a pack to each of its customers. The cards, of course, are as useful to Japanese, Korean and Chinese travelers in this country as to Americans visiting the Far East.

The trick for the traveler who needs the right phrase in a hurry is to memorize which phrase goes with which card. In some circumstances the time spent trying to find "where is the men's room?" might seem awfully long. It is the nine of hearts.

NEWS FEATURES

A news feature treats human-interest aspects of current news, its emphasis on human rather than "solid" values. It fleshes out the basic news; it provides information which, though not imperative to knowledge of what's going on, fills in gaps or offers background against which events can be better understood. The example that follows is such a story (as is its companion on page 294). The news impulse for both stories was the fact that Minnesota's new governor, appointed rather than elected, was bringing to his office a folksy flavor and an accessibility that were attracting national attention. This story was written by a Minneapolis *Star* reporter as one of the paper's team covering the recently ended legislative session.

ST. CHARLES, Minn.—A county fair is a place where 4H Club members show their projects, where senior citizens are honored, where almost everybody knows everybody else, and where you can get a glass of lemonade made with big chunks of real lemons.

In Minnesota this year, it's also likely to be a place where you can meet the governor and, if something is bothering you, give him a piece of your mind.

At the Winona County Fair in St. Charles last week, Gov. Rudy Perpich ate a piece of cherry pie, crowned an 85-year-old queen, walked through a junkyard, answered questions for several TV, radio and newspaper reporters and drank a glass of milk.

And, he says, by talking to the people at the Winona fair he learned some things he didn't know. As a result he's going to meet with a group of citizens that felt he had snubbed them, ask some pointed questions of a state commissioner about a park's name, and look into some other problems.

It's no accident that Perpich made some political points in Winona County.

His visit to the fair last week was part of his summer's schedule of traveling around the state. At the Winona County Fair he told about 100 senior citizens, "I think as long as I touch base with the people, I'll be OK."

That's been the touchstone of his seven-month-old administration from his first unannounced visit to western Minnesota in January less than two weeks after he took office to find out about the power-line controversy first hand.

Perpich arrived at the Winona fairgrounds at about 1 p.m. Thursday. The local state senator, Roger Laufenburger, DFL-Lewiston, picked him up at the Rochester airport when he arrived from Camp Ripley. "He was just walking through the airport all alone, like anyone else," Laufenburger said.

The governor, in a slightly rumpled tan suit, showed the effects of the 90-degree-heat. He carried his suit jacket most of the time and his tie was slightly loose. Like just about everybody but the beauty queens—who looked as fresh as the proverbial daisies—the governor looked hot.

The whole affair was handled informally. Perpich, flanked by four area legislators, walked around the fair for a while, chatting with people who came up to shake his hand. Crowds were small; this is farm country and, governor or no governor, people work hard during the day. At night the fair starts going full blast.

After he'd eaten a piece of cherry pie—"I always choose cherry pie if I can"—he participated in senior-citizen day activities, including crowning the king and queen of the Winona fair. The queen was Rose Laufenburger, 85, the state senator's mother.

As the crowd of about 100 listened to the Rose Petals, six gingham-clad women, harmonize on "You Are My Sunshine," "Ring of Fire" and other favorites, Perpich slipped outside the green-and-white tent for television and radio interviews.

A question that comes up frequently was asked again: What are you accomplishing by visiting county fairs, governor?

And the answer was about the same as it had been every other time: "Y'know, I learned three things in my first 20 minutes here that I wouldn't have known about if I'd stayed in St. Paul."

He said he learned that:

A group called Citizens for a Clean Mississippi Inc. was angry because he had refused to meet with them. Not so, he replied, there was a misunderstanding. He promised to set up a meeting soon.

Residents of the area are furious that the Department of Natural Resources' (DNR) acting commissioner renamed nearby Whitewater Wildlife Management Area after former Gov. Karl F. Rolvaag.

"I thought they'd checked and it was all right with the people" Perpich said. "I'll be talking with Mike O'Donnell about it." O'Donnell, the acting commissioner, used to be an administrative assistant of Rolvaag.

"The DNR is not the most popular state agency." Perpich said that kind of general discontent is difficult to deal with, but he promised to discuss it with the department's new commissioner.

He also was asked repeatedly whether this wasn't a campaign trip rather than state business.

"When I start campaigning, you'll know it. I'll be starting at 5:30 a.m. every day," he said. He added that because "there's such a fine line between state business and campaigning" he pays his own way on these trips. But he insisted that meeting the people across the state is essential to doing his job right.

How come, then, so many of his first summer trips have been to the 1st Congressional District, which is represented by Albert Quie, a Republican being courted as an opponent for Perpich?

"That's where the first county fairs are," the governor replied.

Whether the trip is political or official, observers note that DFLers who hoped to run against former Gov. Harold LeVander in 1970 were hitting the county fairs in force in 1969, and the DFL won the election.

Getting out to the fairs is one of the best things Perpich could do, the observers say.

The interviews over, Perpich returned to the tent to hand out awards to senior citizens. Then cookies and punch were served, and he chatted with more residents. Again, Whitewater came up frequently and forcefully.

After a brief live interview by phone on WCCO Radio, the governor toured the 4H building (he rushed to the building because the man who was to lead the tour had to get home soon to start milking), admiring exhibits and chatting with exhibitors.

He also walked a block or so to a junkyard at the request of owner Ervin Unger, St. Charles, who wanted to know whether his efforts to beautify it were in line with the governor's Aesthetic Environment Program.

Perpich later pronounced Unger's efforts "a nice, nice job" and a model of how to clean up junkyards ("they call 'em something else, now, I forget what," the governor said).

That evening Perpich traveled to nearby Hayfield, Minn., to help the community dedicate its new 18-hole golf course and "a really unbelievable golf club" built with volunteer labor.

Perpich got home in St. Paul at 9:45 p.m.

And went straight to bed, right?

Wrong. "We had some people over and worked on the Reserve (Mining Co.) permits until 2:45 a.m.," Perpich said.[3]

The reporter's familiarity with the governor and his environment enabled him to add touches that depart from fully objective reporting, but that most journalists would approve: "that's been the touchstone of his administration," "the answer was about the same as it had been every other time," references to "observers" and political analogies. A photograph of the sweating governor taking a glass of milk from a fresh-looking "dairy princess" added to the flavor.

The slice-of-life narrative that follows is marked by extraordinary restraint—pared to bare detail, no adornment. Its refusal to sentimentalize is one of its virtues; another is that it ends, as do so many minor miseries, in limbo.

The man was about 45 years old and drunk. He'd arrived at the State Capitol with some friends Monday afternoon, looking for a warm place to stand for a while.

But somehow, he was overlooked when his friends moved on, and he was left standing on the Capitol steps waiting for help.

Inside the Capitol, a senate subcommittee was holding a hearing on drug abuse and the need for treating the state's 75,000 alcoholics.

Then a couple who had just testified on alcoholic rehabilitation at the hearing emerged from the building.

"Look at that poor man," said the woman. "He could freeze in this cold. A lot of them do, you know. I wonder if they'd have room for him in a half-way house."

"The least somebody could do," said the man with her, "is call the police."

They got into their car and drove away.

The drunk stopped a visitor and asked for a ride to the West Side. The visitor asked the man to wait in the lobby while he tried to get him a bus.

While he was inside, the visitor asked building attendants if there wasn't a first-aid station or some department that might be able to handle the man's problem.

The attendants said they could call the police, but didn't want to because the man appeared to belong to a minority group, and involving the police might embarrass the governor.

Meanwhile, the drunk wandered down the Capitol steps, his hands shielding his ears from the cold. He turned down Falton St. toward downtown. He mumbled off and on, stopped and threw a few imaginary punches, once threw up his hands in a gesture of despair.

The police were called, and the operator said they'd try to reach the man right away.

But before they could find him, he stopped in front of a church, then turned in a side door. He asked a secretary for a meal ticket or money for food.

"We no longer have this service," the secretary said. "We would rather you be on your way now."

He stumbled as he left, not noticing a sign proclaiming, "Have a Great Day!"

He walked on, asking not for a handout, but for help. But passersby didn't seem to know what to do. People he talked to turned their heads away.

Finally he turned down Temperance St. at the edge of the loop. Then he turned off and was lost.[4]

COLOR IN NEWS STORIES

A wire-service staff memo has this to say about color in news stories:

> Color is part of the news. But news must never be colored.
>
> The distinction is sharp and clear, and artificial coloring is usually easy to detect.
>
> One way to avoid false color is to omit human interest and confine each story to a dull, bald recitation of the barest facts minus all atmosphere. That would be safe; but it would be neither adequate nor complete coverage of the news. *Readers often need to see, feel, sense the complete picture.* They should be able to capture the atmosphere as well as the basic facts.

Color in the news, to put it another way, is the seasoning on the meat—hues, sounds, flavors, looks. It is the *mood* of the crowd that attends the political convention . . . the *setting* of the regatta on Lake Cayuga's waters . . . the *emotional and visual flavor* of the smoke-filled room rather than the decisions made there. It is often secondary news, not the heart of the event—not the essential Ws but the surrounding human or physical background that throws essentials into relief.

[4] Copyright © 1974 by the St. Paul *Pioneer Press.* Reprinted by permission.

Color need not be discoloration. Color is fact; color is reporting, just as genuinely as recital of what the speaker said. The wire-service memo quoted above continued:

> To draw color from the imagination rather than from accurate, unbiased observation is felony. It moves from the reporting to fiction, and fiction has no place in news.

To call the audience "enthusiastic" when half of it went to sleep, to write of a "slashing" game when it was listless, is discolor. It belies the integrity of the reporter; to the consumer who was there it is evidence of irresponsibility and incompetence.

Not every news story has to contain color. Most news is reported flat, without the third dimension that color gives it; much news, especially routine news, does not merit the extra space that color takes. But some news is less than accurate without it. The best newswriting gives color its due.

Color is description Writing a color story is a venture in description, just as surely as is the "descriptive theme" in an English composition class or as a fiction writer's painting of background for a tale. The purpose of color is to take the readers to the scene, to provide the sensory stimulants that the reporter perceived. Its tool is putting into words what would have struck the observers—what they would have heard, seen, smelled, touched, tasted and perhaps breathed.

Color stories, like descriptive essays and fiction, depend on painstaking selection rather than on photographic detail. They grow out of a writer's decision on basic theme—gaiety, confusion, noise, banality, anguish—and the choice of specifics to support it. They shun distracting nonessentials.

But because news color differs in purpose from essays or fiction, it differs also in approach and method. An essay or theme reports from a single, single-minded consciousness: that of its writer. Color's purpose is to tell somebody else what its writer sensed and felt about a scene or an event—how he saw it. Fiction writers compose a picture, describe an Alpine slope, a Victorian drawing room, a bar or a bawdy house, as a background contrived to throw into relief a contrived life situation. They are bound only by the limits of their imagination, knowledge and artistic integrity; essayists by the necessity to be honestly subjective.

Reporters, on the other hand, must seek something loosely called a universal point of view—universal, at least, for whatever universes comprise their audiences. They have to present things as they think their particular universes would see them. Like fiction writers, they must provide backdrops against which events occur, settings that they think will afford the net impressions they think the events have produced.

And—it cannot be said too often—they are rigidly bound by the facts.

Objectivity and color A reasonable and often-asked question: Can writers of color stories maintain the objective approach? Can they keep themselves out of the story?

Rarely. It is comparatively easy for reporters covering a political speech to report impersonally what the man said, who sat on the platform, how many attended. But the attempt to capture the flavor of the event means that complete detachment is impossible. The reporter's obligation to see the event as most of the audience would be likely to see it is conditioned by experience, wisdom and the not-too-common ability to step into the observer's shoes. Some shading of personality or of individual attitude, held within control, is bound to enter the collection of material for either a color story or a story with color. The shading may become deep-hued if the reporter is a "trained seal," a star performer, one who has become known to the audience as a personality. Because most reporters are anonymous, however, the need for objectivity remains.

Where color stories come from Most color stories deal with people-events. The stricken crowd on a Dallas street as a president is shot is the source of a color story. Fans lining up in the rain at a Super Bowl ticket window 24 hours before it opens . . . kids on a beach on the first warm day in June . . . strikers jeering at trucks trying to cross a picket line . . . the circus, the annual parade of gas buggies, the Christmas party for old men on Skid Row . . . such events are magnets for people, because people like to know about other people.

There are other kinds of color settings. A magazine story about a paddle-and-portage trip in Canada's Algonquin National Park took its savor from the very lack of people. A vigil at an isolated forest ranger's station, Coney Island in midwinter—these lonely scenes

---

"Color" and "With Color"

Make this distinction: A *color story* is one whose purpose is color. A *story with color* is one which, reporting a substantive event, provides enough of its background that the consumer can get an added emotional message. Straight news stories are often strengthened by the judicious injection of color.

Brush or Spray?

More words of wisdom from Theodore Bernstein: "Some writers brush words onto their canvases with gentle precision and the utmost feeling for color; others spray them on and leave them to drip." Understatement and restraint mark effective color writing.

demanded a sharper level of perception than people stories. But—to repeat—most color stories grow out of settings rich in human interplay.

Gathering material Three short sentences hold the key to reporting for color stories: *See* what you see. *Hear* what you hear. *Smell* what you smell.

You start with keen perception of the facts. Then you add the skill to winnow, to select, to discard, to pick details that will paint your description in honest shades. Suppose the subject is the crowd at the homecoming football game. A burst of rain in the second quarter soaks 40,000 fans. The rain and what it does, you decide, gives you your theme—your focus and your springboard. You observe the sodden hats, the newspaper-sheltered coiffures, the rush for the exits. You find out what the downpour did to the sale of coffee and hot dogs, you report the instant mire on the gridiron. You keep ears open for pungent comments. You note the bare stands across the field that five minutes ago were jammed.

Equally important is your decision what not to use. The bit about the sharp new band uniforms goes out (or should you keep it for contrast with the soggy cheerleaders?). You throw out the notes you took when nobody sang "The Star-Spangled Banner." As for the welcoming speech by the president of the alumni association—well, it was dull anyway.

All of this points up several characteristics of color stories: they start with central ideas or themes; they get vividness and credibility from careful choice of detail; they depend on specifics to convince readers that they are real. Fact-gathering can't be too careful or too thorough. A reporter on a color story becomes both spy and eavesdropper. It is vital to note the adoration on the face of the little girl cuddled under her father's plastic raincoat; to listen to the good-natured complaints of a plump matron that she's wet to the skin; and to make quick notes of her exact words, asking whether to use the simile that flashed to mind: "She looks like a drowned rag doll." And to get her name and address.

Of one unfailing aid experienced reporters are always aware—audience imagination. News consumers do not have to be told that there are 9,247 soaked topcoats in the crowd, for description of one

Falsehood Will Out

Fabrication of detail in color stories is hard to conceal. One of America's most competent reporters who was also a fiction writer covered the funeral procession of a president in Washington. The story was widely praised for its warmth and color. But in one respect it came a cropper. It reported a man and his small son as spectators at the Pennsylvania Avenue curb, and quoted them five times in a long story. Each time they "spoke" they became less real. The reason: The writer gave them no clear personality or physical reality, and their dialogue sounded bookish. Correctly or not, a reader is inclined to think that the reporter put fictional words into fictional mouths because they were routine words.

of them suggests the scene. Readers can generalize from the specific; when reporters give a sharp detail, they place it in a context created out of their own knowledge and experience.

The color story has no characteristic pattern. Because it is an appeal to the senses, it will more likely follow the suspended-interest model than the conventional; but it appears in a thousand forms. Often it is episodic, stating the theme in a lead section and supporting it with evidence in one specific after another. The simple color story is less difficult to compose, in one way, than the story with color, for the story with color emphasizes a news event against color background. The interweaving that combines the two elements in proper proportion and order is anything but easy.

The long story that follows is pure color. Its purpose is to paint a sordid scene, to let the reader experience what the reporter experienced. It may also have a social purpose—to arouse public concern. (Facts may stir citizen opinion more quickly and deeply than a sheaf of editorials.) This story is one of detailed description; it opens with a specific scene and goes on to a series of sharp vignettes. (Note that its reporter refers to himself only in the third person.)

The black snub-nosed police van, manned by three shirt-sleeved civilians, stopped quietly in a warehouse section near downtown at 10:30 one night last week.

Crouching through the darkness, the three searched quickly by flashlight beneath parked semi-trailers to find what they were looking for.

Moments earlier, the police radio had crackled the word: A man has passed out beneath one of the semis.

The man turned out to be Francis Alton, 62, craggy-faced and grayhaired, his body wedged against a pair of the trailer's wheels.

"Francis, what are we gonna do with you?" one of the men half-joked as they gently guided the wobbly man toward the black van.

Alton eased himself through the van's side door and maneuvered his grease-stained body onto the dusty, carpeted floor. "I guess I gave up," he said.

Several minutes later the van delivered Alton to the County Alcoholism Receiving Center, commonly called "Detox," and another night in a month-old experiment was well launched.

The experiment involves the use of a

pickup van manned by civilians. No police are on board, although police squads can and do pick up drunks.

Before July 1 the van duties were shared experimentally by police and civilians. Long before that, picking up drunks and drug addicts was exclusively a police chore. Many of the "victims" landed in the local jail's "drunk tank," and many were then sentenced to the workhouse.

But the Legislature declared drunkenness no longer a crime, and detoxification centers were established to dry out the nuisance inebriate and treat his behavior as an illness.

For nearly two years the main Detox Center has been housed in a nursing home, at 22 27th Av. From 900 to 1,000 inebriates are brought there each month.

The men in the van are two experienced Detox staff members—health aides or nursing assistants. They usually are joined by a civilian volunteer, frequently a Jaycee. They tour the city's central area nightly from 4 p.m. to midnight.

The unspoken assumption is that inebriates will get more humane treatment from paramedical personnel, whose goal is rehabilitation, than from policemen, who are used to dealing with criminals. The experiment also frees police time. But there is no expectation, according to Karl Parkins, director of the county's Alcoholism and Inebriety Program, that police squads ever will be entirely free of such duties.

The night that Francis Alton was led from underneath the semi, the van crew consisted of John Sample, 24, a health aide; John Fitzsimmons, 25, a nursing assistant; and a reporter acting as a volunteer.

During the night the crew made 10 contacts with drunks, eight of whom were taken to Detox. One man, found huddled in the vestibule of St. Julien's Catholic Church, was allowed to go on his way. Another was taken to a neighborhood shelter for Indians.

When Alton climbed into the rear of the van, the volunteer stepped in with him for a bumpy, circuitous ride that included a swing around Foster Park, a common collapsing place for the over-drunk.

The van's "passenger section" is barren except for wooden benches on opposite walls. There are two small windows, but they don't open. The air quickly becomes stale, stifling and hot. Nobody complained but the volunteer.

The back door is securely bolted—a fact tested by one of the evening's passengers. This passenger lay on his back and gave the door all he had with the heels of his shoes. Other passengers ignored him.

The volunteer wanted to know how Alton ended up with a pair of big truck wheels jammed against his body.

The van lurched forward and the man swayed. "I don't know how I got there," he said. "I don't know where I come from, and I don't know where I'm going."

Food? "I ain't had nothing to eat in three days," he said.

This was not Alton's first visit to Detox. Sample and Fitzsimmons knew him well, and the old man himself admitted to being in Detox, jail and the workhouse on many occasions.

There was no question about his preference. Detox, to him, was a place to "meet friends." Jail he described only in expletives.

In an expansive moment, bouncing along on the wooden bench, he said he was so glad to be going to Detox that "I hope to stay there the rest of my life."

But that isn't likely. Warren Illings, Detox administrator, explains that the average stay is just over three days. The law allows the center to hold a patient for 72 hours without a criminal charge.

Whenever possible, Illings said, the policy not only is to dry patients out, but also to refer them to Alcoholics Anonymous or other treatment programs.

A "shelter care" section of the center, however, is set aside for drying out chronic repeaters for whom there seems little hope of rehabilitation.

At least some of those encountered by Sample and Fitzsimmons the other night appeared to fall into that category. Nearly all the men—there were no women—were known to them as former Detox patients.

John, for example. He was found lying face down in a toilet stall in the basement of the Employment Service building.

And Ray, picked up on Potter Avenue after a wobbly bit of joshing with two policemen.

In the van, Ray said he has been picked up for drunkenness "a hundred times," makes his living by panhandling, sleeps "under the post office," and lays claim to being "one of the best bums there is."

Ray said he is 60 years old, and he laughed heartily before he said it. He has never been married, he said, nor has he ever gone hungry. He guessed that he makes $15 a day panhandling.

The van door opened and an aging man with dark glasses entered. Ray knew him at once as "One-Eye." They shared a bottle of wine which one of them had concealed in his clothing.

Francis Alton was the last man checked into Detox that night. Like the rest, he was given a rudimentary physical examination and issued clean pajamas. The center, clean and modern, looks like a hospital ward.

Fitzsimmons, who shared the driving with Sample, seemed pensive before quitting time.

"What's the problem?" he was asked.

"Oh, I don't know," Fitzsimmons said. "I was just thinking about the other guys out there who will be sleeping under semis tonight."

Whether such civilian concern is an argument for keeping the pickup chores out of police hands is a matter of opinion. The all-civilian setup is not totally without problems.

The presence of a police uniform, for example, may be a protection in the search of warehouse areas for men like Alton. After that search was over, the volunteer confided to Sample that he was envisioning a night watchman taking a shot at what might appear to be three burglars.

"I thought about that while we were doing it," Sample replied.

The following day at Detox, the new arrivals shuffled about the halls in pajamas and paper slippers with sobriety bordering on depression. Ray, the garrulous panhandler of the night before, was too sick to talk.

But Alton was all right. "I'm a little shaky, but not bad," he said, sitting on his white bedsheet.

He recalled nothing of the night before and had no idea how he had landed under the truck trailer.

"Trouble with me," he said, "I get to drinkin' and I'll lay down anywhere and go to sleep."

Sober now, Alton said he was born in Wisconsin, worked as a railroad section foreman for more than 10 years, "never had time" to marry, and has a room in a Potter Av. hotel.

He said he lives on a railroad pension of "$62 or $64" a month, much of which goes for wine. He used to belong to Alcoholics Anonymous, he said, but it didn't take. "It's pretty hard," he observed, "to change the spots on a tiger."

Several floors below, food carts were being loaded onto elevators for distribution to the approximately 110 temporary Detox residents. Some stared at television sets in corner lounges; others milled about trying to light cigarettes with trembling fingers.

Alton was asked what he would want from Detox if he could have anything at all that would help him. There was no hesitation.

"To stay sober," he said.[5]

The story below would not have been published—even locally—as straight news. But its graphic retelling put it on the wires. Two characteristics are worth note: first, its straight-news form, with a short summary lead, a second paragraph of secondary facts, and a third that introduces the narrative; second, its color words and color facts ("calloused mitts," "pretty even when drenched," "swaying gently," "big man with a voice to match").

NEW YORK, N.Y.—One hundred thirty steel-muscled longshoremen flattened their calloused mitts against the side of a 10,000-ton ship Wednesday, pushed it away from a Brooklyn pier, and held it back to save a 4-year-old girl from being crushed to death between the vessel and the pilings.

The feat was performed with a slight assist from three small loading machines and a large assist from a daring stevedore who was lowered by the heels into the narrow space between the ship and dock to help bring the child to safety.

The girl is Diana Svet, a blue-eyed blond, pretty even when drenched. The villain of the piece was the Yugoslav ship Srbija, hitting 10,000 tons with her cargo.

The Srbija docked Wednesday morning. In the afternoon the stevedores began unloading her. In mid-afternoon, Diana came to the pier with her mother, Anna, 25, to visit one of the vessel's officers, a cousin of Mrs. Svet.

They went aboard, learned that the cousin wasn't there, then began descending the stairway leading down the ship's side.

The lowest step of the stairway was one foot above the pier. Mrs. Svet, holding onto Diana's left hand, made it, but Diana, who jumped, didn't.

The jump carried her out of her mother's grasp, and into the 10-inch space between ship and dock outer-structure.

Screaming, she plunged 15 feet into the water, where she managed to grab a slippery piling.

The Srbija was swaying gently. But even the slightest sway, with 10,000 tons behind it, could be fatal.

Pier superintendent Ignatio Scibilia, a big man with a voice to match, bellowed an order, and 130 stevedores scrambled off the ship. The two lines holding the ship to the dock were cut.

Then the men and the three little machines pitted themselves against the ship. Inch by inch, it gave away.

John Balzano, 45, Giuseppe Gambino, 49, and Joseph Zapulla, 25, went into action.

Balzano and Gambino lowered Zapulla, head down. Diana's strength was waning as Zapulla dropped a noosed rope and pulled it taut. Then he and the girl were pulled up to the pier.

Outside of a scare and a thorough wetting, Diana was all right. Mama took her home.

Zapulla, who had taken a banging around against the piling, went home, too.

STUDY SUGGESTIONS

1. What would you expect to be the essential differences between, say, a *news* story about the adjournment of a session of Congress and a *feature* story about the event?
2. How—using terms different from those on pages 302–303, would you define the journalistic concept *human-interest story*?
3. Define the term *suspended interest* as

applied to news stories and give examples of stories treated in the suspended-interest manner.

4. Define the term *news feature* so as to make clear its distinguishing characteristics.
5. Would you describe the drunken derelict story (page 313) as a news feature? Explain your answer.
6. Differentiate between color in news reporting and colored news reporting.
7. Name some of the distinctive problems you might face in gathering material for a color story and in writing it.
8. "Most color stories deal with people-events" (page 316). Why?
9. In the story about the pickup patrol (page 318), the reporter refers to himself three times, always in the third person. Do you think he should have stressed his part in the event more heavily? less? or omitted it entirely?

PRACTICE ASSIGNMENTS

1. Extract from the pickup patrol story (page 318) all the references to and facts about Francis Alton (the first man you meet in the story). With all these facts, write a brief suspended-interest story beginning and ending with Alton's experiences.
2. From a newspaper, select a "parent" story and its accompanying sidebar—for example, a political convention story and a sidebar about the collapsing stage—and combine the two. Which is the better treatment?
3. Cover an event of local significance—a senator's campaign talk, dedication of the new city hall, a three-alarm fire. Write the straight story the event calls for and also a color sidebar.
4. Make a list of five or more topics on which you could write human-interest stories. Write them.
5. When you come across amusing or odd incidents that could be treated as human-interest or suspended-interest stories—events that might not "make the paper" in any other form—write them. You can't try too many. And you can't keep them too short.

RELATED READING

Snyder, Louis L., and Richard B. Morris, eds. *A Treasury of Great Reporting.* Simon & Schuster, 1949. See page 109.

16 News Below the Surface

PREVIEW

Much news lies below the surface. In-depth reporting, the kind that looks under carpets and seeks causes, explanations or probable outcomes, is in short supply today. Though a lot of news work is hit-and-run, journalists and their audiences join in demanding more cause-and-effect reporting.

Enterprisers, also called "made stories," are in-depth tools. They result from recognition that surface reporting has not yielded enough enlightenment and that further investigation, new questions, added sources are needed. Among types of enterprise reporting:

- Investigative reporting (see Chapter 17)
- Features of many kinds
- Follow-up reporting
- Campaign and crusade reporting
- Historical features
- Special occasion stories

The surface of the news is thin, but it is often opaque.

Editors at conventions talk soberly about "reporting in depth." Critics of the news media ask, with considerable naiveté, why every newspaper does not report as fully as the New York *Times* or as thoughtfully as the *Christian Science Monitor*. They frown at broadcast journalism for hop-skip-and-jump reporting. They demand of all of the media the cause-and-effect reporting[1] that digs for the *how* and the *why*. Nobody argues the assertion that photographic reproduction of the veneer of events does not reveal what lies below.

Getting beneath the surface is the essential challenge of today's reporting.

[1] The term used by Dr. Harold L. Nelson, School of Journalism and Mass Communication, University of Wisconsin

HIT-AND-RUN REPORTING

"The hit-and-run reporter," says one observer of the journalistic process, "partly through production pressures and partly because of personal inadequacy . . . appears content to grab a few facts, bang them into a story, and turn to something new." Stories that report faithfully the *who, what, when* and *where* may be barren if they do nothing more. Elmer Davis said that reporting that is *merely* objective isn't good enough (see page 39). Examples of stories whose writers stopped too soon:

- The report that postal inspectors "swooped down" on the Boston post office to check on suspected fraud, but that did not identify the fraud or the reason for thinking it existed
- The report that the state commissioner of human rights resigned after two weeks in office, without indication of what led to the resignation
- The report that plans for a big local factory have been canceled, but that gives no reasons

Reporting that pierces the crust depends on news imagination, energy, perception and a burning drive to find causes. It is sometimes a luxury—expensive in dollars, time, manpower and gray matter. Harry Ashmore, whose stubborn war on a segregationist governor won him a Pulitzer Prize when he was editor of the Arkansas *Gazette,* said that "we can't expect a local tea kettle radio station to do much costly reporting in depth—especially when the great newspapers, the networks and even the wire services do so little of it." Without it the public, like a passenger in a Concorde SST at 45,000 feet, sees land from such a distance that even the Eiffel Tower looks flat.

Most followers of the news have seen news coverage that stopped too soon. Why, in the story about a basketball team's walkout after the coach fired a player, weren't you told why the man was fired, whether the team will come back to play Friday's game, what avenues of appeal are open? When two local clinics catch fire in two days, you want to know whether arson is suspected, how the patients will be served, when reopening can be expected. How does the latest Supreme Court decision about control of obscenity affect *your* community: What is the local definition of community standards? Will children's attendance at movies be affected? How do local citizens feel about it?

News enterprise that asks questions going beyond the instant news is a reasonable minimum to expect of reporters. Interrogation marks are elementary in reporting a PTA meeting or an airplane smashup, a Sunday school picnic or the outbreak of a new kind of flu. They are basic to the craft.

They are especially vital, though in a different way, to the kind of reporting to which this chapter is devoted: enterprise reporting.

ENTERPRISERS

Some newsrooms, print or air, misapply the term *enterpriser* or its equivalent *made news* to the elementary reporting process. The terms mean something else. Enterprisers and made-news stories grow from a reporter's or editor's "news imagination," from a realization that spot news often is not enough. They often are *sequels* to spot news. They come from asking the right follow-up questions in the right places, the right kind of digging in a library, the approach to a condition of life—contemporary or ancient, human or geological or theoretical—from a new angle. Such stories may be spot news; they are often suggested by current events; they may be entirely free-standing. They develop from curiosity about subjects like these:

- How each councilman has voted on tax issues since the last election (from council records)
- Trends in local real estate transfers in the last *xxx* years (from real estate dealers and public records)
- The probable impact on farm income of a current corn borer infestation (from agricultural economists, pathologists, county agents)
- Success of the municipal heating system installed two years ago in a nearby small town, and possibility of its use in other communities (interviews in the nearby town, records, queries of local energy authorities)
- Changes in reading habits and book borrowing in recent years (from local librarians and library records)
- Turnover of small businesses, vacancies in commercial property, number of tax delinquencies in a "blighted" area of a city (real estate dealers, Chamber of Commerce, local businesses)
- Out-of-the-ordinary ways people make their livings: the woman who runs a yarn import shop in her living room, the Ph.D. candidate who earns his tuition by writing other students' term papers, the man who traces family trees for local citizens of Swedish descent
- The fortunes of the local family that moves each April to the north woods to live off the land
- Prospects for another mass influenza inoculation program in your community this year

- Success—or lack of it—of the small plant in a suburb that started making running boards for autos

Reports of public opinion polls are *made* stories. They take their cues from current events; but they elaborate or amplify rather than report them. When a newspaper, a commercial polling company hired by a TV station, or the Associated Press, Gallup or Harris survey organization asked a cross section of citizens whether they thought Bert Lance should resign as director of the Office of Management and Budget in 1977, it was "making" news.

Such stories go beyond current events; they add depth to people's understanding of the life of which they are a part; they show how some of the other half live. They inform and entertain audiences, and they often make a reporter's life more interesting.

They can take any journalistic form. When you develop a story beyond the call of duty, it is news imagination that you add, not new rhetorical pattern. Though made stories are usually what were defined in Chapter 15 as features—stories whose time element is secondary—they can take any form the news craft or your own invention suggests. Often they use the suspended-interest form.

"Creative" Writing

Can journalistic writing be "creative"?

The question comes up because of a thoughtless distinction between the writing demanded in composition courses and that in newspaper-magazine-advertising-broadcasting writing. The first is creative, so it is implied, because it is the stuff of the imagination or the intellect; the second is something else because it grows out of actualities.

This is nonsense.

Creative writing is not limited to belles lettres—to fiction, poetry and the essay (though these kinds of writing are sterile without creativity).

Creative writing springs from creative imagination . . . writing that calls up lucid, living images, that breathes vitality into emotive concepts and hard realities. It is evoked by lively and probing vision. It demands innovative attitudes toward the routine or the arcane—toward dramas or news interviews, novels or event-centered spot news, poems or personality portraits. Its agent is rhetorical or "literary" sensitivity that makes language provocative, impelling.

Creative imagination in news starts with theme and purpose. It continues with curiosity, inventiveness to guide planning and collecting materials, and wisdom to choose between the superficial and the essential. It depends on a subtle alliance of art and craft.

"The truly creative writer or artist," wrote Norman Cousins in *Saturday Review/World*, "never has to choose between the ivory tower and the arena. He moves freely from one to the other according to his needs and his concerns. Nothing is more vital for the creative artist than access to the arena . . ."

Creative writing is a totality. It is a proper goal for any worker with words, not the property of one lonely genus of writer.

Newspapers now use more made-news stories than they did a few years ago—television newsrooms too—but few media can free reporters regularly for the time depth reporting demands. Reporters, aware of the need for more such enterprise, complain that newsroom purse strings aren't elastic enough. Whatever the cause of missed opportunities, the stories you remember are often those that have departed from routine in favor of getting behind the scenes.

EXAMPLES OF ENTERPRISERS

The examples that follow show how stories grow beyond the spot news impulse. A reporter or an assignment editor somehow envisions that "the right questions in the right places" will lead to a story. The writer of the story below took a cue from a national magazine article:

> Though local parks are safe, Capt. Elmer Bednagl, head of the park police, said yesterday, he "would not advise using them after midnight."
>
> Bednagl was commenting on a national magazine article that called his city's parks "among the safest in the country."
>
> "I'd hesitate myself to walk through our parks at night," Bednagl said, "especially in the early morning hours."
>
> The parks close officially at midnight.
>
> "Some of these parks have dark, wooded areas," Bednagl explained. "People shouldn't use such areas at night—and fortunately most people don't."
>
> Park police statistics show that there have been only three molestings and five robberies reported in city parks in the first eight months of this year.
>
> There are 152 parks in the police jurisdiction of the county. Twenty-four patrolmen work the 600,110 acres of park property lying within and without the city.
>
> "Lighting is a deterrent to crime," Bednagl said. "The lighting is good now, especially at Franklin, North Side, Wilbur and Pleasant Parks."
>
> Since the lighting was improved at Franklin early last year, Bednagl said, only three reports of crime have come from there. During the preceding two years there were 30.

A story in the Milwaukee *Journal* published when college and high school students were about to begin classes attacked a question thousands were asking: How important are grades? No references to its timeliness are needed. Excerpts from the story appear here:

> Some employers really care what kind of grades you get in high school or college. Others don't.
>
> There are companies that say, "We won't even look at any college graduate with less than a 3-point average" (on a 4-

point system). Generally they mean it.

Public accounting firms usually demand high grades. So do several prestigious, big name companies. Freezing out anybody under a 3-point may seem unfair or elitist, but these companies get swamped with applicants. And grades are a handy screening device.

If you have a 2.3 average, you probably should forget about such a company for the time being. That doesn't mean you're barred from the company for life. You might land a job there after you get experience somewhere else. (Or you might find you like your career elsewhere and decide that the company that wouldn't talk to you can go climb a rope.)

These general statements can be made about grades:

Good grades can never hurt you, particularly in a tight job market.

Ed Wild, director of employee relations for the Ball Corporation of Muncie, Ind., said, "Anything over a 3-point receives instant recognition."

Bonnie Cready, employment supervisor for Owens-Corning Fiberglas in Toledo, hires very few secretaries right out of high school. But, she said, "If someone with an A or A-minus average was on the honor roll all four years, I may make an exception."

In most cases good grades alone will not get you the job. Recruiters look at the whole package . . .[2]

[*The story continues with comment on other aspects of the subject, following the same pattern—summary statements by the writer, direct quotations from employment directors, and division under other subtopics.*]

The story about motels, below, was born in the perceptive curiosity of Andrew H. Malcolm of the New York Times Service on a cross-country motor trip. Though he based it largely on what occurred on "one recent day" at a specific motel in New Mexico, he bolstered on-the-spot material with facts from Holiday Inn central-office statistics and other outside sources. The story would not have been written without the impulse to find out "how it works." Notable in the story are the conviction and pace it gains from specific names and details:

ALBUQUERQUE, N.M.—"Do you have a room for tonight?" the rumpled father asks wearily.

"For how many?" the desk clerk responds.

Out in the car a rumpled mother, three rumpled children, and a rumpled dog watch intently. When the father reaches for a pen to fill out a form, a soft cheer seeps from the air-conditioned station wagon.

Everyone begins gathering up coloring books, dolls, handbags, toy pistols and swim suits. And another motel room is rented.

It is a ritual as old as the automobile itself: Americans on the road in search of a night's lodging.

And across the land on these warm summer evenings during the peak vacation period, it is a ritual that is performed perhaps two million times a day, about once for every one of the 2,551,007 rooms in the 52,000 motels in the United States.

Here in New Mexico at the intersection of two major interstate highways, the cars

[2] Copyright © 1977 by Summit Press Syndicate. Reprinted by permission.

begin streaming down the cement exit ramps soon after 2 p.m.

For many travelers, a computer has already made their reservations and promised to bill them, even if they do not appear. In fact, the computer based in Omaha, Neb., or Memphis, Tenn., or Phoenix, Ariz., has determined, in effect, how far each family will drive each day.

It does not matter to these travelers in search of some vacation Valhalla that a few years ago the land around here was a sandy waste beyond the city limits.

Few people except the scouts for Holiday Inns knew that this property was destined to become, in effect, a new "transient town" dedicated to the needs of those thousands who pass through daily.

On Sept. 2, 1966, the interstates opened here. On Jan. 11, 1967, they began construction of a motel. The motel opened on Oct. 1, 1968. It was followed by several other motels, truck stops and restaurants. And now just about anyone driving through this city passes by what the Holidex computer calls H.I. No. 126AB.

The result is an average annual occupancy rate of 98 to 99 percent, compared with the national average of 70 percent and the break-even average of 60 percent.

"And summertime," a motel official said here, "is family time when you really make your money."

Long before the sun came up one recent day, the innkeeper, Murphy Jenkins, and his assistant, Jim Sanders, knew very well that they would have no vacancies for the coming night, and, for that matter, the next night and the next night.

Frank Cortese, the bellboy, knew he would make close to $30 in tips. And Joe Roloson, the bartender, know he would sell a case of beer and a quart of vodka every hour. Bennie Davis, the housekeeper, knew she would lose about 75 ashtrays and 50 towels and two families would forget luggage. And Sanders knew the morning mail would bring 10 keys that yesterday's guests had carried off. But Mrs. Margaret Parker could not know that there would be no room at the inn for her.

The day began at 4 a.m. when Steve Dillon, the night clerk, started the wake-up calls for travelers anxious to get on the road. At 6:30 a.m. Agnes Martinez arrived to handle the remaining guests checking out and, with colored paper slips in numbered slots, to begin plotting which guests, some of them still asleep hundreds of miles away, would stay in which room.

By 8 a.m. almost every guest had hefted his bags into gaping car trunks or tied them on rooftop luggage racks. The long hallways were empty, but silently they began to look like narrow, carpeted battle zones.

The maids, 18 of the inn's 96 employees, were attacking each of the inn's 192 rooms, tossing the soiled linens and towels out the doors, emptying the trash, vacuuming the shag rugs, and setting the partly used soap bars aside for charity.

The washing machines began to chew on the day's 550 sheets and 970 towels. The swimming pool, out where the construction crews were working on an additional 108 rooms, was little used. Jenkins, the innkeeper, was in Phoenix for an emergency regional meeting to update menu prices for this month's inflation. And Amos Wack had just left a motel in Lubbock, heading west.

Slowly the seven ice machines recovered from the onslaught of tourists surreptitiously swiping scoopfuls for their portable coolers. Then, at 2:30 p.m., Connie Brown and Loretta O'Brien, the two receptionists who would handle the brunt of the day's tourist barrage, went on duty.

Minutes later, like clockwork, the barrage began. Mrs. Rosalie Simon checks into Room 333. George Tarleton checks in with his wife and child. Mrs. Simon returns. Her room faces the highway.

"I need my sleep," she says. She gets Room 305. The Tarletons march by in their swim suits.

"You have to be very patient with people," says Mrs. Brown, who, like many out here, fled from the East.

"Families are the messiest guests of all," says Mrs. Davis, the housekeeper. "Businessmen use one towel, one bed, one ashtray and that's it. Not families. And families seem to steal more, too."

At 5 p.m. Ramsay Conyer of Morristown, N.J., arrives with a reservation. The motel does not have his name, but he gets one of the few remaining rooms and never learns of the error.

Shortly before 6 p.m., Wack, an airlines pilot being transferred from Florida to San Francisco, drives in from Lubbock.

A young man comes in. He wants a good stationery store. Miss O'Brien directs him. Mrs. Parker, who is driving from Nashville, Tenn., to Los Angeles at 50 miles per hour, arrives. All the rooms are full or reserved. She is sent to another motel. One-half hour later she could have had one of the unused 6 p.m. reservations.

And so it goes into the evening, each traveler another face and another room number. Stretching their arms, rubbing their eyes and sucking their sunglass earpieces, they fill out forms, submit credit cards, get directions and become new numbers on the board.

At 7 p.m., Room 157 calls for more towels. Room 407 has toilet trouble. A young couple shuffles to the desk. They are ill at ease and smile often.

Mrs. Brown looks at them briefly. "You're honeymooners, aren't you?" she says. The newlyweds look stunned.

"In that case," Mrs. Brown continues, "let's give you a room with a king-sized bed." The couple blushes. "Aren't they cute?" says Mrs. Brown.

Room 435, Eric Dickman, checks out. He prefers to sleep by day and drive by night.

At 9 p.m., 19 guaranteed reservations are unclaimed. Mrs. Brown rents out a couple to a lucky few travelers. For the others there is no room.

At 10:30 p.m. Robert Keats, 10 hours out of Dallas, drags himself to the desk and pleads, "I can't go another mile. Anything?" He gets a couch in a meeting room.

At midnight there are 13 unclaimed reservations. Dillon, the night man, starts renting them to "walk-ins," travelers without reservations.

At 4 a.m., Katherine Golden checks in and becomes Room 249. As it has been for 10 weeks, the inn is full.

Moments later Dillon begins the wake-up calls.[3]

Made stories appear every day in all the news media—stories short and long, solemn and light, color, personality, historical. Identifying them and examining their qualities with critical eye is a way to learn. (Some of the stories in other chapters are enterprisers—the poll of high school students on page 289, the North Dakota blizzard recap on page 147, and others.)

Made stories can be short. The one that follows seems little more than a synopsis:

> Nonfiction books, especially about sports, child care, personal and family adjustment, and current events, continued last year as most in demand at the Winton Public Library.

> "Not more than half as many fiction books circulated as nonfiction," Amanda Sharpe, librarian, said last week. "It's a trend we've experienced ever since the Vietnam War and Watergate."
>
> Ms. Winthrop said that books on politics are "big sellers."
>
> "We never had enough copies of the Woodward-Bernstein books about Watergate and Nixon," she said. "And books like 'The Boys on the Bus'—about politicians if not politics—are being widely read."
>
> Books on soccer, women's sports, mental hygiene for children and "self help" get wide circulation, she said. "Lots of people seem to want to be their own psychiatrists," she added.
>
> A count on circulation of all types of materials will be a part of the library's annual report next July.

Broadcasting in recent years has made increasing use of its own varieties of enterprisers, often in documentary series. Many readers will recall the "Nixon on Nixon" collection of excerpts from Nixon speeches that was broadcast in 1974. Such subjects as abuses in nursing and senior citizen homes, lack of sanitary regulations in grocery stores and meat markets, the decay of schools in the inner city, and the notable career of Edward R. Murrow have been investigated. A radio broadcast from a Great Lakes port described the shabby reception facilities for visitors coming to the city by ship.

FOLLOW-UP

The complaint that news media forget a news event when it has cooled is well based. Emphasis on *today's* news has often meant that sequels to the first chapter are ignored. When 164 guests at a Kentucky nightclub died in a fire they couldn't escape, it was screaming news in print and on the air. When a fire marshal's report a few months later showed criminal negligence by owners and officials, the story got seven inches on an inside page. Not many know today what happened to the Watergate burglars, the Hanafi terrorists in Washington or the restored monarchy in Spain. And how many read or heard the shocking report of experts six months after the Teton dam disaster in Idaho? The report got lost—not by evil intent, but because such a report isn't very exciting, and because its topic was "old."

The media know the problem and increasingly try to meet it. Newspapers and radio or TV newsrooms have followed up on the use of federal money to restore water supplies to farms after a drought; on whether people who telephoned President Carter on his radio call-in program got answers to their gripes; and on the success of new measures to control forest fires following the disastrous 1976 summer. The Associated Press took a long look at the new government in India six months after it replaced Prime Minister Indira Gandhi's regime (it was "caught in a web of unhappy dilemmas"); the New York *Times* checked up on federal policing of Medicaid abuses a year after a new system was installed (much of the waste was continuing).

The most meaningful follow-ups are likely to be those developed at the instance of the media themselves—enterprisers, in other words. It isn't good enough to sit back and hope that George, the government or God will do it.

OTHER USES OF MADE STORIES

The campaign or "crusade" Newspapers, and radio and TV less frequently, undertake stories—often in series—to reveal corruption, to present community needs or to promote special causes. Chapter 17, Investigative Reporting, has more to say about this type of journalism.

Series An Albany newspaper assigned a reporter to write a series of stories about the city's amusement and recreation facilities for use by visitors to the city in summer. Dozens of media, in the face of inflation and "consumer protection" needs, developed stories in the 1970s about comparative prices, reasons for rising food costs, the decreasing value of the dollar. The New York *Times* once put 20 experienced reporters to work on 20 stories about contemporary changes in the city and its suburbs. Most people have seen series about teen-age drinking, drug use and response to new voting responsibilities; governmental and private intrusion into citizens' privacy; the effects of "affirmative action" requirements; the need for more mental health facilities; the Equal Rights Amendment; pornography; why Johnny can't read, though Nancy can. A reporter finds out how a candidate won an election he was supposed to lose, and writes a string of stories about it.

Such investigations, demanding time, money and reportorial skills, provide more material than one story can accommodate. Most media, air and print, hold series to four or five installments. Audience interest declines perceptibly when series run longer.

Historical features are made stories. So are many features in science, medicine, industry, sports, finance, education. The business section of one Sunday paper contained these made stories:

- The increasingly sober and businesslike behavior of conventioneers
- The prospects for a profitable shipping season in a nearby port
- The growth of "professionalism" among secretaries in local offices

- The importance to retailers of good weather as Easter approaches
- What price-support legislation might mean to area farmers
- The rousing success of a new local pizza emporium

Most such stories are built around cores that would yield similar features any place. City and assignment editors and reporters who are alert check regularly on media in other communities.

Stories for special occasions Reporters mutter "not again!" when they are assigned special-occasion stories—the usually brief pieces that are routine when a holiday or an annual event rolls around. These stories tell you how Labor Day came about, what really happened to Washington's father's cherry tree and the way they celebrate April Gowks' Day in Scotland. The mutterers aver that every approach known to man has been exploited (how many times, come February 2, have you seen a cute interview with a groundhog?). But the stories continue, and now and then somebody thinks up something new to do with them.

A special-occasion story is not often spot news. It is timely general information (or whimsy)—timely because it must be published *now* or not at all. Often, however, it is also timeless—it would be as apt in 1980 as in 1960. It gives the reader something novel or amusing to suit the flavor of a familiar holiday or season. Often it's a sidebar.

Materials for these stories often came from printed references: histories, encyclopedias, almanacs. A February 12 story telling the world that Lincoln was the first president to wear a beard came from an old biography; one about the origin of Memorial Day from an almanac; one on December 7 from 1941 newspapers. A long feature reporting that only two men actually signed the Declaration of Independence on July 4, 1776, was drawn from histories.

Special occasions also generate spot news. They report community celebrations, patriotic parades, fireworks; at Christmas, church services, retail sales, the family that can't afford turkey and fixin's. Spot news may follow as well as precede the occasion. The Associated Press for a Labor Day Tuesday brought together a story with this opening:

> For most Americans, Labor Day means leisure at the end of summer—picnics, county fairs or a long drive back home. From organized labor, there were reminders that for many it had been a summer of discontent.
>
> In Detroit, union officials . . . [*the story continues with a column of Labor Day news from all over*]

And a morning paper, on one February 15, carried a long human-interest story about the marriages that had been celebrated in local courts the day before . . . and the divorces that had been granted.

A classic special-day story came from Drew Middleton of the New York *Times'* Paris office on V-E Day anniversary in 1965. Middleton buttressed historical material and his own past experience with on-the-spot reporting. Here is his comment on the story's development:

> A good deal of the story originated in my memory; it was not easily forgotten. The description of the school room and its surroundings on the day was reporting on the spot. I spent the day in Rheims talking to people in the city. By luck, I had come through the city earlier in the month and had met five couples, two American and three British, who had stopped to see the place "where it ended." These provided me the material about the middle-aged men from Oklahoma and Yorkshire.
>
> I also looked through the *Times* files in Paris to check some of the facts about the surrender and to get some of the atmosphere of the time.
>
> The genesis of the story was this: I thought we should have a piece from Rheims rather than Paris, told the foreign desk in New York, and went up to Rheims to write it.

Middleton's background combined with current reporting to produce the story:

RHEIMS, France, May 7—Up the street the boys were waiting for the girls to come out of school. When they walked off arm in arm in the soft May air, none gave a thought to the dusty room in the school where it all ended.

The room nowadays has that unreal air that haunts all shrines. The battle maps still hang on the walls. But the armies marked on it, and even the place names, seem irrelevant to the busy life that flows around the school.

A long plain table stands at one end of the room. There are seven chairs on one side, three on the other. On that other May 7 the three were occupied by Adm. Hans Georg von Friedeburg, Col. Gen. Alfred Jodl and Major Wilhelm Oxenius.

At 2:41 in the morning Jodl and Friedeburg signed the instrument that signified the unconditional surrender of the Third Reich. It was over, in Europe at least.

History chooses strange sites for her great acts of surrender.

Someone knew that the McLean house at Appomattox was undamaged and Lee rode up in his best uniform. There was a convenient railroad siding at Compiègne and to it came the Germans of 1918 and the French of 1940.

In May, 1945, Rheims was the advance command post of the Supreme Headquarters Allied Expeditionary Force Europe. Millions of men over half a continent answered the orders that came from the big red brick school.

Great men came and went: Eisenhower, Montgomery, Bradley, Tedder, Spaatz. Here were planned the last blows that felled Hitler's Germany.

But today the people of Rheims couldn't care less. The schoolroom, once General Eisenhower's "war room," is closed to the public Sunday because it is being used by a television company for a program.

No one is going to miss it. The kids waiting outside the school know there was a war but they are a little vague about what actually happened there. And in the good cafes in the arcades of Rheims the surrender is good for perhaps two minutes of personal reminiscence, and then on to today's business: the next vintage, the new car, the trip to the Riviera.

They may be callous to the touch of Clio, the muse of history. Or perhaps Rheims knows the lady too well. What is the date May 7, 1945, to such a city?

Not far from the school, the great Mars Gate built by the Romans in the third century still stands. The archbishops of Rheims consecrated kings of France from the time of Philip Augustus to that of Charles X. Outside the medieval walls Joan of Arc dispersed an English army.

So, a generation after, this is a shrine for that one generation among many. They come, of course. Middle-aged men from Oklahoma or Yorkshire with rather impatient wives who can't understand why their husbands are interested.

The men, however, won't be hurried.

They look at the maps and point. "There's where we were, Edna," or "The map must have been bloody well out of date. We were well east of Hamburg."

The room, the school, the city amount to a punctuation point for a whole generation. This was the end of the belly-tightening, desperate years.

It is not dramatic now and it was not dramatic then. A friend once asked Lieut.-Gen. Walter Bedell Smith, General Eisenhower's chief of staff, who signed the document for the Allies, what he had thought of when it was all over.

"To tell you the truth," he said, "I thought of all the damned paperwork this was going to mean in the morning."

The only touch of drama was provided by Jodl, the schoolbook soldier with the face from a medieval painting and the mind of a computer.

When he had signed, he stood at attention and said to General Smith:

"General! With this signature the German people and the German armed forces are, for better or worse, delivered into the victor's hands. In this war, which has lasted more than five years, both have achieved and suffered more than perhaps any other people in the world. In this hour I can only express the hope that the victor will treat them generously."

Outside the street is almost deserted. The few passersby don't even glance at the door with its brass plaque. After all, it was a long time ago.[4]

Few special-occasion stories have the richness of Middleton's—most are simple brighteners. A Friday the 13th story offers mock-serious interviews about ways of avoiding bad luck. April First rarely passes without leads that say something like "income taxes will be abolished if . . ." or "now that we have put a man on the moon, green cheese imports are feared by the Wisconsin dairy industry." An inland New York paper published a doctored photograph showing an ocean liner in the town's small lake harbor. Oslo newspapers urged readers to pour boiling water down their drains to melt ice in Oslo Fjord. And an American editor is still wondering why so many people called in after he ran this story:

> The Mocha-Java Grocery on East Main Street is doing something about the price of coffee. For one day only the

owner, who signs himself Loof Lipra, is offering all brands for 29 cents a pound. "It won't make me much money," Lipra explains, "but I have too much cash in the bank anyway."

The day of the sale is today, April 1, and the offer expired at 7:30 a.m. Lipra opened for business at 8.

STUDY SUGGESTIONS

1. Define the term *enterpriser* as a description of a type of reporting.
2. What can the enterpriser provide to news audiences that "ordinary" reporting may not offer?
3. What is the difference between *made news* and *invented news*?
4. What do you understand to be Norman Cousins' meaning when he says that "nothing is more vital for the creative writer than access to the arena"?
5. Suggest some specific examples of the use of news interviews as enterprisers related to the current news.
6. Would you surmise that the Andrew Malcolm story about the motel business was on assignment or that it was the outcome of Malcolm's own curiosity and perceptiveness? Do you agree that it "answers a lot of questions many travelers ask themselves"?
7. Explain the difference between a news story reporting plans for a local Fourth of July celebration and a Fourth of July special occasion story.

PRACTICE ASSIGNMENTS

1. Get the facts for and write a story that brings readers up to date on the progress of integration in your city's public schools; or what several local industries are doing to assure their energy supplies in the next decade; or the effects in your community of the drive for equal rights for men and women; or some other problem that your community's citizens have been thinking about. Include not only factual material but also, when it's appropriate, opinions representing different points of view.
2. Events at state or national levels often suggest development of local-angle stories—how the rise in minimum wages will affect local industry, whether a change in the pattern of federal funding for highways will be felt in a state, county or city. Identify such a news topic, gather facts and write a story for your local newspaper.
3. Rewrite the Assignment 2 story for a local radio station.
4. Try an April 1 or Friday the 13th story, making it frankly a lampoon. Or do a more serious one for Labor Day, Easter or some other major holiday. Do a number of them.

17 Investigative Reporting

PREVIEW

Though investigative journalism became the vogue of 1970 journalism, it is not new. Any good reporting is investigative reporting. But the term has come to mean reporting in depth to reveal public or private behavior that otherwise might go unseen—usually criminal or antisocial behavior, but not always. Investigative reporting can disclose a trend in real estate sales or a future health hazard as well as corruption in City Hall.

This kind of reporting, though it uses the tools of day-by-day journalism, uses them with more vigor, more determination, often more preparation and more time allowance, and always more patience and perseverance. It is often "team reporting"—collaboration among two or more reporters. It sometimes resorts to infiltration or undercover methods, sometimes methods criticized as unethical. But its results are almost always admired and frequently of high public service.

"Investigative reporting" is a catchword of American journalism in the late 20th century. Newsrooms label some of their reporters "investigative"; columnists write about the sins and virtues of the art; journalism students set their sights on the path of Woodward and Bernstein, whose Watergate reporting focused the world's eyes on the "new" kind of newswork.

It is not new. The New York *Herald* prevented conviction of the wrong man for murder in 1836 by producing proof of innocence. Joseph Pulitzer's *World* caused a cleanup, early this century, in life insurance companies' misuse of policyholders' investments. The hard-nosed reporting of the muckrakers, in both magazines and newspapers, exposed crime and antisocial behavior in government and business, in industry, politics and welfare work.

Though the Watergate achievement is the century's most notable example of investigative reporting, it is not alone. Don Bolles, a Phoenix reporter, was murdered in 1976 after his series of stories alleging that a dog-racing enterprise had ties to organized crime (a Chicago *Tribune* reporter was similarly murdered in the 1930s). More than two dozen *Wall Street Journal* reporters revealed payoffs, kickbacks and bribery among giant corporations (see page 346). The Los Angeles *Times* unmasked municipal financial misbehavior involving the Long Beach city government and a Long Beach paper (see page 348). Joe Rigert of the Minneapolis *Tribune* won a Society of Professional Journalists award for a 15-part series on the staggering problems of peoples in South Africa. The Philadelphia *Inquirer* showed up brutality and murder in a Pennsylvania state hospital, and the New York *Times* found criminal behavior in a New Jersey hospital; the Cleveland *Plain Dealer* exposed corruption in a county office.

There are limits Reporting in depth to unearth vital information about matters of public policy is a prized tool of responsible news media. But it is apparent that most of the media that undertake it are the ones that have the finances and staff to support it. And too many, large and small, limit themselves to the passive comfort of covering surface news. Caustic critics like H. L. Mencken and A. J. Liebling protested what they considered the apathy of 20th century journalism. Silas Bent, however, whose book *Newspaper Crusades* recounts many notable feats of investigative journalism, thinks the charge poorly founded. One of the judges of an annual Heywood Broun competition said that the entries gave him "renewed confidence in the performance of the working journalist. . . ."

Credit . . . But Where It's Due

Americans applauded the news media when they brought word, in the early 1970s, of political and personal corruption in Washington—Watergate, a bribed vice president, scattergun invasion of privacy, falsehoods in the White House. But, as David Halberstam and others noted, it wasn't so much "the media" as a handful of reporters and publications that earned the credit. It wasn't "the media" that broke Watergate open—it was two reporters and the backing of their paper, the Washington *Post*. It wasn't "the media" but two or three loners that defied Washington to publish the Pentagon Papers. After they found leadership, "the media" rode along. But only a few reporters, almost all from the print media, put forth the effort and the daring to achieve what has properly been called "great journalism."

The kudos gained by the *Post*, the New York *Times*, the Los Angeles *Times*, and *Time* and *Newsweek* gratifies journalists and encourages them. There is currently far more emphasis on depth reporting, in print and on the air, than there was before 1972. But investigative reporting, more by circumstance than by choice, remains the rarity rather than the rule.

A reporter interviews a resident of a public-housing development. *(Bill Anderson photo from Monkmeyer Press Photo Service)*

When newsworkers hold conferences, they rarely fail to talk about investigative reporting. They talked loud and long about it during the post-Watergate years (investigative reporting supplanted the interpretive reporting vogue of a generation earlier). Though everybody agrees that greater emphasis on depth reporting is vital, not everything said about it has been positive. Douglass Cater warned a conference on government and the media that "the task of organizing intelligence and presenting a more adequate picture of reality is going to require initiative and discipline . . . really important reporting is expensive in time and money." Gerald Warren, a Nixon press aide and speechwriter, looked with suspicion at the "post-Watergate syndrome," which he said led to "jugular journalism" preoccupied with sensational news and minor scandal. Others, like Warren, have inveighed against investigating for investigation's sake, digging for dirt because dirt—particularly off the shoes of people you don't like—is so seductive. A senator asserted in 1977 that investigative reporting had "victimized" Bert Lance, President Carter's appointee as U.S. budget director, by forcing inquiries into Lance's personal finances.

Reporting is not the only journalistic weapon to serve public purpose. Editorial pages, which bring interpretation and sometimes moral reflection to support reporting, often give the final thrust to crusading. Investigative reporters form part of some editorial-page staffs, a reflection of the knowledge that editorials without thorough fact-gathering have not won many wars.

Two kinds of investigative reporting A California editor, speaking before a newsworkers' conference at Stanford University, distinguished between two species of investigative reporting:

- Reporting to expose corruption in public places. This produces the most dramatic news, though not always the most important.
- Solid community-interest reporting to lead to positive social action or, in many cases, simply to add to public understanding of current affairs or social, economic, artistic or political trends. This kind does more to justify the privileged position of the news media than reporting that, however exciting, is trivial.

The second kind of investigation is becoming more and more common. One newspaper in a single season used its investigators to report on rising hospital costs; to find out whether, in its area, the day of the small farmer and the family farm was passing; to try to learn how the late-1970s college generation differed from that of the late 1960s, and why; to discover the effects of "equal employment" practices in local industries and businesses; and, in satiric vein, to make critical analysis of the kind of talent, eye and hair color, height, weight, bust and hip measurements, career plans and taste in pastry, pop and pantyhose that characterize candidates for the homecoming queens, Miss Downtowns and other aristocracy.

IS INVESTIGATIVE REPORTING "DIFFERENT"?

No new reporting techniques had to be invented for investigative reporting. It differs from day-to-day legwork not in methods but rather in the circumstances that surround it. The story tip or news idea is usually obscure rather than there for all to see. The fact-gathering calls for more patience, perseverance and imagination than does everyday reporting. The reporter is likely to meet roadblocks, hostility, attempts to deceive and sometimes personal peril. The deadline may not be tomorrow but months in the future.

Look-Ahead Reporting

Most reporting tells about events after they have become history. "Why not," some press critics ask, "dig out the roots of disaster in time to prevent it?" Pinpointing social, economic or political trends before they turn into triumph or catastrophe takes time, money, manpower and forethought. "Well," say the critics, "isn't that what investigative reporting is all about?"

Look-ahead reporting by two Philadelphia *Inquirer* reporters warned of the 1974 energy crisis in America. They told of forecasts of oil shortages and of heavy supplies abroad, and showed that similar crises in earlier years had worked out to oil industry profit. American stockpiles, they said, were the biggest in history; plenty of foreign oil was being imported; tanker sailings from Arab countries were increasing. Yet shortages were said to be imminent.

The *Inquirer*'s revelations did not prevent panic or price rises in the United States. If more American media had taken long looks at the problem, would the 1974 crisis have been another story?

The investigative reporter usually is no beginner. Reporting-in-depth techniques are sharpened by experience and by the polish that comes from thoughtful analysis of experience. Clark Mollenhoff of the Cowles newspapers in Des Moines, one of America's most relentless investigative reporters, translated his knowledge gained from digging into local government practices into a checklist for use by other reporters. The list shows "some common evils" found in local government—payroll padding, false billing, misused expense accounts, nepotism; it catalogs the principal city and county agencies to be checked, and the kinds of questions useful for each; it suggests sources of personal information about people in the news. Few reporters systematize their procedures so carefully, but Mollenhoff's orderly methodology is similar to guides prepared by other reporters. Here, for example, are the principal suggestions in a survey among large-city newspapers reported by the American Society of Newspaper Editors:

1. *Evaluate tips carefully.* Make sure there is "something worth going after"; don't be misled by tipsters with axes to grind: do enough preliminary investigation to avoid wasting time and money.
2. *Pick the right reporter.* Often the veteran "who can ask a direct question without flinching" or the specialist with expertise is the right choice. But one newspaper selected two young reporters with almost no experience to do a series on radical left- and right-wing organizations. Sometimes a black reporter can get into places nobody else can go; sometimes a woman can do what a man can't (or vice versa). The Kansas City *Star* "turns loose one

reporter each month" to work on special projects. The St. Louis *Post-Dispatch* holds that "virtually everyone on the staff is an investigative reporter." Good reporting is good reporting.

3. *Investigative reporting needs strong backing.* It is costly and slow-moving. Months may pass without a line of publishable copy. The St. Petersburg *Times* sent a man to Brazil as part of an investigation; the *Post-Dispatch* sent one to Turkey on what turned out to be a false lead. The same paper offered $20,000 to an informer (most papers, however, stop short of paying informers).

Investigative reporting puts heavy weight on showing up bribery, graft, error, deceit and incompetence in public places. The seed of this kind of reporting is hard to identify; it almost always is hidden. The situation may be peaches and cream on the surface; it becomes worth looking into only when a discriminating eye or an educated hunch perceives that its color is murky purple. It is not news that a councilman has bought himself a Buick. But when the three county commissioners who voted in favor of the glossy new stadium start coming to work in glossy new Cadillacs, reporters get busy.

The increased investigative reporting done by the New York *Times* in recent years has been concerned largely with social, economic or political trends and developments. Often a reporter or a team of reporters is released from other duties to give full attention to a particular investigation. But it is also common for a reporter to carry the search for hidden answers alongside beat or other regular work. "You just have to keep everlastingly at it," explains Gene Goltz (see page 345). "You do a little now, and a little tomorrow. Sometimes you think you're getting nowhere. But you keep plugging, working plenty of nights and weekends that don't show on your overtime card. Eventually, if you juggle the pieces often enough, you find that they start fitting together."

Team investigation Investigative reporting by teams of two or more newsworkers, increasingly common in the 1970s, is not new. For years major news organizations have assigned teams to specific news explorations. The New York *Times* used teams for in-depth reporting in the 1950s on segregation in 18 Southern states, the extent of support for Eisenhower (1956), Middle East tension and danger spots, and other subjects. Usually such assignments are opportune—problem areas show up, and reporters or their editors start digging. The new attack is the organization of teams whose permanent assignment is investigative reporting. Few media have gone beyond assigning more than one or two reporters solely for such work, however. But the Long Island newspaper *Newsday*, under the guidance of Pulitzer Prize winner Robert W. Greene, established in the early 1970s a "projects department" with a sociological investigative team to "probe the root causes of suburban concerns, such as justice, housing and drug use." *Newsday*'s success in revealing political graft and corruption on Long Island is considered a model. *Quill* magazine (February, 1974) described the team's assignment:

> In theory, the team could function in a variety of ways. Employing *Newsday* experts in medicine, religion, minority affairs, media, consumer affairs, education, environment, politics, courts and police, as well as general assignment reporters, it could take a look at a group—for example, Puerto Ricans on Long Island—and assess their problems, needs and accomplishments. It could use those same specialists to dissect a community and put it under a journalistic microscope.

Other journalistic investigations by reporter groups have made press history. A joint team from the Chicago *Daily News* and the St. Louis *Post-Dispatch* exposed the corruption of reporters who were getting illicit income directly from the Illinois capitol. Accomplishments of a two-reporter team in Philadelphia and of other teams are cited in this chapter and Chapter 19. Three top reporters spent three months on "juvenile justice" for the Minneapolis *Tribune*, and a team on its sister paper, the *Star*, produced a series on conflicts of interest in the Minnesota legislature. A remarkable investigative reporting project followed the murder of Don Bolles, the Arizona reporter who had dug into crime in the state. Thirty-six reporters from around the country, on vacation, unpaid, or on employer-supported time, worked from four weeks to four months as a team, under the aegis of the Investigative Reporters and Editors Association and the direction of *Newsday*'s Bob Greene, to find out what had happened; their efforts led to 23 articles on corruption in Arizona, some clean-ups and some $60 million in libel suits, and were followed by the conviction of two men of murder. The Association's 1977 convention at the School of Journalism, Ohio State University, which had established a center for information exchange and research to advance investigative reporting, drew 300 participants. . . . In Boston, WBZ-TV has its vigorous "I-Team," and the *Globe* its "Spotlight" team.

Consumer reporting and "action line" In the 1960s Ralph Nader and others made "consumer protection" a fashionable issue, and the news media were quick to pick it up. They centered on two approaches: consumer reporting, much of it investigative; and "Action Line" or "Your Money's Worth" columns or broadcasts. These two should be carefully differentiated.

Investigative consumer reporting ranges from routine market-basket reports—price comparisons for items at a number of groceries—to the elaborate effort of one three-reporter team to assess the quality of their city's hamburgers. Getting samples from groceries was no problem; to get raw hamburger from restaurants, they drove up in a camper truck with a friend's beagle, Emily, wagging her tail. The raw patties went to a laboratory for analysis (Emily got dog biscuits). The lab's analysis showed good meat and bad, lean beef and rat hairs. The resulting articles ran for six days; some advertisers howled; the series was overwhelmingly popular.

"Action line" features depend primarily on reader or listener questions. At best such columns are conscientious efforts that investigate scrupulously, keep merchants and other service enterprises on their toes, and don't hesitate to say when the questioners are wrong. At worst they are superficial and sometimes little better than blackmail. They are widely read, whatever their quality; they make friends for newspaper or broadcaster; they are as high in human interest as the columns of Ann Landers and her twin, Abigail Van Buren.

Infiltration reporting A Washington newspaper assigned a woman reporter to attend a meeting of a chapter of a "white citizens council" in Maryland. Her identity unsuspected, she was elected recording secretary; her lawyer husband became the group's legal adviser, and they brought in another reporter and some friends as members. Their enclave gained control. They persuaded the national headquarters to bar segregationists from the chapter, and ended by affiliating it with the Congress for Racial Equality. The reporter had a sparkling exclusive for her paper.

This comedy ended as comedies should—happily. But it didn't face up to the ethical quandary posed by the reporting method. When Philadelphia reporters, unidentified, joined far-left and far-right organizations, they wrote a descriptive series on "The View From Within." Nobody complained about its accuracy. But a member of one group asked, "Did you have to do it secretly?" From the other group: "We wouldn't have let you in if we had known who you were."

The reporters, justifying the tactic, quoted John Milton's classic 1644 plea for press freedom, "Areopagitica." A reporter whose identity is not known, they said, is uninhibited, has no worry about offending news sources, and has the clandestine privilege of observing news figures when they are off guard. But they also said:

> The moral issue posed by infiltration journalism is not unlike the free press-fair trial controversy, and it is just as difficult to resolve. In abstract terms, the public's right (or need) to know is pitted against the person's right to privacy. . . . [The reporters,] by maintaining a shield of secrecy while seeking information, had . . . been deceiving the public. . . . To say there are circumstances in which infiltration journalism can be morally justified is not to say it can't be abused. When it is, the quality of the finished product is likely to be small.

Disagreement on this difficult question is a constant in journalistic life. When a Houston reporter posed as a former friend of a murdered man, gained admission to a postfuneral gathering and interviewed the dead man's mother, he had an exclusive story. But his paper, the *Chronicle,* did not use it. The news editor, calling the reporter "inexperienced," said "printing it would not be honest."

The case contrasts with the award-winning feat of a New York *Daily News* reporter who exposed abuses in the Medicaid program he had uncovered while pretending to be a Medicaid beneficiary. The cases are not parallel, for one was secret invasion of a private group and the other probing into a public enterprise. The contrast is worth noting.

Most reporters believe that the obligation to reveal significant information the public can't get otherwise overbalances the question of impropriety in the method used to obtain it. The end justifies the means—that is to say, if the end itself is justifiable. It is not a totally satisfying conclusion.

THREE CASE HISTORIES

Goltz got suspicious Gene Goltz, a Houston *Post* reporter, was also an accountant. Assigned to a suburban beat, he began to scent irregularities in city financial procedures in one of his suburbs. He began to investigate rumors about the curious ways six million dollars from a bond issue were being spent; for six months he ran into records he wasn't allowed to see, denials of irregularities, secret meetings of officials and, finally, threats. At length he had enough evidence to assure him and his city editor that behind the smoke burned a fire.

His first stories told of no illegalities, but they triggered midnight telephone calls, anonymous voices, veiled hints that opened new avenues of investigation. One led him to proof that a 2 percent commission for handling city bond sales (quadruple the usual rate) had been partly kicked back to city officials. Others developed information that mayor, councilmen and others had paid themselves illegal fees.

And one led to an encounter with the suburban police commissioner, whose furious punch broke Goltz's nose. His wife's safety was threatened. Though citizens of the suburb didn't want to believe Goltz's stories, the facts eventually won. A grand jury indicted city officials. The voters, at length convinced, cleaned house.

And the *Post* and Goltz got an armful of prizes—the Broun, a Pulitzer, a National Headliner.

All this came from the classic tools of investigative reporting: open eyes and ears; patient, tireless digging; persistence over weeks and months; courage (and, says Goltz, a wife who can take it). A truism the campaign reinforced was that many sources knew the facts Goltz excavated, but that to open mouths it took the revelations that Goltz and his paper provided.

Business corruption; newspaper corruption The two investigative reporting achievements described in the following pages were 1977 winners of Sigma Delta Chi awards—the first for newspaper public service, the second for general reporting. Both accounts appeared in *The Quill,* June, 1977.

THE BIG DEAL OF CORPORATE CORRUPTION
by Kay Lockridge

Sometimes a seemingly routine press release can start the ball toward a blockbuster series. Such a release led the *Wall Street Journal* to an international investigation of corporate payoffs, kickbacks and bribery.

The series began in 1975, when the *Journal* picked up a tip involving "a clear case of corruption" at United Brands Co. Three reporters in three cities began working on the story.

"Our coverage started with an isolated case and widened as we followed up," Managing Editor Frederick Taylor says. The follow-up led to the possibility of corruption at other companies. The *Journal* "capitalized on disclosures forced by the Securities and Exchange Commission" and produced articles about Lockheed, Exxon, Del Monte and Union Carbide.

The investigation "was given direction from New York in terms of overall encouragement and praise of individual stories, some prodding for certain kinds of stories and investigations of individual cases, and some coordination to make sure we weren't overlapping or being redundant.

"But most of the coverage stemmed from individual enterprise." Taylor notes that "almost all editorial staffers" (there are about 200 worldwide) took part in producing some 470 articles, including spot news, and that perhaps two dozen reporters developed major features over a two-year period.

Under the direction of Taylor and Laurence O'Donnell, assistant managing editor, the *Journal* followed up tips for fresh investigations of corporate activities and covered early reform efforts and the debate over disclosure and its effects.

"During the first year—1975—the emphasis was heavy on what happened. We tried hard to avoid judgments—let the facts and situations speak for themselves. The second year the coverage widened substantially, mainly because the list of companies admitting payoffs grew sharply and because the disclosures were triggering extensive repercussions.

"I was amazed as hell at what we found was going on. The attitude of some people was, 'What's the big deal? It's standard operating procedure.' But I couldn't believe the corruption. The *Journal* is not a mouthpiece for business, and we believed that exposure of this corruption would ultimately strengthen business and private enterprise."

Not all corporate heads agreed with this conclusion, but Taylor says there has been "no pressure directly from inside or outside ownership to cease or tone down" the coverage. Criticism has come from businessmen in private conversations, Taylor admits, but he says he knows of "no case where a corporation threatened or suggested it might withdraw its advertising. They're too sophisticated for that."

He says he has "no idea" of the *Journal's* advertising department's reaction to the series because the editorial and advertising departments are "totally separated."

Some of the major stories were run past the *Journal* lawyers for a libel check. "Our lawyers never say, 'Don't run it'; they show us how to run it. They help us, not stop us."

The biggest flak from business came from stories originated in Pittsburgh concerning the Gulf Oil Corp., Taylor says.

"Our . . . coverage was the outgrowth of tenacious work by Barney Calame, our Pittsburgh bureau chief. It was difficult for him personally because Pittsburgh is a close corporate community and his persistence was misinterpreted within the community as some sort of vendetta."

Taylor says the *Journal* received a "relatively strong" expression of reader sentiment in letters to the editor—"a lot of people were bewildered by it all." The mail ran about 50-50 in terms of reader support

Meanwhile, the *Journal* plans to continue its investigative efforts into business and is looking into IRS and SEC reports of unaccounted-for corporation slush funds used by executives, although "it looks as though the major stories have run out.

"There is a big corporation awareness now, and they know they can't get away with it because we're watching them. The SEC is all over them, too, and business in general is pretty careful of anything that even hints of corruption.

"There is probably less to report now, but that's the idea. By keeping an eye on business, we'll be serving both business and the public."

SCANDALS IN CITY HALL, GOVERNMENT BY NEWSPAPER
by DeWayne B. Johnson

The city of Long Beach, Calif., had been wracked by a series of mini-scandals over a period of years. They culminated in the ouster of the city's planning director, Ernest Mayer, Jr., indicted on bribery charges.

The events had aroused the curiosity of all of Southern California and in particular that of Mark Murphy, metropolitan editor of the Los Angeles *Times.*

Murphy wanted to know how the city had managed to squander millions of dollars in oil revenues and why the governmental processes had failed to stop it. He assigned Mike Goodman and George H. Reasons to find out.

Persistent rumors about the city's power structure—rumors not a great deal unlike those in any city—said that Long Beach's was government by newspaper. Against a backdrop of cynicism and hostility, the reporters soon found story after story that was not being covered in the local paper, the Long Beach *Independent-Press-Telegram,* a member of the Knight-Ridder chain.

They found a city government controlled by a handful of men on various commissions—some holding several positions. They learned that the city manager for years had had a drinking problem. They found that Long Beach City Hall reporters were not writing about it. They wondered why.

They decided to investigate the Long Beach hierarchy and the newspaper hierarchy. They went to the records—civil records, court records, land records. They heard stories—and later printed them—of how Editor-Publisher Daniel H. Ridder had killed stories of the city's Economic Development Corp., in which the newspaper's upper echelon had a significant involvement. They and their editors realized that a story of a city scandal had grown into one involving the city's major newspaper.

Goodman and Reasons had developed credibility among sources through earlier reporting on the city planning director, the $40-million financial disaster of the Queen Mary and other failures. More and more of Long Beach's insiders, people not inclined to speak to reporters, came forward. The reporters began getting telephone calls leading to other stories—the looting of a landmark building by city employees, a lucrative Centrex phone system installed in the new City Hall and Library without benefit of contract. They also found that city officials spent public funds to subsidize a private company that promoted two Grand Prix races despite a promise "not to spend a dime of city money" on them.

The story grew. A federal investigation into allegations of "massive fraud" in the operation of poverty programs in Long Beach was ordered.

Finally, after every word was tested by the Los Angeles *Times*' attorneys, the main story appeared under the headline "Long Beach—Government by Newspaper." The lead read:

> Top executives of Long Beach's only daily newspaper played active roles in key governmental decisions while the newspaper shielded much of the city's business from public view, an investigation by the *Times* has revealed.

The newspaper was characterized as the city's "king-maker." Its influence was traced into vital city offices, agencies, commissions and boards. The newspaper hierarchy was described as so powerful that "its voice, in effect, was the city's voice. When it spoke everyone listened."

Reasons and Goodman knew that if they made one mistake both they and their newspaper would suffer. They felt they were in a "no win" situation—one newspaper telling tales on another.

Editor-publisher Ridder limited his rebuttal—at a Long Beach Rotary Club luncheon—to accounts of his role in suppressing news stories about the city-sponsored Economic Development Corp., of which he was president. (Two *I-P-T* reporters had resigned from the paper, saying Ridder had killed stories critical of the agency. A story by one of them, rejected as "unprintable" by the *I-P-T* appeared in *New West* magazine.)

Since the series appeared, not all has been set straight in Long Beach. But there is talk of pending shake-ups. The new city manager has been engaged in a thorough housecleaning. The *I-P-T* seems to be reporting on things it would not in the past have touched. And follow-ups are planned.[1]

STUDY SUGGESTIONS

1. Define the two kinds of investigative reporting.
2. Chapter 16 speaks of cause-and-effect reporting, this one of "look-ahead" reporting. Could it be said that the two are differing manifestations of one kind of reportorial purpose?
3. It has been said that "investigative reporting is merely good reporting, intensified." In what ways, if any, does investigative reporting differ from the "regular" day-by-day work of most reporters?
4. Investigative reporting "remains the rarity rather than the rule." If you agree with this statement, what do you consider the principal causes?

PRACTICE ASSIGNMENTS

1. Reporting that investigates corruption or misbehavior at any level has to start with evidence that corruption or misbehavior exists; such evidence is not easy to find. But investigative reporting of the kind that develops information about a condition that is not purposely and consciously concealed but is merely unseen is possible in many areas of modern life (see page 340). Make a list of as many such unseen topics for deep reporting as you can. Explain what you consider that the goals or purposes of the investigations should be, why they are needed, why they have not been undertaken, and what you think they might accomplish.
2. Select one of your Assignment 1 topics and outline a thorough investigative reporting effort—nature of the problem, sources of information, fore-

[1] Reprinted by permission from *The Quill*, published by The Society of Professional Journalists, Sigma Delta Chi, June 1977.

seeable obstacles, number of reporters needed, principal subtopics, timing.

3. Undertake a "consumer investigation" in your community, one in which you gather information about comparative costs or quality of a group of consumer products so as to flesh out an informative feature. (Such a story, written for a local paper or broadcasting station, does not have to be an expose.)
4. The section of this chapter about infiltration reporting concludes that the view that in such reporting "the end justifies the means" is "not a totally satisfying conclusion." Several of the reading citations below discuss this topic. After reading as much as you can on it, and talking with experienced journalists about it if you can, write a statement of your own opinions.

RELATED READING

Anderson, David, and Peter Benjaminson. *Investigative Reporting.* Indiana University Press, 1976. A textbook by two successful investigative reporters. Methods, sources, use of public records, six case histories. The authors cynically affirm that "dishonest, fraudulent, immoral, and perhaps even illegal" methods are justified by defensible ends.

Bernstein, Carl, and Bob Woodward. *All the President's Men.* Simon & Schuster, 1974. Two reporters' story of their Watergate revelations. Candid account of methods, frustrations, successes and failures.

Downie, Leonard, Jr. *The New Muckrakers.* New Republic Book Co., 1976. An award-winning investigative reporter takes an "inside look" at widely known investigative reporters of the last decade and at some who are less touted but also worth examining.

Dygert, Dames H. *The Investigative Journalist: Folk Heroes of a New Era.* Prentice-Hall, 1976. This book looks at the "folk heroes" with too-wide eyes, but it makes realistic appraisals of what investigative reporting demands.

Hage, George S., Everette S. Dennis, Arnold H. Ismach and Stephen Hartgen. *New Strategies for Public Affairs Reporting.* Prentice-Hall, 1976. An excellent textbook, especially helpful on use of public information.

Mencher, Melvin. "The Arizona Project." *Columbia Journalism Review,* November–December 1977. Detailed account and evaluation of the team investigative reporting following the Bolles murder.

Stanford, Phil. "The Most Remarkable Piece of Fiction I've Ever Read." *Columbia Journalism Review,* July–August 1976. Subtitled "A Problem for Investigative Reporters."

18 Interpretive Reporting

One interpretive story can weigh more than a hundred "items" a reporter dredges up on his beat.
Erwin D. Canham, editor emeritus, Christian Science Monitor

Reporters count how many times an audience applauds a speaker. Analysts study what gets applause and try to figure out why.
Anonymous

PREVIEW

The distinction between interpretive reporting and editorial comment is this: Editorial comment—editorials, articles or analyses by authorities, and the like—is personal and subjective; interpretive reporting is the presentation of relevant fact (either objective fact or pertinent opinion or expertise from qualified sources) that helps readers to understand current affairs. Interpretive reporting seeks not to persuade but to illuminate—not to lead thinking, but to provide information so that opinions can be formed with perspective and knowledge.

Interpretive reporting—often under a label like "What the News Means" or "News Analysis" or "News Background"—is a major service of 20th-century journalism. It employs a number of devices, prominent among them the news interview and the "backgrounder." Some reporters acquire specialized competence that permits them to combine reporting with qualified opinion.

The two aphorisms above make a distinction between news reporting and news interpretation. Though they oversimplify, the heart of the matter is in them.

Interpretation of the news—illumination of what the news means—is older than investigative reporting. In earliest American journalism the news was reported in whatever way would make it mean just what its editor wanted it to mean. Objective reporting changed all that. By the 1930s and the Depression that drove Herbert Hoover out of office, news that was merely objective was not good enough. News consumers were asking, "Why didn't we see this coming? What caused it? What will it do to us? Will there be more of it?"

And they were asking, "Isn't it the job of the news media to let us know?"

Attempts to answer these questions began to appear in the 1930s, first on the editorial pages, then in syndicated columns. Columnists in print and on radio (radio called them "commentators") became fixtures: pundits like Marquis Childs, Raymond Clapper and Dorothy Thompson in the papers, Raymond Gram Swing and H. V. Kaltenborn on radio. Daily these men and women, and a lot of others, sought to tell a troubled world why things were the way they were. Some of what they said made sense, some only pious nonsense.

However wise, news explanation became established. And it didn't take long for personal, subjective opinion-explanation to be supplemented by a "new" brand of explanation that consisted primarily of reporting. Journalists like Elmer Davis and Edward R. Murrow in broadcasting and Erwin D. Canham and James B. Reston—four of the best-known—developed the technique soon styled news analysis. Murrow explained his view of the distinction between interpretation, or commentary, and analysis:

> News periods should be devoted to giving facts emanating from an established newsgathering source, to giving color in the proper sense of the word, without intruding the views of the analyst.
>
> The news analyst can often give light on the meaning of events. The analyst should not say that they're good or bad, but should analyze their significance *in the light of known facts,* the results of similar occurrences, and so on.
>
> He should always be fair. He should give the opinions of various persons, groups or political parties when these are known, leaving the listener to draw his own conclusions.

Murrow was drawing a fine line, and whether it was too fine—whether analysis could remain objective—is vigorously debated. Some journalists deny both the possibility and the desirability. "What's important," they assert, "is the judgment about news events that knowledge of the facts makes possible." Eric Sevareid, Murrow's CBS colleague, accepted the Murrow thesis but doubted that complete objectivity could be attained. The New Journalists of the 1960s and 1970s scoffed. They not only believed that reporters should say what they thought about the news they covered but that it was less than self-respecting to try to achieve the impossible.

The continuing dispute becomes less heated as a distinction in somewhat different terms gains acceptance: the distinction between commentary and background. *Commentary* is now generally taken to mean what the word denotes: comment, criticism and illumination of the news in light of whatever knowledge and opinion—competent or not—the commentator can bring to it. Thus a departure from rigid objectivity has been reintroduced to news presentation. It is recognized that responsible journalism calls for responsible subjective analysis, always clearly identified for what it is and from whom it comes, always founded on dependable information.

Background, in contrast, is the body of facts underlying, surrounding or affecting a news event, presented on its own merits to help news consumers place the event in proper context. This is no more a 20th-century novelty than is editorialized comment. But it has gained increasing status as essential to news media service. The listener or viewer, to grasp the news about protection of human rights as a keystone in United States foreign policy, has to know a great deal about what Washington believes the principle means and about relevant attitudes and actions in other countries. When readers discover in a news column that air pollution in their city has doubled in 10 years, they must be told what air pollution is, why it has grown and (background can look ahead as well as behind) what it will be in another decade. Backgrounding may or may not evaluate meaning for consumers; but it must free them to pursue the evaluation themselves.

The interpretive approach to reporting helps the press to serve another purpose, one that gets little attention: providing a two-way pipeline between the people and government. As editor C. A. McKnight of the Charlotte, N.C. *Observer* has pointed out, "the media must report back to the government what the people are thinking and feeling and believing."

Straight Reporting as Interpretation

That day-by-day news, published to inform more than interpret, nevertheless can serve the interpretive function is recognized in a book devoted to speech communication:

One spectacular example of the media's ability to clarify a wild confusion of data through presentation came during the Watergate investigations, with their array of names, committees, titles, statutes, and contradictory allegations. In addition to their general news coverage, many of the news media provided a periodical summary of events; gave pertinent background information regarding sophisticated electronic equipment and procedures; and devoted special programming to discussions, reviews, and interpretations . . .—Michael Burgoon and Michael Ruffner, *Human Communication* (Holt, Rinehart and Winston, 1978), page 353.

Awareness of the need for news clarification has led to development of a number of helping devices. Among them:

- Insertion of background paragraphs to provide clarification with a news story. The "background precede," explanatory material at the head of a story, is one form. Another is material inserted into the body of a story, often in parentheses or contrasting type.
- Regular use, on the editorial page or elsewhere, of background columns. A paper in Ohio used a staff-written column called "Reviewing the News." A London paper called its similar column "The World This Morning."
- Use of sidebars, sometimes with such labels as "What the News Means" or "News Analysis"
- Use of news interviews and other made stories to provide competent explanation of complex events
- Development of weekly news review departments (one of the first of these was the New York *Times'* Sunday "The Week in Review" section, both summary and explanation)

REPORTING THAT EXPLAINS

Most such approaches, however, are attempts to do big jobs in small ways. A better way is true interpretive reporting—reporting whose purpose is to explore topics that are not understood and to clarify the meaning of facts or events which, standing alone, have little meaning or the wrong meaning for most news consumers. Interpretive reporting is a relative of investigative reporting, which often has the same purpose. The differences are that interpretive reporting isn't primarily aimed at revealing evils or hidden facts, though it may do just that: and that interpretive reporting can often be carried out in the most prosaic way, in libraries or easy and harmonious interviews, whereas investigative reporting is likely to have the flavor of conflict, peril or adventure.

Interpretive reporting is not solely American. The *Times* of London spent millions of pounds to set up an eight-reporter research team assigned to "give the fullest explanations of news events." French, English, Italian and other papers emphasize interpretive articles. Such writing is not reporting unless it involves a fact- or opinion-gathering process; it often includes opinion. It commonly appears under a byline, so that its reader knows whom to credit (and sometimes whether to trust it).

Those who worry about the quality of American news performance—journalists and their audiences alike—think the interpretive reporting tool is too little used. The fact that a whole battery of magazines—*Time, Newsweek, U.S. News & World Report* as well as *Harper's*, the *Atlantic, Saturday Review*, the *Progressive*, the *Nation* and scores of others—carry current affairs analysis is evidence that the news media go only part way to meet the need. News backgrounding by TV commercial and public networks, sometimes in the form of documentaries or featured programs like "60 Minutes" and "Eyewitness" (public TV), and in small doses by individual stations, has helped to fill the gap. "Face the Nation" and "Meet the Press," reporting significant views by letting the viewers express them, are interpretive efforts.

Nonopinion backgrounders The classic backgrounder takes off from a current news event or circumstance and reports facts or relevant opinions (not the reporter's) to lay a setting for the event. You have seen several such stories in this book: One is the combination of news interview and spot reporting suggested by the gasoline shortage (page 277). The story is a backgrounder all the way, though it also fits other categories. It reports competent opinion to help troubled motorists understand what's happening to them, then goes (in paragraph 10) into spot reporting of facts that help people to see how it may affect them. (Among other examples of interpretive reporting in this book—some of them combining spot news with background—are the stories on bus riding (page 88), the importance of grades (page 327); the football player (page 275), delinquency in high schools (page 289), the Perpich biographical sketch (page 294) and the brief one on park safety (page 327).

Interpretation vs. Opinion

"What," asks the perplexed journalism student, "is the distinction between news interpretation and editorializing?" A fair question.

Sometimes there is no difference. An explanation of the meaning of an event may be the sharply personal view of its author, an attempt to persuade readers or listeners to a point of view.

But there are differences:

The prime purpose of interpretive reporting is just what the term connotes: to use reporting to add meaning to the news. Editorials may be used for many purposes: clarification, illumination, opinion-shaping, incitement to action, entertainment. Reporting can be used toward any of these ends; but if its intent is any of the last three, it twists the definition.

An editorial is usually the voice of an institution. The interpretive news story represents nothing but the goal of service to an audience.

Editorials typically are anonymous. The interpretive reporter is usually identified. If the story includes personal opinion, identification of the writer is a must.

Lester Markel, for years a ranking editor of the New York *Times,* once said it more briefly: That a question was asked or a condition arose would be a fact. Stating why the question was asked would be interpretation. Saying whether the interpretation was correct would be opinion.

TWO INTERPRETIVE STORIES

The year 1976 was one of ruinous drought in northern California. A calamity for the farmers of the Sacramento Valley, it also had more distant implications. Much of the nation's food supply—especially fruits and vegetables—comes from the Valley. All over the United States people feared increasing rises in food prices. The Minneapolis *Tribune* sent a staff writer, Bernie Shellum, to examine the problem throughout western United States. Excerpts from one of his stories illustrate the use of individual news sources, direct quotation and anecdote to tell what he found.

Levi M. Turner is an Okie, a tall, slow-moving man who left his dust-blown Oklahoma farm decades ago and carted his family to California's Central Valley in a truck.

They were among the 350,000 migrants who fled the Plains during the drought of the 1930s, drawn west by California's promise of a more hospitable climate and more fertile soil.

Settling in Selma, a small town south of Fresno, Turner drove a meat truck and grew grapes and eventually retired. Like most of the Okies, the Turners have moved to the suburbs. There is a Cadillac in their garage on the outskirts of Fresno.

Next door the Turners' oldest son, Clayton, operates the Hard Times Gallery, where he sells ink drawings that are slowly building his reputation as a western artist.

He is a quadraplegic who paints with the pen held in his mouth.

"We thought it would be better out here," Mrs. Turner said the other day, "and it was."

"It's a good country," the elder Turner added.

But history is repeating itself. Drought has dried up the hay in the foothills of the Sierra Nevadas, forcing cattlemen to trim their herds and buy expensive feed. Drought threatens the grape vines that sustain many of the small farmers in the eastern part of the valley and provide much of the nation's supply of raisins. Drought has caused a sharp reduction in the flow of irrigation water to fruit and vegetable farmers, taking some land out of production.

The Turners already are paying 89 cents a pound for tomatoes, twice the usual price. Lettuce, which usually sells for 15 to 20 cents a head, is 50 cents.

"It's drier than it's ever been," said Turner. "A little farmer can't make it. It costs too much money for him to operate. He has to borrow, and when his crop doesn't come in he's out of business."

The impact of the drought extends beyond the hardships of individual farmers, for the Central Valley produces 25 percent of the nation's entire food supply and 40 percent of its fruits and vegetables.

California's drought is described by Robert J. C. Burnash, a hydrologist who has charge of the California-Nevada River Forecast Center, as the fourth worst weather-related disaster in the nation's history. It is exceeded, he said, only by Hurricanes Agnes, Betsy and Camille, which ripped through southern and eastern states in 1962, 1965 and 1969.

Gov. Jerry Brown has said that 1976 drought is unprecedented and that it "conjures up memories of the Dust Bowl."

A spokesman for the state's Department of Feed and Agriculture has estimated the loss in farm production at $791 million to $2.1 billion.

But such calculations may be premature. Some of the big corporate farms in the valley are believed to be shifting from water-intensive crops such as vegetables to cotton and other crops that need little water.

Moreover, the Sacramento *Bee* has

quoted farm spokesmen as admitting "they are making the effect of drought appear as bad as possible in an effort to condition shippers to expect an increase in food prices."

"Maybe we can get people to accept a rise in the wholesale price of canned peaches a penny or two," the newspaper quoted one farm adviser. "The housewife won't notice it, and it will allow the grower to recover the cost of this thing and also not show as much red ink as last year."

The newspaper quoted an expert on the fruit and vegetable trade as acknowledging, "They're talking about a disaster in tomato production so women in the East will go out and buy 30 cans of catsup and 30 cans of tomato paste. It's a self-fulfilling prophecy that these prices will rise if you stampede the consumer."

[*Four following paragraphs describe the impact of the drought on prices, and 11 tell of the vast California water supply system, pictured as "the one man-made structure identified by astronauts from the surface of the moon." The story continues:*]

To try to comprehend the drought, said George Ballis, "is like trying to get a handle on the fog. We know it's there. We can see it and feel it, but we can't grasp it."

Ballis is executive director of National Land for People, a Fresno-based organization bent on breaking the grip of corporate farms in the 600,000-acre Westlands Reclamation Project.

"We have a northern California drought, but not a statewide drought," Ballis noted. "There is a surplus of water in Southern California."

To relieve Marin County and other drought-stricken communities in the San Francisco Bay area, Southern California has agreed to sell 300,000 acre-feet of water from the state water project. "The water being sold to the north comes from the north," Ballis said, "so the so-called sale is accomplished by not delivering the water to the south."

Ballis said he has been told by the California Tomato Growers Association that growers this year will plant some 250,000 acres and that there will be adequate water to bring in a crop of 6.8 million tons, nearly a million tons more than last year.

"The irony here is that as this good news was being reported, some canners began announcing price hikes," he said. "This irony is further confused with the realization that the tomato is a minor item in a can of tomatoes. The can, the label and the sugar in the can each cost more than the tomato in it.

"When farmers lost 25 percent of their crop last year, they still got $47 per ton for tomatoes, but canners raised the prices anyway."

Oh, yes, the Turners. They've raised five children in California and have seven grandchildren, and they have no plans to head back to Oklahoma.

"I haven't encountered any disenchantment from the progeny of the Okies," said Jerry Haslam, who grew up near Bakersfield and lives in Petaluma.

The son of Okies and now director of the Okies Studies Project at Sonoma State College, Haslam said, "If we have one more year of serious drought, then we'll have Okies harking back to 1934 and 1935.

"But one of the reasons the Okies were attracted to the valley and stayed was the similarity of the climates. There were consistent drought cycles. It's not a place where small farmers can make it. Most of the Okies are no longer on the land anyway. They're living in stucco suburbs." [1]

A reader of the Seattle *Post-Intelligencer* story below may say that it should appear on the editorial page. The writer clearly means to show inconsistency between what Washington's first woman governor says and what the story reports. It is nonetheless interpretive reporting: fact presentation to put a current event into context. Could it have been done without its sardonic tone?

The governor's hands grasped the lectern and she was rising up on her toes for emphasis. "It's a serious situation," the governor was saying in the hotel ballroom that afternoon. The Rotarians had finished their veal and dessert and now they sat in folding chairs and listened to the state's governor talk about energy problems.

"We must conserve our energy in all possible ways," Dixy Lee Ray said. "We must"—she paused, lifted a finger, "must," she repeated—"conserve the fuels we have."

Applause rippled through the audience.

Down the stairway and out through the glass doors to the Olympic Hotel's U-shaped drive-in entrance off University Plaza, the governor's poodle waited for her.

The little wide-eyed pooch was standing on expensive rolled and puffed upholstery, looking out tinted glass windows from the back seat of a 1977 fully equipped Mercury Grand Marquis four-door sedan. It is a beautiful car.

In the hotel parking zone, it glittered in the play of afternoon shadows, a great machine heavy with chrome, a glossy royal blue with vinyl top and three radio antennas poking up from the fenders.

The Marquis is one of the biggest cars on the road. It has tilt steering, electric rear-window defrosters, power seat, power antenna and air conditioning. It is an expensive car to buy and operate.

New, this car would cost between $7,000 and $8,000. The governor has it on a lease at $1,700 a year from the Ford Motor Co. It is a special deal extended by Ford to the governors of most states, and includes insurance and maintenance. A state spokesman says it is a "giveaway price."

The Environmental Protection Agency says the 1977 Mercury Marquis gets 11 miles per gallon around town.

The President of the United States says cars getting this kind of mileage are gas guzzlers.

Three new cars purchased for members of the governor's cabinet come off a little better than this. These are 1977 Ford deluxe model LTDs, 302-inch-engined four-door sedans, costing just over $5,000 apiece.

These new cars have gone in the past two-and-a-half months to Dr. Harlan McNutt, director of the Department of Social and Health Services; Kaz Watanabe, director of the Department of Commerce and Economic Development; and Web Hallauer, director of the Department of Ecology. . . .

The three new LTDs, according to the Environmental Protection Agency, get up to 13 miles per gallon around town.

Actually, eight other new cars purchased for the state in the last half year get even better mileage. Although they are also Ford LTDs, they are standard and not deluxe models like the agency heads'. . . .

The EPA says these standard model 1977 Ford LTDs, priced at $4,500 each, get up to 15 miles per gallon around town.

"It has been policy and precedent over many years to make full-sized cars available for state officials," says a spokesman in the General Administration Department's purchasing division.

"When we award a bid, we do take into

account the performance, economy and so on of the particular car. But we will continue to purchase full-sized cars. There has been no declaration that the state should or must buy smaller cars."

On the stage at the hotel where she was speaking that afternoon a few weeks ago, Dixy Lee Ray was up on her toes again for emphasis:

"We will continue to urge the public," the governor said with determination, "to be prudent . . . in the use of all forms of energy."

Downstairs, the little poodle waited in his big car for the chauffeur and the governor to come back. In a few moments, they would be dashing along the Seattle freeway, where the EPA says the Mercury Marquis gets all the way up to 16 miles per gallon.[2]

An interpretive story of a different sort was compiled by a newspaper copy desk following the kidnapping of Patricia Hearst in 1974. Pulling together information "from our wire services," copy editors provided answers to some of the questions it was sure readers were asking: What was the Symbionese Liberation Army? How did it grow out of meetings of radicals in a California prison? Who was Cinque, the group's leader? Whence the nickname, and how had he been identified? How did the group move from intellectual left ideology to terrorism?

The Houston *Journalism Review*, one of the critical journals that flourished in the mid-1970s, emphasized that the opportunities for such stories in complex news situations are close to endless. After sexual abuse and murder of a score of Texas teen-agers came to light, the *Review* listed questions the media had not answered:

> Why have so many teen-agers left home for a lifestyle of sex and drugs? Why have conventional social services failed? What could have been done to help these youths? What good will the state and national proposals do? What causes families to break down? What effects do broken families have on children? What can be done to alleviate the problem?

Among backgrounders or interpretive stories that followed a Nixon "Watergate explanation" speech were:

- A Chicago *Tribune* news analysis with opinion that "Nixon offered little," that the speech was "imprecise" and "a delicate balance of self-defense and attrition"
- A New York *Times* collection of opinions from cabinet members, a labor leader, a left-wing commentator, some politicos, a former Nixon aide
- A combination of the two methods in the *Christian Science Monitor*
- An Associated Press "Background of the News" dispatch with its

[2] Copyright © 1977 by the Seattle *Post-Intelligencer*. Reprinted by permission.

single theme supported by excerpts from the speech: "Nixon's survival strategy is built on belief that Americans . . . are willing to forgive."

- A London *Times* opinion that Americans would not support Nixon's wish that "Watergate be forgotten"

STUDY SUGGESTIONS

1. Why have news interpretation and analysis increased steadily in importance in the American news media?
2. What is the "fine line" drawn by Edward R. Murrow?
3. Is there common ground on which interpretive reporting and investigative reporting stand, or are they entirely disparate?
4. Comment on the assertion that "an editorial may be interpretive without being subjective."
5. In what ways does the story about Governor Dixy Lee Ray (page 358) depart from straight reporting? Would you call it biased? colored? sardonic?

PRACTICE ASSIGNMENTS

1. Write a series of brief definitions to denote similarities and differences in *follow-up reporting, enterprise reporting, investigative reporting, background reporting* and *interpretive reporting.*
2. Select a current event of significance in your community (or, if you are well versed in it, an event in state or national politics or social policy) and write a background story—no opinion—for a local medium.
3. List a dozen or more current "news streaks"—continuing news developments—that might be treated by the interpretive reporting process. Suggest specific approaches for each one.
4. Carry out one or more of the stories suggested in Assignment 3.

RELATED READING

Copple, Neale. *Depth Reporting.* Prentice-Hall, 1964. A book about "reporting in depth," written before the term became a fad.

MacDougall, Curtis D. *Interpretative Reporting.* Macmillan, 1977. A textbook treating all aspects of reporting.

UPI

NEWS PROFESSIONAL PROBLEMS

19 Pressures on Reporters

PREVIEW

Reporters face pressures that may, unless they are on guard, make their reporting misleading. Some come from within the media, some from outside; some are benign, others ominous. Among the influences that need watching are these:

- Journalism must make money, must be financially sound to survive
- Media ownership, especially in broadcasting, is more conservative and profit-oriented than its editorial employees
- Concentration of media control in fewer hands, as it strengthens media independence, reduces the number of "voices" heard in the land
- Newsmakers, from the White House to the church down the street, have become adept in news manipulation and increasingly ready to benefit by doing it
- Journalists' participation in political, civic, economic or other public affairs may create conflicts of interest or give the appearance of such conflicts

Though journalistic freedom from government interference is established by the First Amendment, newsworkers' performance is conditioned by a body of legal restrictions: the laws of libel, copyright and property ownership, and often statutory restriction of reporters' rights to shield their sources of information.

The principal reportorial procedures—newsgathering and newswriting—are the subject of preceding chapters. This chapter looks at some of the pressures reporters face, inside and outside their "shops"—some that help, some that hurt; some ignored, some accepted. Over some, reporters have little control. Many involve moral and ethical judgments, decisions on social or professional propriety. To inventory the entire roll would be an infinite task.

In Utopia no selfish interest would influence what a news medium publishes or what a reporter finds out. That isn't, and never will be, the way it is. A thousand forces shape and manipulate what people want and what the news media report. Reporters who know that they will confront new pressures every day are forearmed. They dare not see these pressures through half-open eyes; they must maintain a controlled skepticism that things are really what they seem.

NEWS IS A BUSINESS

It is a fact of journalistic life that the news media are profit-making enterprises. This does not have to mean, and usually does not mean, that they are up for bids or that they are unaware of social needs, civil justice and the rights of the people on the other side of the tracks. But to remain alive they need the support of the economy in which they live.

The media, at every level from ownership and management to editorial comment and the newsroom, are under pressures to provide "favorable treatment." Happily, self-seeking pressures do not influence news policies as much as people think. The American newspaper, traditionally jealous of its independence, is usually strong enough to resist duress. Broadcasting does not differ much from the printed press in financial stability; but it has never had the newspaper's devotion to news service as a principal function, a fact that sometimes modifies its approach. Elsewhere in this book it has been said that broadcasting is show business, its primary purpose to entertain.

Newspaper Funerals

The Chicago *Daily News,* "the writer's newspaper," gave up in 1978 because it could "no longer earn the revenues for any healthy, sound business operation." The *Daily News* had won 15 Pulitzers, created a brilliant pioneer among foreign news staffs and undertaken courageous investigative reporting "when Woodward and Bernstein were toddlers." It had graduated such writers as Carl Sandburg, Ben Hecht, John Gunther and scores of other notables. But changes in reader habits—including the turn to TV and the rise of suburban living—had halved its peak circulation, and it faced the prospect of an $11-million loss in 1978. About the same time, in New York, America's youngest big-city paper—*The Trib,* only three months old—died. It had been welcomed by thoughtful New Yorkers and had had lip service from the business community. But, facing problems akin to those of the *Daily News,* it had lost $5 million, and its paid circulation was below 40,000. Months earlier the admired *National Observer,* though the wealth of the Dow Jones publishing firm was behind it, ended its 15-year struggle to get enough readers to get enough advertisers to stay alive.

"Cronyism"

"The cozy atmosphere surrounding publishers and their peers, business tycoons and government leaders" is a threat to free and full reporting, in the opinion of David Halberstam, Pulitzer prize reporter. Halberstam says that reporters who get chummy with presidents and cabinet members tend to accept and report official views rather than to seek qualifying information. If you get close to officials, if you have cocktails with them, you may be careless in analyzing their views or the "facts" they give you; and you may be reluctant to report news they don't want reported. Such influence is not limited to news sources with impressive titles or bank accounts. Reporters sometimes have to cover news that their butchers, candlestick makers or back-door neighbors would like to keep hidden.

Pressures from within A common complaint of journalism's critics is that newspapers, broadcasting stations and the business world that supports them are all run by the same people. It takes money to operate a business, and people with money have kindred interests and values. Publishers, broadcasters and their advertisers—say the critics—all belong to the same country clubs. The publishers mostly are members of generally conservative groups like the American Newspaper Publishers Association, and the broadcasters of the National Association of Broadcasters. They like good cars and good living, and they need profits to stay in business. Though newspaper and broadcasting ownership is not the monolith that aggrieved assailants make it, in general it obeys one set of economic and social rules.

Nobody believes that ownership never colors news selection. It was said of two Florida newspapers owned by railroad interests that their front offices let the staff know that "derailments aren't news on these papers." Patrick Owens, a labor reporter with editorial management experience, criticizes what he describes as "indifference to working people" and an impulse in the American press to use news space for private or institutional benefit. In Albany a mildly critical review of a soprano recital by the wife of a former publisher of Albany's two Hearst papers was edited to omit its adverse comments. When a publisher tells his city staff that "we're going to go all out to promote the Fall Festival," it may be hard to let solid news judgment be the guide. Views of top news executives, fortunately, are usually acceptable, for managing and city editors are hired for expertise and good sense. But their biases need watching. In one newsroom reporters used to say, "If you want a byline, write a piece about a cat. The city editor loves cats."

There are opposite influences. Hundreds of journalists have bosses like the Midwest radio station manager who told his news staff, "I have no rights in this newsroom. Kick me out if I ever try to tell you how to play a story." The reporting staff, the men and women at the desks around you, are commonly more "liberal" in social and political views than the occupants of the front office.

A trend is growing concern among reporters and editors about "power in the newsroom," a voice in shaping news policies. The rebellious underground press of the 1960s that developed into the alternative press of the 1970s was characterized by anger at establishment conservatism and by moral vigor, logic ranging from sober to passionate, and strong social purpose. Local journalism reviews—critiques by newsroom staffs of their own media—blossomed in more than a dozen cities after the first influential one, the Chicago *Journalism Review,* appeared in 1968. (Their number declined through the '70s as inflation climbed and the job market weakened. But a vigorous newcomer entered the field in 1977: the Washington, D.C., *Journalism Review.*)

Monopoly ownership The attrition of newspaper competition in American cities—not 5 percent of cities with daily newspapers have more than one ownership—concerns not only journalists but also any believer in the American sociopolitical system. Democracy depends on many voices, on hearing all the sides of every story. There are a thousand fewer dailies in the United States today than when William Howard Taft was president, and 2,000 fewer weeklies. The nearly 10,000 broadcasting outlets are only a meager replacement for the lost newspaper voices. Radio is heard everywhere, and TV sets serve nearly every American home. But broadcasting, though its news services improve steadily, does not equal the printed press in quantity, variety or interpretation of news. Radio, which served up an impressive array of commentators and documentary programs in its first quarter-century, now does little but present a skeleton of the news; TV's great potential for news coverage is only rarely realized.

The decline in newspaper competition furrows the brows of thoughtful observers—"if nobody's barking at you, you stop trying." The concern is lessened by the number of monopoly ownerships that use their strength to maintain newspaper quality. But there never was a time when competition guaranteed excellence; in the big cities there were more "bad" newspapers than "good" in the years when newspapers were plentiful. Competition has frequently been a degrading influence. New York City had three widely circulated but disreputable papers in the 1920s, during the circulation wars of the sensational tabloids. In Detroit in the same period, when Hearst journalism entered the scene with its lurid tactics, the other papers tended to fight it by imitating it.

Monopoly ownerships, almost always strong financially, have the means to develop and maintain high standards of news and editorial performance. Not all local monopolies take advantage of their opportunity; but on the whole the level of newspaper service has been high in the United States in the last third of the 20th century. At least a third of the papers on "best newspapers" lists are in monopoly cities. In some of the few cities where competition exists, newspapers range from "mediocre to miserable," as one editor said of the newspapers in Boston.

Excellence does not depend as much on the presence of competition or its absence as on quality of ownership. Observers of American newspapers remark on the notable advances in the Los Angeles *Times*, the Chicago *Tribune* and the Hearst papers when younger generations took over after the despotism of the older Chandlers, McCormick and Hearst. The Twin Falls (Idaho) *Times-News* (in the words of the *Columbia Journalism Review*) had been "all boost and no bite" until the 23-year-old son of a major owner became publisher in 1973. The "new" paper undertook investigation of secret payments of $600,000 to staff members in the city's hospital, an effort that led to changes in the system; and editorials and news questioned the activities of a local insurance company whose operations were under investigation in Wyoming, Utah,

---

Cross Ownership—Chain Ownership

Cross ownership is the term that means financial control of newspaper and broadcasting outlets in one community by one ownership. Articles in the October, 1977, *More* ("The Media Magazine") analyze the spread of cross ownership in the United States and conclude that "though the damage done by cross ownership [to full dissemination of news and opinion] is modest," it is enough to cause concern. The U.S. Supreme Court in 1978 broadly supported this view when it approved Federal Communications Commission authority to prohibit such ownerships in granting new broadcasting licenses if it should believe that diverse ownerships would serve the public better. The Court decision left intact most existing cross ownerships (involving 150 newspapers and more than 200 broadcasting stations in 44 states), but ordered that 16 be severed. Thus a 1975 policy opposed by newspapers and broadcasters but generally favored by lay and public-interest groups became the law of the land.

Chain ownership, the possession of two or more newspapers by one owner, has also been regarded with misgiving by social critics. Newspaper chains are expanding (about two-thirds of the 1,760 U.S. dailies and more than two-thirds of their circulation were under about 70 ownerships in 1978). As John Hulteng says (Related Reading, page 387), "Some owners . . . choose to keep hands off their properties most of the time. They give the local publisher or the chief editorial executive fairly free rein in putting out the news product." Some chain owners are also involved in cross ownerships. The danger of limitation in the "free market of ideas" is a major concern among analysts of the American scene. (A study of newspaper chains is reported in the September–October, 1977, *Columbia Journalism Review*.)

North Dakota and Oklahoma (libel suits did not deflect the paper).

Publishers who are strong financially can readily turn dedication into performance, just as they can most easily abort it. In practice, monopoly newspapers seek fair presentation of most news and multisided comment on most topics. There are more dailies that are politically independent every presidential election year; though this might mean that more are dodging the responsibilities and the headaches that go with political commitment, it usually doesn't work that way.

Pressures from other directions Every news medium and every reporter is besieged by groups or individuals trying to get something into the news or keep it out. Most governmental offices larger than that of dogcatcher have public relations (or, pompously, community consultant) offices. News media get mountains of mail every day—releases offering "news" of employees, auto models, political candidates, art shows. One big-city editor says he has "more trouble" with church groups seeking free space than any other. Some requests are legitimate; some stories would be covered without outside pressure; some the newsroom could get in no other way. But all have to be sifted, and their chaff bulks larger than their yield. (Pressures to report only "good news" are discussed in Chapter 4.)

Advertiser pressures The lore of the "news business" bulges with tales of advertisers who want to get news space or time, or to avoid it. More and more of the tales tell how the efforts have failed. A small-town Iowa merchant threatened to withdraw his advertising if the local weekly published a piece about his son's drunken driving; the paper published the story and the merchant pulled his ads . . .

Pressure From the Oval Office

President Carter, fearing that a 1977 story about CIA payments to foreign governments might compromise imminent discussions with King Hussein of Jordan, asked the Washington *Post* to withhold the story. When the *Post* declined, the President issued a statement deploring failure to "respect confidentiality on sensitive government matters." Editor Norman Cousins of the *Saturday Review* commented that "the *Post* did what it is supposed to do." Cousins held that it was the job of the newspaper to tell its readers what the CIA had done, that the government must bear responsibility for its acts, and that the President does not "strengthen himself or the nation by invoking national security as justification for corrupt practices." If national security "is an acceptable excuse for secret payoffs why is it not an acceptable excuse for denial of human rights?" asked Cousins.

But he was back, full force, in a month. General Motors canceled a quarter-million-dollar advertising contract with the *Wall Street Journal* because it published advance news of next year's models; but GM ads returned in weeks.

On the other hand, there's that Florida city where railway trains don't strike cars (the cars strike the trains). A movie house stopped printing its flyers in the plant of the newspaper that wrote its own movie criticisms, instead of using canned reviews from the movie makers (but it didn't withdraw its advertising). A newspaper withheld a story about a teen-ager's drug use—a type of story it had used before—when the youngster's advertiser-father made loud enough noises. Broadcasters have complied with many such requests from advertisers. One would be deaf not to know that in a lot of cases money talks.

The evidence seems to show that, when a newspaper refuses to comply, it is usually the winner. In a day when newspapers in most communities are financially strong (often it's *the* newspaper), there's truth in the axiom that "the advertiser needs the newspaper more than the newspaper needs the advertiser." A reporter threatened by an advertiser usually has only to inform his editors to make sure the "objectionable" story will be published. Some papers fall over backward to demonstrate rejection of attempts at control. One big paper front-paged a story about an accidental death in a department store elevator (the store was the paper's largest advertiser), giving the story more prominence than other such news received. Sordid divorce charges against a local grocery chain owner, in another case, were played big by a paper whose policy was to ignore divorce news. Of different color but the same cloth was overplay of paternity charges against a member of the paper's executive staff. The same paper used big type over a story about the charge that one of its circulation employees used "vacation stop" orders as tips for burglaries. On the contrary, it barely mentioned the fact that one of its executives had become director of an annual community fund campaign.

A reporter asked to twist, withhold or publish news in any "improper" manner can always say "no," subject to review by his editorial superiors, whom he should inform. He will usually get support.

Commercial names For many years news media shied away from names of specific businesses or products, especially in local news. For a number of years everybody knew that the term "a small foreign car" meant Volkswagen, before the invasion of other European and Japanese cars made the phrase ambiguous. Today many media

Censorship of Ads?

The Los Angeles *Times,* in 1977, announced that it would henceforth refuse ads for pornographic movies. The policy followed complaints from citizens and local groups; the *Times* said in announcing its policy change that it had been in error in accepting such ads, and offered an apology. (Similar screening instituted in the 1960s had been relaxed.)

have policies that permit use of commercial names when they add meaning to the news. The New York *Times* directs its staff to use commercial names

> if they provide necessary information (the brand name of the poisonous food); if they provide pertinent information (the name of the local firm that sponsors the Soap Box Derby); if their omission is curiosity-rousing (which self-adjusting camera are you writing about?); if to omit them seems niggardly (writing that the greyhound in the picture is "identified with a bus line" is pretty silly).

But, the instructions continued, you don't have to say "Scotch-taped" if "taped" does the job.

The spread of consumer columns and broadcast programs—"Action Line," "Your Dollar's Worth"—in which commercial names are essential to meaning has made their use frequent. The TV program that reported that "nineteen percolators, all of one make, were found to be dangerous" reported worse than nothing. The letter to the editor that says slyly "you won't use this because it will offend an advertiser" is naive. Newspapers (broadcasters less commonly) mostly follow guides like those of the New York *Times.* (The practice of advertisers of referring to competing products by trade name, introduced with a bang in the mid-70s, may have been helped along by relaxation in the news columns.)

"FAVORS"

An ancient—and hardly honorable—practice among journalists is the acceptance of "considerations" from news sources. It used to be that freebies all the way from movie tickets to junkets to Paris were general and almost unquestioned. A radio station news director reported one winter that he was "still entertaining with the booze he received at Christmas a year ago." A professional journal reports the comment of an editor attending an Associated Press Managing Editors convention: "Every corner suite at the Waldorf has some company (paper suppliers, news syndicates, travel agencies) handing out free drinks." Hundreds of reporters, from top echelon to bottom, have traveled millions of miles (first class) as "guests" of airlines, foreign governments and big businesses.

Why not? Does acceptance of a fifth of Scotch, a Dior gown, a sports jacket or tickets to the World Series obligate a reporter to "favorable" treatment of news about the donor?

Many journalists, beneficiaries of the practice or not, deny that freebies affect news handling. "I always tell the fight promoter that I'll go on his fishing trip," one sportswriter asserts, "but I also tell him that it won't affect what I write about his shows." The reporter covering the Rotary meeting doesn't think, "Good free meal. I'll make the dull talk sound interesting." The meal ticket is looked on as a routine aid to coverage. "I judge the news on its merits."

If freebies have no effect on news treatment, millions of dollars have poured fruitlessly down the sluice. Sportswriters, print and broadcasting, are favorite targets of this kind of persuasion; their Christmas stockings don't stretch enough to hold the bottled goods, tickets to Las Vegas or casting rods that come their way. Football writers who covered the Green Bay Packers were accustomed to getting 20 passes for each game. Theaters traditionally give free seats not only to critics but also to others on news staffs willing to accept them. Transocean junkets "to observe foreign politics" are offered and taken by reporters and editorial writers (apparently in the belief that a journalist—if accompanied by spouse or guest—can learn all about the Common Market in 12-hour visits to two countries). The professional journalism societies have only recently given up elaborate convention entertainment by such hosts as Sears Roebuck, Chrysler, Ford, big oil.

The American Society of Newspaper Editors, the Society of Pro-

---

Editorial Space for Sale?

Direct purchase and control of "editorial" space—news or any other kind—is a violation of the unwritten journalistic law that such space is not for sale. It is not often transgressed by American newspapers, though use by some papers of "canned" editorials and publicity releases favoring special interests is not a novelty, and commercial or advertiser pressure on broadcasters as well as sponsor control of program content is common. A remarkable variation on the practice occurred in 1976. *Esquire* magazine published an article by a distinguished newspaperman, Harrison Salisbury, for which he was paid $40,000 plus expenses—not by *Esquire* but by the Xerox Corporation. Xerox also bought advertising space at more than $100,000. Nobody suggested that the article promoted Xerox; but E. B. White, the pungent *New Yorker* editorialist, argued that in a press whose editorial space is for sale "the truth becomes elusive and the light fails." It would mean, he said, that the facts and opinions the people receive would come from fewer and fewer mouths—and the mouths would become those of special interests. To its credit, a Xerox spokesman thanked White for "telling me what I didn't want to hear" and forswore doing it again.

---

fessional Journalists and the Radio-TV News Directors Association, however, are among major professional groups that now reject this kind of bounty. The freebie practice is under fire. A number of newspapers, and some broadcasters, have adopted codes of practice that outlaw gratuities; the Louisville *Courier-Journal* and *Times*, whose procedures seem to have eliminated acceptance of freebies, are "the acknowledged Messrs. Clean of the newspaper industry." Major league athletic teams used to pay the freight for the sportswriters who covered their wide-ranging schedules; now at least a few newspapers bear the costs. The Chicago *Tribune* is one of the scores of papers that pay for seats their theater critics sit in; the sheaves of "comps" that Ringling Brothers used to pass around in newsrooms (sometimes in batches of 50) are often refused. Some employers stand on a sneaky middle ground: "Never take anything too big to hold in one hand." Two Chicago newspapers intercepted employees' mail and returned gifts that were suspect. The Chicago Newspaper Guild, approving "the policy of not accepting gratuities," asked in 1970 that newspaper executives reject "educational trips" and other hospitality offered them (but the Guild's national office in 1977 demanded that taboos on gifts be written into codes of ethics only upon Guild membership-and-management negotiation). The Memphis *Press-Scimitar* staff voted to "reject all gifts that could be construed as forms—subtle or otherwise—of 'payola,' bribery or coercion."

Few journalists think their integrity so fragile that it can't withstand a hand-holdable gift now and then. But journalists are human, and they don't always read their subliminal impulses correctly. A reporter who values personal independence and the dependability of the news knows that hands can't be too clean. Every favor accepted shadows not only its recipient but everybody working in journalism.

Walter Lippmann told the International Press Institute in London in the mid-'60s that "the powerful are perhaps the chief sources of news. They are also the dispensers of many kinds of favor, privilege, honor and esteem . . . The temptations are many: some are simple, some refined; often they are yielded to without the consciousness of yielding. Only constant awareness offers protection."

Checkbook journalism The reverse of purchase of news favors in wampum, whiskey or wardrobes is purchase of news itself. Is buying news facts proper? The answer is frequently "yes." Compensating people for information they hold, especially when it is personal or private or the product of their own efforts, is both common and appropriate. Exclusively held information is often a form of private property: It may be honorably bought and sold.

But when the information has public impact, the complexion of the problem changes. Exclusivity is the key. When a news medium sews up newsworthy figures so that no other medium can get significant information they possess, the competition—and, more important, the public—can justify feeling shortchanged.

Checkbook journalism has for years been big business. *Life* magazine, during its affluent years, was an aggressive buyer of "exclusive rights" (among them the personal stories of 47 astronauts—not all of them very good stories). In 1927 the New York *Times* and the St. Louis *Post-Dispatch* sewed up the first-person story of Charles A. Lindbergh, the "Lone Eagle" Atlantic flier. CBS paid one of the Watergate notables, H. R. Haldeman, $100,000 for two 1975 interviews and NBC is said to have bought five annual broadcasts, beginning in 1978, from Henry Kissinger for a million dollars. NBC helped finance the building by young East Berliners of an escape tunnel under the Berlin Wall, and only NBC was on hand to cover the exploit. The Nixon-Frost interviews are mentioned elsewhere in this book. (An attempt by an eager opportunist to peddle what he called the "Son of Sam murders story" was rejected by several media.)

Among criticisms of the purchase of news are these:

- That exclusivity automatically limits the number of media that offer a story and thus limits the breadth of its audience
- That news sources with information they think has cash or other value (a kidnapper offered to surrender if he was assured of national TV coverage) may refuse to divulge it if the price isn't right
- That the most prosperous media (great dailies, networks, syndicates) dominate the bidding, squeezing the little fellows out
- That the holders of the news are in prime position to manage it, to put out as much or as little as they choose, to color it to suit their fancy

Only a small portion of the news can be thus packaged and marketed. A spot news story has to be covered on the run, and its facts are usually as readily available to the 15th reporter as to the first. You can't bottle up actions of courts and most other governmental bodies, or of natural catastrophes, or of events open to the public. But you can sign up an All-American basketball player to talk only to you about professionalism or such searching questions as whether lady tennis players ought to engage in matches with gentleman tennis players.

Reporting is healthier when it is not at the mercy of the bankroll.

Conflicts of interest A cousin of the favors problem, and one just as durable, is that of journalists' affiliation with newsmaking groups.

On this issue today's news practitioners are widely divided. The problem: How fairly, how objectively, can you report news that relates to a community action group or a golf club you belong to, a business some of whose stock you hold (it is a little-known fact that some reporters own stocks), a political party you love or despise? Here are some of the pros and cons:

Pro:

- Reporters associated with public, community-service and many other kinds of organizations are informed on and close to current trends, significant events and the people who make news. Can a political reporter report politics if he doesn't know politicians, party management and political shenanigans firsthand?
- When readers and viewers know that newsworkers are active in civic affairs, they will respect both journalists and their media.
- No employer has the right to say to a man or woman, "You're a journalist by your own choice. This means that you're willing to give up being a citizen."

Con:

- A reporter affiliated with a newsmaking activity is under suspicion. How can school board news be trusted if its writer, or the editorialist commenting on it, is a member of the board?
- Newsmen need to keep their distance from the *making* of news in order to view it objectively.

The pro side seems to be gaining. Reporters and their editors and managers commonly take part in community activities. Direct political activity is rare, however. When the Newspaper Guild's Washington office demanded impeachment of Nixon in 1973, a number of local Guild chapters issued disclaimers. Some newspapers and broadcasters try to have it both ways by establishing community relations officers who, without news responsibilities, provide public service in the names of their media without commitment to party, race, religion or economic interests. The Des Moines *Tribune* dropped William F. Buckley's column because of doubt that Buckley's business interests would permit him to write objectively on a number of subjects (Buckley responded acidly that he should be judged on what he says, not on his outside interests). The appointment of a newspaper's "outdoors writer" to a state natural resources agency was criticized on the ground that he might not be able to write without bias about the agency. Jack Anderson, the muckraking Washington columnist, gave up a bank directorship after a Miami editor rejected part of one of his columns that dealt with actions of a bank stockholder.

In a remarkable effort to play fair with readers, the Philadelphia *Inquirer* published a 17,000-word report that a woman formerly its political reporter had carried on a love affair with a state senator through a period in which she covered his political activities. Two of the paper's investigative reporters worked six weeks, on assignment, to produce the "special report on an *Inquirer* conflict of interest." The paper said it wanted to "allow readers to reach their individual conclusions" about the episode. The journalistic magazine *Quill* recommends the report (Oct. 16, 1977) to journalists for "what it has to say about professionalism and human nature." Publication of the article, acknowledging as it does the *Inquirer's* "lapse of editorial vigilance," is a monument to editorial responsibility.

Most laymen doubt that Olympian disinterest is possible. But the record holds scores of tales of reporters who reveal the illegal duck bags of their own gun clubs or the civil rights violations of organizations they belong to. There is no sure or ready answer. The problem is pragmatic, philosophical, human and ethical—not legal or journalistic.

THE NEWS COUNCILS

How can a private citizen or an unofficial group get a hearing for a complaint about news media performance? The First Amendment means that any law seeking to compel or prevent publication of news or modification of press attitudes is unconstitutional. The press, in effect, can behave as it likes. How can a mere reader-listener bring it to heel if in his opinion it behaves badly?

One answer has taken form through the 1970s: the news council, a voluntary body of lay and professional citizens charged with rendering judgment on allegations of journalistic behavior. Britain has had a Press Council—unofficial and with no powers of sanction—for a generation; though it has not purged the British press, consensus says that it has observably upgraded news performance and press

A Case in Point

The National News Council, in 1977, considered whether it was proper for a TV station executive to sit on a court-appointed body examining Boston busing desegregation and busing problems. The station had carried statements urging parent cooperation in meeting the problems. The Council decided that it was "improper" for the executive to serve on such a body. "Such involvement can only create doubts about the objectivity and balance of his organization's news coverage." But one member of the Council, agreeing with the general conclusion, objected to "the notion that . . . the journalist is subject to limitations on his freedom of speech, association and action that are not applicable to others."

responsibility. In the United States proposals for such a plan were ridiculed or ignored when they were made at the time of World War II. But in recent years local councils have appeared in a number of towns and cities. The National News Council, with a five-year $2-million grant from the Twentieth Century Fund, was organized in 1973, an "experimental" panel with nine lay and six journalist members. Its charge: to hear complaints about news and editorial actions of major news media—wire services, "national" and other principal newspapers, *Time* and *Newsweek*, national broadcasting networks—and to render judgments of fault or merit. Not everybody liked the idea. The New York *Times* refused both cooperation and acceptance of Council criticism; the Council, said the *Times*, would be grand jury, prosecutor and judge; it left out most of the media. But in its first four years it heard and rendered opinion on more than 50 complaints, and its judgments at the minimum brought to public attention not only pluses and minuses in news media behavior but also competent judgment about specific accusations against the press. Among the complaints it considered in the last half of 1977 were these:

1. That a syndicate and some of its clients had failed to retract properly an unproven allegation about misuse of funds contributed to relieve suffering caused by a Central American earthquake. *Conclusion:* The charge was "warranted."
2. That a network broadcast came at a time to influence a jury decision. *Conclusion:* Unrestricted reporting is vital to public understanding, and "fair trial . . . can be preserved, if necessary, by sequestering the jury."
3. The Boston conflict-of-interest case (see page 377).
4. That a Cape Cod magazine had failed to correct properly an inaccurate article about water fluoridation on the Cape. *Conclusion:* The charge was warranted.
5. That a network broadcast on radioactive waste was unbalanced and "replete with major factual errors" (*conclusion:* charges warranted), and that it used "show-biz gimmicks" and was poorly edited. *Conclusion:* "This Council should not substitute its producing judgment for that of a news organization".

The Council also urged news media to conduct coverage of terrorism to guard against "reckless rumors and exaggerated, word-of-mouth reports" and to forgo interviews with terrorists or hostages during negotiations. (The Council offered to become a repository for media guidelines designed to avoid such coverage, and urged television to make sure that "docudramas" be guarded against "the dangers of public confusion and historical revisionism or inaccuracy.")

Local news councils follow less ambitious procedures and often operate with weak financing—sometimes a single broadcaster or newspaper is the sponsor. The successful Minnesota (statewide) Press Council, in one report, tells of a judgment against a small-city daily paper which, it said, was deficient in coverage of a local dispute (not enough expertise and depth of reporting, and biased treatment of letters to the editor); criticizes another small daily for changing its letters-to-the-editor policy without informing readers, and for failure to assure that letters published "reflect fairly the diversity of opinion on each issue"; and rejects a complaint that a reviewer in a metropolitan paper had made false imputations and uncorrected errors in a column (some of the column, the Council decided, was "in poor taste").

LAWS AND THE NEWS MEDIA

Confidentiality Respected and generally observed among American journalists' ethical concepts is the principle governing release of information given them "in confidence."

When news sources tell reporters, "I'm revealing such-and-such to you for your private information, but not for publication," they can be sure that only once in a blue moon will their confidence be misplaced. A practical, down-to-earth reason is that a betrayed news source becomes a news source no longer. But equally compelling is journalists' professional and personal belief in the sanctity of such a promise.

The strength of the belief, however, causes problems. Among them: manipulation by shrewd news sources to dam up information that ought to become public property; and protection of the identity of informants.

The news management problem, familiar under the term *off the record,* is discussed in Chapter 12. The second, revealing or concealing news sources' identities, is one of journalists' most burdensome—grave enough to send some of them to jail. "Sure, go ahead and use it," says the source. "But don't let on that I told you." The tactic may be used by an informant to cover carelessness in his own behavior or to plant lies, libel or information impelled by self-interest. The danger is always present, and reporters learn to keep their guards up. Most give the promise to withhold a source's name, or information that would identify the source, as rarely as possible.

Sometimes concealment is appropriate and defensible. When you are sure of the accuracy and reliability of the source, when revealing a man's name would put him into an unjustly embarrassing, compromising or perilous position, and when you can make the news just as meaningful without a name as with it, you may find it proper to refer to him as "a New York broker with local connections," "a responsible party official" or even "a Skid Row pusher who says he would be rubbed out" if he were known. But your own confidence in the source's dependability (or clear warning in your story of any doubt) is a minimum precaution.

Refusal to reveal information or its source has sent a number of reporters to jail for contempt of court in the last half-century; some have paid fines. Recent conspicuous cases (both involving New York *Times* reporters) gave no comfort to the press. Earl Caldwell, in 1972, refused to give a grand jury the notes on his Black Panther investigation; the U.S. Supreme Court confirmed the contempt-of-court judgment against him. In 1978, Myron Farber, withholding files on a murder case involving 12 "mysterious" hospital deaths, was jailed, and the *Times* was given a heavy fine; the Court refused to review the penalties. But the Court had upheld the right to publication of the "stolen" Pentagon Papers—a case that supported "the values of freedom of expression and the right of the people to know" even though all newsgathering procedures were not revealed. Other courts have upheld this principle; some have denied it with stated reluctance, saying that the welfare of society or the right to fair trial demands the broken promise.

About a third of American states have adopted "shield laws" that outlaw or limit the power of the court to penalize reporters (usually by contempt-of-court action) for declining to reveal sources of information. Attempts to pass a federal shield law have repeatedly failed. Most such laws make immunity an "absolute privilege," though some provide that the court may demand information if "justice depends on it." Most journalists favor absolute privilege (news

---

Is Privacy Private?

The Supreme Court of the United States, in a dubious decision in 1978, extended the use of search warrants to permit:

- surprise searches of homes and businesses for documentation—pictures, letters, notes, diaries—to be used as evidence in court
- seizure of the records of ministers, physicians and lawyers (in contravention of the traditional confidentiality of such material)
- unannounced inspection and confiscation of anything in news media files, whether relevant to legal proceedings or not, and whether gathered under promise of anonymity or not

Civil libertarians as well as professionals whose work involves guarantees of protection of privacy—including journalists—looked on the decision as potentially violating First and Fourth Amendment rights; journalists could see news sources dry up and capacity to report many kinds of news evaporate. As this is written, Congress is being asked to legalize protection against unreasonable invasions.

---

media professional associations have been influential advocates of protective laws), but a minority has doubts. The executive editor of the St. Petersburg (Fla.) *Times* told editors of his state that such legislation would "be an erosion of the First Amendment . . . an admission that somehow the First Amendment is less than adequate." An attorney for the Gannett newspaper chain told the same meeting that "the courts will try to balance the various interests" and make reasonable decisions without the law. But an attorney for the Miami *Herald* expressed fear that only wealthy newspapers could afford "the tremendous legal costs involved" in protection of confidences.

Disagreement also exists as to whether a reporter's fidelity to a promise should be regarded in the same light as that of the clergyman, the lawyer or the physician. These professionals are universally permitted to protect individual clients; in news reporting, however, it is the interest of the public that is at stake.

An enlightening discussion of aspects of confidentiality, especially of the growing use of subpoenas to bring reporters and sometimes their notes into courts or before grand juries, appears in the *Aspen Notebook on Government and the Media,* pages 66–66 (see page 387).

A final comment from Robert W. Greene, the seasoned investigative reporter of *Newsday* (Long Island):

> Shield laws give government the power to define what a newsman is. This . . . gives government a foot in the door.

That is to say, if law defines who is protected, it can also decide who is not protected. This is a distant danger, but it is not an unthinkable one.

Who owns news? Most news information is everybody's property. An event open to all comers—inauguration of a bridge, a ballyhooed revival meeting, a football game—gives all the right to observe and report. Semipublic events such as theater productions and church services, though their managers may deny admission and usually have the right to do so, may be reported by anybody who gets information about them. An event in a public street or one observable from a public vantage may be turned into news by anybody who sees and hears it.

Managers or participants in private events may refuse to give reporters information, just as they may refuse to talk about public events. But information about them is public property if a fact-gatherer—a reporter, a policeman, the woman next door—finds a legal way to get it (see Chapter 12). Reporters who get such information may make their own decision about its use; they may withhold it, turn it in to the city desk with or without recommendation, or throw it into the trash can. They may decide that is is unnewsworthy; they may fear that it contains libel they cannot defend; they may believe that it might cause damage or pain beyond its public value, or that it is the concern of nobody but those involved in it.

Information growing out of government activities, however, is almost always public property, open to any citizen who demonstrates reasonable need or use for it. Acquisition of public information about laws and lawmaking, governmental records, court proceedings and the like, as a basis for news, is a legally reasonable need. So is the public's right to know. (Out-of-bounds information includes that affecting national security and certain types of economic or personal data.) The fact that some public officials try to keep information under cover does not affect the principle; injunctions and other stratagems may enable the journalist to gain access.

A legal approach considered a threat to freedom of the press surfaced in the 1970s: the definition of information as property subject to laws governing ownership and theft. In 1971 the federal government tried to prevent publication of the Pentagon Papers on this legal base, though decision in the case was made on the constitutional prior-restraint base. A Washington reporter was arrested by FBI agents in the early '70s for "possession" of Bureau of Indian Affairs papers; a grand jury refused to indict him. The threat to press freedom and public information in such cases is not in restriction on the right to publish, but in the use of property laws to achieve *de facto* censorship.

Who owns the news a reporter gathers? This is a knotty question to which there is no all-or-none answer.

Traditional definitions rely on the fact that a reporter is a paid agent and that disposition of materials such an agent collects is ownership's prerogative. Ownership may publish it, sit on it or toss it. If ownership has not decided whether to publish (or broadcast) it, the reporter is generally considered to have no more right to use it for private purposes than the hired trainer of a race horse has a right to enter the horse in a race. The trainer must acquire and train his own horse; the reporter is usually expected to gather information for personal use on personal time.

But what if ownership decides not to use it? It is a legal principle that "literary properties . . . are products of the mind plus skill" and that such properties belong to their producer until he releases them (by publication, by sale, by written or unwritten contractual arrangement). A Washington lawyer argues in the *Columbia Journalism Review* (May–June 1978) that property law indicates a reporter's work should be open to personal use, especially after obligations to the employer have been met.

In practice this hair is not often split. News materials ordinarily are used or promptly thrown away. Once published, their facts (though not their literary style or expression) are anybody's property. If a reporter wishes to make personal use of them later, asking the publisher's permission is a courtesy rather than a legal necessity. Some employers, by contract or otherwise, restrict free-lancing; but doing so is regarded by most reporters as cruel and unusual, and restrictions are often blinked at by employers and employees.

In brief, a reporter's efforts are formally the property of whoever pays for the time and skill, until they are released—to the writer or to somebody else, gratis or for "valuable consideration." Or until they are published.

Copyright The copyright laws are designed to protect "the products of the mind." They say you cannot make more than limited verbatim quotation of a copyrighted news story; its style and mode of presentation belong to its owner, usually the employer of the writer. Most news media do not go through the copyright process; those that do are sometimes willing, on request, to register the copyright in the name of the writer. The copyright holder may sell or give away the copyright. Under the new federal copyright law, the copyright ownership expires after 75 years for most newspaper material. In the case of a work by an individual, such as a book or a play, the copyright expires 50 years after the author's death. Until the copyright period expires, the owner can control exact reproduction.

But content is something else. The substance of a news story, its facts, become anybody's property—go into the public domain—when publicly released. This means that you can't *reprint* your competitor's copyrighted news story, but you can use its facts—as a tip for further investigation, or as material for a rewrite (in your own words).

Reporters don't often have copyright problems—fortunately, for the intricacies of copyright law are more involved than this brief résumé suggests. Anybody with questions should go to the company lawyer or the library. But it won't have to be done often.

Libel "Libel," says the AP "Libel Manual," "is injury to reputation. Words, pictures or cartoons that expose a person to public hatred, shame, disgrace or ridicule, or induce an ill opinion of a person are libelous." Libel is defamation that is printed, written or pictorial. Before radio, defamation by spoken word was slander—derogatory statement by use of the vocal cords. Since a person's voice doesn't go as far as a printed page can be circulated, it was generally held that slander—though similar in many ways to libel—wasn't likely to be as damaging; therefore the penalties to which it might lead were less severe. But radio, and later TV, range as widely as print, and defamation by broadcasting is looked on as libel.

But defamation by itself is not always actionable—not always an act for which the individual defamed may get damages through court action. The defamation must also be untrue; and if it deals with a public man or matter, it must be what is called malicious—that is, uttered with intent to injure, or without good reason to think it is true. Examples will show this difference:

- A published or broadcast news story says that a citizen was seen breaking a window in a home not his own, climbing inside and later emerging with a well-packed burlap bag. The factual statement is true: The citizen was so observed, and the paper can prove it. The defamation therefore is not actionable.
- The same story is published or broadcast, but it is false. The citizen is therefore falsely derogated, and his suit for damages would be likely to succeed.

Now inject malice, or lack of it:

- In the second case the citizen may be able to show that the newspaper reporter or broadcaster put forth the allegation knowing that it was false; or that, knowing it or not, he had made statements that he was "going to get" the citizen. Courts would usually take proof of these facts to indicate "actual malice," intent to injure, and might award both general and punitive damages—the latter considered punishment of the libeler, the former compensation to the libelee.

Take another case: A newspaper opposes a candidate's election to the city council. It publishes an editorial (editorials can be as libelous as news stories) saying the candidate has not always paid state income taxes. The candidate sues for damages, calling the statement false and malicious. Under the so-called New York *Times* decision of 1964, he cannot recover damages if the newspaper can prove that it honestly believed the statement to be accurate (this interpretation was later extended by the Supreme Court to "public figures" of almost any kind). Some lawyers, journalists and others think the interpretation too broad, but one Supreme Court justice, Hugo Black, thought it too narrow. Reporters should know the law books, especially those of the state in which they work, and keep abreast of current court decisions.

Several rules of thumb help reporters (usually poor lawyers) assess most libel problems:

1. Truth of a statement is in most cases a full defense against libel actions. In rare cases absence of malice must also be shown.
2. "Privilege" that attaches to governmental and judicial proceedings is usually a full defense. "Privilege" is the right to make accurate reports of court and other public or governmental proceedings and all the charges and testimony that are a part of them, no matter how defamatory, if the *reports* (not necessarily the testimony) are accurate. Inaccuracies in reporting on privileged material may destroy the privilege and may be taken as indications of malice.
3. The laws of fair comment and criticism permit journalists or others to express honest opinions or judgments on all kinds of "public" actions, from government and judicial proceedings to public performance of actors, musicians, public speakers or athletes. Such comment must be based on the pertinent actions, and it must be reasonable and fair (even if adverse). You can call a man a grotesquely inept tennis player if he plays before an audience (whether others agree with you or not), as long as you evidence no malice. But you cannot say of him that "a man who makes passes at his secretary ought to make better lobs" unless you're prepared to prove there's a relationship.
4. You may say anything for which someone has given consent (but you'd better have the consent in writing).
5. The "right of reply" permits you to respond to an attack in kind—to attack back. Your response can be strong, but it can't be false or malicious.
6. Many states have retraction-and-apology laws under whose provisions you can reduce or remove liability for actionable statements.

Many more libel suits are threatened or brought to court than come to trial or to decision by judge or jury. Libel suits are expensive, and suers and sued often prefer to settle out of court. And some libel suits are simple efforts at vindication. Theodore Roosevelt once sued for, and was awarded, six cents.

Somebody once said, "Write correct, don't write mean, and you've got 'em cornered"—oversimplification that will take you a long way.

STUDY SUGGESTIONS

1. In what ways does the fact that "news is a business" affect the work of reporters?
2. What are the relationships between a news medium's financial strength and its editorial and news-treatment freedom?
3. What does the concept "cronyism" have to do with news coverage? If you see it as a threat, how serious do you think it is?
4. Name some of the "pressures from within"—auspicious or destructive to reporting—that may face modern journalism.
5. State your beliefs about the effects of advertiser pressure on news handling.
6. Do you see gifts and "favors" to reporters and editors as a menace to the integrity of news reporting? Or as something of little weight? On what do you base your opinions?
7. The news council concept has been cheered and derided. After studying a dozen of the National News Council judgments reported in *Columbia Journalism Review* (see page 387), write your views of the news council plan and what you see as its effectiveness.
8. Journalists have long argued about the privilege of confidentiality—should a reporter have free choice whether to reveal news sources or do demands of society (usually represented by the courts) sometimes take precedence? After studying some of the references suggested on pages 387–388, state your own views.
9. When is news defamatory of an individual not "actionable"—not subject to suit for damages?

PRACTICE ASSIGNMENTS

1. From current issues of your local newspaper, list at least 10 news story references, *by name*, to advertisers, trademarked products or other commercial enterprises. Make a second list from radio and TV newscasts. Interview a news executive from each medium you have studied about its policy concerning use of commercial names. Write an analytical report of your findings.
2. A TV news reporter refuses to tell a court the sources of information in his stories about use of angel dust in the local high school. He presents two justifications for refusing: first, that he has made a promise not to name names; second, that revealing one set of sources would close many other kinds of sources to him ("he has a loose lip"). Without his evidence, charges of dope-peddling collapse; the court charges him with contempt and jails him. (a) Would such a finding be possible in your state? Does the state have shield laws or other protections for reporters' confidential information? (b) If there are no such laws, what arguments could be presented on each side of the question: required revelation of the sources and continued concealment?
3. Discuss with a newspaper or broadcasting news executive one of the following topics and write an analysis of what you learn:

The pluses and minuses of forming a news council in your area

Should reporters be permitted to take on writing or other journalistic work for other publications, on their own time?

The extent to which local advertisers seek to influence news or editorial content

Should a publication or a broadcaster censor advertising?

Can reporters report fairly on news events or projects in which they are personally involved?

RELATED READING

Ashmore, Harry S. *Fear in the Air.* Norton, 1973. Subtitled *Broadcasting and the First Amendment: The Anatomy of a Constitutional Crisis.*

Auletta, Ken. "Bribe, Seduce, Lie, Steal: Anything to Get the Story?" *More,* March 1977. Cynical defense of the end-justifies-the-means school of reporting.

Bagdikian, Ben H., "Newspaper Mergers—the Final Phase." *Columbia Journalism Review,* March–April 1977. A leading journalism critic and scholar expresses deep concern over "chains devouring chains" in American newspaperdom.

Cannon, Lou. *Reporting: An Inside View.* Praeger Publishers, 1976. Critical view of news reporting by an experienced national affairs reporter. Commercialism, suppression, news management, bias, other topics.

Gora, Joel M. *The Rights of Reporters.* Discus Books, 1974. In Q-and-A form, this American Civil Liberties Union handbook explains and suggests protections for reporters under the law.

Gormley, William T., Jr. "How Cross-Ownership Affects Newsgathering." *Columbia Journalism Review,* May–June 1977. Report of a careful study that leads the author to believe that the growth of cross-ownership is a threat to thorough reporting.

Hulteng, John L. "The Performance or the Power?" *Quill,* October 1977. Penetrating analysis of "the Panax case," an intrusion by a chain owner into the news columns and the independence of his newspapers.

Kennedy, George. "Processing of the Beefs." *Quill,* October 1977. Description of the pioneering work of a state Press Council.

Levine, Victor. *Your Guide to the New Copyright Law.* Freelancer's Newsletter, 1977. Clarification of the first changes in copyright procedures in nearly 80 years, in a "practical 27-page booklet in nonlegal language."

Masters, W. H., Rinker Buck and Peter M. Sandman. "Media Monopolies." *More,* October 1977. Three articles about the monopoly ownership problem.

"National News Council Report." *Columbia Journalism Review,* March–April 1977, and subsequent issues. Details of complaints heard and decisions rendered by the National News Council.

Pember, Don R. *Mass Media Law.* William C. Brown, 1977. A complete and careful work, described as "not a book for lawyers or law students" but "a journalism or mass media book *about* the law." Press freedom, libel, privacy, copyright, access to information, confidentiality, free press-fair trial, broadcasting law and other areas are covered.

Report by the National News Council, 1973–75. National News Council, 1976.

Rivers, William L., and Michael J. Nyhan., eds. *Aspen Notebook on Government and the Media.* Praeger Publishers,

1973. Comments by a score of leaders in many contemporary activities on current press problems. They cast light on many of the topics treated in this chapter.

Rivers, William L., ed. *Aspen Handbook on the Media.* Praeger Publishers, 1977. The 1977–78 edition greatly expands this reference guide to the communications media. Required reading in many communications courses.

Schmidt, Benno C., Jr. *Freedom of the Press vs. Public Access.* Praeger Publishers, 1976. Overview of demands for access to the media and their constitutional ramifications.

Sheehan, Neil, and others. *The Pentagon Papers.* Bantam Books, 1971. Narrative of the effort by news media to publish the "secret history of the Vietnam War," together with many documents and photographs. The story of a massive effort to reveal historical materials marked "secret" by the Department of Defense. In the words of Justice Hugo L. Black, "the newspapers nobly did precisely that which the founders hoped and trusted they would do."

Zuckman, Harvey L., and Martin J. Gaynes. *Mass Communication Law in a Nutshell.* West Publishing Co., 1977. A compact and understandable discussion of libel and other press law problems.

20 Reporters and the Public

PREVIEW

Reporting is generally looked on as a professional occupation—one conducted under ethical controls that take into account the dignity and prerogatives of people involved in news events and of news audiences, as well as the self-respect of those who do the reporting. In addition to the journalistic attitudes and practices that protect these rights cited in Chapter 19, other important ones are:

- Care in use of names so that their owners will not be unfairly or unjustly brought before the public
- Regard for the privacy of citizens in areas that are not properly open to news attention
- "Good taste" in reporting so as not to offend public mores needlessly or to capitalize on the anguish, joy or personal oddities of people, when doing so serves no useful journalistic or public purpose
- Avoidance of "sensationalizing" in reporting, either in broad strokes or fine
- Refusal to "serve two masters," to dilute or disguise professional activities by mixing them with service to other causes, public or private

---

American journalists and most of their clientele look on reporting as a professional occupation. A reporter is expected to be more than an artisan; the work of newsmen and newswomen is conducted under defined and socially approved characteristics:

- Its principles and practices can be handed down from one worker to another, by formal or empirical education.
- It operates with a recorded and expanding body of knowledge.
- It has its base in the culture and mores of its times.
- Its practitioners are concerned about human welfare, and most of them are motivated by a drive to meet its demands.

- It is responsible to principles of ethical conduct.
- It has an awareness of its own shortcomings and a desire to correct them.

Acceptance of professional principles as the base for responsible newswork is implicit in this book. The principles should be the property of and guides for all journalists—the brass in the front office as well as the men and women on the action front. A reporter's charge is to behave so as to serve the large and the small interests of the community, to take account of broad social imperatives as well as narrower community affairs and relationships.

The first responsibility is to be as good a reporter as the gods permit—to gather information as searchingly, evaluate it as carefully and present it as effectively as personal capacities allow. The specifics of reaching these goals are given attention in other chapters in *Reporting.* But reporters recognize that personal as well as communal values concern them. Those who merit the term *professional* respect individual dignity and the private prerogatives of citizens; sometimes they regard them as overriding.

And they respect both their own dignity and that of those they hope to serve. They earn the confidence of others as a consequence of what they think of themselves.

This chapter deals with specific circumstances in which professional journalists believe the personal lives of people in the news deserve protection. Some of these circumstances are examined else-

---

To Be or Not to Be

The first effective news-editorial labor union, The Newspaper Guild, was organized in 1933. Publishers and employers of newsworkers have continually sought to have them classified by the National Labor Relations Board as "professional employees"—a classification that would exempt them from the provisions of the National Labor Relations Act and bar them from the advantages of collective bargaining. The Guild is, however, a horizontal union—its membership includes many media employees other than the news-editorial. In 1976 the NLRB repeated earlier rulings: "The contention that journalists are 'professional' employees . . . has been fully litigated and rejected by the Board."

Thus journalists who take pride in the professional character of their occupation support a legal definition that denies professional status, in order to maintain their prerogatives as union members.

Law Professor Roger Fisher of Harvard points out that compulsion or legal techniques do not guarantee "professionalism." Of reporters, he says, "We must always ask more than we require . . . . Society can define the functions it thinks the media ought to perform, without requiring them by law or professionally established guidelines to do so." Professional conduct comes from within, not from without.

As the latest edition of a newspaper comes off the press, newsmen examine copies. *(James H. Karales photo from Peter Arnold Photo Archives)*

where, as problems that impinge on newsgathering practices (the right not to be libeled, for example, and the right of property in literary or intellectual achievements). But at times reporters must consider the sensitivities, the privacy and the dignity of people they write about—times when such considerations carry more weight than the right of the community to information. Shielding those who make the news is sometimes as "professional" as opening them to public scrutiny.

And there are values in the rights of the audience—the right not to be offended unnecessarily, the right not to be exposed to false valuations, the right to be told displeasing facts that they ought to know.

NAMES AND IDENTIFICATION

The uses of names get serious attention at newsroom policy conferences. Reporting is usually not complete if participants in events are not identified. Yet the news media are in consensus that some circumstances call for anonymity. A conspicuous example is in reporting juvenile misbehavior.

Most news media agree that leaving teenagers nameless when they get into trouble may be a service to them and to society. The boy or girl in midteens who is caught shoplifting, runs the argument, is not likely to be a habitual evildoer. Rehabilitation is of more concern than punishment; through 80 years since a county judge in Illinois established the first American juvenile court, courts and newspapers have moved toward the belief that "the important thing is not what can be done to the child but what can be done for him." By common consent, reporting of "atrocious" crimes—murder, rape, sadism—or spectacular or repulsive public offenses, should include names. When a 15-year-old took a rifle, walked into the family living room and shot his mother, news media thought the public should know his identity. But if he had heaved a rock through a school window—especially if it had been his first offense—few papers or broadcasters would have named him.

This approach is not universal. A Montana judge, insisting on naming boys and girls charged in his court with felonies, asserted that his practice decreased crime in his district. Helena and Great Falls police statistics, where some of the media followed his advice, did not bear him out. But a six-month trial of complete suppression of *all* news (newspaper and radio alike) of juvenile vandalism in a small Iowa city ended with a 30 percent drop in vandalism.

A writer in *Quill* said that "the sad truth is that no one really knows the answer." No one has figured out how many youngsters have been "rehabilitated" because they were unnamed. Nevertheless, American media usually believe in giving misbehavers under 18 the benefit of anonymity.

Names in sex crimes The media are surer of their ground in withholding the names of women who have been raped and of children who have been sexually mistreated. The justification is, however, quite different: protection of victims from embarrassment or humiliation. Few dispute this practice or its rationale.

Names in "in-house news" The media are sometimes accused of protecting their own—staff members, officers, relatives, social or business associates. Lack of competition, it is said, may induce the cover-up of news that ought to be published. But some monopoly papers fall over backward to demonstrate their objectivity. A publisher of a daily in the Southwest once complained to his city editor, "Do you have to report every parking ticket I get?" He answered his own question: "Yes, I guess you do."

Minority identifications Identification of members of minority groups by racial, religious or national labels is no longer a common pattern. Usual policy is to describe a man or woman in the news by such a word as *black, Chinese, Indian, Jewish, Polish, Italian* . . . only if the news can't be understood without the tag.

This enlightened policy is less widely accepted in areas with heavy minority populations. Even in the South, however, habitual identification by skin color is declining (as is the policy of "no black news except bad black news" once followed by many Southern media).

The dilemma cannot be swept away by blanket rules. In New York City with teeming Puerto Rican, black and other minorities—most at ruinous economic levels—it may be both good reporting and fair reporting to say that the muggers in Central Park were white. In Decorah, Iowa, description of the man suspected of a dozen purse snatches as black may aid in his capture. A Minneapolis newspaper story about a rally protesting minority admission policies of a law school identified the protesters only as "law students"; the TV report showing many of them to be members of minority groups was more meaningful.

First names Newspapers and news announcers occasionally have to refer to people in the news by first names. When the news figure is a child, or when everybody uses a given name or nickname, the last name might sound stuffy. In a personality story about the grade school janitor whom everybody in town has known for 50 years as "Chris" it would be pompous or puzzling to call him Mr. Sutherland. Nobody—himself least of all—objected to reference to the Great Crooner as Bing, or the Greatest as Ali. Circumstances, custom and the nature of the news often justify familiarity.

But what about these cases?

> Police arrested Mrs. Janet Stringster yesterday on a charge of shoplifting. Janet told the police . . .
>
> College kids don't like former Sen. Eugene McCarthy as much as they used to. When Gene spoke yesterday to students . . .
>
> Mabel Hopkins, 77 years old, was evicted because she couldn't pay rent, electric or gas bills. Mabel told police . . .

Broadcasters—somewhat more than print journalists—often use given names for women. And the lower the woman's social level (thus the more needful of respectful protection), the more likely the first-naming.

Why object?

- The practice violates accepted social custom (even in a society where everybody calls everybody Hank or Peggy the first time round).
- It is subtly demeaning, especially when applied to men and women involved in questionable behavior or subject to social disadvantage.

A suggested guide: Use first names only when everybody would; be chary of them when the news is disparaging.

Names in "injurious" news Names often must be used in news that casts their owners in unfavorable light. But a problem is suggested in a "cardinal, unbreakable" instruction given to reporters and copyreaders on the New York *Times:*

> If a person is mentioned derogatorily in a news story, he should be given immediate chance to respond. If he can't be reached, the story should be held over if possible. If it's something that ought to have instant publication, the story should say the person was not reachable, and efforts to get him should continue until he can be heard from.

(The *Times* didn't say it, but careful reporters and editors try to avoid the nearly meaningless cliché "he was not immediately available for comment." When he can't be reached, better say something like "telephone calls to his home and office were not answered.")

The *Times* rule does not usually apply to news on the public record—court news, grand jury indictments and the like. Formal charges of illegal activity have opportunity for defense built into them. But the charges must be filed; news media carefully avoid using names of "suspects" not yet officially charged.

Names in news involving homosexuality A fire in a Washington, D.C., theater heavily patronized by homosexuals killed nine persons. Among the dead were "prestigious members" of the Capital community. The Washington *Post*, after some fumbling, adopted a no-names policy "to protect the families" of those who died. The competing *Star* identified the dead because "it was our responsibility to report" the news. It is a reasonable prediction that the *Star* practice will become general if the stigma of same-sex preference continues to diminish.

Are Laws Needed?

Protection of privacy by statute has been so complicated a problem—the danger that privacy laws might infringe First Amendment principles is one of the complications—that few laws have been passed. Congress and some states have considered them, and news media violations of privacy have stimulated interest in toughening restrictions. But an HEW study concludes that laws of personal record-keeping "do not add up to a consistent body of law." A Midwest police chief a few years ago ran "record checks" on newcomers to his town at the request of landlords and employers, apparently without violating any law.

PRIVACY: RIGHT OR PRIVILEGE?

"The right to be let alone" has long been acknowledged as a characteristic of American life. "A man's home is his castle"; people's private acts and thoughts are their business and nobody else's. Within broadly defined limits they may reasonably expect to live as free from outside observation and interference as they wish. But the question remains: Is the "right of privacy" a right or a privilege? The Constitution does not establish it, though the first eight Amendments and the 14th are considered by lawyers to support the principle by implication.

One misapprehension should be dispelled: *Secrecy* and *privacy*, in the news sense, are not synonymous. Secrecy means concealment of information—justifiably or not—at the source: refusing to reveal facts about matters of public concern. Privacy goes to the person, the individual: maintenance of silence about matters that are are personal, *not* of public concern. Reporters generally respect the secrecy of a fact given them in confidence (pending its later release if it becomes a public matter); they respect the privacy of a news figure's home life if it has no external political, social, economic or other communal impact.

Massive intrusions on privacy have occurred in recent years: hidden cameras observing private, non-newsworthy activities, development of a national data bank with detailed information about millions of citizens, records in credit bureaus about habits good and bad of local residents, "security checks" by government agencies. Thousands of such records, their illegal existence revealed, have been destroyed. Laws have been developed to curtail wiretapping, to control government collection and distribution of personal information, and to assure the citizen the right to examine public files and the secrecy of personal data.

Journalistic invasions of privacy, though they relate to the broader problem, pose particular difficulties for reporters. The question does not often arise in reporting acts of government or events planned for public attention. It does come up in reporting events that have no overt public character and that take place outside the public spectrum. Specific cases illustrate aspects of the problem:

- Mastectomies became newsworthy when First Lady Betty Ford underwent breast surgery. Even a sore throat in the White House is news; but the clinical spotlight the press trained on this essentially personal matter seemed excessive. Mrs. Ford's grace softened the indignity; and Eileen Shanahan of the New York *Times* said that the news treatment "saved millions of lives." Columnist Erma Bombeck, however, expressed a different view on the day President Carter was inaugurated: "There are a lot of things I don't want to know about him . . . his golf scores . . . his spills if he is a skier . . . his scars if he has had surgery, especially if it means taking off his necktie . . . I don't want to know if he and the First Lady share a double bed or go singles . . . or how he felt about Rhett Butler or whether he would have married Melanie or Scarlett . . . . I don't want to intrude on the Carter joy, grief or the dignity of their private lives."
- A Midwestern state's first swine flu victim authorized the release of his name. A newspaper editorial commented: "The patient was so swamped by TV cameras and calls from reporters that he probably wished he was back in his sick bed, or at least a little contagious. The poor guy didn't run for election as a flu victim, and it was patently unfair for him to be harassed by a lot of nosy reporters and photographers. His privacy was not merely invaded; it was demolished."
- Patty Hearst's life while she was at home awaiting trial on criminal charges was the subject of dozens of stories low on fact and high on speculation (no reporters talked to her). The New York *Times* did the job in five columns that described the joy and tragedy of her homecoming, her work with a psychiatrist, the color of dye her beauty parlor used on her eyelashes, and her attitude toward the man with whom she had once lived.
- A woman obviously hysterical after watching her children die in her burning home was interviewed for 10 minutes, on camera, by a TV reporter.
- A reporter badgered a young man whose home had just been destroyed by a tornado with such questions as "how did you feel when you saw your roof blow off?" and "do you have any savings?"

Some generalizations apply to meeting privacy problems:

- Wiretapping and bugging are looked on as invasions of privacy unless they have legal authorization.
- Photographs of individuals or their testimonials may not be used in advertisements in most states without written consent.
- Public figures, either in government or in industries and activities that invite public attention, surrender privacy in their public actions, but not in their private lives. The cost of redecorating the White House would generally be considered public information; that of a shopkeeper's home in Arlington would not.

To summarize: There is small justification for reportorial invasion of privacy unless it relates to a person of demonstrable interest to a news audience. The problem is often ethical rather than legal, especially since statutes on privacy are few. It would entrance TV viewers to see that members of the Methodist Ladies' Aid Society shoot craps for high stakes every Tuesday afternoon; it would be a violation of no law to report the fact if it's true. But what about the ladies' private right to have their fun, unbeknownst to the Baptists?

"GOOD TASTE"

One reason that reporters do not always observe an individual's right to privacy is that privacy and the right of the public to information may be at odds. In the case of the woman who saw her children die, the facts—though not in a broad sense important—ought to be reported. But the intrusion into the woman's grief, the manipulation of tragedy for the titillation of the TV audience, is something few journalists would defend (the reporter involved said he couldn't). It is "bad taste" to use human misery for no newsworthy end.

"Good taste" in news handling is a term that frustrates definition. One attempt is this: "Good taste in reporting is behavior that does not violate the sensitivities of the community, its readers and viewers, and—sometimes most delicate of all—of the people it involves." When the feelings of news consumers or of news figures conflict with the mandate to report what ought to be reported, the decision may be easy: The audience wins. But every medium has a dozen opportunities each day to decide between protection of feelings and audience excitation—between informing appropriately and informing only to stir passions or adrenal glands. A morning newspaper used a column and a half to catalog the horrid beating that had killed a handsome young call girl; it described her mangled body, quoted a policeman who mused that she had been "a good whore," and reported her meticulous bookkeeping. The competing

Memo on a City Room Bulletin Board:

"This paper does not use profanities and obscenities except in direct quotations. Determining factors are the person quoted, the circumstances and the importance of the quotation. If an obscene or vulgar word is necessary to accurate meaning of a significant comment on a significant subject, we print it . . . It will usually occur in a spot news story in which it is spoken in public . . . In some cases, exact words are necessary . . . to reflect a philosophy or personality. The test is whether the words are essential to the purpose."

Even so precise a guide will not always meet all needs. When the U.S. secretary of agriculture made remarks in 1976 that were offensive not only in word choice but also in their references to blacks, the media were in no agreement as to how to handle them. Most described them in carefully guarded paraphrase, some so vague as to be meaningless. One that quoted them exactly explained: "We reluctantly concluded that we had to tell readers what it was that was so vile that its user was fired from a president's cabinet. We found it highly distasteful, and we assumed that a lot of readers would tell us they were offended. We have heard from just 13 readers: six objected to our use of the words, five approved and two simply asked why we decided as we did."

afternoon paper used three paragraphs, with principal facts; it gave the news and stopped.

Matters of taste are ill-defined because yesterday's coarseness is today's routine usage. Four-letter words that were taboo in the 1950s became commonplace—in print, on the air, in living rooms, bars and beauty shops—in the 1970s. The U.S. Supreme Court geed and hawed in its attempts at defining obscenity—each new decision, it seemed, making the problem more amorphous. (One in 1978 was a widely debated opinion that seven specific words are unfit for use by broadcasters. Russell Baker of the New York *Times* pointed out that all seven are Anglo-Saxon terms whose Latinate equivalents are "commonly used without producing a blush.") Times change, customs change, and what hurts or offends loses its poison among new proprieties.

The late 1970s became a period of unprecedented candor and "freedom of expression" in the news media. Exploitation of sex news was nothing new: James Gordon Bennett did it in the 1830s; the New York tabloids gloried in the Lolita-like adventures of Daddy Browning and his "Peaches" in the 1920s; the "sex scandal" that lost a British cabinet minister his job was followed by lurid treatment of the careless amours of American congressmen. Few defenders of this kind of sensationalism are discernible. The Chicago *Tribune*, in announcing that it would give up printing the "sordid and depraved" testimony about the British scandal, said it was doing so "because we cannot feel our readers would be improved by acquaintance with it."

Some who deplore the use of news of this kind think they see declining interest among audiences in it, with bedroom romps becoming as common on the TV screen as on Broadway. Stage and broadcasting candor, new attitudes on marriage and man-woman relationships, relaxations in family patterns and lifestyles—however one views them—have begun to take the magnetism out of such news.

Offense by camera News photographs are sometimes prime offenders against the dignity of their subjects:

- A mother bows, shattered, over the blanket on the pavement covering her child.
- TV catches a man groaning in anguish as he is taken from an auto wreck.
- A young couple, their baby in the woman's arms, sleeps sprawled on a bench in a bus depot. The story with the picture says that, unable to find work, they are penniless. Even when the picture is taken with their permission, it opens them to humiliation. What if the reporter, instead of calling for a photographer, had pointed out some of the dignified ways to meet their emergency?

Of similar cloth was the shocking television sequence of the Indianapolis man who, his shotgun wired to a hostage's neck, proclaimed himself a "goddamned hero." The event and his action certainly demanded report. But did it require protraction on the screen, especially since the anguished victim received as much public display as the abductor?

Pictures of human anguish often have the beauty of tragedy. They tell stories powerfully. And they are more likely to be talked about the next day than the mug shot of a visiting prime minister. But grief and pain are deeply personal emotions, and they rarely belong to the public.

There are justifiable cases. One postwar photo showed a returning soldier—one leg gone—descending from a plane; his wife faced him, her hands pinched to her cheeks; a small boy stared immobile at the father he had never seen. The deeply emotional picture won prizes—not because of its excellent photography but because it was moving social commentary.

"THE ANGLE"

Every well-built news story has an angle—a focus that gives the story its character. As you approach a story, you hope for an angle that hasn't been worn thin—a unique one, if you're lucky. Often the search is fruitless. Football games, burning buildings, civic improvement association meetings follow consistent and all-too-familiar patterns. Though each has an appropriate point of emphasis, what you write about it may sound distressingly like what you wrote yesterday.

So reporters are led into excesses or, regrettably, banality. They develop minor themes at the expense of major. Sports stories for afternoon papers, when the morning papers or the broadcasts have used up the cream, put emphasis on what the pitcher said and forget to tell about the game. "I wasn't thinking of a no-hitter when that guy walloped my ninth-inning two-out slider into the gap. All I was trying to do was win for the team." This kind of "angle," a cliché of today's sportswriting, is not only flat but also unbelievable. Does any baseball player talk like that?

Questionable emphases can crop up in any kind of newswriting:

- What did the housewife wear when she went to jail for shoplifting? A stole.
- What followed when a dreary derelict entered his 92nd "guilty" plea to the drunk-and-disorderly charge? "Smitty was sent to the city lockup to sober up for appearance No. 93."

Ridicule is not a tool of responsible reporting. Art Buchwald, Russell Baker and others of their skill and standing use it, under bylines and with tongues in cheek. Ellen Goodman removes the sharp points from her verbal jabs with perceptive wit and clear love of the human race. Satirical writing like that in the wire-service story below, which is cruel in its disrespect for personal dignity, is not to be tolerated:

> NEW YORK, N.Y.—Those three rude hotel detectives who burst in on Angelo del Carlino and his pretty wife Leonora on their wedding night bruised them $10,000 worth. This was disclosed in a sealed jury verdict opened Monday by Judge Nathan Edwards.
>
> Injuries to Angelo, owner of a beauty shop, were physical, he testified during trial last week. Leonora had the marriage annulled two years after that humiliating night. She said her wounds were spiritual.
>
> She had so wanted a beautiful evening, she said, but it wasn't beautiful because of "those awful men."
>
> Jurors scorned defense testimony that the trio burst in on

the Del Carlinos because they had been creating a disturbance.

TRIAL BY NEWSPAPER

The overplay of the "Son of Sam" murders in New York City in 1976 and 1977 focused new attention on the journalistic phenomenon called "trial by newspaper." The New York case was of note because it went unsolved for a year; but it became spectacular because the news media made it so. As the murders continued, they drew more and more news space and time, and the reporting persuaded New York that no street corner was safe. During the intense hunt just before the capture of the suspect, as well as afterward, two of the New York newspapers—the *Post* and the *Daily News*—spent hundreds of man-hours and many columns of space (much of it in giant type) on "developments"—not only the fairly meager facts, but also speculation, average-citizen interviews, stories on distant sidelights, reviews of other such cases. A woman reporter for WABC-TV "managed to get in the back door of a precinct house," close enough to the prisoner to be able to report triumphantly that he had "cold, very blue, piercing eyes." It was not a surprise that, when psychiatrists reported to the court that the arrested man was mentally incompetent to stand trial, part of the response was that "it might be impossible to give him a fair trial anyway." Could the court find an unbiased jury, one whose members had not judged the man guilty before the trial started, when so much of the "news" had assumed guilt in advance?

The "Son of Sam" case was not a first. A Cleveland doctor, convicted of murder and in prison for 10 years, was given a new trial (and found not guilty) after the U.S. Supreme Court decided that Cleveland newspaper excesses had made his first trial one conducted in an atmosphere of prejudgment and unfairness. John Ehrlichman, in 1974, pleaded (unsuccessfully) that he could not get a fair trial in Washington because he had already been tried by the media. Through the 1970s there were frequent cases of judges or prosecutors demanding that news information be withheld before trial—always drawing cries of unconstitutional suppression—in order to avoid prejudicing juries. The fears were not always soundly based, and the cover-up orders were usually voided by higher courts. But newsworkers learned to be on guard.

In 1974 a dozen news media in Pennsylvania agreed to honor a judge's request to withhold news of a murder trial (to avoid prejudicing future jurors in related trials, he said). The news was withheld, but since hundreds of spectators attended the trial, the result was only to keep accurate information away from the thousands who couldn't get in. One of the newspaper managing editors who agreed to the judge's request said later that "I was ashamed of myself the minute that I walked out of the judge's chambers."

Loaded language Overplay of spectacular news is not the only peril. Carelessness with loaded rhetoric may be just as harmful. A common error is the substitution of "admitted for "said."

> The bank president *admitted* that he owned stock in the bankrupt company. He *denied* that he voted to protect personal interests.

What if the banker neither *admitted* nor *denied*, but rather merely described or stated? The words suggest something quite different.

Other examples of loaded language:

> . . . arrested *for stealing* . . . (should be arrested *on a charge of stealing* unless you want to say flatly that he did it)
>
> He exited from Soviet *tyranny* . . . (*Tyranny* is the writer's word)
>
> The grand jury investigating *welfare fraud* . . . (To most people "welfare fraud" means chiseling by welfare recipients; in the case from which this example comes it was welfare agency employees, not recipients, who were under investigation)

SERVING TWO MASTERS

As knowledge of the tactics of the Central Intelligence Agency broadened in the 1970s, questioning of CIA use of the news media burgeoned. After World War II the CIA made secret arrangements to use journalists from the New York *Times*, CBS, *Time*, and other media as information sources, and some of the larger news organizations as covers. The CIA was not alone. The FBI sought and got "cooperation," and dependence of local law-enforcement agencies on reporters who cover them is common. The exploits and associations of a Nashville woman reporter who worked with the FBI for 15 years are called by the *Columbia Journalism Review* "not really unusual." (See Related Reading, page 406.)

Most journalists agree that a reporter cannot serve two masters. Charles B. Seib expresses a typical view—that noninvolvement is an imperative if reporters and the media are to maintain public confidence and credibility. Stanley Karnow, for years a foreign reporter for the Des Moines *Register* and *Tribune*, though he found CIA news sources indispensable in his work, says that "journalists have

Fast-moving trucks deliver just-printed papers to street corners, where newsstand operators and carriers pick them up. *(F. B. Grunzweig photo from Photo Researchers, Inc., New York)*

no business signing contracts with the CIA, and those who do ought to be exposed."

Why? Because reporters depart from their prime function, getting news for the public, if they serve another master; because they open themselves to the chance of "influence," even though most resist; and because, once found out, their usefulness as agents of the press and the public withers. (See conflicts of interest, Chapter 19.)

The reverse may also be threatening—permitting police, CIA or FBI agents and others to pose as reporters. Examples have surfaced frequently in recent years. Usually the law enforcers are the instigators—the plainclothes detective, for example, who declares himself a reporter for a day. The masquerade is usually disowned by the pretender's news medium (though a West Virginia publisher who allowed a state trooper to pose as his reporter defends the policy: "What's wrong with cooperation with authorities?"). Law, order and justice may or may not be served by such playacting; journalistic credibility can only suffer. It makes "real" reporters suspect, and sometimes rejected, by news sources who fear they may be cops.

GUIDES AND SAFEGUARDS

Journalistic misbehavior can be avoided. One guide lies in familiar reportorial tenets: triple-checking, slow movement and acceptance of three values: the respect due the people making news, the needs of the people reading or hearing it and the integrity of those reporting it. Without precautions reporting may deserve some of the censure it receives.

There are external formulas for professional behavior. More than 50 years ago the American Society of Newspaper Editors adopted a "code," the Canons of Practice. They are honorable in principle and concept, but they often gather dust in frames on editors' walls rather than flow in journalists' bloodstreams. A basketful of codes to guide the practices of newsworkers has been formulated by newspaper and broadcast editors and reporters.

No tenets or truisms can alchemize a reporter, beginning or old-time, into professionalism. But they represent the thinking of men and women who affirm (and most of whom act by) their principles, who believe out of their own experiences that journalism is a mode of life with an exalted ceiling. They are a promise to their followers—a promise of service, growth and infinite reward.

STUDY SUGGESTIONS

1. What is your explanation of the conflict between the National Labor Relations Board's denial that journalists are "professionals" and Roger Fisher's statement (see page 390) about "the functions . . . the media ought to perform"?
2. Write a statement of your opinion about the Montana judge's view (page 392) that society and juvenile misbehavers are served best by making antisocial behavior fully public.
3. Periodicals today are widely adopting the omission of Miss, Mrs., or Ms. in second mention of a woman's name, in the interest of parallel treatment of the sexes. Do you perceive informational problems in this practice?
4. Consider the guidelines in the bulletin board memo on page 398 dealing with the use of "offensive" words. If you think it either too weak or too strong, write your own rule.
5. Do you think the Chicago *Tribune's* concern about "improving" its readers (page 398) one of the appropriate guides to selection of news?
6. Define the term *angle* as it is used in journalistic jargon.
7. On page 400 you are told that the

story following the statement "is not to be tolerated." Note the loaded words in the story: *rude, bruised,* and others. Rewrite the story in straight news form. Then contrast the two stories.

8. Define the terms *trial by newspaper, invasion of privacy.*

PRACTICE ASSIGNMENTS

1. Examine five or more news stories reporting juvenile misbehavior; catalog what seem to be their guidelines for use of juvenile names. On the basis of what you find and what this chapter says on the subject, write a one-page memo to guide reporters on "your" newspaper.
2. Write a similar statement on identification by race, religion, sexual orientation, skin color or national origin—taking into account whatever local factors may be involved—for the bulletin board of "your" paper.
3. Watch TV news and newspapers to spot "offense by camera"—photography that in your opinion invades personal privacy or presents people in a ridiculous or demeaning manner. If you find cases, express your views in the form of a letter to the editor (you may even want to mail it).
4. It has been said that "if God lets it happen, it's news." That is to say, there are no limits on subjects with which news media may deal. This chapter suggests that there may be intimate areas that are not properly open to the public eye. Write an essay giving your own answers to this question: can newsworkers properly be called on to act as censors? Then write a newsroom guide to help reporters implement the policy you approve.

RELATED READING

Bernstein, Carl. "The CIA and the Media." *Rolling Stone,* Oct. 20, 1977. Exposé by a "Watergate reporter" of CIA relationships with American journalists from 1950 to 1977. Names, dates, events. Many of its charges have been denied by those at whom they are leveled.

Crewdson, John M., Joseph B. Treaster, and others. Series of articles on the CIA and the media. New York *Times,* Dec. 25, 26, 27, 1977. Typically thorough and searching *Times* history and analysis.

Gerald, J. Edward. *The Social Responsibility of the Press.* University of Minnesota Press, 1963. A sober and searching examination of its far-reaching topic. The last chapter explores problems surrounding the development of the professional spirit in journalism.

Gillmor, Donald M. *Free Press and Fair Trial.* Public Affairs Press, 1966. Authoritative book on legal and journalistic aspects of the problem. Accounts of the Lee Harvey Oswald, Sam Sheppard and other cases.

Lahr, John. "Notes on Fame." *Harper's*, January 1978. The cult of fame: If you get your name up in lights, it doesn't matter how you did it. Thoughtful ruminations on the American passion for visibility.

"Talk of the Town." *The New Yorker*, Aug. 15, Sep. 5, 1977. Two editorial articles on treatment of "Son of Sam" news by the New York *Daily News* and the *Post*. Angry, well-documented, enlightening.

Tucker, Carll. "The Night TV Cried Wolf." *Saturday Review*, Oct. 1, 1977.

Ungar, Sanford J. "Among the Piranhas: A Journalist and the FBI." *Columbia Journalism Review*, September–October 1976. Detailed account of the adventures of Nashville reporter Jacque Srouji with the FBI.

Ungar, Sanford J. "The Forgotten Case of Sam Jaffe." *Columbia Journalism Review*, November–December 1976. The long-lasting "unusual ties" between a *Life*-CBS-NBC correspondent and the CIA and FBI.

APPENDIX A

Preparation of Copy

A page of copy for the biggest newspaper looks a lot like one for the smallest. Standard editing practices and symbols, widely accepted and used, simplify copy writing and editing because they say the same things to all who use them. As described here for paper-and-pencil editing, they are the basis for and similar to the new electronic practices (see pages 205–206). Every newsworker needs to know and use them.

PAPER-AND-PENCIL COPY

1. Always typewrite copy, double- or triple-spaced. Make sure the typewriter ribbon is in good condition and the keys clean.

2. Type on only one side of soft-finish copy paper. Copy paper is often newsprint cut to the standard 8½-x-11-inch size (some newsrooms use half-sheets, 5½ x 8½ inches; some use tinted paper). Never use onionskin; avoid hard-finish paper—you can't erase copy pencil marks from it.

3. Keep copy "clean"—not necessarily stenographer-perfect, but always legible and unmistakable. If typing errors, strike-overs or editing make it hard to read or follow, retype it.

4. Put your name and a short slugline at the upper-left corner of page 1, with the page number, thus:

```
Cooper – Valley basketball – 1
```

or

```
Cooper – 1
Valley basketball
```

If you need to give other information to the city or copy desk, type it under the slugline or in the upper-righthand corner: "For release March 16," "Hold for name check," "High school sports page."

5. Leave the upper third of page 1 blank except as directed above. This provides space for headlines, a new slug or typographical or other instructions. Leave margins of 1 or 1¼ inches at sides and bottom.

6. Indent paragraph openings five to 10 spaces from the left margin.

7. Write name or slugline and page number at the upper left of pages following page 1, thus:

Cooper – 2 or Valley basketball – 2

Some newsrooms prefer to number the second page "add 1" or "1st add" and succeeding pages correspondingly. Thus the third page becomes "add 2." Continue the copy just beneath (no extra blank space).

8. Avoid hyphenating words at the ends of typewritten lines, and do not break sentences or paragraphs from one page to the next. Some newsrooms require the word "MORE" at the bottom of each page whose copy continues to another page.

9. Write an endmark, either by typewriter or pencil, at the end of a story; circle it in pencil to make it unmistakable. Endmarks in common use, placed below the final line of copy (don't use both), are:

Some writers like to use their initials, lower case—a practice borrowed from the wire services, whose writers thus "sign" their stories.

10. Edit all copy completely with a soft black pencil. Use the copyreading symbols accepted in your office (the traditional symbols are shown on page 412). Do not use proofreading symbols, and remember that only amateurs refer to copyreading as proofreading. Mark all paragraph openings. Make a final check of each story, confirming facts and clarifying anything that might puzzle or be questioned.

11. If it is your office's practice, paste sheets of a story together to produce one continuous piece of copy. Never put more than one story on a page.

Writing electronically "The tube" does away with copy pencils, copyreading marks and erasers. Every newspaper—whichever of the new electronic systems it uses—develops its own pattern for identifying a story (the slugline), its writer and where and when it is to run. One caution: Copy on the screen *looks* perfect. It has no uneven lines, no strikeovers, no copyreading marks to call attention to errors or needed changes. Reporters need to be on double alert for such faults as transpositions, misspellings and—above all—mixed-up numerals.

Some newspapers still use paper-and-pencil copyreading in one form or another, so it's important to learn the craft.

COPY FOR BROADCASTING

Some newspaper copy-editing practices apply to broadcast copy; others vary widely, because of the different methods of production and delivery. A principal difference is that errors in copy as it moves to the printed page can be caught at several later points, but mistakes in copy read into a microphone are instantly transmitted, and correcting them is clumsy. Copy for radio and TV, therefore, must be sparklingly accurate, and it must be totally legible and understandable. When it isn't, its errors or muddiness may go on the air.

Fewer conventional symbols are used in editing for broadcast than in newspaper editing. Every change or correction must be lightning clear to an announcer's eye. For this reason, corrections are written in full rather than by symbol or abbreviation.

Another difference is that readers don't have to be sure how words are pronounced—whether you say Row-se-velt or Roo-se-felt. In broadcasting you must say it right. So phonetic spellings appear in broadcast copy: "the Yugoslav sculptor Mestrovics (MESH-tra-veets)."

Here are the usual broadcast editing practices:

1. Typewrite copy with black ribbon and clean keys, double- or triple-spaced. Some newsrooms type local copy in caps because wire service copy comes in caps. (Ease-of-reading experts say that copy in caps is harder to read than that in caps and lower case.)
2. Write on only one side of paper. Use soft-finish paper that won't crackle into a microphone.
3. Make paragraph indentations deep—10 to 15 spaces—so they'll surely be noticed.
4. Put a slugline and a page number at upper left of each page.
5. Never split words at ends of lines, or sentences at ends of pages. Paragraphs ought not to be split at page ends. An end-mark (usually a typewritten or longhand ###) or a "continued" line should end each page.
6. Edit copy scrupulously, using editing marks that cannot be misunderstood. Messy copy must be retyped. Never strike over a typing error—pencil it out and type it again. This rule is triple-

strength for initials, capital letters and numerals.

7. Provide phonetic spellings as needed, for unfamiliar foreign words and names and for words often mispronounced (clan-DES-tine, HAR-ass, sac-ruh-LIH-jus, chaise LONG).
8. Use periods, commas and dashes generously to indicate voice or meaning pauses or inflections. Overuse capital initials to identify important words. Underline words that should get special attention from the announcer—names, difficult words, points of emphasis.
9. Use few abbreviations, or none. Write out such titles as Mister, Doctor, President. Write figures and numerals precisely as they should be spoken: sixteen hundred, not 1,600. Use round numbers when you can: 9,000 families.
10. Put on the copy paper *only* what is to be read aloud, except clearly identified instructions and such conventions as sluglines and page numbers.
11. Avoid most copy-editing symbols. In newspaper copy a circled numeral tells the compositor to spell it out. In broadcast copy it might trip up the announcer.

The example of broadcast news copy on page 411 is typical.

COPY-EDITING AND PROOFREADING SYMBOLS

On page 412 is an example of a reporter's copy marked for the composing room, with the commonly used editing symbols explained at the left. On the facing page is the galley proof of the story, corrected after it comes from the typesetter. For illustration, it contains a most unlikely assortment of errors—"typos"—all marked by a proofreader for correction. Alongside is the corrected story, ready to print.

There's only one undefeated team LEFT in the Valley conference. THAT team is Mitford, which beat Perkins last night by five points -- 59 to 54.

That leaves Mitford's Ponies one game ahead of Port Arthur. Port Arthur has won fourteen games since December first, One of them was over Shantietown last night -- the score was 59 to 54.

To get back to the Mitford-Perkins game, it was close until the last few minutes. It was the fourth victory in a row for Mitford.

Two other Valley games were played last night. Both were close. Washburn beat Retreet BY THREE POINTS, 70 to 67. And Alhambra had to rally to edge LITTLEDALE by one point, 52 to 51. Dave Larson of Alhambra had 15 points. And the Alhambra coach, Peter Edmond, said that he "felt lucky to win."

######

Typical edited broadcast news copy

Italics Center in column	Other basketball news on Page 11
Paragraph Insert letter	Mitford remaind the only undefeated team
Insert word or phrase	in the Valley school basketball race Thursday
Substitute phrase Delete word and letter, draw together	by beating Perkins on the big Perkins floorr
New paragraph	in a tight game, 59 to 54. The victory, fourth
Delete fault Clarify bad typing	straight fon for the ponies, kept them
Spell out figure Spell out abbreviated word	1 game ahead of Pt. Arthur, which has won
Use figure instead of word Abbreviate word	fourteen games since December 1.
Insert comma Remove space	Perkins always trou blesome for Mitford
Insert space Capitalize	athome, carried the ponies right down to
Use small letter	the wire, But the closest game of the night
Transpose words Transpose letters	Alhambra found egding Littledale 52 to 51.
Continue without paragraph break	Dave Larson scored 15 points in the
Period (or ⊙)	last period, when Alhambra rallied to win
Overline longhand o, m, n, underline a, w, u Insert quotation mark	"We felt lucky to win that won, Peter
Ignore change; "let it stand"	Edmond, Alhambra coach, said.
Boldface	Other results last night:
Correct spelling—do not change	Port Arthur 62, Shantietown (CORRECT) 41
Spelling correct—do not change	Washburn 70, Retreet 67
Endmark (or ###)	

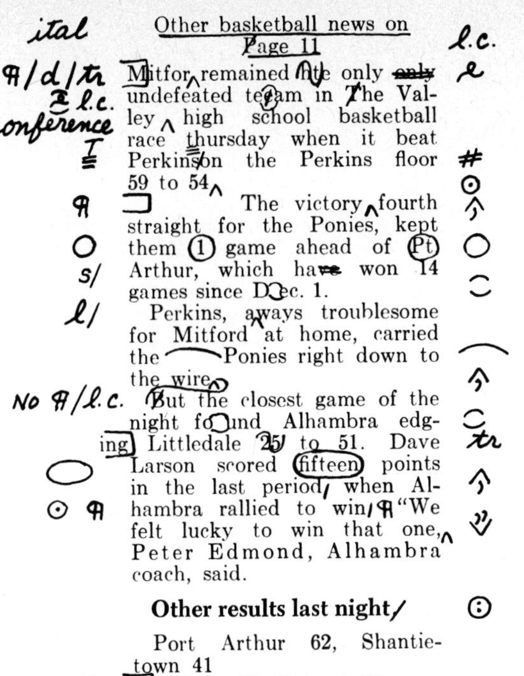

Other basketball news on Page 11

Mitfor remained hte only only undefeated teeam in The Valley high school basketball race thursday when it beat Perkinson the Perkins floor 59 to 54

The victory fourth straight for the Ponies, kept them 1 game ahead of Pt Arthur, which have won 14 games since DDec. 1.

Perkins, aways troublesome for Mitford at home, carried the Ponies right down to the wire But the closest game of the night foound Alhambra edging Littledale 25 to 51. Dave Larson scored fifteen points in the last period when Alhambra rallied to win "We felt lucky to win that one, Peter Edmond, Alhambra coach, said.

Other results last night

Port Arthur 62, Shantietown 41

Washburn 70, Retreet 67

Proof from the composing room, with the proofreader's marks

Other basketball news on page 11

Mitford remained the only undefeated team in the Valley conference high school basketball race Thursday when it beat Perkins on the Perkins floor 59 to 54.

The victory, fourth straight for the Ponies, kept them one game ahead of Port Arthur, which has won 14 games since Dec. 1.

Perkins, always troublesome for Mitford at home, carried the Ponies right down to the wire, but the closest game of the night found Alhambra edging Littledale 52 to 51. Dave Larson scored 15 points in the last period, when Alhambra rallied to win.

"We felt lucky to win that one," Peter Edmond, Alhambra coach, said.

Other results last night:

Port Arthur 62, Shantietown 41

Washburn 70, Retreet 67

The story as it appears on the printed page

APPENDIX B

Two Codes of Ethics for Journalists

Groups of professional journalists traditionally lay down "codes of ethics" to guide the conduct of their members. The American Society of Newspaper Editors did so in 1923, the Radio-Television News Directors Association soon after its organization in the 1940s. The largest such organization in the world, the Society of Professional Journalists, Sigma Delta Chi—born three quarters of a century ago as a campus journalists' group but now with hundreds of campus and community chapters—updated its statement of journalistic standards in 1973. The statement, slightly abridged, follows:

The Society of Professional Journalists, Sigma Delta Chi, believes the duty of journalists is to serve the truth.

We believe the agencies of mass communication are carriers of public discussion and information, acting on their Constitutional mandates and freedom to learn and report the facts.

We believe in public enlightenment as the forerunner of justice, and in our Constitutional role to seek the truth as part of the public's right to know the truth.

We believe these responsibilities require journalists to perform with intelligence, objectivity, accuracy, and fairness.

To these ends, we accept the standards of practice here set forth:

RESPONSIBILITY: The public's right to know of events of public importance and interest is the overriding mission of the mass media. The purpose of distributing news and enlightened opinion is to serve the general welfare. Journalists who use their professional status for selfish or other unworthy motives violate a high trust.

FREEDOM OF THE PRESS: Freedom of the press is to be guarded as an inalienable right of people in a free society. It carries with it the freedom and the responsibility to discuss, question, and challenge actions and utterances of government and of public and private institutions. Journalists uphold the right to speak unpopular opinions and the privilege to agree with the majority.

ETHICS: Journalists must be free of obligation to any interest other than the public's right to know the truth:

1. Gifts, favors, free travel, special treatment or privileges can compromise the integrity of journalists and their employers.
2. Secondary employment, political involvement, holding public office, or service in community organizations should be avoided if it compromises the integrity of journalists and their employers. Journalists and their employers should conduct their personal lives in a manner that protects them from conflict of interest, real or apparent. Their responsibilities to the public are paramount.
3. Communications from private sources should not be published or broadcast without substantiation of their claims to news value.
4. Journalists will try constantly to assure that public business is conducted in public and that public records are open to public inspection.
5. Journalists acknowledge the ethic of protecting confidential sources of information.

ACCURACY AND OBJECTIVITY: Good faith with the public is the foundation of all worthy journalism.

1. Truth is our ultimate goal.
2. Objectivity in reporting the news is the mark of an experienced professional. It is a standard of performance toward which journalists strive.
3. There is no excuse for inaccuracies or lack of thoroughness.
4. Newspaper headlines should be fully warranted by the contents of the articles they accompany. Photographs and telecasts should give accurate pictures of events.
5. Sound practice makes clear distinction between news reports and expressions of opinion.
6. Partisanship in editorial comment that knowingly departs from the truth violates the spirit of American journalism.
7. Journalists recognize their responsibility for offering informed analysis, comment and editorial opinion on public events and issues. They accept the obligation to present such material by individuals whose competence, experience and judgment qualify them for doing so.
8. Special articles or presentations devoted to advocacy or the writer's conclusions and interpretations should be labeled as such.

FAIR PLAY: Journalists at all times show respect for the dignity, privacy, rights and well-being of people encountered in the course of gathering and presenting the news.

1. The news media should not communicate unofficial charges affecting reputation or moral character without giving those accused a chance to reply.

2. The news media must guard against invading the rights to privacy.
3. The media should not pander to morbid curiosity.
4. The news media should make prompt and complete correction of their errors.
5. Journalists should be accountable to the public, and the public should be encouraged to voice its grievances against the media. Open dialog with readers, viewers and listeners should be fostered.

• • •

Six suggested specific guidelines for journalists were drawn up by a "news media-government consultation" group convened by Freedom House in 1973 to evaluate the "changing perception of the news media in American society" and particularly the areas of press-government conflict. The guidelines:

1. A journalist should report the news impartially and fairly.
2. A journalist should assume full responsibility for the accuracy and truthfulness of any news he reports. He should adequately qualify the reliability of any unidentified news source whenever making public information from such source, to enable the public properly to decide the weight to be given to the information.
3. A journalist should protect the freedom of the press, while giving due consideration to the rights of others, including the right of persons accused of crime to due process of law.
4. A journalist should avoid activities which might create a conflict of interest and should promptly disclose to his employer any actual or potential conflict.
5. A journalist should file with his employer regular reports of outside compensation and financial interests.
6. A journalist should refrain from publicly undisclosed extracurricular activities which might raise questions about his professional objectivity.[1]

[1] From Peter Braestrup, *Big Story: How the American Press and Television Reported and Interpreted the Crisis of Tet 1968 in Vietnam and Washington* (Westview Press, 1977; published in cooperation with Freedom House). Reprinted by permission.

APPENDIX C
The Jargon of Journalists

Newsworkers, like specialists in other fields, have a private language—a jargon made up largely of common words given uncommon newsroom meanings. It's simple, informal and practical, and every reporter learns it. Fast.

Like other dialects, it changes some of its forms from area to area; but most are generally understood. (Some technical printing and broadcasting terms are omitted from the list that follows.)

A matter Advance matter. Background material prepared in advance about an expected event

ad Advertisement

add Addition to a lead or a story

advance Story about a coming event. *See* **prelim**

agate Smallest type used in newspapers (for box scores, tabular matter, want ads). It measures $5\frac{1}{2}$ points, about 14 lines to the inch. *See* **point**

air **1.** To broadcast news (or anything else). **2.** White space on a page

AM Morning newspaper

angle The approach or perspective from which a news fact or event is viewed, or the emphasis chosen for a story. *See* **slant**

AP Associated Press

art Photographs, drawings, charts or other illustrative material used with printed matter

attribution Identification of the source of a fact, interview, judgment or quotation

audio The aural (sound) portion of a telecast

background Factual material illuminating a current event, presented to increase understanding

backgrounder A background story

bank A section of a headline. *See* **deck, drop head**

banner A headline the width (or nearly the width) of a page, at or near page top. Same as **line, ribbon, streamer**

beat **1.** The area or subject field assigned to a reporter. Same as **run.** **2.** A story published or aired ahead of the competition. Same as **exclusive, scoop**

bf Boldface, blackface—heavy black type **like this**

blind head "Teaser" headline, usually on a feature, that seeks to attract attention without revealing the event's essence

blurb **1.** A short story used to fill space. **2.** A device to call attention to a feature elsewhere in the paper or in a broadcast. Same as **squib**

body type Small type in which most news stories are printed. Usually 8 point (9 lines to the inch) or 9 point (8 lines to the inch)

boil, boil down Shorten or condense copy

boldface *See* **bf**

box Typographical enclosure for a story or picture to set it off from surrounding material

break 1. The moment at which news material becomes available for publication. 2. The point at which a printed story moves from one column or one page to another (*see* **jump**). 3. (In this book) A structural or meaning division in a news story

bridge Transition from one element in a printed or broadcast story to another, or from one broadcast story to another. Noun and verb

bright A story (usually short) about an odd or comical occurrence

budget Wire-service or newsroom list of the day's major stories

bulldog An early—usually the first—edition of a newspaper

bullet A heavy dot (•)

bulletin Brief story on a late-breaking news event. In broadcast news, bulletins often break into other programs; in print they usually get prominent display. *See* **flash**

byline Writer's name, usually at the head of a story. Wire services use the term **signer** both for the byline and the stories under them

cap Capital letter. Same as **uc** and **upper case**

caption Title or headline above a printed picture. Often used to refer to any text with a picture. *See* **cutline**

center spread Side-by-side pages in the middle of a section, made up as one page. Also called **double truck**

city editor Director of a newspaper's local news operation

clc or **c&lc** Normal capitalization, using capital and small letters

clip A clipping, usually from a newspaper

clip sheet A sheet of printed stories, often publicity stories, from which an editor may clip for reference, publication or further development

cold type Typesetting process in which "type" is a positive image on paper rather than a raised symbol in metal. Usually used in offset printing. *See* **hot type, offset, paste-up**

column 1. A periodical feature or opinion article, usually written continuously by one person. 2. A space on a printed page the width of a line of body type, running the depth of a page

composing room Area where printers set type and headlines and make up pages

copy 1. A news story, feature, headline or caption on paper as it is given to a printer or newscaster. 2. Written matter in a computer system before it is published

copy editor A worker on a copy desk who edits and sometimes rewrites stories and writes headlines. Also called **copyreader** or **rim man**

copyreader *See* **copy editor**

copywriter One who writes advertising or public relations copy

correspondent A reporter who works at some distance from the home office and delivers copy by wire, radio or mail

CQ Symbol inserted in copy in parentheses to assure editors that unlikely spellings, names or facts are correct

crash Computer malfunction

credit, credit line 1. Printed or spoken acknowledgment of the source or ownership of a story or picture. **2.** Attribution: "he said," etc.

crop To edit photographs by trimming off unwanted parts

CRT Cathode-ray tube (the television display screen in a computer terminal). Often used to denote the entire terminal

cut **1.** Metal or plastic plate from which an illustration is printed. **2.** The printed illustration. **3.** To condense copy

cutline Descriptive text accompanying an illustration. *See* **caption**

dateline Identification of place and often date and wire service at the beginning of a wire story

deadline The final moment at which news material can be sent to the desk or composing room and still "make" the paper or broadcast

deck *See* **bank**

delete Take out, remove. Primarily a proofreading term. Often shortened to **dele**

desk Copy desk or city desk

dingbat A star, asterisk, bullet (large dot) or other small type symbol used to mark a break in a story

dog watch Last shift on a morning paper or (less commonly) earliest on afternoon paper. *See* **lobster trick**

dope story Story of speculation, prediction, comment or background. Most common in sports and political reporting

double truck *See* **center spread**

down style Editing pattern using a minimum of capital letters

drop head A **bank** in a headline, usually a secondary bank

dummy Chart or drawing showing how a page is to be made up. *See* **makeup**

dupe, duplicate A carbon or facsimile copy

ear Upper corners of a page (usually page one)

edition A single regularly scheduled version of a newspaper. Not the same as **issue,** which comprises all editions of a single date

editorial An article or essay that reflects opinion or analysis of an event, public question, person or other event. Usually anonymous, as distinguished from **column**

editorialize To express opinion or attitude toward a news topic. Properly confined to editorial pages or signed columns and stories

effects Sound or music to back or support voices or action in a broadcast

em Unit of typographical measure about as wide as it is high, varying in size with the type size (an em in 12-point type is 12 points wide, in 10-point, 10, and so on). *See* **pica** and **point**

en Half an **em**

exclusive *See* **beat**

face Characteristic design of a family of type, such as Bodoni, Tempo, etc.

feature **1.** A news story other than straight news (*see* Chapter 15). **2.** To emphasize or play up a story or particular elements of a story

file To send a story to the home office, usually by wire; to put a story on news-service wires

filler Minor or untimely material used to fill extra news space or time

flak Derogatory term for a public relations worker

flag The printed title of a newspaper at the top of page one. *See* **logo**

flash Brief wire-service news bulletin of high urgency (more emphatic than bulletin), taking precedence over all other matter

fluff Announcer's error on the air, analogous to **typo.** Also called **beard, boo-boo**

flush Type, illustrations or headlines set

even with column margin. Material can be set flush left, flush right or flush both sides

folio Page number and date of a publication on an inside page (usually in the top margin)

folo A story that follows an earlier report on an event, bringing it up to date

format The pattern or structural outline of a newscast or a printed page

free-lancer Self-employed reporter who works without assignments and offers his product to media for sale

futures book Reporter's or editor's calendar of future events

galley Metal tray for carrying or storing type

galley proof Print-off from type in a galley

glossy Photograph with a hard, shiny finish, most suitable for **halftones**

graf or **graph** Paragraph

guide or **guideline** Identification at top of a copy page to facilitate handling. Similar to **slug 2**

gutter Margin separating newspaper pages

halftone Metal or plastic plate from which a photograph is printed; or the printed photograph itself. *See* **line cut**

handout *See* **release**

head, headline Display type above a news story, or the concise introduction of a story in a newscast

headline count The number of units (large and small letters, spaces and punctuation) in a given size and face of type that a **column** (**2**) will accommodate

hell box Bin for discarded type

hole **1.** Extra space on a page after all scheduled ad and news copy has been placed. **2.** Total space in a newspaper for non-advertising material; usually called **news hole**

hot type **1.** Solid lines of type cast from molten metal. **2.** The typesetting method using hot type. *See* **letterpress**

HTK Copy-desk shorthand for "hed to kum," which tells printer that the headline will move separately

hype An event staged to gain publicity

insert Material to be added to previously prepared copy

issue All editions of a publication on a given date. *See* **edition**

italic or **ital** Type designed to slant to the right *like this*

jump To continue a story from one page to another; also the material continued. *See* **runover, break 2**

jump head Headline on a jump

jump line Line where a jump occurs, to tell readers where it continues

kicker **1.** A short story, usually comic, used to close some newscasts. **2.** A secondary line in a subhead, usually above the main line

kill **1.** To destroy type. **2.** To eliminate all or part of a story **layout** *See* **makeup**

lc Lower case—small letters rather than capitals

lead **1.** (pronounced *leed,* often spelled *lede*) The opening paragraph or introductory section of a news story. **2.** (pronounced *led*) Thin metal spacing between lines of type. To lead out, blow up or air out a story is to space out its lines so that it takes up more room and appears more legible

lean against To be contiguous to. A local newscast leans against a network newscast it immediately precedes or follows

legman A reporter, especially one who telephones stories to a rewrite desk

letterpress Printing directly from type or from plates cast from type. *See* **offset, stereotype 2**

line See **banner**

line cut A plate that prints line drawings, maps, charts and graphs in solid black lines, as distinct from photographs; or the printed illustration itself. *See* **half-tone**

live Broadcasting from an event rather than from a recording

Linotype Machine for casting metal type lines or slugs

lobster trick *See* **dog watch**

lower case *See* **lc**

logo Logotype, a head used regularly for a column or section of a newspaper (particularly the paper's page one name-plate). *See* **flag, standing head**

make over Rearrangement of content or design of an existing newspaper page

makeup Arrangement of type, illustrations and white space on a page (spelled *make up* as a verb)

masthead Formal statement of a newspaper's title, ownership, officers, point of publication and other such information. Usually appears on editorial page

morgue A newspaper or broadcasting station library (the term is becoming passé)

move To send a story by wire. *See* **file.** Also to send a story to its next step in the publication process

must A story whose publication or broadcast is imperative

net Network

news hole All the space in a newspaper allotted to editorial (non-advertising) matter

news peg The timely element on which a story hangs

news service *See* **press association**

obit Obituary

off the record Not-for-publication information given to a reporter

offset Lithographic method of printing from photomechanical plates. *See* **letterpress, cold type**

op-ed page The page opposite the editorial page, customarily devoted to opinion and non-news materials

one-shot A news story that is not part of a series or continuing pattern

overhead A story filed by commercial telegraph rather than by leased or news-service wire

overset News in type that is held for later use or discard. Also called **slop**

pad In writing, to fill out, extend, stretch a story, usually with secondary information

paste-up 1. A newscast composed of wire service copy pasted or arranged in desired order. **2.** Arrangement of type, proofs, illustrations, etc., on a dummy sheet to be photographed for offset printing. *See* **cold type, offset**

pica A typographical measure equal to 12 points (about one-sixth of an inch). *See* **em** and **point**

pix Picture or pictures

plate *See* **stereotype**

play Emphasis given to news. A story may be "played up" or "played down"

play story The story given greatest emphasis in a newspaper or newscast

PM Afternoon newspaper

point Smallest unit of type measurement, 1/72 of an inch. *See* **em** and **pica**

pool One reporter or a small group designated to cover an event for other reporters when the number of reporters allowed is limited

PR Public relations

precede A descriptive or explanatory passage preceding a story's lead

prelim Story announcing a future event. *See* **advance, folo**

press association An organization that collects and distributes news to many news media by wire (AP, UPI, Reuter and others)

press run The number of copies printed of a given edition or issue

printer A teletypewriter or teleprinter, used in wire service and other interoffice transmission

proof A print-off of type to be read and corrected

proofreader One who reads proof for corrections (distinguished from **copyreader**)

publicity Promotional matter presented as news

punch Emphasis on a word, story or idea in a broadcast

put to bed To complete all work necessary before a press starts to "roll"

query A correspondent's or free-lancer's inquiry about whether to cover a story

quotes **1.** Quotations. **2.** Quotation marks

release A story provided to news media by an individual or organization interested in getting it before the public, usually for use at or after a stated release time

revise (noun, pronounced *REE-vise)* Corrected or rewritten version of a story a story

rewrite (pronounced *REE-write*) **1.** Same as **revise.** **2.** Newsroom operation in which writers take information from legmen and write the stories

ribbon *See* **banner**

rim The outer rim of a horseshoe-shaped copy desk around which copyreaders work; sometimes the copyreaders (use of the term is declining as electronics takes over)

rip and read To "rip" copy from a teleprinter and read it onto the air with inadequate editing

roman Vertical type like this, in contrast to *italic*

rule A thin printed line separating one column or type segment from another

roundup **1.** A newscast summarizing late news. **2.** A story bringing together diffuse parts of a wide-ranging story, such as a five-state blizzard

run *See* **beat 1**

running story A news development continuing for two days or longer

runover Same as **jump**

scanner Device that "reads" news copy or other graphic images electronically and actuates machines that translate them into type

scoop *See* **beat 2**

script Copy for broadcast

sectional story One treating different aspects of an event in several stories

shoot To take photographs

short A short story used as filler

sidebar A secondary story that amplifies a facet of a main story

slant **1.** Same as **angle.** **2.** To shape a story to lead readers' thinking; to editorialize in news; to color or misrepresent

slot The inside rim of a horseshoe-shaped copy desk. *See* **rim**

slot man Copy desk chief

slug **1.** A metal bar (6 points) placed between lines of body type to provide **air** (*see* **lead 2**). **2.** (also **slugline**) Brief identification of a story placed at top of copy or proof. *See* **guide**

sob sister A reporter (male or female) who specializes in tearjerkers

spike To hold back a story, to place it on a spindle for future use or to kill it

spot news News printed or aired as quickly as possible

squib *See* **blurb**

standing head A headline used repeatedly for one feature or department

stereotype **1.** A bromide, cliché or hackneyed expression or news concept. **2.** A metal printing plate cast from a paper matrix molded from type. *See* **letterpress**

stet Copyreading and proofreading symbol meaning "let it stand," an instruction to ignore editing and proofreading marks

still A single-exposure photograph, as distinguished from a motion picture

store To place copy or other information in a computer or library for future use

straight news News presented in conventional "straight" news story form, primarily for informational purpose

streamer *See* **banner**

stringer A part-time correspondent, usually paid by the number or length of stories published

stylebook A publication's guide to specific rules for punctuation, capitalization, spelling, grammar, style of numerals and abbreviations. *See* page 139

subhead **1.** A small head used to break up long blocks of body type. **2.** A secondary headline

syndicate A service that sells features (crossword puzzles, comic strips, horoscopes, material for children, opinion and analysis columns, editorials, etc.) to news media

tabloid **1.** A newspaper with pages half the size of the standard newspaper. **2.** By extension, a sensational paper (because many tabloids belong to this category)

tack-up *See* **paste-up**

take One of the successive parts of a story (usually five to 10 lines) rushed from typewriter or VDT to copy desk as deadline approaches

terminal *See* **VDT**

text The full verbatim report of a speech or public statement

30 Symbol widely used as an endmark for news copy

time copy A story that does not depend on the time element

top head Major headline at or near the top of a page

transition *See* **bridge**

trim To cut or condense copy. *See* **boil, cut 3**

typo Typographical error

underline Descriptive text with picture. *See* **cutline, caption**

update To add later information to a story

UPI United Press International

upper case Capital letter. *See* **cap**

up style Editing pattern calling for liberal use of capital letters

VDT Video display terminal—the computer terminal used in a newsroom, including television screen (*see* **CRT**) and keyboard

video The visual portion of a telecast

wf Wrong font—type face that does not match those surrounding it

widow A very short line of type, especially when it falls at the head of a column of type

yellow journalism Sensationalized journalism

INDEX